THE STUDY OF HINDUISM

Studies in Comparative Religion
Frederick M. Denny, Series Editor

THE STUDY OF HINDUISM

Edited by ARVIND SHARMA

UNIVERSITY OF SOUTH CAROLINA PRESS

Published in Columbia, South Carolina, by the
University of South Carolina Press

Manufactured in the United States of America

07 06 05 04 03 5 4 3 2 1

Library of Congress Cataloging-in-Publication Data

The study of Hinduism / edited by Arvind Sharma.
p. cm.—(Studies in comparative religion)
Includes bibliographical references and index.
ISBN 1-57003-449-4 (cloth : alk. paper)
1. Hinduism. 2. Hinduism—Study and teaching. I. Sharma, Arvind. II. Studies in comparative religion (Columbia, S.C.)
BL1205 .S82 2003
294.5'071—dc21 2002041370

CONTENTS

SERIES EDITOR'S PREFACE

This series has as its main goal the publication of books and monographs on a wide range of topics in the general area of comparative studies of religion. The comparative study of religion as a scholarly enterprise is a product of the Enlightenment. And although it sometimes does indeed involve actual comparisons of religious traditions, the field is principally a discourse that develops and applies theories and methods to data in order to discern, explicate, interpret, and understand their nature and meaning. In our postmodern intellectual environment, as much energy and attention are often dedicated to interrogating and problematizing the various ways in which religions have been studied as the object of the study itself. The very term "object," of course, bristles with difficulties and raises fundamental questions of point of view, intellectual and cultural assumptions, definitions, and much more. Further, the term "Hinduism" indicates a modern way of categorizing a vast and complex religious heritage that did not employ the term before colonial-era contact and the emergence of a notion of "world religions."

Arvind Sharma's *The Study of Hinduism* provides an informative, reliable, and detailed guide, not principally to the major long-standing religious traditions of South Asia that are usually included under the umbrella term Hinduism, but to the ways that those traditions have been viewed and understood by modern scholarship over the past two centuries. The study of Hinduism has proceeded in a manner in some ways parallel to the academic study of, for example, Islam, ancient Israelite religion, and

Buddhism. That is, over the past two centuries, (mostly) western scholars have first focused mainly on the major ancient texts of those traditions, with a strong linguistic and philological interest. During the post–World War II era, with the opening of much of the world to trade, mass telecommunications, and travel, field studies of contemporary Hindus, Muslims, Buddhists, and other communities have come increasingly to supplement, if not to supplant, the older studies based largely on classical texts. Field studies of religious adherents is a study of texts that talk back. That approach has provided fresh, often unprecedented glimpses to outsiders of what Hindu, Buddhist, and Islamic texts actually mean within their lived contexts. Finally, religion scholars and cultural critics have come to focus increasingly on the study of religions and religious adherents themselves, as mentioned above.

While *The Study of Hinduism* focuses in detail on ways in which that tradition has been viewed and understood, it also provides much of great value to the furthering of the comparative study of religion as a global discourse. Companion projects could profitably be developed focusing on Islam, Buddhism, and other long-standing traditions that have experienced parallel scholarly scrutiny.

Frederick Mathewson Denny

INTRODUCTION

Although even the early Greeks exhibited familiarity with some forms of Hinduism and even more so the Muslim savants after the rise of Islam, the study of Hinduism as a modern academic discipline is of more recent origin and may be said to have properly commenced with the gradual establishment of British rule in India. Since then the investigation of Hinduism has been a constant, if not always a conscious, process. By now this scholarly enterprise has assumed major proportions. However, no adequate critical survey of the state of the art exists at the moment. Those that exist are either short or, when longer in size, are more in the nature of bibliographic guides than critical surveys.[1] This is true of works that deal either with a period in the history of Hinduism or with Indian religion and culture as a whole, in the broader context of South Asia.[2]

There is thus no work at present that takes stock of the state of the discipline, something every discipline needs to do from time to time; this is particularly true for Hindu studies now that the discipline has become global in scope. The purpose of this book, therefore, is to reflect and to reflect on the state of the art in Hindu studies. Its aim is twofold: to survey what has been done and to indicate what might be done in the study of Hinduism.

The book periodizes Hinduism along conventional lines: Hinduism in the Vedic times; Hinduism in classical times; Hinduism in medieval times;

Hinduism in modern times. It is not intended as a substitute for a textbook on the study of Hinduism, and it will be best to begin this section by clarifying its nature. From one point of view one may view Hindu studies, like Hinduism itself, as undergoing distinct stages of development. In the earliest phase, the emphasis lay on textual studies, with the philological approach in the ascendant. This phase broadly coincides with the period of the British Raj over India. The trend continued after India became independent in 1947, but was supplemented by a greater recognition of the role of fieldwork in the study of Hinduism. This trend became particularly marked after the 1960s, when a new body, and even new generation, of scholars began to combine textual work with at least a stay in the field, if not fieldwork in its anthropological sense. Now a third stage seems to be emerging—one in which the continuing earlier interest in textual studies and more recent interest in field studies is being leavened by critical reflection on the nature of the scholarly enterprise constituted by the study of Hinduism itself.

Following some introductory material, the structure of the book coincidentally, perhaps even serendipitously, reflects these developments. The chapters on Vedic and classical Hinduism are primarily textual in nature, thus reflecting the study of Hinduism's first phase; the chapters on medieval and modern Hinduism continue the textual approach but also begin to reflect the results of fieldwork.

Where this book fits into this scheme of things is as a third-order study of Hinduism. Its goal is to provide a picture of those aspects of Hinduism that have received attention in the recent past and that are currently receiving attention, as well as to offer the opinions of this book's scholar-contributors as to what remains unexplored territory. Thus it will serve to indicate (1) what has been accomplished in the study of Hinduism; (2) where readers may turn in order to familiarize themselves with these accomplishments; (3) what issues are currently engaging attention, and by whom, and (4) what areas await further investigation.

As an example of the latter—the areas that await further investigation—if we consider the study of Hinduism in general, while the philosophical aspect of the tradition has received considerable attention, the political element may have suffered from neglect.[3] Turning to the historical periods, although the various divisions of, for example, Vedic literature (including the Brāhmaṇas) have been explored, there are as yet no translations of three of the five Black Yajurveda Saṁhitās.[4] Similarly, in the study of classical Hinduism, the study of Tantra has been neglected, a neglect that is now gradually being overcome.[5] In the study of medieval Hinduism, the regional language versions of the Bhagavadgītā, which abound, have been overlooked, with the exception of Jñāneśvarī.[6] Similarly, in the study of modern Hinduism the fundamentalist strand in post-Independence Hinduism has been overlooked, and foreign scholars have even been actively discouraged by Indians from studying it, although the situation in this respect is now being rectified as the high price of such oversight becomes obvious.[7]

Even this brief survey discloses the importance of the sociology of knowledge in the presentation of Hinduism at its very source. For instance, it has been claimed that only those parts of Vedic literature have survived that were purposeful from the point of ritual, so that one must take into account "the result of the bias in that direction of scholar-priests, who were responsible for the compilation of the Veda as it has come down to us."[8] In the case of classical Hinduism, it must be taken into account that what we have in the law books are idealized Brahmanical models rather than the field reality itself.[9] And in medieval Bhakti, as in modern Indonesia, the influence of Islam in representing Hinduism as deliberately monotheistic must be considered.[10] Similarly, the fact that modern presentations of Hinduism reach us through an English-speaking Westernized elite cannot be overlooked.[11]

In other words, it is the goal of this book to demonstrate how Hinduism has been and is being studied, and to further locate, whenever possible, both the determination of the aspects studied and the manner of the study thereof in the broader, and hopefully illuminating, framework of the sociology of knowledge and the history of ideas, taking a suggestive look at future trends in terms of their desirability or necessity or both. Hindus may choose to look forward to the past, but that luxury is not available to the students of Hinduism.

Notes

1. For example, Charles Adams, ed., *A Reader's Guide to World Religions* (New York: Free Press, 1983), s.v. "Hinduism."

2. For a work dealing with one period, see R. N. Dandekar, *Vedic Bibliography* (Poona: Bhandarkar Oriental Research Institute, 1973–). For a work on the

broader context of South Asia, see Maureen L. Patterson, *South Asian Civilizations: A Bibliographic Synthesis* (Chicago: University of Chicago Press, 1982).

3. See Karl H. Potter, comp., *Bibliography of Indian Philosophies* (Delhi: Motilal Banarsidass, 1987–).

4. See James A. Santucci, *An Outline of Vedic Literature* (Missoula, Mont.: Scholars Press, 1976), 14.

5. See Troy Wilson Organ, *Hinduism: Its Historical Development* (Woodbury, N.Y.: Barron's Educational Series, 1974), 300.

6. See Winand M. Callewaert and Shilanand Hamraj, *Bhagavadgitānuvāda: A Study in Transcultural Translation* (Ranchi: Satya Bharati, 1983).

7. On discouragement of foreign scholarship, see Philip Ashby, *Modern Trends in Hinduism* (New York: Columbia University Press, 1974), 115. For examples of recent work, see Daniel Gold, "Organized Hinduism: From Vedic Truth to Hindu Nation," and T. N. Madan, "The Double-Edged Sword: Fundamentalism and the Sikh Religious Tradition," both in Martin E. Marty and R. Scott Appleby, *Fundamentalisms Observed* (Chicago and London: University of Chicago Press, 1991), 531–627.

8. See M. Hiriyanna, *The Essentials of Indian Philosophy* (London: Allen & Unwin, 1946), 17–18.

9. See Vincent A. Smith, *The Oxford History of India*, 4th ed., ed. Percival Spear (Delhi: Oxford University Press, 1994), 70.

10. See Ainslie T. Embree, ed., *The Hindu Tradition* (New York: Vintage, 1972), 263.

11. See A. Bharati, "The Hindu Renaissance: Its Apologetic Pattern," *Journal of Asian Studies* (February 1970): 267–87.

THE STUDY OF HINDUISM

ONE What Is Hinduism?

ARVIND SHARMA

The chapters that follow will go a long way toward confirming the description of Hinduism as a religion of mobile and multiple thresholds. This feature of Hinduism, rooted in its pluralistic orientation, makes the question of defining it sufficiently difficult and even contentious to justify a separate chapter. There could be some discussion as to whether such a chapter should be placed toward the beginning or the end of a book on Hinduism. Though much can be said in favor of both the views, we have decided to place it at the beginning on account of the salience the issue has been steadily gaining in the study of Hinduism. There is also the hope that exposure to the problematic at the very start of the study of Hinduism may help the reader to evolve an individual approach to the matter as he or she journeys through its various manifestations.

This chapter is divided into three parts. The first part surveys some of the reasons that have been adduced to account for the problematic; the second part surveys some of the attempts to address the problem; and in the third and final section, a resolution of the problematic for the purposes of this book is proposed.

Defining Hinduism: The Problem

The problem of defining Hinduism has been endemic in the study of Hinduism since the term *Hinduism* was coined and introduced early in the nineteenth century.[1] It has, however, increasingly become more acute. Early scholars do not allude to the problem directly but refer to a feature of Hinduism that complicates immensely the task of defining it; namely, the absence of creedal formulation. It is already identified by Monier Monier-Williams in 1883, in the Vedic-period phenomenon that "each man satisfied his own religious instincts, according to his conception of the character of the supernatural being or beings on whose favour his welfare was thought to depend."[2] When, in another work, Monier-Williams sets out to define Hinduism, he alludes to this aspect and ascribes it to Hinduism proper, as distinguished from Vedism, to which he had attributed it in the earlier citation. He writes:

> And far more remarkable than this—it will be seen . . . that another characteristic of Hinduism is its receptivity and all-comprehensiveness. It claims to be the one religion of humanity, of human nature, of the entire world. It cares not to oppose the progress of any other system. For it has no difficulty in including all other religions within its all-embracing arms and ever-widening fold.
>
> And, in real truth, Hinduism has something to offer which is suited to all minds. Its very strength lies in its infinite adaptability to the infinite diversity of human characters and human tendencies. It has its highly spiritual and abstract side suited to the metaphysical philosopher—its practical and concrete side suited to the man of affairs and the man of the world—its aesthetic and ceremonial side suited to the man of poetic feeling and imagination—its quiescent and contemplative side suited to the man of peace and lover of seclusion. Nay, it holds out the right hand of brotherhood to nature-worshiper, demon-worshiper, animal-worshiper, tree-worshiper, fetish-worshiper. It does not scruple to permit the most grotesque forms of idolatry and the most degrading varieties of superstition. And it is to this latter fact that yet another remarkable peculiarity of Hinduism is mainly due—namely, that in no other system of the world is the chasm more vast which separates the religion of the higher, cultured, and thoughtful classes from that of the lower, uncultured, and unthinking masses.[3]

It is obvious, then, that one reason Hinduism is difficult to define is on account of its diversity. This is also recently alluded to by Gavin Flood, when he writes:

> Because of the wide range of traditions and ideas incorporated by the term "Hindu," it is a problem arriving at a definition. Most Hindu traditions revere a body of sacred literature, the Veda, as revelation, though some do not; some traditions regard certain rituals as essential for salvation, others do not; some Hindu philosophies postulate a theistic reality who creates, maintains and destroys the universe, others reject this claim. Hinduism is often characterized as belief in reincarnation (*saṃsāra*) determined by the law that all actions have effects (*karma*), and that salvation is freedom from this cycle. Yet other religions in south Asia, such as Buddhism and Jainism, also believe in this. Part of the problem of definition is due to the fact that Hinduism does not have a single historical founder, as do so many other world religions; it does not have a unified system of belief encoded in a creed or declaration of faith; it does not have a single system of soteriology; and it does not have a centralized authority and bureaucratic structure. It is therefore a very different kind of religion in these respects from the monotheistic, western tradition of Christianity and Islam, though there are arguably stronger affinities with Judaism.[4]

A second reason given to account for this problem is related to the first, but not identical with it:

> But there are no criteria for determining who is and who is not Hindu. There are no hierarchies of priests, no rolls of congregations, no uniformly accepted sacraments, no creedal statements to be agreed to, no initiatory rites universally accepted by Hindus, and no practices which always distinguish the Hindu from the non-Hindu. Being a Hindu appears to be a matter of individual decision, yet few Hindus have chosen to be Hindu. A Hindu has been described as anyone who does not say no when asked, "Are you a Hindu?" For example, Govinda-Dasa writes that "any and every one is a Hindu who does not repudiate that designation" and who "accepts any of the many beliefs, and follows any of the many practices that are anywhere regarded as Hindu." But Govinda-Dasa does not name the beliefs and practices. Instead, he offers a list of items which he says have been thought by some to be essential to the Hindu, whereas in fact none is necessary: birth from Hindu parents, birth in geographical limits of India, belief in the Vedas, practice of the caste system, belief in sanctity of the cow, belief in God, leaving the

> scalp lock (*shikha*), wearing the sacred thread, observing special rules concerning diet, belief in *karma* and reincarnation, belief in incarnations of gods, belief in the sacredness of *Brahmin* priests, holding to restrictions of race and color, and practice of Hindu law! This list seems extreme . . . but it does serve to call attention to the scarcity of universally accepted beliefs and practices among Hindus. In India today it is not unusual to find a person who denies he is a Hindu but who acts in a manner which others associate with Hinduism. I recall an occasion in India in which a dinner companion who, after assuring me he had completely deserted Hinduism, carefully removed a fly from his glass of water, placed it on the floor, and then observed, "I think it will be all right now." I could not refrain from reminding my friend that his act revealed more about his religion than his words.[5]

This position has been forcefully expressed by R. E. Frykenberg:

> Does the fact that an Untouchable Madiga or Chakriyar leather-worker makes and beats the drums for a civic ceremonial or a common festival make him or his community Hindu? Does the fact that a Muslim mahout cares for and rides the elephant of a large temple make him a Hindu? Does the participation of Parava or Nadar or other Christian communities in ceremonies connected to major or minor local (temple) deities make them Hindu? Does an endowment by a European to a temple ritual make that European Hindu? If Christian doctors and nurses work in a local hospital which is maintained by temple endowments, are they thereby Hindu? What is it that an image-maker makes which he uses the same molds to produce plaster or clay or even metal (*pancaloha*) figurines both of a Blessed Virgin Mary and of a Mariamman? Are we to characterize him and his work as being both Catholic and Śaiva Siddhānta? Is he Hindu or Catholic? And, if one or other or both, how is this so?[6]

The point at issue, therefore, is whether there is any scientific or systematic way to determine who was or who is or who is not a Hindu. However much the Registrar-General of the Census or however much contemporary politicians may insist upon lumping nearly 80 percent of the peoples of India under this categorical designation, it is almost impossible to determine how many of peoples so categorized would identify themselves as "Hindus" and, moreover, what such a self-identity would mean in a religious, as distinct from a cultural or geographical or national or political, context. Context, indeed, may be seen as making all the difference.[7]

A third reason can also be related to both of the previous ones:

> Hinduism is more like a tree that has *grown* gradually than like a building that has been *erected* by some great architect at some definite point in time. It contains within it, as we shall see, the influences of many cultures, and the body of Hindu thought thus offers as much variety as the Indian nation itself. It is not surprising, therefore, that A. C. Bouquet, writing on comparative religion, found that "India in particular furnishes within its limits examples of every conceivable type of attempt at the solution of the religious problem." The cultures of the Dravidian and the non-Dravidian peoples before the so-called Aryan invasion, the actual Sanskritized Aryan culture, the culture of the later invaders, the influences of Buddhism, Jainism, and Sikhism (to which Hinduism gave birth) can be traced at various stages of the evolution of Hindu thought.[8]

The point here is that what Hinduism *is* is also connected with how it came to be—that the difficulty of defining Hinduism comprises both its being and becoming.

Another set of reasons traces the definitional problems not so much to the term Hinduism itself as to the category under which it is being subsumed; namely, "religion." Here again one encounters several distinct but related positions, all essentially having to do with the artificiality of the term when applied to the Indian reality. According to both Wilfred Cantwell Smith and H. von Stietencron, the problem lies with the Western conceptualization of Hinduism—although Smith traces the problem to the term's Enlightenment usage and Stietencron traces it to its Christian deployment.

Smith uses the term to illustrate his more general thesis that *religion*, in the sense we use the term, is a relatively modern invention that came about under the influence of the Enlightenment, when the concept of religions as distinct, identifiable, reified entities came into being. He goes on to say:

> The term "Hinduism" is, in my judgement, a particularly false conceptualization, one that is conspicuously incompatible with any adequate understanding of the religious outlook of Hindus. Even the term "Hindu"

> was unknown to the classical Hindus. "Hinduism" as a concept certainly they did not have. And indeed one has only to reflect on the situation carefully to realize that it would necessarily have been quite meaningless to them.[9]

Smith goes on to make the further point that "while a boundary between non-Muslims (followers of indigenous ways, 'Hindus') and Muslims is sharply drawn, the boundary which demarcates a 'Hindu' community from other Indian groups is not clear."[10] He then adds:

> Indeed it is still not clear today. The census of India, 1941, gave up the attempt of previous British censuses (1931, 1921, and on back) to enumerate Hindus exactly. The census offices reported that they had been forced into realization that the boundaries of Islam and Christianity were reasonably clear, but that those of the Hindu community were not. They could draw a line discriminating Hindus from Christians and Muslims on the one side, but it was not possible to draw one discriminating them from animists on the other. This on the practical, operational side is an unwitting empirical confirmation of my theoretical point, that the concept of a religious system, whether ideal or sociological, is here alien and invalid. It is a Western (and Muslim) concept, which Westerners (and Muslims) have tried to impose upon their understanding of India; but it does not fit. There are Hindus, but there is no Hinduism.[11]

Stietencron, on the other hand, sees in the use of the word *religion* to describe Hinduism an imposition of the word's Christian sense on Hinduism. It does not fit the case because Hinduism is not a single unified tradition but a multiplicity of religions. If for Smith the word *religion* does not apply to Hinduism because there is no Hinduism,[12] for Stietencron it does not apply (in the singular) because there is no Hinduism, only Hinduisms. He writes:

> These or similar arguments contributed to support the westerners' preconceived notion that it was *one* religion they were dealing with. Since they were used to the Christian tradition of an absolute claim for only one truth, of a powerful church dominating society, and consequently of fierce religious and social confrontation with members of other creeds, they were unable even to conceive of such religious liberality as would

give members of the same society the freedom, by individual choice, to practice the religion they liked.[13]

A third approach, which overlaps with the previous two but is also advanced on its own, contrasts the word *religion* with the Hindu word *dharma*, only to conclude that *dharma* is too polysemic and extensive in its semantic range to provide an adequate translation for *religion*. As Stietencron points out,

> Translating our word "Hinduism" into their own terminology, they conceived of it as equivalent to the Hindu *dharma*, often referred to as *sanātana dharma* or eternal dharma in writings of the 19th and 20th century. *Dharma* or *sanātana dharma* is that universal order of things, by which man is born into a certain social stratum and into one of the regional or even local religious traditions and has to behave accordingly. It is the normative basis of behavior in consonance with cosmic order and it operates on all levels of worldly existence. Thus *dharma* may refer to the duties of caste (*varṇa*) and stage of life (*āśrama*), to the nature and tasks of male and female, or to the religious practice of various groups such as *buddha dharma*, *vaiṣṇava dharma*, *śaiva dharma* etc. (Note that the Indians use the same term *dharma* for all three while we use "religion" for Buddhism and "sect" for Vaiṣṇavism and Śivaism). *Dharma* operates also in the animal and plant kingdom and in the laws of nature. It is the *dharma* of plants to grow according to their species and to serve as food for animals. Following their *dharma* the beasts of prey kill other living beings. And it is the *dharma* of fire to annihilate, to transform, and to carry oblations to the gods. Obviously, *dharma* has a much wider semantic dimension than our word "religion." Therefore the Indian acceptance of the term "Hinduism" cannot serve to prove the existence of a "religion" called Hinduism.[14]

These two strands can be brought together in the dual claim that Hindus possess no term that corresponds to either *Hinduism* or to *religion*.

Attempts to Solve the Problem

Attempts to resolve this problem have usually proceeded along two lines, which Richard Davis has characterized as the central and plural approaches to the issue.[15] He then proceeds to describe the two approaches as follows:

> Centralists identify a single, pan-Indian, more or less hegemonic, orthodox tradition, transmitted primarily in Sanskrit language, chiefly by members of the brahmanic class. The tradition centers around a Vedic lineage of texts, in which are included not only the Vedas themselves, but also the Mīmāṃsā, Dharmaśāstra, and Vedānta corpuses of texts and teachings. Vedic sacrifice is the privileged mode of ritual conduct, the template for all subsequent Indian ritualism. Various groups employing vernacular languages in preference to Sanskrit, questioning the caste order, and rejecting the authority of the Vedas, may periodically rebel against this center, but the orthodox, through an adept use of inclusion and repressive tolerance, manage to hold the high ground of religious authority.[16]

This centralist approach is not the only option available. One also needs to take a pluralist approach into account.

> The pluralists, by contrast, envision a decentered profusion of ideas and practices all tolerated and incorporated under the big tent of Hinduism. No more concise statement of this view can be found than that of the eminent Sanskrit scholar J. A. B. van Buitenen in the 1986 *Encyclopedia Britannica:*
>
> "In principle, Hinduism incorporates all forms of belief and worship without necessitating the selection or elimination of any. The Hindu is inclined to revere the divinity in every manifestation, whatever it may be, and is doctrinally tolerant. . . . Hinduism is, then, both a civilization and a conglomeration of religions, with neither a beginning, a founder, nor a central authority, hierarchy, or organization."
>
> Adherents of this viewpoint commonly invoke natural metaphors. Hinduism is a "sponge" for all religious practices or a "jungle" where every religious tendency may flourish freely. Within the pluralist view, the Vedic tradition figures as one form of belief and worship among many, the concern of elite brahmans somewhat out of touch with the religious multiplicity all around them.[17]

It seems to me that the distinction is useful, if broadened. It allows one to identify, initially, a two-pronged approach toward answering the question, What is Hinduism? The Vedic–Sanskritist–Brahmanical tradition is one way of centralizing the tradition. This approach has recently been further developed by Brian K. Smith. If the point is pressed, however, it evokes the kind of criticism voiced by Stietencron.[18]

Sometimes the centralist approach assumes another form. It is then argued that the indefinably vast doctrinal amplitude of Hinduism goes hand in hand with its almost ossifiedly defined caste system, which is then taken to constitute the central core of the tradition. In other words, the problem of defining Hinduism, which seems so insoluble at the level of theory, may be amenable to a solution at the level of practice. In terms of this approach it may be claimed that "a Hindu without a caste is almost a contradiction in terms."[19] However, as Donald Eugene Smith has pointed out, while "in terms of traditional Hinduism this statement is for the most part accurate . . . it does not take into account the many new developments which have vigorously challenged traditional Hindu society in the past one hundred and fifty years. In particular, it ignores the work of the Hindu social and religious reformers, many of whom made a deliberate effort to separate caste from Hindu religion."[20]

This point becomes all the more relevant if we regard the emergence of Hinduism itself as a modern phenomenon:

> In one respect, Hinduism is one of the oldest, if not the oldest continuous recorded religion, tracing itself back to a text that was already edited and put into final shape by about 1200 B.C.E. In another respect, though, it is the youngest, for it was only in the nineteenth century that the many indigenous Indian religious formations were collectively named Hinduism. Before this, not only did these groups not have a name for themselves as a religious unity but for the most part they did not consider that they were members of a single religious collectivity.[21]

And if we consider the present context in which the question is being raised—namely, that of the *study* of Hinduism, which is, even less ambiguously than "Hinduism" a modern phenomenon, at least the way it will be discussed in this book—the argument gains in force.

The centralist approach to defining Hinduism sometimes finds expression not in an attempt to identify one central feature of it, but more broadly in terms of identifying patterns of thought or behavior central to it. Madeleine Biardeau seems to follow such an approach when she writes in favor of detecting a "pattern," as follows:

> This amounts to saying that change, when it does appear, is only superficial and always refers back to a normative foundation, the one source from which spring the most transient phenomena. It is then a question of adopting this language as far as one can, of entering into this world view, forgetting one's own categories so as to discover those of the Other, accepting that its lines of cleavage are not ours, that its values are distributed in a way that for us is unexpected. Such a perspective in fact does no more than reconnect with the very modern and very Western preoccupations of this historians of "mentalities." There is simply a change of scale when dealing with India, because one cannot "periodize" its history as one does for other areas, or divide it into territories as restricted as those of European countries. The documentation available does not lend itself to this either in quantity or, above all, in content, since it speaks of something other than "history." The psychological, the individual, the momentary collective movement escape us—or are they simply absent? A rigorous study of mentalities must in fact take care not to see these lacunae as something negative, as a limit on investigation. On the contrary, they have a heuristic value if they are regarded as indices of what the Hindu will or can say of himself.[22]

Biardeau, however, herself seems to be aware that the pattern may involve the sacrifice of scope, or even precision, when she adds:

> I do not deny that this is a risky undertaking; how can one be sure that the reduction of the fact to the norm does not conceal the intrusion of a historical contingency the data of which elude us? One cannot hope to make a system of Hindu culture as a whole, *without any remainder*. In particular, this would be to make light of the centuries of rationalizations which the Brahmans have accumulated in all good faith, deceiving themselves before catching us in their trap. More modestly, therefore, I shall endeavour to show the probability of an interpretation by examining it from several angles, not forgetting that the most solid pieces of evidence may themselves prove to be deceptive, that the insignificant anecdote takes on the air of a myth the better to charge itself with meaning. In short, I shall place a wager on meaningfulness, while remaining aware that meaninglessness also exists.[23]

Another approach, which looks to social rather than mental patterns and attempts to define Hinduism in terms of social tendencies, may be placed here. The following remarks are suggestive, as they enable us to see some categories already introduced in a new light:

> The great difference between the Hindu conception of the "dharma" and the European conception of "religion" is this. To a European, Christianity or Christian religion are self-defined terms, and the acceptance of those ideas and practices that are indicated by the word would make a man Christian. In the case of Hindu-"dharma," the relation is different. Hindus are a definite body, and Hindu-"dharma" is that indefinite thing which the Hindus consider their own "dharma." . . . The word *Hindu* is itself a foreign one. The Hindus never used it in any Sanskrit writing, that is, those which were written before the Mohammedan invasion. In fact there was no need of calling themselves by any particular name (all the rest of the world being "foreigners" (*mlechchha, Greek BápBapoç*). . . . Hindus define a Hindu as a man who has not fallen from Hinduism, that is, taken up the membership of any community like Christian or Mohammedan, which is not considered as a Hindu community. The distinction between the Hindus and the Animists is based only on ignorance . . . the distinction drawn between a Hindu and non-Hindu is merely a provisional one. It may change any time. Hinduism may in future, include Christians, Muhammedans, and Buddhists. Hinduism is an ever-changing society, which may expand and take in races and peoples irrespective of their religious beliefs. What societies it will absorb depends almost entirely on the circumstances.[24]

While an exercise to discover "deep" structures is illuminating in terms of understanding a tradition, it may not be equally helpful in describing or defining it. Part of the argument here seems to be that while a religious tradition may not possess *integrating* characteristics, it might still possess *underlying* characteristics in terms of which it may be defined.[25] But the problem with restricting the attention to the chassis is that the rest of the truck may go unnoticed.

We turn now to a consideration of some of the plural approaches, which have been adopted in the context of arriving at a satisfactory formulation of what Hinduism is all about. The distinction between religion and culture has now come to play a major role in this context. Stietencron does not hesitate to identify pluralism as a, even the, key aspect of Hinduism, but this leads him to propose that Hinduism should be viewed as a *culture*, characterized by the presence of many (related) *religions*.

> It could be argued that it is precisely the multiplicity of notions and of approaches to the divine, the ever-changing pattern of so many paths for the individual to choose for his progress towards prosperity and liberation, which is the characteristic feature of Hinduism and which constitutes its peculiar attractiveness. This is perfectly true. But nothing is taken away from the justified picture of interacting religious multiplicity and liberality if we conceive of "Hinduism" as a whole group of related but distinct religions.[26]

Vasudha Narayanan implicitly seems to prefer a different resolution of the religion/culture dichotomy in the case of Hinduism by suggesting that the definition of religion when applied to Hinduism be made to include culture. This is at least one way of interpreting her comment that

> subjects such as astronomy and astrology, phonetics, and studies on poetic metre are traditionally considered *vedāṅga* or ancillary to the study of scripture. These subjects would also come under the purview of "religion." While it would be impossible to do justice to all these areas that fall under the rubric of sacred texts and sacrality for the Hindus, our discussion of the Hindu tradition in this chapter will include features not covered by the word "religion" in the Western world.[27]

It is also worth noting that, in premodern India, Hindus, Buddhists, Jains, and Sikhs "perceived themselves as all belonging to the same extended *cultural* family."[28]

A third approach to the issue is represented by a decision of the Supreme Court of India that characterized Hinduism as a "way of life" and not a religion. This is significant because the decision was handed down in a context in which the defendant had been accused of violating electoral law by asking his constituents to vote for him because he was a Hindu. Such appeal to religion for soliciting votes is forbidden under Indian electoral law. The court decreed that the candidate's election was valid because the Hinduism he was appealing to was not that Hinduism that is a religion but that Hinduism that is not a religion but a way of life.[29] The academic context for assessing the significance for this judgment in the context of understanding Hinduism is suitably provided by the following remarks that Stietencron made prior to and independently of the judgment:

> When the search for "essentials of Hinduism" failed, and when it became obvious that it was impossible to harmonize the major conflicting elements of theory and practice, one more suggestion to explain Hinduism was advanced. It claimed that Hinduism was not a religion, but "a way of life." This solution to the problem is an ingenious effort to escape from the impossible task of grasping the "religion" Hinduism. Maybe it is not far from truth. But as a way of life, as a culture or civilization, Hinduism should not be compared with other religions, but with other ways of life and other cultures or civilizations. This solution could be improved and retain its connection with religion, if formulated thus: Hinduism is a civilization formed and enriched by a group of Hindu religions which developed a particularly liberal way of coexistence and interaction between themselves.[30]

This paves the way for discussing what might may be called nominalist approaches to the study of Hinduism, in addition to the centralist and the pluralist ones. In fact the progress of the argument of this chapter up to this point may be summarized as follows: Hinduism is a holdall, and no single belt can hold it together. In other words, the pluralist approach is more satisfying than the centralist in the context of defining it. The question thus morphs now into the following: In what way is its plurality most satisfactorily described? In terms of religion, and/or in terms of culture, or in terms of a way of life?

Those who wish to continue to describe it in terms of religion would like to maintain that, just as some have claimed that there is "no such thing as Hinduism," there are also some scholars who deny that "there is any such thing as religion in general":[31]

> They claim that there are religions, i.e., particular patterns of life and thought, and there are religious attitudes, i.e., particular responses to life experiences, but there is no abstraction known as religion. In similar fashion one could say there is no science in general; there is only chemistry, biology, physics, geology, etc. Yet common usage demands the generic words, religion and science and even though agreement as to their exact meaning is unlikely, the words will probably remain.[32]

This statement assumes significance in the light of the parallel claim that there is no such thing as Hinduism. Arguably there is, now, something like "Hinduism" in the sense of a "field of study"; in any case, that is what one is concerned with here. This prompts the question: How are we now to understand the term *religion*? Sometimes a distinction is drawn between two different meanings of the word:

> Our term "religion" has two different meanings: one general and one specific. Religion (singular) is a general term applied to human attempts to communicate with the divine on all levels and at all times. As a concept it presumes cross-cultural universals in human nature. Religions (plural)—and among these each single religion defined by a specifying term such as Greek religion, Roman religion, Judaism, Christianity, Islam, Shintoism, or religion of the Incas, the North American Indians, the Nuer, etc.,—are concretizations of religious systems in space and time and therefore distinct *historical* phenomena.[33]

Although the distinction between religion and culture was invoked by H. von Stietencron to argue that *Hinduism*, as a term, is not sufficiently specific and should be disaggregated into Vaiṣṇavism, Śaivism, etc., which would then place these on par with Judaism or Sikhism, for instance, Allie M. Frazier proposes to apply a somewhat analogous distinction between broad and narrow senses to Hinduism itself.

> What is Hinduism? In a broad sense, Hinduism is the whole complex of events, beliefs, practices and institutions that have appeared in India from the time of the ancient Vedas until the modern age. In a more narrow sense, Hinduism could be defined as that social and religious system which developed in India after the third century B.C. But whether broadly or narrowly conceived, Hinduism represents an extraordinary spectrum of belief and practice ranging from polytheism to monotheism, from pluralism to monism, from ceremonialism to mysticism, and from religious moralism to secular amoralism.[34]

According to another approach, we should understand the term *religion* somewhat differently in the context of Hinduism. Gavin Flood offers here an understanding of religion as a category that seems to marry the centralist and pluralist approaches. He writes:

> In other words, "Hinduism" is not a category in the classical sense—to which something either belongs or it does not—but more in the sense of prototype theory. Prototype theory, developed by George Lakoff, maintains that categories do not have rigid boundaries, but rather there are degrees of category membership; some members of a category are more prototypical than others. These degrees may be related through family resemblance; the idea that "members of a category may be related to one another without all members having any properties in common that define the category." Hinduism can be seen as a category in this sense. It has fuzzy edges. Some forms of religion are central to Hinduism, while others are less clearly central but still within the category.
>
> To say what is or is not central to the category of Hinduism is, of course, to make judgements about the degree of prototypicality. The question of the basis of such judgement arises. Here we must turn, on the one hand, to Hindu self-understandings, for Hinduism has developed categories for its own self-description, as well as, on the other, to the scholar's understandings of common features or structuring principles seen from outside the tradition.[35]

We have already alluded to the categorical interface of religion and culture. According to Robert Baird, however, what is important in the Indian context is the distinction between the legal and "religious" definitions of Hinduism.[36] Very briefly, the legal definitions of who is a Hindu in India tend to assimilate the Buddhists, Jains, and Sikhs in this category. In the study of religion in the West, however, Hinduism is typically distinguished from Buddhism, Jainism, and Sikhism. The fact that in India there is a strong tendency to homogenize these four complicates the situation.

The difficulty in defining the word *religion* itself might offer another clue. Some scholars have argued that, in face of the bewildering variety of definitions of religion available to us, only a *stipulative* definition would do.[37] Some seem to propose a similar procedure when faced with the bewildering variety of Hinduism. Louis Renou seems to hint at both the inevitability and the limitations of such a procedure when he remarks:

> Can one rather define Hinduism by its elements? Actually, this will have to be done; but in attempting to find such a unifying definition we run the risk of generalizing to such an extent that we fail to grasp the infinite diversity of forms which constitute Hinduism.[38]

Significantly, Renou is led to this because an initial attempt at a geographical definition of Hinduism as "the totality of religious forms which originated and developed on Indian soil"—minus Buddhism, Jainism, Christianity, Judaism, Zoroastrianism, [Sikhism, Islam,] and Animism—fails him because Hinduism cannot be confined to the "circumference of India" on account of extension beyond India in both ancient and modern times.[39] The concept of Hinduism as a subject of study as a religion may have to be guarded against a *geographical* fixation with India and a *cultural* conflation with other religions of Indian origin.

What, then, are we to do, apart from throwing up our hands in despair? For readers of this book (as well as the contributors to it), the situation is not desperate since this book is about the *study* of Hinduism, and the study of a religion, in the Western sense of the term, is virtually (though not altogether) unknown in India. Further signaling that the book's perspective is Western is the fact that the book is about the *study* of *Hinduism*, which itself originated in the context of interaction between India and the West and reflects a Western perspective. The present enterprise is thus doubly Western in nature.

In such a context, one could define Hinduism as what remains of the reality *after* it has been emptied of first Judaism, Christianity, and Islam, and *then* of Buddhism, Jainism, Sikhism, and Bahai.[40] In the end, then, we have opted for a stipulative resolution of the matter. Note, however, that this definition is stipulative in terms of scope, rather than subject matter. The question of defining Hinduism remains, but it need not detain us, thanks to the deus ex machina in the form of the Western academic intervention.

Notes

1. See Robert Eric Frykenberg, "The Emergence of Modern 'Hinduism' as a Concept and as an Institution: A Reappraisal with Special Reference to South India," in Günther D. Sontheimer and Hermann Kulke, eds., *Hinduism Reconsidered* (Delhi: Manohar, 1989), 43 n. 7; Richard King, "Orientalism and the Modern Myth of 'Hinduism,'" *Numen* 46 (1999):165.

2. Monier Monier-Williams, *Religious Thought and Life in India* (1883; reprint, New Delhi: Oriental Books, 1974), 6.

3. Monier Monier-Williams, *Brahmanism and Hinduism* (London: Murray, 1891), x–xi.

4. Gavin Flood, *An Introduction to Hinduism* (Cambridge: Cambridge University Press, 1996), 6.

5. Troy Wilson Organ, *Hinduism: Its Historical Development* (Woodbury, N.Y.: Barron's Educational Series, 1974), 2.

6. Frykenberg, "Emergence," 41–42.

7. Ibid., 42.

8. K. M. Sen, *Hinduism* (Harmondsworth, Eng.: Penguin, 1961), 14–15.

9. Wilfred Cantwell Smith, *The Meaning and End of Religion* (New York: Macmillan, 1963), 63.

10. Ibid., 65.

11. Ibid.

12. The point, however, can be overstated; see Smith, *Meaning and End of Religion*, 65–66.

13. H. von Stietencron, "Hinduism: On the Proper Use of a Deceptive Term," in Sontheimer and Kulke, *Hinduism Reconsidered*, 14–15.

14. Ibid., 15.

15. Richard H. Davis, introduction to Donald S. Lopez Jr., ed., *Religions of India in Practice* (Princeton: Princeton University Press, 1995), 6.

16. Ibid.

17. Ibid., 6–7. For a felicitous extension of the arboreal analogy, see Julius Lipner, *Hindus: Their Religious Beliefs and Practices* (London and New York: Routledge, 1994), 5–7.

18. von Stietencron, "Hinduism," 15: "Major sections of bhakti religions have, for many centuries, rejected the authority of the Veda. This is true for the Vaiṣṇavas and important parts of the Śaivas and Śāktas, as well as for the devotees of Kumāra and Sūrya, as is testified by numerous texts. A single song in praise of Kṛṣṇa (or Śiva, Devī, etc.) has, according to many texts, more value with the sixteenth part of one's own sacred scriptures. Of course, when an increasing number of brahmins turned to these bhakti faiths and became devotees to Viṣṇu, Śiva etc., they brought with them all their Vedic learning. Brahmins did play an essential role in the literary expression of bhakti religions. But what they introduced, in course of time, into Purānic and Smārta and Āgama religious literature was neither a genuine Vedic polytheism nor the Vedic sacrifice; it was mainly the *samskāras*, the protective and initiating sacraments of the *smṛti* tradition which accompany human life from conception to death, and Vedic technical scholarship. The Veda itself has astonishingly little impact on high-class and middle-class bhakti religion. We should also remember that Vedic religion was

at all times totally inaccessible to śūdras and outcastes who form the vast majority of the Hindus: they were, according to orthodox law, prohibited under penalty of death to hear the Veda or to take part in Vedic rituals and sacraments. It is thus obvious that at no time in history the Vedas were the sacred scripture of all Hindus."

19. L. S. S. O'Malley, cited by Donald Eugene Smith in *India as a Secular State* (Princeton: Princeton University Press, 1963), 294.

20. Smith, *India as a Secular State*, 294–95.

21. Davis, introduction to *Religions of India in Practice*, 5.

22. Madeline Biardeau, *Anthropology of a Civilization* (New Delhi: Oxford University Press, 1989), 3.

23. Ibid.

24. Shridhar V. Ketkar, cited in *Encyclopedia of Religion and Ethics* (1914), 6: 698, s.v. "Hinduism," by W. Crooke. This entry constitutes an early attempt to grapple with the issue under discussion.

25. Davis, introduction to *Religions of India in Practice*, 5: "It is important to bear in mind, however, that Hinduism does not share many of the integrating characteristics of the other religious traditions we conventionally label the "world religions." Hinduism has no founding figure such as the Buddha Śākyamuni, Jesus of Nazareth, or Muhammad. It has no single text that can serve as a doctrinal point of reference, such as the Bibles of the Judaic and Christian traditions, the Islamic Qur'ān, or the Ādi Granth of the Sikhs. Hinduism has no single overarching institutional or ecclesiastical hierarchy capable of deciding question of religious boundary or formulating standards of doctrine and practice."

26. Von Stietencron, "Hinduism," 17.

27. Vasudha Narayanan, "The Hindu Tradition," in Willard G. Oxtoby, ed., *World Religions: Eastern Traditions* (Toronto: Oxford University Press, 1996), 16–17. See also Arvind Sharma and Katherine K. Young, eds., *Feminism and World Religions* (Albany: State University of New York Press, 1999), 36.

28. Lipner, *Hindus*, 14 (emphasis added).

29. *Supreme Court on "Hindutva" and Hinduism* and *L. K. Advani's Statement* (New Delhi: Bharatiya Janata Party Publication, 1995).

30. Von Stietencron, "Hinduism," 16.

31. Troy Wilson Organ, *The Hindu Quest for the Perfection of Man* (Athens: Ohio University Press, 1970), 13.

32. Ibid.

33. Von Stietencron, "Hinduism," 19–20.

34. Allie M. Frazier, ed,. *Hinduism* (Philadelphia: Westminster Press, 1969), 5–6.

35. Flood, *Introduction to Hinduism*, 7. For a strikingly similar proposal made earlier in relation to the term *religion* itself, see John H. Hick, *Philosophy of Religion*, 4th ed. (Englewood Cliffs, N.J.: Prentice Hall, 1990), 3.

36. See Robert Baird, ed., *Religion and Law in Independent India* (New Delhi: Manohar, 1993).

37. Melford E. Spiro, "Religion: Problems of Definition and Explanation," in Michael Banton, ed., *Anthropological Approaches to the Study of Religion* (London: Tavistock, 1966), 85–87.

38. Louis Renou, ed., *Hinduism* (New York: Braziller, 1962), 16.

39. Renou, *Hinduism*, 15, 16 (emphasis added).

40. The logic of the two steps consists of the recognition (1) that degrees of differentiation characterize Islam and (2) that the Indian religious reality includes "Greater India" (i.e., Indian expansion outside the boundaries of subcontinental India).

TWO The Study of Hinduism

The Setting

ERIC J. SHARPE

Behind the simple words *the study of Hinduism* there is an enterprise of great complexity. No one reading these pages is likely to be under any illusions as to the intricacy of the subject matter: what custom has taught us to call Hinduism is a network of phenomena as rich, complex, and varied as the land and life of India itself. The point has been made so often as to have almost become a cliché—that no one label is comprehensive and flexible enough to perform all the services we require of this single term. Still, we are used to *Hinduism*, and we have learned to make allowances. *Study*, similarly, is by no means an unambiguous term for what may be a structured and systematic process (although it is often a haphazard one) of acquiring and digesting information and impressions. Further, we need constantly to be reminded that study is never carried out in a vacuum: behind the study there is the student, and behind the student there is the society of which the student is part, with all its presuppositions, expectations, and constraints.

In my library I have a curious volume, published in Poona (as it was then still called) in 1938, a series of 103 photographs of "the eminent Indologists—living and dead—of the West," and called *Picturesque Orientalia*.[1] But how little the photographs convey on their own! Some are not even dated as to birth and death. Some I am entirely unable to place, though others again are still household names wherever India is studied. This may perhaps serve as a parable. We at the beginning of the twenty-first century do not live in the atmosphere in which the Indologists of 1938 (let alone 1838) worked, and it is idle to pretend that we do. We are, on the other hand, still building on the foundations they laid, and it may be salutary to recall both who they were and the conditions that shaped their achievements. We sometimes forget that it may be as difficult to come to grips with those former students of Hinduism whose tomes still stand on the library shelves as it is to approach Hinduism itself: it may be that in some ways Friedrich Max Müller is as hard for the twenty-first-century student to "understand" as the Veda to which he devoted so much of his scholarly life. Either attempt may fail. That, though, is no reason for either possibility to be dismissed.

What is true of Max Müller is true, to a greater or lesser extent, of every student of Hinduism. Each is the child of a time and a place and is impelled by various combinations of circumstances to ask questions of India. Merchants, soldiers, lawyers, missionaries, philologists, historians, anthropologists, economists—all have had reasons of their own to approach India from a certain angle and to entertain a certain range of possible questions and answers. The answers they obtain are inevitably determined by the questions they ask: so much is obvious. In our present climate of opinion it is almost painfully obvious. If study in any branch of the humanities involves an initial motive on the student's part, acquaintance with a given body of material, and the application of one or other method, since the 1960s we have witnessed a gradual drift away from intense concentration on the material, by way of a nervous preoccupation with method, back to the intractable question of what motivates the investigator to ask questions in the first place.

There is, however, a good deal of difference between doing one's best to uncover and where necessary to make allowances for scholarly presuppositions—which is part of the serious business of historiography—and dismissing a branch of scholarship wholesale on the grounds of its real or imagined ideological shortcomings. It is my impression that Edward W. Said, in his enormously influential book *Orientalism*,[2] while carrying out to a high degree of professionalism the first of these exercises, may have pushed the less discerning in the direction of the second. And it is an unavoidable fact of history that where the study of Hinduism is concerned, throughout most of the period under review, the greater part of India was ruled from London by men who were not Hindus and who were ultimately answerable to the British Parliament. Some of these rulers made notable contributions to Indology, which indeed they often saw as a necessary aspect of the serious business of government. Does that, though, vitiate the result? More seriously, there is the question of missionary scholarship.[3] There has been in India a constant Christian missionary presence since the early sixteenth century, at first Roman Catholic but during the eighteenth century locally Protestant as well. Free access having been granted to missionaries by the East India Company in 1813 and 1833 (previously missionaries were not permitted into territory administered by the company for fear that they might "preach the natives into insurrection"), thereafter the Protestant as well as the other Catholic missionary presence in India was considerable. Some were minimally educated and poorly prepared. Others were outstanding scholars by anyone's standards. A few gave themselves, as time permitted, to the study of the land, life, and religion of India, and published their findings. Without these, the volume of European and American literature on Hindu subjects would be much smaller. What, though, are we to say about its quality?

Much might be said either way, and there is a body of opinion that insists that to belong to one religious tradition automatically disqualifies the individual concerned from pronouncing on any other. The insider-versus-outsider argument is an old and a persistent one. Very possibly it will never be settled. At least, though, one may allow that what the insider gains in immediacy is often lost in perspective, and vice versa. Best of all is perhaps to know one tradition or part-tradition intimately, but to see it in relation to others. Often this principle has been applied by the West, consciously or unconsciously, as India and Hinduism have been made to serve as a focus of ambition, admiration, proselytizing zeal, self-congratulation, self-criticism, deference, and attempted domination on the part of Christians. The study of Hinduism therefore may be seen not only as the material and method of a straightforward enquiry, but equally as a clue to Western self-understanding, of which a considerable part has been Christian.

Early Missionary Accounts

In April 1988 an Indian bookseller advertised, for the price of Rs. 2000, a two-volume work in reprint, William Hurd's *A Universal History of the*

Rites, Ceremonies, and Customs of the Whole World, calling it "encyclopaedic in nature" and pointing out that it would be useful to "the scholars of Religion, History, Anthropology, and Sociology all over the world." What was not made clear in the catalog was that Hurd's book had in fact been published in London precisely two hundred years earlier, in 1788. A copy of the folio first edition is among my most prized possessions. In 1788 the Asiatick Society had been in existence in Calcutta for four years; Sir William Jones had been in Calcutta for five. Three years earlier, Charles Wilkins had published his celebrated translation of the *Bhagavadgītā,* the *Bhăgvăt-Gēētā.* However, if we examine Hurd's encyclopaedia with an eye to the state of the study of Hinduism in 1788, we are bound to be disappointed—if at times amused. Hurd's was a work of Christian apologetics, parading the religious "rites, ceremonies, and customs" of the world only to dismiss them as shoddy (and in all likelihood satanic) counterfeits of true religion. India he clearly saw as being a land of grotesques and gargoyles: "There is a pagod near *Naugracut,* a considerable city between Indus and the Ganges, and in it an idol, which the Brahmins honour by cutting off part of their tongue. This, however, is done but once during their lives"—understandably so, on the whole.[4]

Popular images (such as this) of other people's religious traditions ought not to surprise anyone. It is, though, worth pointing out that even at the end of the eighteenth century, information about India and Hinduism was by no means unavailable to the West.[5] Much depended on where in the West one happened to be. On one level, the classically educated could begin with records first made in the wake of the expeditions of Alexander the Great by Megasthenes, and subsequently quoted by Diodorus Siculus, Strabo, and Arrian.[6] Principal William Robertson of Edinburgh published *An Historical Disquisition Concerning the Knowledge which the Ancients Had of India* in 1791 (4th ed., 1804), to which he added observations on Indian civil policy, laws and judicial proceedings, arts, sciences—and religious institutions, in all of which areas he was infinitely better informed than Hurd. That "the Ancients" provided a point of departure, was simply assumed, especially since the otherwise supremely authoritative biblical record stretched no farther east than to Mesopotamia. (A Bible-reading age could not on the other hand overlook condemnations of "idolatry" where India was concerned.)

On a quite different level, there were the "modern" firsthand accounts of India and things Indian that had been accumulating since the early sixteenth century. We who are accustomed to having easy access to information quite fail to appreciate the sheer effort required of whoever would study a people, a country, a language, a religion, without the help of the grammars, dictionaries, textbooks, and the other tools we so casually take for granted. This, however, was precisely the situation in which the pioneer European Indologists found themselves. A Roberto de Nobili found himself (as a Jesuit missionary in Madura) in a position to learn Sanskrit and even gain illicit access to a few Vedic texts: this was very early in the seventeenth century. It would not be appropriate, though, to claim that de Nobili was in any way interested in Hinduism for its own sake. A few years later, in the 1630s, Abraham Roger was serving as a chaplain of the Dutch East India Company in Madras.[7] He acquired a Portuguese-speaking Brahmin informant and proved to have considerable gifts as a reporter. His book "Open Door to Hidden Heathenism" appeared first in Dutch in 1651 and in a German translation of 1663 (*Offene Thür zu dem verborgenen Heydenthum*), and was notably free of theological, or other, special pleading. Roger had grasped matters that were not to become tolerably common knowledge for many years after his death (he died in 1649) and had classified what he had learned of Hinduism on what might almost be called phenomenological principles.

Moving on a further half-century, the first decade of the eighteenth century saw the commencement of the first Protestant Christian mission to India. Financed from Denmark, staffed from Germany, and administered from England, this international enterprise is known either as the "Danish-Halle" or the "Tranquebar" mission; its outstanding pioneer was Bartholomäus Ziegenbalg (d. 1719), who very quickly became proficient in Tamil, produced the first translations of Tamil into any European language (German), and in 1715 published the first Tamil grammar.[8] Ziegenbalg's two books about Hinduism, *Genealogie der Malabarischen Götter* (Genealogy of the Malabarian gods) and *Malabarischer Heidentum* (Malabarian heathenism), though written in the 1710s, were not published until 1867 and 1926, respectively, since the church leaders in Europe to whom they were sent told Ziegenbalg sourly that he and his colleagues had been sent to India to root out heathenism, not to propagate it in Europe by writing books about it. Copies of the missionaries' letters were on the other hand translated into English and published in London (3rd ed., 1718). The translation has its own charm: "They have many Books, which they pretend to have been deliver'd to them by their Gods, as we believe the Scriptures to be delivered to us by our God. Their Books are stuffed with abundance of pleasant Fables and witty Inventions concerning the Lives of their Gods. They afford Variety of pretty Stories, about the World to come."[9]

Colonial Origins of Indology Proper

Ziegenbalg and Plütschau were only the first of many missionaries of German (or in some cases Scandinavian) origin to work in South India. Always they prided themselves on the superiority of their ability to learn (usually) Tamil and to come to terms with Hindu culture and religion. However, by the end of the eighteenth century their work had fallen away. Following the battle of Plassey in 1757, the East India Company had found itself, somewhat to its surprise, in the position of having to administer areas of Asia vastly greater than the whole of Britain. From the first, "John Company" had determined to give the whole of religion—whether Hindu, Muslim or Christian—as wide a berth as was humanly possible, while trying to maintain a laisser-faire policy over against whatever religion happened to be practiced in their territories. This did not mean that Hinduism was deliberately favored. But laisser-faire will always favor the sitting tenant, especially where, as in this case, pragmatic and moral issues seemed to coincide.

That rebellion is bad for trade is a principle almost too obvious to need stating. That an administration such as that of the British in India had first of all to learn to manage India's intricate legal system was the complementary principle that helped to create the modern study of Hinduism. The lawyer-orientalist Sir William Jones arrived in Calcutta in September 1783.[10] By common consent, Jones's arrival began an epoch in Indology. Precisely why this should have been so is not so simply stated. Jones's time in India was not long; he died prematurely in 1794. In law, politics, and religion he was a Whig—a parliamentarian and populist who "declined to be governed by a single man whatever."[11] Like many other Whigs, Jones's religion took the form of deism: a Christianity purged of accretions and supernatural furniture and reduced to moral essentials, which essentials he was only too ready to find in Hinduism as well as in Christianity. His profession, however, was that of a lawyer, and his approach to India was by way of its codes of law. As S. N. Mukherjee has rightly observed, "Just as the scientific revolution of the seventeenth century was stimulated by the needs of navigation, so Oriental Studies was stimulated by the birth of colonial rule."[12]

Totally disinterested scholarship in any area may be a great rarity. In this case, Jones and his contemporaries among the merchants and lawyers of the East India Company in Bengal embarked upon the study of Hinduism, not simply because it was there but because *they* were there, and were responsible for administering Bengal's laws with as little friction as possible. This meant, among much else, the codification, translation, and publication of whatever *Shastras* were deemed the most important. Trade and turmoil did not sit well together; let the administration therefore interfere as little as possible with local religious practices (provided that they did not conflict with *universal* law, most particularly that forbidding the nonjudicial taking of human life), and offer them gentle support wherever possible. As to its own employees, the Company sensibly held that time spent in acquiring accurate knowledge of Hindu and Muslim belief, practices, and (especially) laws could never be time wasted.

The record of these years has been admirably set out by P. J. Marshall in *The British Discovery of Hinduism in the Eighteenth Century* (1970). Marshall passes in review the work of John Zephaniah Holwell, Alexander Dow, Nathaniel Brassey Halhed, Warren Hastings, Charles Wilkins, and of course William Jones.[13] A somewhat longer view is taken by George D. Bearce, in *British Attitudes towards India, 1784–1858* (1961), in which Hastings and Jones again figure largely. Bearing in mind the point about administrative responsibility, Halhed's *A Code of Gentoo Laws* (1776) may serve as an illustration of the problems early Indology had to face. The laws it contains were assembled by eleven *pandits* in Sanskrit, translated into Persian, then retranslated into English. There were further translations from English into French and German.[14]

The two most influential products of Bengal orientalism in the 1780s and 1790s were both fairly slight in comparison. Charles Wilkins's translation of the *Bhagavadgītā* (1785) and William Jones's translation of Kālidāsa's play *Śakuntalā* (1789).

Both translations were designed to appeal more to the aesthetic than to the religious sentiments of the West. Wilkins's *Bhagvat-Geeta, or Dialogue of Kreeshna and Arjoon* seems originally to have been no more than a pilot project on the way to a translation of the whole of the vast *Mahābhārata* (which Wilkins never completed). That it was published separately was thanks to the support of Warren Hastings in recommending it to the East India Company. Even so, Hastings had to argue his case since the Sanskrit language had no "official" status in India, and its study therefore could not be "applied to official profit." Wilkins's work he thought might serve in future to entertain the curious, as no doubt it did. What neither patron nor translator could have foreseen was the incalculable impulse given to the study of Hinduism in the West by this one work—a process about which I have written in some detail elsewhere.[15]

The Wilkins *Gītā* was not however to come into its own before the cool antiquarianism of the 1780s had given way to the enthusiasms of the age of romanticism, and then only in second place to William Jones's *Śakuntalā*.

Indology and the Romantic Movement

The turn from the eighteenth to the nineteenth century was a time of intellectual and spiritual turmoil in the West. The ingredients are well enough known: revolution in America and France, growing urbanization and industrialization, the partial collapse of the old hierarchical order, followed far too quickly by the phenomenon of Napoleon. The four-square classical model gave way to the freer romantic, the wit in his city coffeehouse to the ordinary man and woman in the village and field. The word *nature* took on an entirely new meaning as the countryside over against the town (in northern Europe; *forest* had similar overtones) as a place of refuge from the pressures of city life.[16] In the midst of nature, one could be closer to God's created order and therefore to true social and moral values. As always, the presence of a nearby tyrant (in this case, Napoleon) prompted peoples under threat to affirm each its own national identity, language, character, and traditions; in short, its own *Kultur* (to use a German term in a somewhat Germanic situation). India entered this drama of identity not so much as a present actuality, needing to be governed; rather, as a distant pastoral idyll, scented with jasmine and sandal, warm and friendly and peaceful. For this, William Jones's *Śakuntalā* was very largely responsible.

Jones's translation of Kālidāsa's play was first published in Calcutta in 1789. However, it was its further translation into German, by Georg

Forster in 1791, that made the greater impression.[17] Goethe's couplet from 1819 sums it all up:

> Willst Du den Himmel, die Erde mit einem Namen begreifen,
> Nenn ich, Sakontala, dich, und so ist alles gesagt.
> [Wouldst thou embrace heaven and earth with one name,
> I name thee, Sakontala, and all has been said.]

From *Sakontala*, from Friedrich Majer's German translation of Wilkins's *Gītā*, and from the French adventurer Anquetil Duperron's translation of a selection of Upanishads (from Persian into Latin, published in 1802–3) there developed Europe's romantic obsession with India and things Indian.[18] Also that of the New England transcendentalists, Emerson, Thoreau, Alcott, and the rest.[19] In these circles, "study" was a totally subjective notion, though this is not to say that the Germans in particular were not capable of serious and sustained effort. To the brothers August Wilhelm and Friedrich Schlegel, to Novalis (Friedrich von Hardenberg), to Schopenhauer, Humboldt, and others, India was not a territory to be administered; it was a landscape of the mind, to be contemplated less for its own sake than for its pleasant effect on the observer's imagination. For all that, wrote A. Leslie Willson, the image was "a figment of diverse imaginations, basically unreal, compounded through centuries of half-knowledge and suddenly focussed into illusory sharpness and brightness and with equal suddenness eclipsed."[20]

Max Müller and Others

The eclipse of which Willson speaks cannot be dated with precision, though the years around 1860 mark something of a watershed. One may speculate freely as to its causes. One was undoubtedly the Rebellion (or Mutiny, which technically it was) of 1857–58, which convinced the West, almost overnight, that human nature in extremis is much the same in India as elsewhere in the world. Another was the onset of critical scholarship, not directly linked either with the conversion or the administration of India. Friedrich Max Müller, around whom so much of the scholarly study of Hinduism in the second half of the nineteenth century circles revolved, observed in a Cambridge lecture in 1882 that his teacher in Paris, Eugène Burnouf, would never, like Sakuntala, have spent his life on "pretty Sanskrit ditties"; what he wanted, thundered Müller, was "history, human history, world-history."[21] Eight years earlier, addressing the International Congress of Orientalists in London, Müller had noted with satisfaction a shift toward the earliest accessible Sanskrit literature as being one of a change "from the purely aesthetic to the purely scientific interest in the language and literature of India."[22]

The existence of the four Vedas, and even (more or less) their names, had long been known outside India. Little, on the other hand, was known of their actual contents.[23] I do not wish to anticipate what my colleagues will write later in this volume; suffice it therefore to say that Max Müller had gone to Paris in 1845 to study the Veda under Eugène Burnouf at the Collège de France and to prepare for publication a definitive edition of the text of the *Rig Veda*, with Sāyaṇa's commentary. The whole of the project, incidentally, was financed by the East India Company, as had been the publication of Wilkins's *Gītā*. Müller bestrode the narrow world of late Victorian Indology like a colossus. He was born in Germany in 1823, but political turmoil in Europe in 1848 helped bring about a move to Oxford, where he spent the remainder of his life, dying a mere two months short of the twentieth century, on October 28, 1900.

Müller, his later scientific enthusiasm notwithstanding, was a child of the German romantic movement, the son of one of its great poets and friend of some of its great musicians (had he not chosen the academy, very likely he would have made his name as a pianist). He was not, on the other hand, an orthodox Christian: rather a broad-church liberal theist. By contrast, his slightly older contemporary Karl Graul was an excessively orthodox Lutheran, while being equally indebted to the romantic movement.[24] While Müller was laboring over his Vedic Sanskrit manuscripts in Paris and Oxford, Graul, perhaps no less gifted, was in South India, working not with Sanskrit but with Tamil sources. He died at the age of only fifty. Even so, his achievement was remarkable. To English missionaries, he was something of a bogeyman;[25] his Tamil Grammar of 1855, his five-volume *Reise nach Ost-Indien*, and especially his four-volume *Bibliotheca Tamulica*, containing texts and translations, nevertheless represent scholarship of the highest order.[26] That they are scarcely known outside a very narrow circle of German missiologists and Dravidologists may be a symptom of a common tendency to omit Tamil sources from consideration where Hinduism is concerned.

We cannot rectify this omission on this occasion, other than to refer to a symposium volume, *Tamil Studies Abroad*, published in Malaysia in 1968, and by quoting the name of one more nineteenth-century Tamil scholar, G. U. Pope, whose important edition of *The Tiruvāçagam* of Māṇikka-vāçagar appeared in 1900. Pope, like Graul, represented the Christian missionary movement, in which connection it is perhaps relevant to observe that Indian Christianity has always been far stronger in the "Dravidian" south of India than in the "Aryan" north. Other outstanding missionary scholars in this area include the Germans H. W. Schomerus, whose masterly study of Śaiva Siddhānta was published as long ago as 1912, but for some inexplicable reason has never been translated into English;[27] Arno Lehmann, translator of Tāyumānavar and author of *Sivaite Piety in Tamil Devotional Literature* (1948); and the Swede Carl Gustav Diehl, to whose field studies we owe two important later works, *Instrument and Purpose* (1956) and *Church and Shrine* (1965).

After this excursus we may return to the second half of the nineteenth century and to Max Müller. It has often been noted with surprise, and sometimes with disapproval, that despite having had many opportunities, Max Müller never actually visited India, no doubt preferring the ideals of an imagined past to the actualities of a stressful present.[28] Certainly he had a low view of "Brahmanism," and an even lower view of popular Hinduism, feeling it to belong to "a stratum of thought which is long buried beneath our feet: it may live on, like the lion and the tiger, but the mere air of free thought will extinguish it."[29] The Hindu reform movements of the nineteenth century were another matter entirely.

Müller's philosophy of history was one in which initial purity of perception of the divine had been allowed to become corrupted by the casting of natural phenomena (and especially the sun) in mythological form. Although he did urge an audience in 1871 to think of the sun "awakening the eyes of man from sleep, and his mind from slumber! Was not the Sunrise to him the first wonder, the first beginning of all reflection, all thought, all philosophy? was it not to him the first revelation, the first beginning of all trust, of all religion?"[30], sunrise exultation and the sense of the infinite that it prompted was still not enough: there also had to be the sense of moral obligation after the manner of Kant. "True" religion, therefore, is "the perception of the infinite under such manifestations as are able to influence the moral character of man."[31] Alas, thereafter the human record had been one of steady decline into troughs of mythology, metaphysics, priestcraft, and special pleading, exemplified at a very early stage in India, so Müller thought, by the ritual treatises the *Brāhmaṇas*. Still, what has been obscured can be revealed afresh, if only accretions can be cleared away. This was what Gautama Buddha had done in his day. It appeared to be what Hindu reform, spreading in concentric circles from the Brāhmo Samāj, was doing at the end of the nineteenth century. In various places Müller wrote warmly about the Brāhmo leadership, about Rāmakrishṇa, about Dayānanda Sarasvatī, and about Vivekānanda:[32] for the Theosophists, on the other hand, he had no time at all. In 1893 he might have shared the Chicago platform with Swāmī Vivekānanda, had not ill health prevented his going—and what was the World's Parliament of Religions, if not a demonstration of universal theism? Naturally he was not in favor of Christian missions in any proselytizing sense (and a storm blew up when he said as much in Westminster Abbey);[33] he would, one fancies, have been a warm supporter of the principle of interreligious dialogue as a means of bringing about a parallel, and ultimately converging, reform in both partners' perceptions.

What Clemenceau once said of Lord Curzon ("orgueil immense—justifié") might well have been said of Max Müller. His very distinction was such as to arouse envy and resentment in lesser mortals, added to which some of his theories did not sit easily with the post-Darwinian climate of opinion and came in for a constant challenge from such as Andrew Lang.[34] In Indology, however, his chief opponent was the abrasive William Dwight Whitney, professor of Sanskrit at Harvard, who (for reasons unknown to me) seldom missed an opportunity to belittle Müller's work. Müller for his part seldom replied, and then always in a tone of chilly politeness.[35] Arguably his two major achievements were his *Rig Veda* and his *Sacred Books of the East*. For the rest, he is no doubt seen rather as the last of the romantics than as the first of the moderns in the study of Hinduism.[36]

Indology: The Latter Half of the Nineteenth Century

Elsewhere I have singled out the mid-1880s as a time of serious realignment in the West's perceptions of India, due almost entirely to the rise at that time of a new national consciousness in India. Keshab Chandra Sen, Dayānanda Sarasvatī, and Śrī Rāmakrishṇa died within not many months of one another; the Theosophists migrated to Adyar by way of Bombay, there to carry out their extraordinary career of power brokerage. In 1883 P. C. Mozoomdar published *The Oriential Christ*, J. R. Seeley *The Expansion of England*, and Henry Drummond *Natural Law in the Spiritual World*. In 1885 Madame Blavatsky left India for the last time, her reputation in tatters, and the Indian National Congress met for the first time. In 1884 Max Müller was writing about the new reformers in his *Biographical Essays*. In 1885 Edwin Arnold brought the first century of English-language *Bhagavadgītā* interpretation to an end with *The Song Celestial*. Finally, in this deliberately haphazard list, in 1883 an apparently minor adjustment to the legal system of India, the Ilbert Bill, which first opened up the theoretical possibility of Europeans in India being tried by Indian judges, passed through the legislative machinery and sparked waves of resentment and counterresentment, in the worst outbreak of racial feeling India had experienced since the Mutiny. The young (seventeen years old in December 1882) Rudyard Kipling had just returned to India to work as a journalist on the Lahore *Civil and Military Gazette*. By the decade's end, having published *Departmental Ditties* and *Plain Tales from the Hills*, his name was a household word all over India. (The reading of Kipling, incidentally, supplies insights into life in late-nineteenth-century India that are not easily come by elsewhere. His masterpiece, *Kim*, appeared in 1900.)

In one respect the developing political and religious situation in India between 1880 and 1914 brought about a partial return to earlier conditions relative to the study of Hinduism; namely, in the supplementing of literary sources by firsthand observation. This did not always then (nor does it now) meet with the unqualified approval of philologists and historians of the severer sort. But the shift in wind direction was not to be overlooked.

By 1914 practically the whole of the edifice of modern Indology was in place, as far as the foundations were concerned. This is not the place to pass in review all the individual contributions. It might be observed though that an elementary bibliography, such as that placed by J. N. Farquhar at the end of the second edition of *A Primer of Hinduism* (1914), includes some ninety titles (plus a dozen on "Hinduism and Christianity")—surveys, texts, translations, commentaries, and the like—many of which are still eminently usable today. Had it been only a matter of studying Hinduism in the light of history (and fairly remote history at that), then aside from adjustments, little thereafter need have changed. In fact far-reaching changes did take place. Perhaps the greatest single error of

Western Indology has always lain in its tacit assumption that "essential" Hinduism (whatever that might turn out to be) must somehow be immune from the pressures of secularization, and that mutant forms of Hindu belief and praxis must therefore be treated with excessive caution. From one point of view this was a sensible assumption since the historical-philological method was an unsuitable (or at least inadequate) tool to use on some of the emergent problems of the turn of the century. But from another, it caused academic Indology in particular to neglect much of interest and importance. Faced with a hermeneutical problem in any tradition, the indignant response, "But this is not what it was intended to mean" may be up to a point understandable. Often it is not helpful.

We might take as a case in point the curious fate of the terms *Indo-European*, *Aryan* and *Vedic* in relation to linguistic, racial, and national patterns, respectively. The relationship between Sanskrit, Latin, and Greek verbal roots and grammatical forms having prompted Jones in 1786 to hypothesize that they might have "sprung from some common source, which, perhaps, no longer exists,"[37] and having been established on sound linguistic principles by Franz Bopp in his epoch-making *Vergleichende Grammatik* (1833–52), the Indo-European "family" was thereafter accepted as having been made up of Sanskrit, Old Persian (Zend, Avestan), Greek, Latin, Lithuanian, Old Slavonic, Gothic, and German components. Common sense dictated that if this "common source," this common *Ursprache*, once existed, someone, somewhere must once have spoken it. And certainly it is hard not to draw some such conclusion. Who were they? According to the great Swedish linguist Björn Collinder, "It is probable that the ancestors of the Indo-European peoples began, about six thousand years ago, to spread out from a homeland north of the Black Sea."[38] Possibly. One can never, in the absence of reliable archaeological evidence, know. As to the later evidence, some mythological resemblances are almost too obvious: the Scandinavian Thorr to all intents and purposes *is* the Hindu Indra. But to proceed from there to conclude that everything identifiable as Indo-European, Indo-Germanic, or Aryan might have been set to music by Wagner, is simply not justified.

The time would come when Max Müller would be hailed by Indian nationalists as *mokṣa mūla*, and even Hitler would be admired by some Indians as a masterful fellow Aryan. But was not the Veda the oldest recorded repository of "Aryan" wisdom, established long before the Germanic peoples began to emerge from their forests into the light of (comparative) civilization? The equation was almost too obvious: Aryan equalled Vedic; India and Europe, East and West, were hyphenated after all, and India could bask in reflected glory while awaiting her own national vindication. Germans might think of themselves as the "most Aryan" of Aryans, and in the years before 1914 said so, loudly and often. India knew better. Still, a very few years ago it was possible to read in the Indian press the claim that until just sixteen hundred years ago the whole of Europe was "a non-Christian, Hindu, Vedic region."[39] Seldom can a simple academic observation have been sent forth on a more intricate journey to reach a more unlikely result.

A more easily traced realignment of traditional hermeneutical principles concerns the *Bhagavadgītā*, that most widely read and deeply loved of Hindu metaphysical treatises. Over the past few years I have written extensively on this subject and will therefore be brief. Before about the 1880s, students of Hinduism almost all regarded the *Bhagavadgītā* as an interpolation in the *Mahābhārata*, and its problems as belonging to India's fairly remote past. Then came the "Krishṇa renaissance" of the 1880s, the identification of Krishṇa as the *avatāra* the times required, his cause as India's cause, his doctrine of "selfless endeavor" (*niṣkāmakarma*) as the perfect creed for a national movement—and the *Bhagavadgītā* as his scripture. It has been said that Bankim Chandra Chatterjee had been reading Renan and that Keshab Chandra Sen had been influenced by Seeley's *Ecce Homo*, with the result that the "new" Krishṇa had taken on some of the features of the liberal Jesus. Some Christian missionary interpreters could argue that Jesus' record was "historical," as that of Krishṇa was not. That argument, however, could appeal only to those prepared to respect the rules of historical evidence. In passing, one might perhaps reflect upon the ease with which legends concerning Jesus' basic training in Ladakh and death in Kashmir were launched and accepted, both, as it happens, in the 1890s. In face of such apparent aberrations, those heirs of the age of reason who studied India needed to learn one lesson above all: that where incontrovertible evidence meets and comes into conflict with established authority, there can be only one victor. Generally speaking, it is not often the evidence.

Concerning the "original" life-setting of the *Bhagavadgītā*, we are hardly better informed today than we were in 1785. Sacred scripture, however, is always contemporary. It was in the 1880s that the *Bhagavadgītā* began to acquire its latest contemporaneity, as first the Bengali Vaiṣṇavas, then the Theosophists, then the political radicals around Aurobindo Ghosh, took up the subject of its political implications. Not before 1903 was any assessment even attempted.[40]

The Development of Archeology

Between 1899 and 1905, India's viceroy was Lord Curzon. Depending on one's point of view, Curzon was either the best or the worst of viceroys. The Bengali radicals hated him for partitioning Bengal (in 1905), for casting aspersions on their truthfulness, for being skeptical about the reality, as opposed to the rhetoric, of Indian nationalism, and for much else besides. Ask India today to whom she owes the restoration of her major tourist attraction, the Taj Mahal, and it is unlikely that anyone would mention the name of Curzon.

Curzon, however, was a well-informed and energetic patron of Indian archaeology. In Vrindaban in 1899, he said, after having pointed out how many temples there had been built and restored at government expense, "I accept the conservation of the ancient monuments of India as an elementary obligation of Government."[41] To the Asiatic Society in Calcutta in 1900 he said, in terms his opponents would scarcely have credited,

> If there be anyone who says to me that there is no duty devolving upon a Christian Government to preserve the monuments of a pagan art, or the sanctuaries of an alien faith, I cannot pause to argue with such a man. Art, and beauty, and the reverence that is owing to all that has evoked human genius . . . are embraced by the common religion of all mankind. Viewed from this standpoint, the rock temple of the Brahmans stands on precisely the same footing as the Buddhist Vihara, and the Muhammadan Musjid as the Christian Cathedral.[42]

Curzon's restoration of the Taj Mahal—an involvement that extended to the removal of cobwebs from the staircase of the west pavilion[43]—is not central to our subject. His appointment in 1902 of John Marshall ("rather distinguished in appearance and quite becomingly keen") as director-general of the Archaeological Survey of India, was a step the long-term consequences of which no one, and least of all Curzon himself, could possibly have foreseen.

In any comprehensive study of an ancient, and living, religious tradition, it is customary to combine three types of approach: the textual, the archaeological, and (where appropriate) the method of direct observation following the techniques of anthropology and folklore. Archaeology, anthropology, and folklore are however all relatively young sciences, having begun to acquire a measure of academic respectability only toward the end of the nineteenth century. Before that time, such interest as there was in "antiquities" tended to be found only among well-meaning but untrained amateurs, typified by Sir Walter Scott's Jonathan Oldbuck (in *The Antiquary*, 1816). The principles of stratification, classification, and recording came to be applied only gradually.

For India's part, the first of the archaeologists had been James Fergusson, who had begun his work in the 1840s and whose books "sound one unending note of passionate protest against the barrack-builder, and the military engineer."[44] An Archaeological Survey of Northern India had been created by Lord Canning in 1860, and two years later General Sir Alexander Cunningham had been appointed archaeological surveyor to the government. The move was a promising one, but the survey was inadequately financed and after 1889 fell into abeyance, until reestablished by Curzon in 1900–1905. Curzon, who left India in 1905, died in 1925, not living to see the publication of the most spectacular results of his policy.

The first task of the original archaeological survey was the maintenance of existing monuments, rather than the opening up of entirely new sites. This changed dramatically after World War I. As with the Mesopotamian mounds, the existence of massive prehistoric sites in the northwest of India (now Pakistan) had always been known, though not what they were. One, the later famous site of Harappa, was cannibalized in 1856 for use in railway construction.[45] Marshall began serious excavation at another site, Mohenjo-daro, in 1922. His work, and later that of E. J. H. Mackay, M. S. Vats, and Mortimer Wheeler, completely revolutionized our picture of prehistoric India, and with it many hitherto unchallenged assumptions about Hindu origins were thrown open to fresh debate.[46]

Still, in the 1920s it was customary to see the "Aryan" entry into India as a process in which cultured newcomers ("the Aryans") overran a rabble of savages ("Dasyus"): "These Dasyus were of a dark complexion, eating beef and indulging in Goblin worship (!). When the Aryans met them they desired to keep themselves aloof from them."[47] The massive and well-ordered remains of Mohenjo-Daro were clearly not built by India's equivalent to the crudely shapeless "Ancient Britons"; who *had* built them was another matter, especially since the Indus script has so far resisted decipherment. Concerning the by-now-famous images—the proto-Śiva, the limbless Naṭarāja, the "priest-king," and the rest—we may speculate, but we are not permitted to know.

In one respect the identity of the Indus Culture was of more than antiquarian importance, especially in the tense political atmosphere of the 1930s. Length of tenure will always be important where rule is disputed, and part of the traditional Hindu argument had had to do with chronology. As we have seen, nationalism had made "Vedic" and "Aryan" into evocative terms. Suppose now that archaeology should demonstrate conclusively that India's very own high civilization had not been Aryan at all, but (perhaps) Dravidian; and that on the point of entry into India, the Veda was actually an unsafe guide. The archaeologists were fortunately untroubled by such questions as these. Now it is the question of prehistory that most clearly distinguishes older from newer scholarship in Hinduism, and does so on the basis of solid evidence. Concerning the interpretation of that evidence, and the reading of the Indus script, on the other hand, there is still a fairly high level of uncertainty. In the absence of the Indian equivalent of the Rosetta Stone, the precise identity of the Indus Culture, and its relationship to later Hinduism, will however remain a mystery.[48]

Max Weber

Indology having developed in the nineteenth century as a largely literary exercise, it has always been rather too easy for the student of Hinduism to overlook that vast body of supplementary evidence having to do with the land and life of Hindu India, assembled by Europeans—administrators, missionaries, and others—of long residence in India, generally on a basis of firsthand observation. This was, as we have seen, where the study of Hinduism had started before the texts were available. In the nineteenth century, a rough distinction was commonly drawn between "higher" and "lower" (or "popular") Hinduism, the former being textually based and Brahmanical, the latter being virtually unclassifiable, though described in the 1901 census report as "the medley of heterogeneous and uncomfortable superstitions now known by the not entirely appropriate name of

Animism."[49] Information on such matters could be obtained only by very few investigators, and could be written up by even fewer.[50]

A related, and yet vastly different, development is associated with the name of the celebrated German sociologist Max Weber and with his attempt to bring the religions of India within the orbit of what was then the relatively new science of sociology. Weber's pioneer sociological study of Indian religion was written at the time of World War I and represents the state of scholarship as it was before 1920. It is not, however, translated into English, as *The Religion of India* until 1958.[51]

The book's background is of unusual interest. At the time at which it was written, the West tended to vacillate between two contrasting images of India: one as the home of timeless wisdom, the other as a case of arrested socioeconomic development. Both were put down to the same cause; namely, the dominance of Hindu and Buddhist "otherworldliness" over the land and life of India. Weber took the second of these views. Hindu philosophy, thought Weber, having been permanently focused on "individual salvation—striving," had "served as a barrier to the development of special science as well as to a framing of the problem of thought in general."[52] In fact, Weber's study was a by-product of his wrestling with the problem that had exercised Germany since the 1870s—that of why some nations (of which Germany up to then was not one) had industrialized and turned to capitalism more rapidly than others. We cannot go into this intriguing question further here. Suffice it to say that Weber was persuaded that India had always been culturally conditioned against economic enterprise by a number of interrelated factors, of which religion (philosophy, ideology) was the chief.[53] At this time, incidentally, there was a growing tendency to blame colonial rule for India's chronic economic plight. Weber certainly did not share this reading of the situation.

Modern Imaging of Hinduism

The interwar years—the 1920s and 1930s—were years during which India occupied a prominent position on the world political stage. Analyses and commentaries were legion, and, naturally enough, the religious question bulked large in the discussions—especially the place of India's various religious traditions in the country's hoped-for future. On the popular level, Hindu voices most often heard by the West included those of Rabindranath Tagore, Śrī Aurobindo, and Sarvepalli Radhakrishnan, as well as the omnipresent Mohandas Karamchand Gandhi and (though leaning far in the secular direction) Jawaharlal Nehru. None was "orthodox" in the strictest sense. All however helped to create a modern image of Hinduism, an image not always congruent with Indian actualities.

No doubt the process had begun when Swāmī Vivekānanda stood to address the delegates to the World's Parliament of Religions in Chicago in 1893, proclaiming the all-embracing nature and boundless tolerance of his tradition. Between *Gītāñjali* in 1912 (and the Nobel Prize for literature in the following year) and *The Religion of Man* twenty years later, Rabindranath Tagore presented India to the world much as the German romantics had done, as an oasis of spirituality and beauty amid arid wastes of materialism and ugliness. Gandhi's way was that of moral intensity, Aurobindo's (once his earlier political activism had been put behind him) that of metaphysical subtlety. But it was left to Radhakrishnan to carry the word to the West, and virtually to define "Hinduism" to a large proportion of subsequent students.

Radhakrishnan's 1926 lectures on *The Hindu View of Life* certainly comprise the most widely read statement of Hindu apologetics ever.[54] They are on the other hand neither simple in their background nor straightforward in their implications. To read them with full understanding (if such indeed be possible) requires an extensive exercise in the history of ideas and the tracing of many a subtlety of East-West, Hindu-Christian relations, idealist philosophy, internationalism in the style of the League of Nations, and much else besides. The heart of the matter is perhaps contained in the statement that says: "Leaders of Hindu thought and practice are convinced that the times require, not a surrender of the basic principles of Hinduism, but the restatement of them with special reference to the needs of a more complex and mobile social order."[55] Radhakrishnan actually achieved such a "restatement." His Hinduism however was an ideal; for Hindu actualities he had very little time. Nevertheless, he supplied students with widely read translations of and commentaries on the *Bhagavadgītā*, the *Upaniṣads*, and the *Brahmasūtra*, and cannot be overlooked where it is a matter of modern images of Hinduism.

Radhakrishnan, despite (or perhaps in part because of) having attended the Madras Christian College, did not much care for most Christian missionaries;[56] nor, with the odd exception, did Gandhi, who on one occasion in the mid-1920s solemnly lectured a group of the most liberal

Calcutta missionaries on the need to abandon the attitudes of ignorant intolerance that had characterized the least liberal half a century earlier. Ignorant tolerance had not been overcome in the 1920s; in some quarters it has still not been overcome, which is perhaps why missionary contributions to the study of Hinduism tend often to be ignored or dismissed as Machiavellian devices to entrap the unwary. This is unnecessary. The missionary generation of which J. N. Farquhar (d. 1929) was doyen, and may serve as representative, made a notable contribution to the study of Hinduism.[57] Of Farquhar's own works, mention may be made of A *Primer of Hinduism* (2nd ed. 1914, long a standard elementary textbook), and *An Outline of the Religious Literature of India* (1920), a remarkable tour de force. As editor, he presided over works as varied as Henry Whitehead's *The Village Gods of South India* (1916), A. B. Keith's *The Sāṁkhya System* (1918), Margaret Stevenson's *The Rites of the Twice-born* (1920), Keith's *The Karma Mīmāṁsā* (1921) and *Classical Sanskrit Literature* (1923), and H. A. Popley's *The Music of India* (1921)—all of them admirably clear and concise statements. Conspicuous by its absence from his lists was, however, anything to do with Tantra.

The principle that the student seldom sees what he or she is not looking for applies most forcefully in the case of Tantra. The existence of a secret *cultus*, in which common taboos were reversed and in which sexuality and metaphysics entered into a strange alliance, had been known to Western orientalists throughout the nineteenth century.[58] There were, however, obvious reasons why it was little known in detail. For one thing, it really was secret, and impossible of access to the uninitiated. For another, sexuality and sexual symbolism, though not the whole of Tantra, was enough of it to make the Victorian age acutely uncomfortable. Not everything sexual in the Hindu world is Tantra; but the connection having been made, it could not easily be unmade.[59] To the barrier of secrecy, there was added the barrier of taste; and to the barrier of taste, the barrier of public morality. A turn-of-the-century missionary summed it up, when he stated that, in his view, Tantra contained "an amount of evil which is certainly unsurpassed, we believe unequalled, in any other system."[60] Even Farquhar, who otherwise always went as far as possible in the exercise of imaginative sympathy for things Hindu, called the rituals of Left-Handed Tantra "foul beyond description."[61]

Tantra, however (not necessarily of the left-handed variety), was certainly an element in Bengali nationalism. Bankim Chandra hinted at it; Rāmakrishṇa appears to have had a Tantric guru; Aurobindo's *śakti* speculations pointed toward a territory of which Tantra was the furthest point. Bearing this in mind, its reappearance in some neo-Hindu movements of the period post–1960 ought not to occasion too much surprise. On the scholarly level, the poineer interpreter was Sir John Woodroffe, a writer better known under the pseudonym of Arthur Avalon. Sir John was a judge of the Calcutta High Court in the tradition of Sir William Jones—hence no doubt the use of the pseudonym. In the early years of the century he published a number of Tantric texts, with introductions and commentaries, the best known of which appeared under the titles of *Tantra of the Great Liberation* (1913) and *The Serpent Power* (1919).[62]

As in so much else, World War I marked a watershed in the study of Tantra. It is hardly likely that there was more Tantra being practiced in, say, 1930 than in 1910; very likely there was less. But in the West, the 1920s marked the beginnings of that shift in sexual perceptions and politics that has been so characteristic of Western modernity. Sigmund Freud perhaps led the onslaught; by the 1960s, the bastions had fallen completely.[63] By 1971 a Tantra Exhibition was being mounted in London, with the public display of much that a century earlier might well have aroused the attentions of the police.

Along the way, another shift in perception had taken place, a shift that is not easily characterized but that might perhaps be styled "reflexive." The post-Napoleon romantics had wallowed in their images of India, in the interests of their own feelings. Their post-Kaiser counterparts sought to contemplate India, and with it the images and symbols of Hinduism, as a microcosm of universal humanity, a peaceable kingdom seeking to be set free from the blight of Western influence. The 1914–18 war having loosened the West's trust in—and grasp of—rationality, in the 1920s and 1930s many desperate attempts were made to recreate a universe of discourse on alternative foundations. Not surprisingly, art came into its own as an alternative to verbalization (which is not to say that the flood of words was ever interrupted), and with it there came a heightened interest in the intricate symbolism of Hindu iconography.

To be sure, for the West's part this was an aesthetic rather than a performative matter. That, though, suited the mood of introspection that came over so many Western intellectuals in the middle years of the century. In the quest for wholeness (what the Jungians taught us to call "individuation"), signs and symbols of transcendence might be of so many kinds. Words were blunt instruments, when compared with the subtleties of dance or a *rāga;* and to many it seemed that the troubles of the West had been not unconnected with its habit of obsessive verbalization.

It is impossible to write concisely of the experiential wave that has swept over Western spirituality since the early 1920s. Its effects—to some, insidious, to others, liberating—have been felt everywhere and show up in the work of all but a very few scholars. Acknowledged leaders in relation to the study of Hinduism included Ananda K. Coomaraswamy;[64] his fellow-pilgrims on the way of the *philosophia perennis;* and Heinrich Zimmer.[65] The work of both Coomaraswamy and Zimmer was completed by the early 1950s.

That ecstasy should have so far cooled down as to become aesthetics, and that Tantra should have been similary tamed (though the late Mircea Eliade certainly knew differently), should surprise no one. Mysticism has been given the same treatment by being scaled down to the level of common comprehension. One wonders, this being so, whether the nonrational aspect of Hinduism—or any other religious tradition, for that matter—can ever be brought within reach under the normal ministrations of the academy, most of whose members can hardly be said to be specialists in the ecstatic. However, as the *Bhagavadgītā* says, it is bad work to attempt to perform *dharma* to which one is not born.

Epic and Myth

In the eighteenth century, the modern study of Hinduism had begun with the pragmatic need to grasp the intricacies of "native" codes of law and with a largely antiquarian interest in Indo-European epic. In the early part of the nineteenth century, while various European epics—the Edda, the Nibelungenlied, the Kalevala, the Mabinogion, the Tain—were finding their place afresh as part of the collective memory of their respective peoples, Indology was tuned in largely to either Vedic antiquity or what it imagined to be timeless metaphysics. Certainly the epics were being discussed as the literary structure of the Old Testament or Homer was being discussed.[66] The *Mahābhārata* was assumed to be the more important of the two great epics (which for India's part it was not), and it was further assumed that it had come into being by stages, after one of which (according to one theory), the original Kaurava heroes had become the villains, as the Pāṇḍava villains had become the heroes. This theory was given textbook form by Adolf Holtzmann Jr. in *Das Mahābhārata und seine Teile* (1895). Mention may also be made of E. Washburn Hopkins's *The Great Epic of India* (1901) as a summing up, without extravagances, of nineteenth-century scholarship in the area. But as J. A. B. van Buitinen pointed out in the early 1970s, for many years the epics were far from being a popular field of scholarship.[67] The exception was of course the *Bhagavadgītā* episode, which has continued throughout our period to generate translations, commentaries, and a considerable popular following. Some of this I have attempted to sum up elsewhere and will here pause only to observe that, in most instances, the *Bhagavadgītā* was treated more or less as a free-standing entity, linked with but hardly dependent upon the remainder of the epic.[68]

Of the vast importance of myth in the spiritual and intellectual history of the human race, no one now needs to be reminded (except perhaps those journalists and others to whom *myth* is inevitably treated as error and untruth, and juxtaposed with *fact*). So central is it, that the whole of this survey might well have based on shifting theories and perceptions of myth. As Mircea Eliade noted in his foreword to the Feldman-Richardson anthology *The Rise of Modern Mythology* (1972), "the evaluation of myth goes together with a specific understanding of religion and, accordingly, with a specific conception of man."[69] From "savage superstitions," by way of nature—and solar mythologies, Darwinian speculations, myth-and-ritual, functional and structural models to whatever is uppermost at the present day (a matter on which no one can be absolutely certain), the constant factor has been the human propensity for image making and storytelling.

At this point the Indo-European connection takes on a renewed importance. In the 1930s, the myth and ritual school around Elliot Smith, Perry, Hocart, and Hooke had its sights set chiefly on Egypt, Mesopotamia, and the ancient Near East generally, only Hocart extending his investigations into the Hindu world.[70] Similarly with the Scandinavian (chiefly Swedish) "traditio-historical" school that flourished between the 1940s and 1960s. In this case, however, there was the additional factor of the role of Iran in the cultural pattern of the ancient Near East as a bridge between the Indo-European and Semitic worlds. Nathan Söderblom (d. 1931) had always been more of a generalist than a specialist Iranist. In the interwar years, however, Iranian studies were represented in Uppsala by the formidable H. S. Nyberg, among whose pupils were Geo Widengren and Stig Wikander. It also happens that in the late 1930s there was at the University of Uppsala a French *lecteur* by the name of Georges Dumézil.[71]

Dumézil is of course a great celebrity in modern Indo-European studies, with a vast (and often controversial) output dating back to the 1920s. Readers of C. Scott Littleton's excellent "assessment" of Dumézil's work in *The New Comparative Mythology* (2nd ed., 1973) may on the other hand be surprised to see how often the name of Wikander appears in his account (twenty-four times in all), as "the earliest and by far the most original of Dumézil's true 'disciples.'"[72] Actually the two were in each other's debt. Wikander cited Dumézil frequently, and vice versa. Especially important was an eleven-page article published by Wikander in Swedish in 1947, *Pāṇḍava-sagan och Mahābhāratas mytiska förutsättningar* (The Pāṇḍava saga and the mythical background of the Mahābhārata).[73] Oddly enough, in view of its stated importance (and its brevity), no one appears to have taken the trouble to translate it into English. Wikander's thesis was that in the *Mahābhārata* the sons of Pāṇḍu were to all intents and purposes human representations of the gods of Dumézil's celebrated "three functions." In Dumézil's own words, "Step by step, over twenty years or so, the interpretative method thus disclosed proved capable of extension to most of the important characters of the poem, and even its subject: it (the Epic) is an entire archaic mythology, more archaic on several counts than the Vedic mythology, that has been transposed to provide these epic characters and their exploits."[74]

Space does not permit further consideration of the historical and literary problems connected with the Dumézil heritage. Reference may be made to the symposium volume *Myth in Indo-European Antiquity*, though with the caveat that the functions of myth—even of archaic myth—are by no means restricted to antiquity, whether Indo-European or any other.[75] A volume spanning the ages is *Krishna: Myths, Rites, and Attitudes*, in which a mixed company of specialists in various academic disciplines joined forces in an excellent interdisciplinary project edited by Milton Singer.[76] This may also be the place to mention Singer's important study *When a Great Tradition Modernizes* (1972), of which more in a moment.

Indology after Indian Independence

It is to state no more than the obvious when we say that beginning in the mid-1960s, there took place a sudden expansion in the study of Hinduism in Western tertiary institutions. The causes are well enough known, up to a point. The advent of jet travel in a time of relative affluence made India accessible to young Europeans and Americans and created a new phenomenon in the West itself: the jet-age guru. Everywhere values were being questioned. To the post-Napoleon, post-Kaiser, and post-Hitler phases there was added (and not only in the United States) the post-Gandhi, post-Kennedy, post–Martin Luther King age. Always India was made to stand for spirituality in a time of materialism, for pacifism in a time of violence, for beauty amid the filth of the megalopolis, for the spontaneous and instinctive over against the rationally calculated. To this was added in some cases the lure of cheap drugs and in others the vague promise of power. TM, ISKCON, Divine Light, Ananda Marga—everyone knew what they were, and to a certain extent what they stood for. But the alienation factor was often there; in 1970, say, a student would happily admit to being a meditator, outside evangelical circles not to praying regularly.

All this was a mixed blessing. It was good for university lecturers to have respectably sized classes, however varied they were in their motives and capabilities. It was good to have publishers beating a path to one's door in search of *oeuvres de vulgarisation* (not however of scholarly monographs: these one had to pay for oneself), of which there were a great number produced in these years. Some writers achieved miracles of condensation. Rather than embarrass others, I will cite my own *Thinking about Hinduism* (1971), a mere sixty pages in length and an example of the farthest limits of this approach. But as my first teacher of comparative religion, S. G. F. Brandon, was in the habit of saying when the popularization question came up, if qualified academics would not do it, the task would be taken up by the less well equipped, as indeed it was.

Modernity and Indology

Since the 1960s the study of Hinduism has proceeded on a great many fronts simultaneously, only a very few of which can be accessible to a single observer at any one time. A rough line of demarcation has been between "pure" and "applied" studies, in line with trends in the humanities and the study of religion generally. The former aims at the acquisition of hard evidence on the principles of historical (including archaeological) and philological research, though increasingly modified by the techniques of the social sciences and the insistence that modern India actually *is* a modern nation.

Rather than attempt a catalog, let me here cite the work of M. N. Srinivas and Milton Singer. Srinivas, a pupil of E. E. Evans-Pritchard, is perhaps best known as the author of *Social Change in Modern India* (1968), in which he established Sanskritization, Westernization, Secularization, and Caste Mobility, both as terms and research priorities, and ended with some important methodological observations on "the study of one's own society."[77] One of these was semipolitical: "The sociologist's commitment to democratic processes is fundamental, and is derived from his commitment to his discipline, for unfettered social inquiry cannot exist and flourish in totalitarian systems."[78] Delivered in 1963, the lectures were not published until 1966. The timing could not have been bettered.

Milton Singer's *When a Great Tradition Modernizes* took up Robert Redfield's 1950s distinction between Little Tradition and Great Tradition (corresponding roughly to what previous generations had called "popular" and "higher" Hinduism) and Srinivas's research among the Coorgs, supplemented by fieldwork in Madras, to describe and illustrate a process of social change. Singer refers at some length to the work of Weber, clearly establishing a lineage.[79] Also, as it happens, in December 1972 Trevor Ling was lecturing in Leeds on "Max Weber in India," hinting strongly that Weber's eminence notwithstanding, he could never have written as he did had he actually spent some time in India.[80]

Before leaving the social-scientific approach to the machinery of Hindu society, it may be worth recalling that India since 1947 has been a "secular" state. I recall an Indian government film on hydroelectric power stations, advertised in about 1970 as Temples of Tomorrow. It was ironical that, just then, the disinherited and alienated young of the West were beginning to flock to India in search of the spirituality they claimed not to be able to find in their own culture. In the Indian context, "secular" has more than one meaning. An old-style socialist like Jawaharlal Nehru could, and did, complain bitterly and often that religion had always been the chief hindrance to India's progress, and needed to be dispensed with.[81] The great Swedish economist Gunnar Myrdal, in his massive *Asian Drama* (1968), agreed. So, too, did P. N. Bazaz, who like Nehru was a Kashmiri Brahmin. In his polemical book *The Role of Bhagavad Gītā in Indian History* (1975) Bazaz argued similarly that because of its endorsement of caste, the Gītā was no work for the right-thinking socialist.[82]

Social science and socialist theory notwithstanding, and despite the severe demands made of the student by historical and philological discipline, the study of Hinduism in recent years has in many cases proceeded on a far more superficial level. To study a complex web of traditions, such as "Hinduism" undoubtedly is, may be an art or a science: it certainly involves the mastery of a craft, the first steps of which involve passing through the needle's eye of philology—a craft to which not all are equally fitted. The end result will as a rule be, if the hard conditions are respected, on the micro, rather than the macro, level.

There are, however, varieties of gifts, and faced with the choice between analytical precision and comprehensive overall judgment, some will always choose the broader option. If they have taken the trouble to inform themselves on matters of detail, all will no doubt be well: the reason why scholars translate and publish texts, and write books and articles, is after all hermeneutical, informative, explanatory. The enterprise may fail: but at least one will have a tolerably clear conscience at having done one's best. Hermeneutics, however, may be a dangerous pastime—never more so than when harnessed with the dialogical imperative.

It was, I think, Wilfred Cantwell Smith who coined the epigram that the Hindu does not reverence the cow we see, but the cow he or she sees. To *see* is not merely to register a sense-impression: it is, in this context, to have that sense-impression conjure up associations that fall into place alongside others, all beneath the canopy of Hindu identity. The principle is capable of almost infinite expansion, on the lines of, "the Hindu/Christian does not read the Gītā/Bible the Christian/Hindu reads," and vice versa. As with associations, so with memories. It is a matter of the utmost importance, where dialogue is concerned, to recognize that one cannot enter into dialogue unbidden with another person's memories; and that while some memories may be more or less public knowledge, others again may be surrounded by a wall of impenetrable secrecy. Of the existence of some, even the subject may be totally unaware: so much we have learned from the depth psychologists. Let the dialogical enthusiast therefore remember (or perchance learn) that where the study of Hinduism by the non-Hindu is concerned, the only condition any of us has the right to impose upon the encounter is that it shall proceed with mutual courtesy and respect, and that it shall not transgress the Judaeo-Christian commandment that forbids one from bearing false witness against a neighbour.[83] The commandment does not use either of the words *knowingly*, or *deliberately*, it might be well to add.

Otherwise, much has always depended on contextual relativities. The study of Hinduism in 1790, 1890, and 1990, respectively, is different in ways other than the purely factual. Between the study as carried out in Calcutta, Concord, Calgary, and Canberra there will be a broad overlap of material; as to the hermeneutical factor, nothing whatever is guaranteed. Another matter involving relativity is more subtle than the geographical setting and harder to express in a few words. Let me approach it obliquely.

As has so often been observed, the "classical" way of religion is one of submission, and of obedience to properly constituted authority. The *chelā* cannot under any circumstances lord it over, or even stand on an equal footing with, the *guru*. The *chelā* is the seeker and the suppliant, the *guru* the provider, who speaks with supreme authority on all matters involving the spiritual life—including the interpretation of sacred scripture, for while the scripture may in theory be supreme, in common practice it is the interpretation that serves as the disciple's rule of faith and practice. The disciple may be obedient to a spiritual director, to a scripture (with or without recognition of the interpretation factor), to a community and its representatives. In their teaching function, these will decree what the disciple needs to learn, what the disciple may learn, and often what the disciple should shun, to the end that the tradition may be kept alive. To speak of "the study of Hinduism" against this group of presuppositions is to speak of a study unlimited as to depth, but severely circumscribed as to extent.

At the opposite extreme to this path of submission is the way of domination, which classical scholarship in the West has for two centuries past seen as the proper goal of study. To be sure, the beginnings of study even here involve submission on the part of *discipuli* to a *magister*, within the accepted limits of a *disciplina*. In time, however, the *studiosus* becomes a *candidatus* (still under discipline); thereafter the grades of *magister* (master) and *doctor* (not medical practitioner, but one qualified to speak with authority as a teacher) speak for themselves. In this setting, "the study of Hinduism" means in principle not submitting to the tradition, but attempting to gain a superior vantage point from which to examine it critically.

One might reexamine the whole course of the study of Hinduism in the light of who, at any given time and in any given place, occupied (or believed themselves to occupy) a position of intellectual or spiritual or economic or political superiority, vis-à-vis whom, and why. This is too large and complex an issue to introduce at the end of what has already become a longish essay; but it is too important to omit entirely. Stated briefly: while the rationalist strain in Western thought has as a rule taken for granted its own right to make authoritative pronouncements on matters Hindu, the romantic strain has always been more or less prepared to defer to insight—its own, Hinduism's, or the two in combination. In religion, the liberal Christian wing has followed the second of these ways, the conservative wing, its apparent supernaturalism notwithstanding, the first. Authoritative pronouncements may be of more than one kind, of course; but what they have in common is the bringing into play of an authority—Bible, law, moral consensus, good taste, "progress"—that the Hindu initially has no reason to recognize and that might indeed be viewed with considerable resentment. The liberal alternative, by contrast, sets up few rigid barriers, tries to argue inductively, thinks in terms of what it believes are universals, and will do all it can to avoid giving offence.

Before World War I, the study of Hinduism was carried on either by those to whom the West was in a position of moral, religious, intellectual, and economic superiority vis-à-vis India; or by romantics whose idealized images of India bore little relation to the often chaotic actualities. But beginning in the mid-1880s, strongly after Amritsar 1919, and irresistibly since 1947, the moral and spiritual superiority passed to India, and to Hinduism—a circumstance of which successive generations, from Vivekānanda, by way of Aurobindo and Gandhi and Radhakrishnan, to today's neo-Hindu movements, took fullest advantage. To be morally superior and economically inferior was by now more of an advantage than a handicap, it might be added. Once more India became a refuge. Once more Hinduism became an ideal way to "be religious" in a secular age. Of course the impression of "spiritual" India, present in the world as a corrective to the "materialist" West, was actively canvassed.

The more severely academic might wish to argue that images, ideals, and impressions are far too indistinct and "unscientific" factors to deserve a place in such a symposium as this. No one, however, enters any field of study for exclusively "scientific" reasons, as I am reminded every time I look up from my desk and see the photograph of my father, army-uniformed and pith-helmeted, taken in the northwest of India in the early 1920s. I do not wish to attribute to the influence of my father (who died when I was an undergraduate) the course my academic career has subsequently taken—except in one particular.

The history of scholarship is by no means unrepresented in relation to the history of religion(s) and its branches: it is underrepresented, however. One reason for this might be that although scholarship does not become dated as fast in the humanities as in the natural sciences, it does age; and being considerably more closely linked with time and place and context, requires a considerably greater effort to grasp as it was when newly minted. I have, however, a strong sense of *pietas* where former generations are concerned; and especially so where their contributions are judged not by their best intentions but by their all-too-obvious faults and failings. It requires no very great scholarly acumen to criticize a representation figure of the past for having had the misfortune (or the temerity) to have been born a century too soon, or for having been in the grip of the wrong set of ideals. None of us would, I think, wish to be so judged. Why then should we be so ready with our caricatures and condemnations, when a little imaginative sympathy (which we expect of every Western student who takes up the study of Hinduism) would be so much more to everyone's credit?

I have written to the best of my ability and in the broadest of terms about the historiography, and a little about the history, of Hinduism as viewed from the only perspective I know—my own. The more detailed work, the filling out of details, I leave now to my colleagues. My exercise has been a little like writing an overture to an opera I have never heard, and at whose contents I can only guess. I trust that I have hit upon one or two leading themes—or at least set up some appropriate stage properties for the drama that follows.

Notes

1. R. N. Sardesai, ed., *Picturesque Orientalia* (Poona: Oriental Book Agency, 1938).

2. Edward W. Said, *Orientalism* (London: Routledge & Kegan Paul, 1978).

3. I make no apology for drawing special attention to this aspect, the interplay of missiology with orientalism having been one of my major areas of concern since the early 1960s. See especially my *Not to Destroy but to Fulfil* (Lund: Gleerup, 1965) and *Faith Meets Faith* (London: SCM Press, 1977).

4. William Hurd, *A New Universal History of the Religious Rites, Ceremonies, and Customs of the Whole World; or, a Complete and Impartial View of all the Religions in the Various Nations of the Universe, Both Antient [sic] and Modern, from the Creation Down to the Present Time* (London: Alexander Hogg, 1788), 67.

5. Cf. G. D. Bearce, *British Attitudes towards India, 1784–1858* (London: Oxford University Press, 1961).

6. Cf. the controversial account of Allan Dahlquist in *Megasthenes and Indian Religion* (Stockholm: Almqvist & Wiksell, 1962).

7. On Roger [Rogerius], see A. Leslie Willson, *A Mythical Image: The Ideal of India in German Romanticism* (Durham, N.C.: Duke University Press, 1964), 8*ff*. I should perhaps add that I have a copy of the German translation of Roger's book.

8. A. Gehring, *Bartholomäus Ziegenbalg*, 2nd ed. (Leipzig: Verlag der Evangelisch-lutherischen Mission, 1907). Cf. Arno Lehmann, "Germans Contribute to Tamil Studies," in Nayagam, ed., *Tamil Studies Abroad* (Kuala Lumpur: International Association of Tamil Research, 1968), 31*ff*.

9. *Propagation of the Gospel in the East; Being an Account of the Success of two Danish Missionaries, Lately Sent to the East-Indies for the Conversion of the Heathens in Malabar*, 3rd ed. (London: Joseph Downing, 1718), 56.

10. S. N. Mukherjee, *Sir William Jones: A Study in Eighteenth-Century British Attitudes to India* (Cambridge University Press, 1968).

11. Ibid., 60.

12. Ibid., 80.

13. P. J. Marshall, ed., *The British Discovery of Hinduism in the Eighteenth Century* (Cambridge University Press, 1970).

14. Ibid., 10*f*.

15. Cf. Eric J. Sharpe, *The Universal Gītā: Western Images of the Bhagavadgītā* (London: Duckworth, 1985).

16. C. S. Lewis, *Studies in Words*, 2nd ed. (Cambridge University Press, 1967), 24*ff*.

17. Willson, *Mythical Image*, 69, 72*ff*.

18. Raymond Schwab, *Vie d'Anquetil-Duperron* (Paris: Ernest Leroux, 1946); idem, *La Renaissance Orientale* (Paris: Payot, 1950). Cf. Nathan Söderblom, *Gudstrons uppkomst* (Stockholm: Gebers, 1914), 328*ff*.

19. Sharpe, *Universal Gītā*, 20*ff*.

20. Willson, *Mythical Image*, 90.

21. Müller, *India: What Can It Teach Us?* (London: Longmans, Green, new ed., 1892), 94.

22. Müller, *Chips from a German Workshop*, vol. 4 (London: Longmans, Green, 1880), 368.

23. They were, for instance, mentioned in Roger's *Offene Thür* (German trans., 1663), 56*f*.

24. G. Hermann, *Dr. Karl Graul und seine Bedeutung für die lutherische Mission* (Halle, 1867); C. Ihmels, *D. Karl Graul und die Leipziger Mission* (Hamburg, 1936).

25. This was because Graul and the Leipzig Missionary Society did not insist, as other Protestant missions did, on converts to Christianity abandoning caste practices. See D. B. Forrester, *Caste and Christianity* (London: Curzon Press, 1980), 18*f*., and Eric J. Sharpe, "Patience with the Weak: Leipzig Lutherans and the Caste Question in Nineteenth-Century South India," in *Indo-British Review* (forthcoming).

26. Cf. Lehmann, "Germans."

27. Schomerus, *Der Çaiva-Siddhanta: eine Mystik Indiens* (Leipzig: Hinrichs, 1912).

28. Nor did James Mill, who argued (not unreasonably) that the longtime resident of India invariably knew some aspects too well, and others not well enough. Cf. *The History of British India* (1817; 3rd ed. London: Baldwin, Cradock, & Joy, 1826), ix*ff*.

29. Müller, *Chips*, 4:263f.

30. Müller, *Introduction to the Science of Religion* (London: Longmans, Green, 1873), 367f.

31. Cf. Eric J. Sharpe, *Comparative Religion: A History*, 2nd ed. (London: Duckworth, 1986), 39.

32. Müller, *Biographical Essays* (London: Longmans, Green 1884); *Râmakrishna: His Life and Sayings* (London: Longmans, Green, 1898); *Auld Lang Syne, Second Series: My Indian Friends* (New York: Scribner's, 1899).

33. Müller, "Westminster Lecture on Missions, December 3, 1873," in *Chips*, 4:251–80.

34. Sharpe, *Comparative Religion*, 60*f*.

35. Müller, *Chips*, 4:447*ff*., 501.

36. Mention should also be made here of the most valuable compilation of John Muir (far more of an orthodox Christian than Max Müller had ever been), *Original Sanskrit Texts on the Origin and History of the People of India, Their Religion and Institutions*, 5 vols. (London: Trübner, 1870).

37. Mukherjee, *Sir William Jones*, 95.

38. Collinder, *Språket* (Stockholm: Natur och Kultur, 1959), 122.

39. Report of the Second European Convention of Vishwa Hindu Parishad, in *Update* 9, no. 3 (1985): 51*f*.

40. J. N. Farquhar [under pseud. Neil Alexander], *Gītā and Gospel* (Calcutta: Thacker, Spink, 1903). Later editions appeared under the name Farquhar.

41. The volume *Indian Archaeology, 1899–1905* (on which this section is based) is hard to describe bibliographically, though it would seem to have been compiled by Curzon himself, or someone close to him, and was (privately?) printed in Simla in 1906. The quotation is from page 71.

42. Ibid., 73.

43. Ibid., 131.

44. Ibid., 77.

45. Walter A. Fairservis Jr., *The Roots of Ancient India* (New York: Macmillan, 1971), 250*f*.

46. Cf. Mortimer Wheeler, *Civilizations of the Indus Valley and Beyond* (London: Thames & Hudson, 1966); *The Indus Civilization*, 3rd ed. (Cambridge: Cambridge University Press, 1968).

47. Sarvepalli Radhakrishnan, *Indian Philosophy* I (London: Allen & Unwin, 1923), 75.

48. Asko Parpola, *Från Indusreligion till Veda* (Copenhagen: Akademisk Förlag, 1980).

49. H. H. Risley and E. A. Gait, eds., *Census of India, 1901* I:1 (Calcutta: Government of India, 1903), 349, 351.

50. The need for accurate information on which to base administrative policies often led indirectly to the gathering of valuable religiohistorical material. For an outstanding example, see William Wilson Hunter et al., *The Imperial Gazetteer of India*, 9 vols. (London: Trübner, 1881) 2nd ed., 14 vols., (London: Trübner, 1885–87). See also Edgar Thurston, *Castes and Tribes of Southern India*, 7 vols. (Madras: Government Press, 1909).

51. Weber, *The Religion of India: The Sociology of Hinduism and Buddhism* (New York: Free Press, 1958).

52. Ibid., 147.

53. Cf. Milton Singer, *When a Great Tradition Modernizes* (London: Pall Mall Press, 1972), esp. 272*ff*.

54. Radhakrishnan, *The Hindu View of Life* (London: Allen & Unwin, 1927). It has been in print ever since.

55. *The Hindu View of Life* (1965 paperback ed.), 92.

56. He was, however, always prepared to make an exception in the case of his first philosophy teacher, Alfred George Hogg, afterward principal of Madras Christian College. See Radhakrishnan, "My Search for Truth," in V. Ferm, ed., *Religion in Transition* (London: Allen & Unwin, 1937), 19*f*.

57. Sharpe, *Not to Destroy but to Fulfil*, passim.

58. There is a surprisingly full account in H. H. Wilson, *Religious Sects of the Hindus* (reprint; Calcutta: Susil Gupta, 1958), 135*ff*. This material was originally published in 1828–32.

59. This was observable at the London Tantra Exhibition, 1971, sponsored by the Arts Council and held in the Hayward Gallery. See also Philip Rawson, *Tantra: The Indian Cult of Ecstasy* (London: Thames & Hudson, 1973).

60. John Murray Mitchell, *Hinduism Past and Present* (Madras: CLS, 1897), 137.

61. J. N. Farquhar, *Modern Religious Movements in India* (1915; reprint, Delhi: Munshiram Manoharlal, 1967), 304; cf. idem, *The Crown of Hinduism* (London: Oxford University Press, 1913), 384, 396*f*.

62. Others of his works included the two-volume *Principles of Tantra* (London: Luzac, 1914–15).

63. Recent works include Agehananda Bharati's *The Tantric Tradition* (London: Rider, 1965); Ajit Mookerjee and Madhu Khanna's *The Tantric Way* (London: Thames & Hudson, 1977); and Ajit Mookerjee's *Kali: The Feminine Force* (London: Thames & Hudson, 1988). Aspects of Tantra were also freely discussed (and possibly practiced) in some of the new religious movements of the 1960s and 1970s. It is unnecessary to identify them.

64. Coomaraswamy, *History of Indian and Indonesian Art* (New York: Dover, 1965; first published 1927); *Hinduism and Buddhism* (New York: Philosophical Library, 1943); *The Dance of Shiva* (collected essays, Bombay: Asia Publishing House, 1948).

65. Zimmer, *Maya: Der indische Mythos* (1936; Zürich: Rascher, 1952) Joseph Campbell, ed., *Myths and Symbols in Indian Art and Civilization* (London: Routledge & Kegan Paul, 1951).

66. For a useful (if at times slightly tongue-in-cheek) survey of earlier literature, see Wendy Doniger O'Flaherty, "In Praise of Nineteenth-century Hindoo Mythologists," in *South Asian Review* (1973):332–35. Wendy O'Flaherty's recent

work has carried the study and analysis of Hindu mythology far beyond this point of almost twenty years ago, but I have not thought it proper in this survey to comment on the ongoing activities of my contemporaries and highly respected colleagues.

67. J. A. B. van Buitinen, *The Mahābhārata I: The Book of the Beginning* (Chicago: University of Chicago Press, 1973), xxxi–xxxv.

68. Cf. Sharpe, *Universal Gītā*, 123*ff*.

69. Burton Feldman and Robert D. Richardson, *The Rise of Modern Mythology, 1680–1860* (Bloomington: Indiana University Press, 1972), xiv.

70. A. M. Hocart, *Kingship* (London: Oxford University Press, 1927).

71. Geo Widengren, foreword to the Swedish translation (*De nordiska gudarna*, trans. Åke Ohlmarks [Stockholm: Aldus/Bonniers, 1962]) of Dumézil, *Les Dieux des Germains*, 1959, 8. On Nyberg, see Sigrid Kahle, *H. S. Nyberg: En kort bildningsroman* (Uppsala: Västmanland-Dala Nations Skriftserie 13, 1977), esp. 24.

72. Littleton, *The New Comparative Mythology*, 2nd ed. (Berkeley: University of California Press, 1973), 156.

73. In *Religion och Bibel* 6 (1947):26–39.

74. Dumézil, *From Myth to Fiction* (Chicago: University of Chicago Press, 1973), viii*ff*.

75. *Myth in Indo-European Antiquity*, ed. Gerald James Larson (Berkeley: University of California Press, 1974).

76. *Krishna: Myths, Rites, and Attitudes*, ed. Milton Singer (Honolulu: East-West Center Press, 1966).

77. M. N. Srinivas, *Social Change in Modern India* (Berkeley: University of California Press, 1968).

78. Ibid., 163.

79. Milton Singer, *When a Great Tradition Modernizes* (London: Pall Mall Press, 1972, 272*ff*.).

80. *University of Leeds Review* 16, no. 1 (1973).

81. Derogatory remarks about organized religion and its inability to move with the times will be found scattered throughout Nehru's works. Fully typical is the passage in *The Discovery of India* (Bombay: Asia Publishing House, 1961), 552*f*., which ends: "India must therefore lessen her religiosity and turn to science."

82. P. N. Bazaz, *The Role of the Bhagavad Gītā in Indian History* (New Delhi: Sterling, 1975). Cf. Sharpe, *Universal Gītā*, 163*f*.

83. Much dialogical writing is unrealistic. But see K. Klostermaier, *Hindu and Christian in Vrindaban* (London: SCM Press, 1969); and idem, "Remembering Vrindaban," in McDowall and Sharma, eds., *Vignettes of Vrindavan* (New Delhi: Books and Books, 1987), 45–61.

THREE Method in the Study of Hinduism

— ARVIND SHARMA

Method in the study of Hinduism is one way of parsing the theme of method in the study of religion. The purpose of this chapter is to supplement the one just read, in which a history of ideas perspective was brought to bear on the study of Hinduism by Eric Sharpe. In this chapter, this broadly historical approach is complemented by an explicitly more methodological orientation, intended to serve a double purpose. Such an approach will enable the reader to examine the extent to which the study of Hinduism, as a religion, has been affected by the methodological pluralism and ferment that characterizes the study of religion. It will also help to supplement the essentially diachronic view of the study of Hinduism that characterizes this book (carried out as it is, within it, in terms of broad chronological periods) with a more synchronic view of it in terms of the various topi of study. Such a study will be far less evocative than the one offered in the previous chapter and may even seem downright pedestrian. The editor therefore has undertaken it himself so as not to embarrass anyone else.

It might be useful to begin by identifying the main methods in the study of religion that hold the field today. They may be enumerated, in the main and not without some overlap, as (1) the historical method; (2)

the phenomenological method; (3) the history-of-religions method; (4) the anthropological method; (5) the sociological message; and (6) the psychological method.[1]

Six Main Methods

The historical method is too well known to require special comment. Any history of India is in some measure a history of Hinduism. Nowhere is it more obvious than in the monumental ten-volume *History and Culture of the Indian People*, published by the Bharatiya Vidya Bhavan, Bombay, under the general editorship of R. C. Majumdar, and soon to be reissued by the Indian Council of Historical Research.

Two points nevertheless deserve notice. The first has to do with the chronology of ancient India. There is a growing sense among many scholars in India, and a few abroad, that the chronology of the Vedic period may have been shoehorned. Some have even argued this in relation to the chronology of ancient India as a whole, for the pre-Harṣa (d. 647 C.E.) period,[2] but this position has fewer takers. On the other hand, issues surrounding the date of the *ṚgVeda*, the role of the Sarasvatī River in this culture, the degree of astronomical knowledge in Vedic times, and the exact relationship of Vedic to Harappan culture, and so on have now become keenly contested sites.[3] Klaus K. Klostermaier echoes the views of an increasing number of scholars when he writes that "the chronology suggested by Max Müller," on which the modern structure rests, "is based on very shaky ground indeed."[4] Attempts to arrive at a consensus on a revised chronology have not succeeded so far, but the fact that the study of India is experiencing chronological turbulence is a useful one to know for a student of this period and of Hinduism in general. Closely tied to this issue is that of the indigenous or external origin of the Aryans, a matter of more than purely historical interest in the political climate of India, apart from its significance for the study of Hinduism. The core of it, however, is constituted by the fact that "the accepted belief in the Indo-Aryan immigration from central Asia depends largely on the interpretation of the geographical allusions in the *Rigveda* and the *Yajurveda*. Direct testimony to the assumed fact is lacking, and no tradition of an early home beyond the frontier survives in India."[5]

It might not be out of place to offer an important clarification here. Although the contending parties on these issues are often characterized as either Western or Indian, they cannot be so pigeonholed without sacrificing a few pigeons, as takers of different positions are found on both sides. The differences between them therefore cannot be unexceptionably correlated with racial, national, cultural, or civilizational boundaries. As a matter of fact, takers of some of the most extreme "Hindu" positions can already be identified among British scholars in the nineteenth century, and even in the heyday of British Empire in India.[6]

The second point has to do with the rise of the school of historical studies in India known as the "subaltern." Its approach is not specifically directed toward Hinduism as such, but it has important implications for the study of Hinduism. This project, which took shape in the early 1980s, sought to steer clear, epistemologically, of the elitism of colonial, neocolonial, nationalist, and Marxist historiography and sought to privilege the subordinated voices in history, in an effort to write history from below. These disenfranchised groups were labeled subaltern; hence, the term *subaltern studies*, an approach pioneered by Ranjit Guha.[7] This approach provides glimpses of Hinduism caught up in the process of societal dislocation at the grassroots level unleashed by colonialism, nationalism, and developmentalism. One wing of it, more Saidian than Gramscian in perspective, is associated with the name of Partha Chatterjee,[8] but focuses on elite discourses, again not without implications for the study of Hinduism.[9] Finally, given the vogue of Orientalism, some studies of that genre in the field should be recognized.[10] It is striking, however, that Said's critique of orientalism has not yet been extended to Hindu studies in any significant way.[11]

The phenomenological method is relevant to the study of Hinduism both on account of its concern with timeless essences and for privileging the insider's point of view (access to which, as distinguished from its acceptance, is now considered de rigueur in the study of comparative religion). The method is discussed by Mariasusai Dhavamony in *Phenomenology of Religion* and is also applied to the study of Hinduism (in combination with the historical) in *Classical Hinduism*.[12]

To the extent that the phenomenological method emphasizes the importance of the phenomenon itself (over against any interpretation of it) and that such a phenomenon often possesses a geographical context, a growing body of literature on the regional diversity and richness of Hinduism may be placed here. The literature on the region associated with Braj in Uttar Pradesh, a land with close links to Kṛṣṇa, is worth mentioning here.[13] Even more impressive and to the point is the body of literature that has grown around Maharashtra.[14] The exploration of regional manifestations of Hinduism in Orissa is also worth noting, as is the ongoing interest in Tamil Nadu.

The history-of-religions method is said to coalesce the historical and phenomenological methods and to harness their powers particularly toward achieving an understanding of myth and ritual in the broadest sense. The application of this method to Hinduism—which is almost scandalously hospitable to both myth and ritual—has aroused much interest. Some of the works of Mircea Eliade (1907–86), a famous exponent of the method, belong here (e.g., *Yoga: Immortality and Freedom* and *Patañjali and Yoga*), as do works by Heinrich Zimmer's (e.g., *The Art of Indian Asia* and *Myths and Symbols in Indian Art and Civilization*) and Joseph Campbell's *The Philosophies of India.*[15]

The anthropological approach to the study of Hinduism, earlier neglected in favor of the historical-philological, is now well established, with the anthropologists hailing both from subcontinental India and the West. The works of Irawati Karve represent this tradition.[16] Among Western anthropologists, the conclusions reached by Madeleine Biardeau, and on another canvas by McKim Marriott, have been influential.[17] The work of Arjun Appadurai, by comparison, is both narrower and broader.[18] Another perspective is represented by the work of Veena Das, the titles of whose works speak for themselves: *Structure and Cognition: Aspects of Hindu Caste and Ritual; Critical Events: An Anthropological Perspective on Contemporary India;* and *Social Suffering.*[19] The approach of Gananath Obeysekere represents another application of the anthropological method, this time in interface with the psychological, in such works as *Medusa's Hair: An Essay on Personal Symbols and Religious Experience* and *The Cult of Goddess Pattini.*[20]

In the context of the sociological method, one may begin by mentioning Professor M. N. Srinvas, who has been called the father of Indian sociology. Some of Srinvas's contributions in the field were noted earlier by Eric Sharpe: his contributions continue to address issues of social change and now also embrace gender issues.[21] Another noteworthy sociologist is Professor T. N. Madan, who has contributed significantly to the discussion of the ethos of Hinduism, as well as that of secularism, with several books and articles (e.g., *Non-Renunciation, Family, and Kinship*; "Whither Indian Secularism?"; and "Secularism in Its Place.")[22]

The caste system has continued to serve as the Rorschack test for Western theorists ever since Herbert H. Risley's *The People of India* offered a racial explanation for it,[23] and Denzil Ibbetson's *Punjab Castes* attempted an anthropological explanation.[24] The ideological explanation offered by Louis Dumont in *Homo Hierarchicus: An Essay on the Caste System* has enjoyed a wide audience.[25] An explanation in terms of contemporary anthropological theory has been offered by Morton Klass in *Caste: The Emergence of the South Asian Social System.*[26] Ketkar (1884–1937) offers a remarkably indigenous perspective on the caste system.[27]

The application of the psychological method to the study of Hinduism was somewhat slow off the mark, although the psychoanalytical tradition made a beachhead in India in Freud's own lifetime through Girindrashekhar Bose,[28] whose doctoral dissertation, "Concept of Repression," was appreciated by Freud. Girindrashekhar Bose founded the Indian Psychoanalytic Society and attempted to locate psychoanalysis in the Vedantic tradition. Despite this head start, the application of the psychological method was curiously delayed until recent times. The method is now being vigorously, even sedulously, applied to Hindu studies. One trend is represented by Sudhir Kakar, who applies it to the Indian reality for deeper psychoanalytical insight.[29] Another trend tends to be more reductive in nature. To this class belong such works as J. M. Masson's *Oceanic Feeling*, N. P. Sil's *Rāmakṛṣṇa Paramahaṁsa*, and, more recently, J. F. Kripal's *Kālī's Child.*[30] Yet another application of the psychological method to Hinduism and, more broadly, to the contemporary Indian reality is represented by the works of Ashis Nandy, such as *At the Edge of Psychology*, *Intimate Enemy*, *The Savage Freud and Other Essays*, and *Creating a Nationality*.[31]

Some methodological approaches relegated to the margins in the study of religion in the West may also be mentioned in the interest of completeness, as, for instance, those associated with parapsychology, the perennial philosophy, and interreligious dialogue. These also bear on the study of Hinduism. The methods of parapsychology have been applied in an innovative way to the phenomenon of rebirth by Ian Stevenson in a series of studies—for example, *Twenty Cases Suggestive of Reincarnation* and *Reincarnation and Biology*.[32] Given Hinduism's self-perception as the eternal religion (*sanātana dharma*), the "perennial philosophy" school has a history of interpreting it. The names of René Guénon, Frithjof Schuon, and, preeminently, Ananda K. Coomaraswamy are worth mentioning here. Coomaraswamy's numerous works include *Hinduism and Buddhism; Myths of the Hindus and Buddhists*, prepared with Sister Nivedita; the widely read *The Dance of Shiva; Transformation of Nature in Art; Time and Eternity*; and *Christian and Oriental Philosophy of Art*.[33]

Recent Developments

One may conclude with some developments in the study of Hinduism in India. Encyclopedic efforts by Hindu scholars continue to flourish. P. V. Kane's monumental studies in *dharmaśāstra* have been followed up by the work of Lakṣmīśāstrī Joshi, the editor of the multivolume *Dharmakośa*.[34] Attempts to bridge the divide between tradition-oriented and West-oriented Hindu scholars are also occasionally made. One product of such an attempt is Daya Krishna's *Saṁvāda: A Dialogue between Two Philosophical Traditions*, which combines reflection by Sanskrit scholars on the Western philosophical traditions with reflections of West-oriented thinkers on Indian philosophy.[35]

Notes

1. For a general survey of the evolution of the academic study of religion in terms of these methods, see Eric J. Sharpe, *Comparative Religion: A History* (London: Duckworth, 1985), and Jan de Vries, *The Study of Religion: A Historical Approach*, trans. Kees W. Bolle (New York: Harcourt Brace & World, 1967).

2. See S. D. Kulkarni, ed., *Study of Indian History and Culture* (Bombay: Shri Bhagavan Vedavyasa Itihasa Samshodhana Mandala, 1988), vol. 1, pt. 6.

3. See Edwin Bryant, *The Quest for the Origins of Vedic Culture: The Indo-Aryan Migration Debate* (New York: Oxford University Press, 2001).

4. Klaus K. Klostermaier, *A Survey of Hinduism*, 2nd ed. (Albany: State University of New York Press, 1994), 479.

5. Percival Spear, ed., *The Oxford History of India by the Late Vincent A. Smith, C.I.E.*, 4th ed. (Delhi: Oxford University Press, 1994), 53.

6. On the indigenous origin of the Aryans, see the views of A. Curzon, in J. Muir, ed., *Original Sanskrit Texts* (London: Trübner, 1974), 301*ff*.; on a "deeper" chronology for ancient India, see the views of Troyer (1859 A.D.), in Kulkarni, *Study of Indian History and Culture*, 1:318.

7. See Ranjit Guha, *Subaltern Studies: Writings on South Asian History and Society* (Delhi: Oxford University Press, 1982–89).

8. Partha Chatterjee, *Nation and Its Fragments: Colonial and Postcolonial Histories* (Princeton: Princeton University Press, 1993).

9. Partha Chatterjee, *Caste and Subaltern Consciousness* (Calcutta: Centre for Studies in Social Sciences, 1989).

10. See Ronald Inden, *Imagining India* (Oxford, Eng., and Cambridge, Mass.: Blackwell, 1992); "Orientalist Construction of India," *Modern Asian Studies* 20, no. 3 (1986): 401–46.

11. For an early effort in the direction, see Kailash Chandra Varma, *Some Western Indologists and Indian Civilization* (New Delhi: International Academy of Indian Culture, 1971). But see Ronald B. Inden, *Imagining India* and Nicholas B. Dirks, *Castes of Mind: Colonialism and the Making of Modern India* (Princeton and Oxford: Princeton University Press, 2001).

12. Mariasusai Dhavamony, *Phenomenology of Religion* (Rome: Gregorian University Press, 1973); *Classical Hinduism* (Rome: Universita Gregoriana Editrice, 1982).

13. See A. W. Entwistle, *Braj: Centre of Krishna Pilgrimage* (Groningen: E. Forsten, 1987).

14. See Anne Feldhaus, *Deeds of God in Rddhipur* (New York: Oxford University Press, 1984); *House and Home in Maharashtra* (Delhi and New York: Oxford University Press, 1998); Eleanor Zelliot and Maxine Bernsten, eds., *The Experience of Hinduism: Essays on Religion in Maharashtra* (Albany: State University of New York Press, 1988); Günther Dietz Sontheimer, *Folk Culture, Folk Religion, and Oral Traditions as a Component of Maharashtrian Culture* (New Delhi: Manohar, 1995).

15. Mircea Eliade, *Yoga: Immortality and Freedom* (New York: Pantheon, ca. 1958), and *Patanjali and Yoga* (New York: Funk & Wagnalls, 1969); Heinrich Zimmer, *The Art of Indian Asia: Its Mythology and Transformations*, 2 vols., Bollingen Series 39 (Princeton: Princeton University Press, 1955), and *Myths and Symbols in Indian Art and Civilization* (New York: Pantheon, 1946); Joseph Campbell, ed., *The Philosophies of India* (Princeton: Princeton University Press, 1951).

16. For example, *Hindu Society: An Introduction* (Poona: Deshmukh Prakashan, 1961).

17. Madeleine Biardeau, *Hinduism: The Anthropology of a Civilization* (Delhi: Oxford University Press, 1989); McKim Marriott, *Village India: Studies in the Little Community* (Chicago: University of Chicago Press, 1955); *Caste Ranking and Community Structure in Five Regions of India and Pakistan* (Poona: Deccan College Post-Graduate and Research Institute, 1960); *India through Hindu Categories* (New Delhi and Newbury Park, Calif.: Sage, 1990).

18. For the narrower view, see *Worship and Conflict under Colonial Rule: A South Indian Case* (Cambridge and New York: Cambridge University Press, 1981); for a broader approach, see *Gender, Genre, and Power in South Asian Expressive Tradition* (Philadelphia: University of Pennsylvania, 1991), and *Modernity at Large: Cultural Dimensions of Globalization* (Minneapolis: University of Minnesota Press, 1996).

19. Veena Das, *Structure and Cognition: Aspects of Hindu Caste and Ritual* (Delhi: Oxford University Press, 1982); *Critical Events: An Anthropological Perspective on Contemporary India* (Delhi and New York: Oxford University Press, 1995); and *Social Suffering* (Berkeley and London: University of California Press, 1997).

20. *Medusa's Hair* (Chicago and London: University of Chicago Press, 1981); *Goddess Pattini* (Chicago and London: University of Chicago Press, 1984).

21. For Srinivas's works on social change, see, among others, *Religion and Society among the Coorgs of South India* (Oxford: Clarendon Press, 1952); *Caste in Modern India and Other Essays* (New York: Asia Publishing House, 1962); *Social Change in Modern India* (Berkeley: University of California Press, 1966); *Remembered Village* (Berkeley: University of California Press, 1976); *Cohesive Role of Sanskritization and Other Essays* (New Delhi: Penguin, 1996); *Caste: Its Twentieth Century Avatar* (New Delhi, Viking; New York, Penguin, 1996). On gender issues, see Srinivas, *Changing Position of Indian Women* (Delhi: Oxford University Press, 1978); *Village, Caste, Gender, and Method: Essays in Social Anthropology* (Delhi: Oxford University Press, 1996).

22. T. N. Madan, *Non-Renunciation, Family, and Kinship* (Delhi: Oxford University Press, 1989); "Whither Indian Secularism?" *Modern Asian Studies* 27, no. 3 (July 1993): 667–97; and "Secularism in Its Place," *Journal of Asian Studies* 46 (1987): 747–60. See also T. N. Madan, ed., *Religion in India* (Delhi: Oxford University Press, 1991).

23. Herbert H. Risley, *People of India* (Calcutta: Thacker, Spink and London: W. Thacker & Co., 1908; reprint, Delhi: Oriental Books, 1969).

24. Denzil Ibbetson, *Punjab Castes* (1883; reprint, Punjab: [Patiala] Languages Department, 1970).

25. Louis Dumont, *Homo Hierarchicus* (Chicago: University of Chicago Press, 1970).

26. Morton Klass, *Caste* (Philadelphia: Institute for the Study of Human Issues, 1980).

27. S. V. Ketkar, *History of Caste in India* (Jaipur: Rawat, 1979).

28. See his "The Aim and Scope of Psychology," *Indian Journal of Psychology* 9 (1932): 11–29; "A New Theory of Mental Life," ibid. 10 (1933): 7–15;

"Sattva, Rajaḥ and Tamaḥ," *Pravāsī* 30, pt. 1, no. 3 (1930): 339–53; "Manuṣer Mana," *Pravāsī* 30, pt. 2, no. 1 (1930): 1–5.

29. Sudhir Kakar, *Conflict and Choice: Indian Youth in a Changing Society* (Bombay: Somaiya, 1970); *Personality and Authority in Work: The Dynamics of Subordinate Behaviour in an Indian* (Bombay: Somaiya, 1974); *Inner World: A Psychoanalytic Study of Childhood and Society in India* (Delhi: Oxford University Press, 1979); *Shamans, Mystics, and Doctors: A Psychological Inquiry into India and Its Healing Techniques* (New York: Knopf, 1982); *Intimate Relations Exploring Indian Sexuality* (New Delhi: Viking, 1989); *Colors of Violence* (Chicago: University of Chicago Press, 1994).

30. J. M. Masson, *Oceanic Feeling: The Origin of Religious Sentiment in Ancient India* (Dordrecht: Reidel, 1980); N. P. Sil, *Rāmakṛṣṇa Paramahaṁsa: A Psychological Profile* (Leiden: Brill, 1991); J. F. Kripal, *Kālī's Child: The Mystical and the Erotic in the Life and Teachings of Ramakrishna* (Chicago and London: University of Chicago Press, 1995).

31. Ashis Nandy, *At the Edge of Psychology: Essays in Politics and Culture* (Delhi and New York: Oxford University Press, 1980); *Intimate Enemy: Loss and Recovery of Self Under Colonialism* (Delhi: Oxford University Press, 1983); *The Savage Freud and Other Essays on Possible and Retrievable Selves* (Princeton: Princeton University Press, 1995); *Creating a Nationality* (Delhi: Oxford University Press, 1998).

32. Ian Stevenson, *Twenty Cases Suggestive of Reincarnation* (Charlottesville: University Press of Virginia, 1974); *Reincarnation and Biology: A Contribution to the Etiology of Birthmarks and Birth Defects* (Westport, Conn.: Praeger, 1997).

33. Coomaraswamy, *Hinduism and Buddhism* (New York: Philosophical Library, 1943); *Myths of the Hindus and Buddhists* (London: Harrap, 1913); *The Dance of Shiva: Fourteen Indian Essays* (New York: Sunwise Turn, ca. 1918); *Transformation of Nature in Art* (Cambridge: Harvard University Press, 1934); *Time and Eternity* (Ancona, Switzerland: Artibus Asiae, 1947); *Christian and Oriental Philosophy of Art* (New York: Dover, 1956).

34. Lakṣmīśāstrī Joshi, ed., *Dharmakośa* (Wai, Dist. Statara, India: Prajnapathashala Mandal, 1937–88).

35. Delhi: Indian Council of Philosophical Research, 1991.

FOUR Vedic Hinduism

STEPHANIE W. JAMISON AND MICHAEL WITZEL

The Vedic period is the earliest period of Indian history for which we have direct textual evidence, but even with this evidence it is difficult to fix even imprecise chronological limits to the period, much less to establish absolute dates within the period. We tentatively suggest 1500–500 B.C.E. as convenient limiting dates of the period, the latter marking the approximate date of the codification of Sanskrit by Pāṇini and the transition from "Vedic" to "Classical" Sanskrit; the former perhaps approximating the beginnings of the Ṛgveda, the earliest Indian text.

Since almost all our evidence for Vedic India is textual, much more fruitful than defining the Vedic period by date is defining it by texts. For purposes of this work, we will define Vedic literature (and hence the Vedic period) as consisting of the earliest texts, the four Vedas proper (Saṁhitās), and texts based on them and the cult in which they were embedded—the Brāhmaṇas and the Śrauta Sūtras, also including the increasingly speculative Āraṇyakas and the older Upaniṣads, as well as the texts relating to the domestic cult, the Gṛhya Sūtras. The content of these texts is wholly religious (when *religion* is defined more broadly than is customary). It may also be added that to call this period Vedic Hinduism is a contradiction in terms since Vedic religion is very different from what we generally call Hindu religion—at least as much as Old Hebrew religion is from medieval and modern Christian religion. However, Vedic religion is treatable as a predecessor of Hinduism.

We owe the transmission and preservation of the texts to the care and discipline of particular religious or, better, priestly schools (or *śākhās*). It should also be emphasized that both the composition and the transmission of the texts were completely oral for the entire Vedic period and some considerable time afterwards—hence the critical importance of the schools in their preservation. From the beginning, the various schools were favored by particular tribes, and later on by particular dynasties. Due to their preservation in various parts of India, a fairly wide spectrum of religious thought of this early period has survived to this day, and we do not have to rely on the authoritative texts of a single school of thought.

Because of these circumstances we are in a reasonably good position to study Vedic Hinduism. We have voluminous texts regarding the religion from various points of view: verbal material internal to the ritual, extemely detailed "handbooks" laying out ritual practice, exegesis of the ritual, both exoteric and esoteric, as well as various views of mythology. However, because of the means of preservation—through schools at once orthodox and intellectual in bent—we have little access to information about either heterodox or popular religious practices, only to the orderly and cerebral system of an entrenched priestly class. We are also almost entirely bereft of information about secular (and indeed religious) history, or political and social matters and their relations to religion, except as filtered through a priestly lens, and as reported, occasionally, often as asides, in priestly texts. Moreover, because we must rely on texts, our knowledge of Vedic religion is entirely verbal; we know nothing of the visual and iconographic aspect of Vedic religion, if such there was, beyond the solemn enactment of the Śrauta and some Gṛhya rites.

Any study of Vedic religion thus must begin with the texts. Fortunately, due to the care with which most of the texts were transmitted and to the last 150 years or so of intensive and painstaking philological work, we are reasonably lucky, in that most of the important texts exist in usable (though generally not, strictly speaking, critical) editions, that many possess careful translations with, at least, minimal commentary, and that the vocabulary and the grammar (morphology and syntax) of the texts have been and continue to be subject to the scientific scrutiny that is a necessary precondition for even first order textual interpretation. Serious lacunae will be noted below. For an overview of the Vedic texts in general see

Gonda, J. A *History of Indian Literature*, Vol. 1 *Vedic Literature* (*Saṃhitās and Brāhmaṇas*). Wiesbaden: Otto Harrassowitz, 1975.

———, Vol. 2: *The Ritual Sūtras*. Wiesbaden: Otto Harrassowitz, 1977.
Santucci, J. A. *An Outline of Vedic Literature*. Missoula, Mont.: American Academy of Religion, 1976.

For Śrauta, Gṛhya, Dharma, and Śulba Sutras, see

Gonda, J. *Vedic Ritual: The Non-Solemn Rites*. Leiden-Köln: E. J. Brill, 1980.
Kashikar, C. G. "A Survey of the Śrautasūtras". *Journal of Bombay University* 35, part 2, no. 41 (1968): vi + 188.
Lingat, R. *The Classical Law of India*. Trans. J. Duncan M. Derrett. Berkeley and London: University of California Press, 1973.
Michaels, A. *Beweisverfahren in der vedischen Sakralgeometrie: Ein Beitrag zur Entstehungsgeschichte von Wissenschaft*. Wiesbaden: Steiner, 1978.

Texts

The texts have traditionally been cataloged into Vedas (better: Veda-Saṁhitās), Brāhmaṇas, Āraṇyakas, Upaniṣads, and Sūtras, in roughly that chronological order. The Indian tradition distinguishes between *śruti* ("hearing") (i.e., texts revealed to the primordial seers), and texts having human authors (*smṛti*, "remembrance"). All texts from the Saṁhitās to the Upaniṣads are *śruti*, while the late Vedic Sūtras are regarded as *smṛti*.

Because their traditional names sometimes misrepresent the type of text contained within, it is useful to speak first of text-type. The Veda- (or Mantra, or Saṁhitā-) text-type consists of collections of liturgical material, the Brāhmaṇa-text-type of ritual exegesis. The Āraṇyaka-text-type often develops the cosmic side of Brāhmaṇa explanations into esoteric speculation about some of the more cryptic and secret of the rituals and generally has served as a catch-all for the later texts of the particular school involved. The Upaniṣad-text-type proceeds further on this speculative path. The Sūtra-text-type, in contrast, contains straightforward, often very elaborate and detailed, directions for ritual performances, with little or no commentary.

However, from the point of view of linguistic development—always a good yardstick for discovering the historical development of text layers—we have to distinguish the following text layers that do not always coincide with the traditional division of Vedic texts given just now: 1. Ṛg Veda (with, as late additions, book 10 and also parts of book 1); 2. the so-called Mantra language (Atharva Veda, Ṛg Veda Khila, the Mantras of the Yajur Veda, the Sāma Veda); 3. the expository prose of the Yajur Veda

Saṁhitā texts (MS, KS, KpS, TS); 4. the Brāhamaṇa prose (including the older portions of the Āraṇyakas and Upaniṣads, as well as some of the earliest Sūtras); 5. the late Vedic Sūtras.

The Saṁhitās

The oldest and most important text, in terms of Vedic ritualism and later Indian religion, is the Ṛg Veda (hereafter also RV).[1] This is a collection (Saṁhitā) of *ṛcs* "verses", forming hymns to be recited during ritual, praising various divinities. They were composed by a number of bards or bardic families, over a period of several hundred years, according to linguistic and stylistic evidence. The ritual, as it appears in these hymns, is earlier and less developed than the "classical" one of the later texts, such as the Yajur Veda Mantras and all of the Brāhmaṇas. The Ṛg Veda has come down to us basically in only one extremely well preserved school, that of Śākalya, who analyzed the traditional text towards the end of the Brāhmaṇa period, apparently in Eastern India (Videha, N. Bihar). His grammatical analysis, in the form of a text without any euphonic combinations (*sandhi*), has been transmitted as the RV-Padapāṭha.

The standard editions of the Ṛg Veda are that of Max Müller (1849–74), incorporating Sāyaṇa's medieval commentary (14th cent.), and the more compact one of T. Aufrecht (1877). The recent edition (1994) of Holland and van Nooten should also be noted. The standard current translation is that of K. F. Geldner (1951) (written already in the 1920s), into German, which supersedes earlier ones such as that of H. Grassman (1876–77). There is also an almost complete French translation by L. Renou (1955–69), and three volumes of a Russian translation by T. Ya. Elizarenkova have recently appeared (1989, 1995, 1999). Unfortunately there is no complete modern English translation, though there are unsatisfactory and out-moded ones by H. H. Wilson (1888), which largely depends on the medieval commentary of Sāyaṇa, and R. T. H. Griffith (1889–92). There are also useful translations of selected hymns, such as that of W. D. O'Flaherty (1981) and W. H. Maurer (1986), which include some of the preceding scholarship. An up-to-date, philologically sound translation of the entire text, incorporating the grammatical and semantic progress that has been made in recent decades, would be extremely welcome.

Other important tools for Ṛg Vedic researches include the invaluable (if somewhat out-of-date) *Wörterbuch* of H. Grassman (1872–75), which lists all the occurrences of all but the most common words in the RV, with definitions, grammatical identification, and contextual information; the concordance of A. Lubotsky; the *Prolegomena* and the *Noten* of H. Oldenberg (1888 and 1909, 1912, respectively), one of the leading Western Indologists; E. V. Arnold's treatise on Vedic meter (1905), one of the first attempts to develop an internal chronology of the text, and also several of M. Bloomfield's reference works.

The Atharva Veda (AV) stands a little apart from the other three Vedas, as it does not treat the *Śrauta* rituals, but contains magical (black and white) and healing spells, as well as two more large sections containing speculative hymns and materials dealing with some important domestic rituals such as marriage and death, and with royal power.

There are two extant recensions of the AV, differing considerably from each other. Currently the more usable one is that ordinarily known as the Śaunaka recension (AVŚ, ŚS). The standard edition is that of Roth and Whitney (1856, corrected repr., Lindenau 1924).

The other, the Paippalāda recension (AVP, PS), was until recently known only in a very corrupt manuscript from Kashmir. The discovery of a much better version preserved in Orissa will now allow the Paippalāda version to take its proper place in the Vedic canon.

The Sāma Veda (SV) is the collection of chants, referred to as *sāmans* "melodies". To each melody a variety of different verses can be sung; these verses are almost entirely extracted from the Ṛgveda. The standard edition of the SV is that of Benfey of the Kauthuma (and Rāṇāyanīya) recension (1848); W. Caland's 1907 edition of the Jaiminīya recension to some extent differs from the Kauthuma version in order and in content. Because of its dependence on the RV (only seventy-five of its mantras are not found in the RV) an independent translation of this text is not particularly crucial. Nonetheless, several exist (e.g., that of R. T. H. Griffith (1893).

The Yajur Veda is a complex entity, consisting of several partly parallel texts, most of which mix mantras (i.e., Veda-text-type) with prose commentary (Brāhmaṇa-text-type). It is divided into two branches: the Black (Kṛṣṇa) YV (BYV) and the White (Śukla) YV (the WYV). It is the Black YV that contains the mixture of text-types; the White YV contains only Mantras, with its Brāhmaṇa separate. Yet it is generally considered that this separation is secondary, that the mantras of the WYV were abstracted from a text that would have looked more like the BYV.

The White Yajur Veda, or Vājasaneyī Saṁhitā (VS), has two very similar recensions, the Mādhyandina and the Kāṇva (VSK). The standard edition is that of A. Weber (1852), which includes the variants of VSK. A separate edition of the VSK has been prepared by D. Satavalekar (1983), and a new edition by the indefatigable B. R. Sharma (1988–) is under preparation. There is a rather unsatisfactory English translation by Griffith (1899). Its massive and important Brāhmaṇa is the Śatapatha Brāhmaṇa (ŚB), the "Brāhmaṇa of the Hundred Paths" (after the number of its "lessons"), also with two similar recensions, likewise Mādhyandina and Kāṇva (ŚBM and ŚBK), whose mutual relationship is rather complicated. The one ordinarily referred to is the Mādhyandina, edited by A. Weber (1855) and translated into English by J. Eggeling (1882–1900). The Kāṇva recension was edited by Caland and Raghu Vira (1926–39). There is no translation of the ŚBK, but it differs little in content and phraseology from ŚBM.

The Black YV is more complex. It exists in three major versions, parallel in great part but often differing fom each other in both phraseology and points of doctrine: the Taittirīya Saṁhitā (TS), the Maitrāyaṇī Saṁhitā (MS), and the Kāṭhaka Saṁhitā (KS), the latter two often agreeing with each other against the (obviously younger) TS. (There is also a fragmentary and somewhat corrupt fourth version, the Kapiṣṭhala Saṁhitā (KpS), which is very close to the KS.) The standard edition of the TS is Weber's (1871–72), of the MS L. von Schroeder's (1881–86), as also of the KS (1900–1910), while Raghu Vira edited the fragments of the KpS (1932). M. Mittwede's useful collections of suggested emendations to the MS (1986) and KS (1989) are important tools in understanding these sometimes corrupt texts, which are based (unlike TS which is still widely recited in South India) only on the traditions of Gujarat/N. Maharashtra and Kashmir. All these texts must have been preceded by an even earlier stage of Brāhmaṇa-style discussion.

Only the TS has been translated (into English, by A. B. Keith 1914). Since MS and KS are generally fuller and more archaic in appearance than TS, translations of these two texts are badly needed. The prose of the Brāhmaṇa portion of these texts is the oldest expository prose in Sanskrit, and its treatment of the ritual and narration of myths is therefore extremely archaic.

References

Arnold, E. V. *Vedic Metre in Its Historical Development*. Cambridge: Cambridge University Press, 1905.

Aufrecht, T. *Die Hymnen des Ṛgveda*. Bonn: A. Marcus, 1877.

Benfey, Th. *Die Hymnen des Sāma-Veda*. Leipzig: Brockhaus, 1848.

Bloomfield, M. *A Vedic Concordance*. Cambridge: Harvard University Press, 1906.

Caland, W. *Die Jaiminīya-Saṃhitā mit einer Einleitung über die Sāmaveda-literatur*. Breslau: Indische Forschungen 2, 1907.

Caland, W., and Raghu Vira. *The Śatapatha Brāhmaṇa in the Kāṇvīya Recension*. Lahore: Motilal Banarsi Das, 1926–39; repr. Delhi, 1983.

Eggeling, J. *The Śatapatha Brāhmaṇa: According to the Text of the Mādhyandina School*. 5 vols. Oxford: Sacred Books of the East, vols. 12, 26, 41, 43–44, 1882–1900. Reprint, Delhi, 1963.

Elizarenkova, T. Ya. *Rigveda. Mandaly I–IV*. Moskva, Nauka: Akademija Nauk SSSR. Literaturnyie Pamjatniki, 1989. *Mandaly V–VIII*. Moskva, Nauka: Rossiiskaja Akademija Nauk. Literaturnyie Pamjatniki, 1995. Mandaly ix–x, Moskva 1999.

Geldner, K. F. *Der Rigveda: Aus dem Sanskrit ins Deutsche übersetzt und mit einem laufenden Kommentar versehen*. 3 vols. Cambridge: Harvard Oriental Series 33, 34, 35, 1951.

Grassmann, H. *Rig-Veda*. 2 vols. Leipzig: Brockhaus, 1876–77.

———. *Wörterbuch zum Rig-Veda*. Leipzig: Brockhaus, 1872–75.

Griffith, R. T. H. *The Hymns of the Rig-Veda*. Translated with a popular commentary. Calcutta: Chowkhamba Sanskrit Series Office, 1889–92. Reprint, 1963.

———. *The Hymns of the Sámaveda, translated with a popular commentary*. Banaras: Chowkhamba Sanskrit Series Office, 1893. [2nd ed. 1916, Repr. 1976].

———. *The Hymns of the Yajur Veda*. Translated with a popular commentary. Benaras: [pub. ?], 1899, repr. Benaras: E. J. Lazarus, 1957.

Keith, A. B. *The Veda of the Black Yajus School Entitled Taittirīya Sanhitā*. 2 vols. Cambridge: Harvard Oriental Series 18, 19, 1914, repr., Delhi, 1963.

Lubotsky, A. *A Ṛgvedic Word Concordance*. New Haven: American Oriental Society, 1997.

Maurer, W. H., *Pinnacles of India's Past: Selections from The Ṛgveda*. Amsterdam/Philadelphia: Benjamins, 1986.

Mittwede, M. *Textkritische Bemerkungen zur Maitrāyaṇī Saṁhitā*. Stuttgart: Steiner, 1986.

———. *Textkritische Bemerkungen zur Kāṭhaka-Saṁhitā*. Stuttgart: Steiner, 1989.

Müller, Max. *Rig-Veda Saṃhitā, the Sacred Hymns of the Brahmins: Together with the Commentary of Sāyaṇācharya*. 6 vols. London: Trübner, 1849–74; repr. Varanasi, 1966.

O'Flaherty, W. D. *The Rig Veda: An Anthology*. Harmondsworth: Penguin, 1981.

Oldenberg, H. *Metrische und textgeschichtliche Prolegomena zu einer kritischen Rigveda-Ausgabe*. Berlin: 1888. Reprint, Wiesbaden: Steiner, 1982.

———. *Ṛgveda. Textkritische und exegetische Noten*. Berlin: Weidmann, 1909, 1912.

Parpola, A. *The Literature and Study of the Jaiminīya Sāmaveda. In Retrospect and Prospect*. Helsinki: Studia Orientalia 43:6, 1973.

Raghu Vira. *Kapiṣṭhala-Kaṭha-Saṃitā. A Text of the Black Yajurveda*. Lahore: Meharchand Lacchman Das, 1932; 2nd ed., 1968.

Renou, L. *Etudes védiques et pāṇinéennes*. Publications de l'Institut de Civilisation Indienne, fasc. 1, 2, 4, 6, 9–10, 12, 14, 16–18, 20, 22–23, 26–27, 30. Paris: E. de Boccard, 1955–69.

Roth, R., and Whitney, W. D. *Atharva Veda Sanhita*. Berlin: F. Dümmler, 1856, 2nd ed. M. Lindenau, Berlin: F. Dümmler, 1924. Reprint, Bonn, 1966.

Satavalekar, D. *Śuklayajurvedīya Kāṇva Saṁhitā*. Pārḍī: Svādhyāya Maṇḍala, 1983.

van Nooten, B. and Gary B. Holland. *Rig Veda: A Metrically Restored Text*. Cambridge: Department of Sanskrit and Indian Studies, Harvard University, 1994

von Schroeder, L. *Maitrāyaṇī-Saṁhitā. Die Saṁhitā der Maitrāyaṇīya-Śākhā*. 4 vols. Leipzig: Brockhaus, 1881–86. Reprint, Wiesbaden: Steiner, 1970–72.

———. *Kāṭhakam: Die Saṁhitā der Kaṭha-Śākhā*. 3 vols. Leipzig: 1900–1910; repr. Wiesbaden: Steiner, 1970–72.

Weber, A. *The Vājasaneyī-Sanhitā in the Mādhyandina and the Kāṇva Sākhā: With the Commentary of Mahīdhara*. Berlin: 1852. Reprint, Varanasi: Chowkhamba Sanskrit Series Office, 1972.

———. *The Śatapatha-Brāhmaṇa in the Mādhyandina Śākhā with Extracts from the Commentaries of Sāyaṇa, Harisvāmin, and Dvivedagaṅga*. Berlin-London: Dümmler, 1855. Reprint, Varanasi: Chowkhamba Sanskrit Series Office, 1964.

———. *Taittirīya-Saṃhitā*. [= Indische Studien, vols. 11–12.] Leipzig: Brockhaus, 1871–72.

Wilson, H. H. *Rig-Veda Saṃhitā*. London: W. H. Allen, 1888. Reprint, New Delhi, 1977.

The Brāhmaṇas

Though the prose portions of the Taittirīya Saṁhitā serve as its primary *Brāhmaṇa*, there also exists a Taittirīya Brāhmaṇa (TB) with additional commentary (and Mantras), unfortunately an inferior text with no standard edition. There are the editions prepared at Calcutta (R. L. Mitra, 1859), Ānandāśrama (V. S. Godbole et al. 1934), and Mysore (Mahadeva Sastri and L. Srinivasacarya, 1908–13); the last has some South Indian phonetic peculiarities. The TB has been partly translated (into English) in a series of articles by P. E. Dumont (1948–69). A late (ca. Upaniṣad period) addition to the Brāhmaṇa is the fragmentary Vādhūla Brāhmaṇa (or Vādhūla Anvākhyāna), which usually is wrongly called Vādhūla Sūtra. About two thirds of the fragments of this Brāhmaṇa text have been edited and translated into German by Caland (1922–28). Neither the Maitrāyaṇī Saṁhitā nor the Kaṭha Saṁhitā has a surviving separate text called a Brāhmaṇa, though a collection of fragments of the original Kaṭha Brāhmaṇa, called Śatādhyāya Brāhmaṇa, is found in Kashmiri ritual handbooks and has been partially edited by von Schroeder (1898) and Surya Kanta (1943); and also Lokesh Chandra (1982, 1984).

The Ṛg Veda has two Brāhmaṇas, the Aitareya Brāhmaṇa (AB) and the Kauṣītaki (or Śāṅkhāyana) Brāhmaṇa (KB), of which the Aitareya is the older and the more extensive. The AB was edited by Aufrecht (1879), the KB by Lindner (1887), and in its Kerala version by E. R. S. Sarma (1968). Both have been translated into English by Keith (1920).

The major Brāhmaṇas of the Sāma Veda are the Jaiminīya Brāhmaṇa (JB) and the Pañcaviṁśa Brāhmaṇa (PB, or Tāṇḍya Mahā-Brāhmaṇa). A carefully, and if possible critically, edited version of the JB is highly desirable. There are several recent partial translations (e.g., H. W. Bodewitz, 1973, 1990) of the Agnihotra and Soma sections, accompanied by detailed philological, though not particularly pioneering, commentary. W. Doniger O'Flaherty (1985) has retranslated some of the narrative portions. R. Tsuchida (1979) and D. Schrapel (1970) have translated parts of book 2. A complete, philologically grounded translation of the JB would contribute greatly to our understanding of middle Vedic religion, but it may be premature to desire one without an accurate text.

The Pañcaviṁśa Brāhmaṇa, which is available only in unsatisfactory uncritical editions, presents fewer difficulties, but also fewer rewards than the JB. For a preliminary critical reading of the text, the old manuscript from Gujarat printed by Lokesh Chandra (1981) and Caland's remarks in his translation, referring to another old MS at Leiden, are invaluable. The text has been translated and copiously annotated, with many valuable references to, and partial translations of, JB, by Caland (1931). There are a number of other, minor "Brāhmaṇas" attached to the SV, most of which rather belong to the category of the Sūtras. Most of them have been edited by B. R. Sharma (1974).

The AV has a very late and inferior Brāhmaṇa, the Gopatha Brāhmaṇa (GB), critically edited by Caland's pupil D. Gaastra (1919). Its first part, in fact, presupposes the grammar of Pāṇini. However, this text, which to a large degree quotes from other Brāhmaṇa-type texts, was probably only an additional Brāhmaṇa (*anubrāhmaṇa*) of the Paippalāda school of the AV, which was, just like some other texts, incorporated into the Śaunaka school of Gujarat only during the Middle Ages, as suggested by M. Witzel (1985).

A collection of fragments of "lost" Brāhmaṇas found in various medieval commentaries has been compiled by Batakrishna Ghosh (1947).

References

Aufrecht, T. *Das Aitareya Brāhmaṇa*. Bonn: A. Marcus, 1879.

Bodewitz, H. W. *Jaiminīya Brāhmaṇa I, 1–65. Translation and commentary with a study of the Agnihotra and Prāṇāgnihotra*. Leiden: E. J. Brill, 1973.

———. *The Jyotiṣṭoma Ritual. Jaiminīya Brāhmaṇa I, 66–364. Introduction, translation and commentary*. Leiden: E. J. Brill, 1990.

Caland, W. *Pañcaviṃśa-Brāhmaṇa. The Brāhmaṇa of Twenty-five Chapters*. Calcutta: Bibliotheca Indica, 255, 1931. Reprint, Delhi, 1982.

———, *Das Jaiminīya Brāhmaṇa in Auswahl*. Amsterdam 1919. Reprint, Wiesbaden 1970.

———. "*Über das Vādhūla Sūtra; Eine zweite/dritte/vierte Mitteilung über das Vādhūla Sūtra*" [Vadhūla Sūtra and Brāhmaṇa fragments (Anvākhyāna)]. AO 1 (1922), 3–11; AO II (1924), 142–67; AO IV (1926), 1–41, 161–213; AO VI (1928), 97–241 [= 1990, pp. 268–541).

———. *Kleine Schriften*. Ed. M. Witzel. Stuttgart: Steiner, 1990.

Dumont, P. E. [Translations of sections of Taittirīya Brāhmaṇa.] *Proceedings of the American Philosophical Society* 92 (1948); 95 (1951); 98 (1954); 101 (1957); 103 (1959); 104 (1960); 105 (1961); 106 (1962); 107 (1963); 108 (1964); 109 (1965); 113 (1969).

Gaastra, D. *Das Gopatha Brāhmaṇa*. Leiden: E. J. Brill, 1919.

Ghosh, Batakrishna. *Collection of the Fragments of Lost Brāhmaṇas*. Calcutta: Modern Publication Syndicate, 1947.

Godbole, V. S. et al. *Kṛṣṇayajurvedīyaṃ Taittirīyabrāhmaṇam*. Poona: Ānandāśrama Saṃskṛt Series 37, 1934.

Keith, A. B. *Rigveda Brāhmaṇas: The Aitareya and Kauṣītaki Brāhmaṇas of the Rigveda*. Harvard Oriental Series 25. Cambridge: Harvard University Press, 1920.

Lindner, B. *Das Kaushītaki Brāhmaṇa*. [Jena:] n.p., 1887. Reprint, Jena: n.p., 1968.

Lokesh, Chandra. *Pañcaviṃśa-Brāhmaṇa with the Commentary of Sāyaṇa*. New Delhi: Śatapiṭaka Series vol. 270, 1981.

———. [Fragments of the Kaṭha-Brāhmaṇas in] *Sanskrit texts from Kashmir*.

New Delhi: Śatapiṭaka Series 298–99, 329–20, 333–35, 1982; *Vedic Texts*, Śatapiṭaka Series Vol. 338, 1984.

Mitra, R. L. *The Gopatha Brāhmaṇa of the Atharva Veda in the Original Sanskrit*. Calcutta: n.p., 1859; 2nd ed. Bibliotheca Indica, vol. 79, 1872; repr. Delhi: Indological Book House, 1972.

O'Flaherty, Wendy Doniger. *Tales of Sex and Violence: Folklore, Sacrifice, and Danger in the Jaiminīya Brāhmaṇa*. Chicago: University of Chicago Press, 1985.

Sarma, E. R. S. *Kauṣītaki-Brāhmaṇa*. Wiesbaden: Steiner, 1968.

Sastri, A. Mahadeva, R. Shama Sastry, and L. Srinivasacharya. *The Taittirīya Brāhmaṇa with the Commentary of Bhaṭṭabhāskaramiśra*. 4 vols. Mysore: 1908–21.

Schrapel, D. *Untersuchung der Partikel iva und anderer lexikalisch-syntaktischer Probleme der vedischen Prosa nebst zahlreichen Textemendationen und der kritischen Übersetzung von Jaiminīya-Brāhmaṇa 2:371–73 (gavāmayana 1)*. Ph.D. diss., Marburg. 1970.

Sharma, B. R. *Ṣaḍviṃśa Brāhmaṇa*. Tirupati: Kendriya Sanskrit Vidyapeetha, 1967.

Surya Kanta. *Kāṭhakasaṃkalana, Extracts from the Lost Kāthaka-Brāhmaṇa, Kāṭhaka-Srauta Sūtra, and Kāṭhaka-Gṛhya Sūtras*. Lahore: Meharchand Lachhman Das, 1943.

Tsuchida R. *Das sattra-Kapitel des Jaiminīya-Brāhmaṇa 2:334–70 nach den Handschriften herausgegeben, ins Deutsche übersetzt und erklärt*. Ph.D. diss., Marburg, 1979.

von Schroeder, L. *Die Tübinger Kaṭha-Handschriften und ihre Beziehung zum Taittirīya-Āraṇyaka*. Sitzungsberichte der Kais. Akad. d. Wiss., phil.-hist. Kl. 137.4. Wien, 1898.

Witzel, M. "Die Atharvaveda-Tradition und die Paippalāda-Saṁhitā." *Zeitschrift der Deutschen Morgenländischen Gesellschaft. Supplementband* 6. 22. Deutscher Orientalistentag, 256–71. Stuttgart, 1985.

The Āraṇyakas

Āraṇyakas are found under this name only in the tradition of the Ṛg Veda (Aitareya Ār., Kauṣītaki or Śāṅkhāyana Ār.) and Yajur Veda (Taittirīya, Kaṭha Ar.). The SV and AV have no texts named in this way. However, the Jaiminīya Upaniṣad Brāhmaṇa may, in part, be regarded as the Āraṇyaka of this Veda, and the Gopatha-Brāhmaṇa plays the same role for the AV. In addition, the first part of Kāṇḍa 14 of the Śatapatha-Brāhmaṇa, which deals with the Pravargya ritual (ŚB 14:1–3), may with good reason be called the Āraṇyaka of the Mādhyandina school of the White YV, for all three Āraṇyaka texts of the YV deal centrally with this ritual.

Its performance and even its acquisition by learning is regarded as too dangerous to be carried out inside the settlement and has to be done "where the houses of the settlement cannot be seen any more." This points to the correct meaning of the designation Āraṇyaka, from *araṇya* "wilderness," which curiously still eludes most modern Sanskritists, though it was established long ago by Oldenberg (1915–16). This oversight also clouds the understanding of the type of text the Āraṇyakas constitute. They are not, as medieval Hindu tradition asserts, the texts of the third stage in life, the Vānaprastha, but deal, quite in the fashion of other Brāhmaṇa type texts, with a particular ritual. In the case of the RV it is the Mahāvrata day of the year-long Gavāmayana, and in the YV it is the Pravargya ritual.

Around this nucleus of dangerous and secret texts (Śaṅkara and others call this sort of text Rahasya) are clustered various additions to the canon: the RV schools add their Upaniṣads and even a brief Sūtra style addition (in AĀ 5, by Āśvalāyana); the Taittirīya school, similarly, begins with one of the eight special Kāṭhaka *agnicayana* rituals, and adds two sections with death ritual as well as all of their Upaniṣads. The White YV contains in its book 14 both the Āraṇyaka and its Upaniṣad, the Bṛhadāraṇyaka Upaniṣad. However, the last sections of this Upaniṣad contain various "strange" materials not expected in an Upaniṣad.

P. Thieme is the first to have correctly understood the structure of this text in his lecture at Kyoto on accepting the Kyoto Prize in 1989. The sections dealing with the procreation of particular types of sons, and so forth belong to the last instructions of a Veda teacher to his departing student. The last sections of Bṛhadāraṇyaka Upaniṣad thus are of Āraṇyaka type and provide a frame surrounding the Bṛhadāraṇyaka Upaniṣad. Its very name may signify this amalgation: it is a Bṛhad-Āraṇyaka-Upaniṣad, a "large (text consisting of) the Āraṇyaka and the Upaniṣad" of the White YV, similarly to the Bāhvṛcya, "the text consisting of many *ṛc*," the RV.

The Aitareya Āraṇyaka has been edited and translated by Keith (1909); the Kauṣītaki or Śāṅkhāyana Āraṇyaka was edited by V. N. Apte (1922) and Bhim Dev (1980) and translated by Keith (1908). The Taittirīya Āraṇyaka was edited by Rajendralal Mitra (1864–72), Mahadeva Sastri and P. K. Rangacharya (1900–1902), and in the Ānandāśrama Series by K. V. Abhyankar et al. in an often incorrect newly set reprint

(1967–69) of the earlier edition of 1897–98; book 2 of TĀ has been edited and translated into French by Ch. Malamoud (1977). The Kaṭha Āraṇyaka has been edited and translated into German by M. Witzel (1974).

References

Abhyankar, K. V., et al., *Kṛṣṇayajurvedīyaṃ Taittirīyāraṇyakam*. Reprint, 1967–69. Poona: Ānandāśrama Saṃskṛt Series 36, 1897–98.

Apte, V. N. *Rgvedāntargataṃ Śāṅkhāyanāraṇyakam*. Poona: Ānandāśrama Saṃskṛt Series 90, 1922.

Bhim Dev. *Śaṅkhāyanāraṇyakam*. Hoshiarpur: Vishveshvaranand Vedic Research Institute, 1980.

Keith, A. B. *The Śāṅkhāyana Āraṇyaka with an Appendix on the Mahāvrata*. London: Royal Asiatic Society, 1908.

———. *The Aitareya Āraṇyaka*. Oxford: Clarendon Press, 1909.

Malamoud, Ch. *Le Svādhyāya. Recitation personelle du Veda. Taittirīya-Āraṇyaka. Livre* 2. Paris: 1977.

Mitra, Rajendralal. *The Taittirīya Āraṇyaka of the Black Yajurveda*. Calcutta: Bibliotheca Indica, 1864–72. Reprint, Osnabrück, 1981.

Oldenberg, H. "Āraṇyaka." *Nachrichten von der Gesellschaft der Wissenschaften zu Göttingen*: 1915/16:382–401.

Sastri, A. Mahadeva, and K. Rangacarya. *The Taittirīya Āraṇyaka with the Commentary of Bhaṭṭabhāskaramiśra*. 3 vols. Mysore: 1900–1902; repr. Delhi, n.d.

Witzel, M. *Das Kaṭha-Āraṇyaka, Textkritische Edition mit Übersetzung und Kommentar (Teildruck)*. Erlangen/Kathmandu: Nepal Research Centre, 1974.

The Upaniṣads

Turning now to the Upaniṣads, we are faced with a dilemma regarding both the actual number of texts belonging to this category as well as their attribution to the four Vedas. There are standard collections, based on their usage in the medieval Advaita and Āgamic traditions of 10, 52, or 108 Upaniṣads, but the texts excerpted in Vishva Bandhu's *Vedic Word Concordance* amount to more than 200, 188 of which have been conveniently edited by J. L. Shastri (1970). The larger collections include even a text as late as the Allah Upaniṣad, which is supposed to be a Śākta Upaniṣad. The standard edition, which contains many useful cross references and a word index but is not a critical edition, is that by Limaye and Vadekar (1958). See now the edition of P. Olivelle of *The Early Upaniṣads*.

The Upaniṣads represent (apart from incidental topics where they overlap with the Āraṇyakas and apart from the final teachings, secrets, and admonitions that a student receives from his Veda teacher) the early philosophy of India, especially that on the nature of the human soul, its fate after death, and its ultimate identity with Brahman, the force underlying the cosmos. Occasionally they also report mystical insights (e.g., BĀU 4.3., KauṣUp 1). Otherwise the speculations frequently take up a ritualistic topic and develop it into a discussion on the ultimate. These topics are often presented in dialogue form, and thus continue the tradition of discussion on ritual topics in the preceding Brāhmaṇas and Āraṇyakas. The word *Upaniṣad* (literally, "sitting close by at the proper place") has found many interpretations, for which Schayer (1925) and Falk (1986) may be consulted.

Usually the Upaniṣads are divided into three broad layers: the older prose Upaniṣads, the middle level of verse Upaniṣads, and the later Upaniṣads, some of which were composed only in the Middle Ages. The late Upaniṣads are traditionally attributed to the AV. The older Upaniṣads comprise the Bṛhadāraṇyaka (BĀU), Chāndogya, Aitareya, Kauṣītaki, Taittirīya, and Kaṭha-Śikṣā Upaniṣads, as well as the Jaiminīya Upaniṣad Brāhmaṇa. To the second level belong the Kaṭha, Iṣa, Mahānārāyaṇa, Kena, Śvetāśvatara, Muṇḍaka, Praśna, and Māṇḍūkya Upaniṣads, as well as four "new" texts, the Bāṣkala, Chāgaleya, Ārṣeya, and Śaunaka Upaniṣads.

Until very recently, most of the Upaniṣads had been translated (Deussen 1897, etc.) following the commentary by Śaṅkara (ca. 700 C.E.) and other medieval commentators, who regard these texts as the scriptures that underlie Advaita (and other medieval) philosophies and religious movements. This is a wrong approach from the point of view of the development of Indian thought. The Upaniṣads are the secondary collections of a whole array of late Vedic teachers (see Ruben 1947) belonging to various Vedic schools; they do not form a single body of texts but represent multiple strands of tradition, often quite individualistic ones. Recent translations, and to some extent Hume (1931), treat the texts with philological correctness; that is, at first as isolated texts and then in their relations to other Upaniṣads and the preceding Brāhmaṇas and Āraṇyakas; see especially Thieme (1966); Rau (1964, 1965, 1971, 1981); Frenz (1969); Witzel (1979–80), and the important new translation of Olivelle (1998). For "new" Upaniṣads, see Belvalkar (1925); Renou (1956); and Tsuji (1982).

References

Alsdorf, L. "Contributions to the Textual Criticism of the Kaṭhopaniṣad." ZDMG 100 (1950):621–37.

Belvalkar, S. K. Four unpublished Upaniṣadic texts. *Report of the Third Oriental Conference*. Madras, 1925.

Deussen, P. *Sechzig Upanishad's des Veda*. Leipzig: F. A. Brockhaus, 1897; 2nd ed., 1985. Reprint, Darmstadt, 1963.

Falk, H. "Vedisch *Upaniṣad*." ZDMG 136 (1986):80–97.

Frenz, A. "Kauṣītaki Upaniṣad." *Indo-Iranian Journal* 11 (1969):72–129.

Hume, R. E. *The Thirteen Principal Upaniṣads*. Oxford: Oxford University Press, 1931; 1st. ed., 1921. Reprint, 1971.

Limaye, V. P., and R. D. Vadekar, *Eighteen Principal Upaniṣads*. Poona: Vaidika Saṃśodhana Maṇḍala, 1958.

Maue, D. *Bṛhadāraṇyakopaniṣad I*. Ph.D. diss., Giessen, 1976.

Morgenroth, W. *Chāndogya Upaniṣad*. Ph.D. diss., Jena, 1958.

Oertel, H. "The Jaiminīya or Talavakāra Upaniṣad Brāhmaṇa. Text, translation, and notes." *Journal of the American Oriental Society* 16 (1895):79–260.

Olivelle, P. *The Early Upaniṣads: Annotated Text and Translation*. New York: Oxford University Press, 1998.

Perez Coffie, C. A. *Bṛhadāraṇyakopaniṣad II: Critical Edition of the Second Chapter of the Kāṇva Recension. According to the Accented Manuscripts with a Critical-Exegetical Commentary*. Diss., Harvard, 1994.

Rau, W. "Versuch einer deutschen Übersetzung der Śvetāśvatara-Upaniṣad." *Asiatische Studien* 17 (1964):24–46.

———. "Versuch einer deutschen Übersetzung der Muṇḍaka-Upaniṣad." *Asiatische Studien* 18/19 (1965): 216–266.

———. "Versuch einer deutschen Übersetzung der Kāṭhaka-Upaniṣad." *Asiatische Studien* 25 (1971):158–74.

———. "Versuch einer deutschen Übersetzung der Taittirīya-Upaniṣad." *Festschrift der Wissenschaftlichen Gesellschaft an der J. W. Goethe-Universität Frankfurt* 349–73. Wiesbaden, 1981.

Renou, L. *Les Upaniṣad III, Kena Upaniṣad*. Paris: Adrien-Maisonneuve, 1943.

———. *Les Upaniṣad XVI. Bāṣkala-Mantra Upaniṣad. XVII Chāgaleya Upaniṣad*. Paris, 1956.

———. *Les Upaniṣad VI–IX. Texte et traduction sous la direction de Louis Renou. Kauṣītaki Upaniṣad* [also contains: Śvetāśvatara Upaniṣad by A. Silburn, Praśna Upaniṣad by J. Bousquet, Taittirīya Upaniṣad by E. Lesimple]. Paris, 1978.

Ruben, W. *Die Philosophen der Upanishaden*. Bern: A. Francke, 1947.

Salomon, R. "Linguistic Analysis of the Muṇḍaka Upaniṣad." *WZKS* 25 (1981):91–105.

Schayer, S. "Die Bedeutung des Wortes Upaniṣad." *Rocznik Orientalistyczny* 3 (1925):57–67.

Shastri, J. L. *Upaniṣat-Saṅgrahaḥ: Containing 108 Upaniṣads*. Delhi: Motilal Banarsidass, 1970.

Thieme, P. "Der Weg durch den Himmel nach der Kauṣītaki-Upaniṣad." *Wiss. Zeitschr. d. Univ. Halle-Wittenburg, Ges.-u. Sprachwiss. Reihe* 1, no. 3 (Halle, 1951/52).

———. "Īṣopaniṣad (= Vājasaneyī-Saṁhitā 40) 1–14." *Journal of the American Oriental Society* 85 (1965):89–99.

———. *Upanischaden. Ausgewählte Stücke*. Stuttgart, 1966.

Tsuji, N. [*alias* N. Fukushima.] "Some Linguistic Remarks on the Maitri Upaniṣad." *Vedagaku Ronsō* (1977):52–67.

———. "Bashukara Mantora Upanishatto to Chagareya Upanishatto," *Tsuji Naoshiro Chōsakushū, Vedagaku* 2 (1982):68–104.

Varenne, J. *La Mahānārāyaṇa Upaniṣad*. Paris: Boccard, 1960.

van Buitenen, J. A. B. *The Maitrāyaṇīya Upaniṣad*. The Hague: Mouton, 1962.

Witzel, M. "An unknown Upaniṣad of the Kṛṣṇa Yajurveda: The Kaṭha-Śiksā-Upaniṣad." *Journal of the Nepalese Research Centre* 1 (Wiesbaden/Kathmandu, 1977):139–55.

———. "Die Kaṭha-Śikṣā-Upaniṣad und ihr Verhältnis zur Śīkṣāvallī der Taittirīya-Upaniṣad." *WZKS* 23 (1979):5–28; 24 (1980):21–82.

The Sūtras

Finally, we turn to the Sūtras. The Indian tradition refers to these texts by the term *Kalpa(-Sūtra)* and regards them as post-Vedic; that is, not as revealed texts (*śruti*) but as texts composed by human authors (*smṛti*), and as such, along with grammar (*vyākaraṇa*), meter (*chandas*), phonetics (*śikṣā*), etymology (*nirukta*), and astronomy (*jyotiṣa*), not as belonging to the body of Vedic texts but to the "limbs of the Veda" (*vedāṅga*). From the point of view of content and language, however, these texts are closely allied to the preceding Brāhmaṇas and Āraṇyakas. Indeed, N. Tsuji, (alias N. Fukushima, 1952) has shown that the Śrauta Sūtras are, by and large, based on the preceding Vedic literature of their particular school (*śākhā*). As we cannot mention each text here by name, we refer to the up-to-date and nearly complete list of editions of the Sūtras, of their often independent appendices (and of most other Vedic texts), as given by Kashikar (1968) and more completely by Gotō (1987, p. 355–71).

References

Gotō, T. *Die "I. Präsensklasse" im Vedischen: Untersuchung der vollstufigen thematischen Wurzelpräsentia*. Wien: Verlag der Oesterreichischen Akademie der Wissenschaften, 1987.

Kashikar, C. G. "A Survey of the Śrautasūtras." *Journal of Bombay University* 35, part 2, no. 41 (1968): vi + 188.

Tsuji, N. [N. Fukushima]. *On the Relation between Brāhmaṇas and Śrauta Sūtras* [Burāhumana to shurauta sūtora to no kanken]. Tokyo, 1952; repr. 1982, 1–124, Engl. summary, 181–247.

Vedic Religion and Ritual

A new general treatment of Vedic religion is badly needed. Those available are, at best, out of date, and often seriously misleading as well. The early massive (3 vol.) work of A. Bergaigne, *La religion védique* (1878–83), in fact, as the rest of its title indicates (*d'après les hymnes du Ṛg-Veda*), essentially limits its purview to the earliest text. It is, moreover, primarily concerned with mythology and should be discussed under that rubric.

The work that remains the most useful treatment is probably H. Oldenberg's *Die Religion des Veda* (1894, 1917; Engl., 1896). This is a balanced account that is not too seriously influenced by the then prevalent nature mythology. Oldenberg is a pioneer in making use of ethnographical parallels. He extracted Vedic religion from the sphere of the "classical" tradition. It is unfortunate that Vedic studies subsequently have disappeared from the view and the agenda of anthropologists. Yet Oldenberg's work, nonetheless, relies too heavily on the evolutionary concept of a still "primitive Vedic mind" preceding the evolution of the structure of our supposedly much more developed mind. As Oldenberg put it: the Brāhmaṇa-type texts represent, after all, "vorwissenschaftliche Wissenschaft," prescientific science. As such, they are the fountainhead of Indian thought and sciences.

A. B. Keith's *The Religion and Philosophy of the Veda and Upanishads* (1925) is also useful, though marred, like most works of the late nineteenth and early twentieth centuries, by an excessive reliance on the nature-mythology paradigm. M. Bloomfield's *The Religion of the Veda* (1908), actually a series of lectures, unfortunately displays a patronizing and superficial attitude to the subject, surprising in one who gave us so many useful research tools and penetrating insights into particular problems.

More recent treatments include Renou's brief but reliable discussion in Renou and Filliozat's *L'Inde classique I* (1947), chap. 5. "Le Védisme" (pp. 270–380)—translated and issued as a separate small volume, *Vedic India* (1957)—and Gonda's survey of 1960, which is sound if uninspired and still somewhat too reliant on the notion of the "primitive mind." Th. J. Hopkins's well-balanced, if necessarily short, *The Hindu Religious Tradition* (1971) is very useful as a general introduction. For certain aspects of Vedic religion, also see Basham (1989); and for the Brāhmaṇas, see Devasthali (1965). A recent edition to this literature is T. Oberlies' *Die Religion des Ṛgveda*, of which two of the projected three volumes have appeared. Despite its title, it is less a comprehensive survey than at first it appears.

References

Basham, A. L. *The Origins and Development of Classical Hinduism*. Ed. and annotated K. G. Zysk. Boston: Beacon Press, 1989.

Bergaine, A. *La religion védique*. 3 vols. Paris: Bibliotheque de l'Ecole des Hautes Etudes 36, 53–54, 1878–83; English translation, V. G. Paranjpe, Poona, 1978.

Bloomfield, M. *The Religion of the Veda: The Ancient Religion of India (from Rig-Veda to Upanishads)*. New York and London: G. B. Putnam's, 1908.

Devasthali, G. V. *Religion and Mythology of the Brāhmaṇas with Particular Reference to the Śatapatha-Brāhmaṇa*. Poona: University of Poona, 1964.

Gonda, J. *Die Religionen Indiens. I. Veda und älterer Hinduismus*. Stuttgart: Kohlhammer, 1960.

Hopkins, Th. J. *The Hindu Religious Tradition*. Encino and Belmont: Dickenson Publishing, 1971.

Keith, A. B. *The Religion and Philosophy of the Veda and Upanishads*. 2 vols. Cambridge: Harvard Oriental Series 31, 32, 1925.

Oberlies, T. *Die Religion des Ṛgveda*, vols. 1 (1998) and 2 (1999). Vienna: Sammlung de Nobili.

Oldenberg, H. *Die Religion des Veda*. Berlin: W. Hertz, 1894; 2nd ed., Stuttgart: G. Cotta, 1917; English trans.: *The Religion of the Veda*, London, 1896, from the 1st ed.; 3rd German ed., Berlin 1923.

Renou, L., and J. Filliozat, *L'Inde classique: Manuel des études indiennes*. Paris: Payot 1947. Reprint, Paris: Maisonneuve 1985.

Ṛgvedic Ritual and Its Forerunners

Early Vedic ritual can be compared not only with what follows it, but with what precedes it—or, rather, it can be compared with cognate ritual tradition(s), and an attempt can be made to reconstruct the shared ritual system from which each of these traditions derived. Striking parallels to

Vedic ritual and religion appear in ancient Iranian religion, as found in the texts of Zoroastrianism preserved in a language closely related to Vedic Sanskrit, namely Avestan. For a convenient collection of technical religious terms shared by Vedic and Avestan, see Hillebrandt (1897, p. 11). For connections between Vedic and Zoroastrian religion in general, see, for example, Keith (1925, 32–36) and Thieme (1957), reprinted with changes in R. Schmitt (1968, 204–41).

Discussions of Ṛgvedic ritual itself are relatively rare and generally purely comparative. Taking the reasonably clear descriptions of middle and late Vedic ritual as their starting points, earlier correspondents of this or that detail or ritual episode are sought, piecemeal, in the Ṛgveda. Examples are the discussions of van Buitenen (1968) of the Pravargya or Gonda on the Sautrāmaṇī Mantras (1980). The only more sustained, if brief, discussion of a "classical" Vedic ritual in the RV is that of the Soma ritual by Geldner in the introduction to book 9 of his RV translation (1951). Also commonly treated is the use or the absence of Ṛgvedic mantras in the later ritual; see Renou (1962), Gonda (1978), and Schneider (1971).

A certain amount of attention has been given to the purpose, function, and context of Ṛgvedic ritual for example, the theory of Kuiper's (going back in part to Ludwig and Hillebrandt) that "the oldest nucleus of the Ṛgveda was a textbook for the new year ritual" (1960, p. 222). This and other suggestions are briefly summarized and a new one proposed in H. Falk (1997). Schmidt (1968) proposes connecting the morning pressing of the Soma ritual with the Vala myth and the new year and the spring season and suggests a connection of the midday pressing with the Vṛtra myth and the rainy season.

However, as we have indicated, relatively little systematic work has been done on assembling the details of Ṛgvedic praxis. Hillebrandt (1897, 11–17) contains a very brief but still useful survey of evidence for Ṛgvedic ritual, especially ritual terminology (see also Keith 1925, 252–56, and Bergaigne, 1878). Both Oldenberg (1888) and Bergaigne (1889) examined the structure of the RV for clues to its liturgical use in the ritual. But what is needed is a thoroughgoing study of the evidence, not only terminological but descriptive, if possible calibrated according to a rough internal chronology of the text and regional differences. Once we know what Ṛgvedic ritual was, we will be in a better position to hypothesize about its purpose (and about its successor, the "classical" Vedic ritual).

References

Bergaigne, A. *La Religion védique*. 3 vols. Paris: Bibliothéque de l'Ecole des Haute Etudes 36, 53–54, 1878–83; English trans., V. G. Paranjpe, Poona, 1978.

———. "Recherches sur l'histoire de la liturgie védique". *JA* 13 (1889):5–32, 121–97.

Falk, H. "The Purpose of Ṛgvedic Ritual." In *Inside the Texts, Beyond the Texts: New Approaches to the Study of the Vedas*, ed. M. Witzel. Cambridge: Harvard University Press 1997, 69–88.

Geldner, K. F. *Der Rigveda*. 3 vols. Cambridge: Harvard Oriental Series, 33, 34, 35, 1951.

Gonda, J. *Hymns of the Ṛgveda not Employed in the Solemn Ritual*. Amsterdam: North Holland Publishing, 1978.

———. *The Mantras of the Agnyupasthāna and the Sautrāmaṇī*. Amsterdam: North Holland Publishing, 1980.

Hillebrandt, A. *Ritual-Litteratur. Vedische Opfer und Zauber*. Strassburg: K. J. Trübner, 1897.

Keith, A. B. *The Religion and Philosophy of the Veda and the Upanishads*. 2 vols. Cambridge: Harvard Oriental Series 31, 32, 1925.

Kuiper, F. B. J. "The Ancient Aryan Verbal Contest." *IIJ* 4 (1960):217–81.

Oldenberg, H. *Metrische und textgeschichtliche Prolegomena zu einer kritischen Rigveda-Ausgabe*. Berlin: 1888. Reprint, Wiesbaden: Steiner, 1982.

Renou, L. "Recherches sur le rituel védique: La place du Rig-Veda dans l'ordonnance du culte." *JA* 250 (1962):161–84.

Schmidt, H.-P. *Bṛhaspati und Indra*. Wiesbaden, 1968.

Schmitt, R. *Indogermanische Dichtersprache*. Darmstadt: Wissenschaftliche Buchgesellschaft, 1968.

Schneider, U. *Der Somaraub des Manu: Mythus und Ritual*. Freiburg, 1971.

Thieme, P. "Vorzarathustrisches bei den Zarathustriern und bei Zarathustra" ZDMG 107 (1956):67–104.

van Buitenen, J. A. B. *The Pravargya*. Poona: Deccan College Research Institute, 1968.

Classical Ritual

In contrast to the sketchy and tentative treatment of Ṛgvedic ritual, "Classical" Vedic ritual—the ritual constantly referred to by the Brāhmaṇas and exhaustively described by the Śrauta Sūtras—has been abundantly studied. A general survey is A. Hillebrandt's important *Ritual-Litteratur: Vedische Opfer und Zauber* (1897), which covers Gṛhya as well as Śrauta rites and offers almost a digest of the relevant *Sūtras*. It sums up the knowledge gathered by the turn of the century and is still a very useful—and the only—compendium.

S. Lévi's *La doctrine du sacrifice* (1898) offers the first intellectual analysis stressing the regenerative function of the ritual; it was a critical source for the general, epoch-making work of Hubert and Mauss, "Essai sur la nature et la fonction du sacrifice" (1898). The general works on Vedic religion mentioned in the section on "Overviews of Vedic Religioin" (Oldenberg [1917], Keith [1925], Renou and Filliozat [1947], Gonda [1960]) also treat the rituals in much detail, and Renou (1954) offers a useful lexicon of ritual terminology, with abundant references to the Sūtras. C. G. Kashikar (1968), one of the foremost ritualists in the footsteps of Caland, has summed up the formal aspects of the Śrauta literature in a handbook. In addition, the introductions and notes to particular text editions and translations are often rich sources of detailed information about rituals and comparison of them across texts.

For individual rituals, there are numerous monographic treatments, which will be referred to in what follows. The great Poona project of a Śrautakośa was intended as a collection of all available Mantra, Brāhmaṇa, and Sūtra passages dealing with each of the Vedic rituals. The New/Full Moon and the Soma ritual have been published in Sanskrit, and in the accompanying English section a translation has been given of the relevant passages from the Baudhāyana Śrauta Sūtra (and other Śrauta Sūtra passages as far as they deviate), but only of non-Mantra texts. Unfortunately the project seems to have ground to a halt after these volumes.

Although many scholars over the last century or so have contributed to our knowledge of Vedic ritual, one must be singled out: W. Caland, whose unequalled command of the massive amount of textual material and inspired ability to make sense of it is always evident in the awe-inspiring flood of his text editions, translations, commentaries, and treatments of particular rituals and ritual types. For a bibliography of his works, see Caland (1990).

References

Caland, W. *Kleine Schriften*. Ed. M. Witzel. Stuttgart: Steiner, 1990.
Hillebrandt, A. *Ritual-Litteratur: Vedische Opfer und Zauber*. Strassburg: 1897.
Hubert, H., and M. Mauss. "Essai sur la nature et la fonction du sacrifice."

L'Année sociologique 1897–1898; English trans., W. D. Hall, *Sacrifice: Its Nature and Function*, University of Chicago Press, 1964.

Kashikar, C. G. "A Survery of the Śrautasūtras." *Journal of Bombay University* 35, part 2, no. 41 (1968):vi + 188.

Lévi, S. *La doctrine du sacrifice dans les Brāhmaṇas*. Paris: E. Leroux, 1898. Reprint, 1966.

Renou, L. *Vocabulaire du ritual vedique*. Paris: Klincksieck, 1954.

Interpretation of Ritual

Though we have a daunting amount of primarily descriptive material about Vedic ritual, there is a relative dearth of interpretive work making use of this wealth of first-order descriptions. In particular, the structure(s) of the ritual, the interrelations of particular rituals, and their internal development (cf. Witzel 1981/2, Falk 1986, 1988) deserve more searching attention than they have heretofore received. Though Thite (1975) assembles a useful collection of statements from the Brāhmaṇas about the meaning, origins, and so forth of sacrifice, the level of analysis is rather unsophisticated. For an approach that reinterprets the ritual through the lens of a single ritual participant, see Jamison's (1996) treatment of the *Sacrificer's Wife*.

In recent years the synchronic question has generally been framed by F. Staal's provocative but oversimple pronouncements about "the meaninglessness" of ritual (e.g., Staal 1979; 1990); (contra, e.g., Penner 1985, B. K. Smith, 1989: 38*ff*., Bodewitz 1990: 7–9, Witzel 1992), which have deflected attention from the more complex issues mentioned above. The main problem with Staal's approach is his refusal to view ritual on several, if not on many, interpretative levels. However, if anything should be clear at the close of this century it is the fact that ritual, like poetry, cannot be grasped by attributing its meaning to a single guiding concept and submitting it to a single "explanation." It is the art of the poet and ritualist to grasp several ideas, concerns, wishes, or fears of mankind in the given form, whether a poem or a rite, and to give expression to it in such a way as to allow multiple interpretations—or in more mundane terms, as to cater to the many different tastes of various individuals and of the various groups in society.

There is another item in Staal's approach that needs more discussion: When he speaks of "meaninglessness," one should not take this word at face value. He has simply redefined, without telling us, the term *meaning*. He does not characterize all ritual or a particular ritual, such as the Agnihotra, as having no meaning or as never having had any meaning (but does not say so expressly). He rather points out the lack of meaning of the various small constituent parts of a particular ritual, just like the various small melodic phrases that make up the particular song of a bird. But he overlooks the point that both ritual and birdsong are a system of signs with a function outside this system.

Just as the "meaning" of ritual has shaped recent discussion of the synchronic questions, diachronic questions have been shaped in response to Heesterman's equally provocative but oversimple theories (see especially the essays of various dates collected in Heesterman, 1993) about the bloodily agonistic background of "Classical" Vedic ritual and its transformation into the (as he sees it) noncompetitive machinery described in the Śrauta texts. This approach views the development of the ritual too much in terms of a sudden revolutionary breakup of the old ritual rather than in terms of observable ritual development. Heesterman specifically does not identify his older ritual stage with that of the Ṛgveda.

References

Bodewitz, H. W. *The Jyotiṣṭoma Ritual. Jaiminīya Brāhmaṇa I, 66–364: Introduction, Translation, and Commentary*. Leiden: E. J. Brill, 1990.

Falk, H. *Bruderschaft und Würfelspiel*. Freiburg: H. Falk, 1986.

———. "Vedische Opfer im Pali-Kanon." *Bulletin d'Etudes Indiennes* 6 (1988):225–54.

Heesterman, J. C. *The Inner Conflict of Tradition: Essays in Indian Ritual, Kingship, and Society*. Chicago: University of Chicago Press, 1985.

———. *The Broken World of Sacrifice: An Essay in Ancient Indian Ritual*. Chicago: University of Chicago Press, 1993.

Jamison, S. W. *Sacrificed Wife/Sacrificer's Wife: Women, Ritual, and Hospitality in Ancient India*. New York: Oxford University Press, 1996.

Penner, H. H. "Language, Ritual, and Meaning." *Numen* 32 (1985):1–16.

Smith, B. K. *Reflections on Resemblance, Ritual, and Religion*. New York and Oxford: Oxford University Press: 1989.

Staal, J. F. "The Meaninglessness of Ritual." *Numen* 26 (1979):2–22.

———. *Jouer avec le feu: Pratique et théorie du rituel védique*. Paris: Collége de France, 1990.

Thite, G. *Sacrifice in the Brāhmaṇa-texts*. Poona: University of Poona, 1975.

Witzel, M. Review of J. Gonda, *The Mantras of the Agnyupasthāna and the Sautrāmaṇī*. *Kratylos* 26 (1981/2):80–85.

———. "Meaningful Ritual: Vedic, Medieval, and Contemporary Concepts in the Nepalese Agnihotra Ritual," in B. V. D. Hoek et al., *Ritual, State, and History in South Asia: Essays in Honour of J. C. Heesterman* (Leiden: E. J. Brill, 1992), 774–827.

Domestic Ritual

The rituals of the Gṛhya (domestic) cult have been less thoroughly studied than Śrauta ritual. While Gṛhya ritual has attracted considerable interest in the last century and well into this one, and was regarded, with a certain justification, as a sort of Indo-European compendium of old rites of passage and of other domestic rites—relatively little work has been done in the past few decades. Some general works exist (e.g., Apte 1939, as well as significant treatment in Hillebrandt 1897), and there has been some discussion, often superficial, about the relationship between Gṛhya and Śrauta ritual (see, e.g., recently B. K. Smith 1986). There is a summary and discussion of the *saṁskāra* by Pandey 1957/1969; cf. also, for many of these aspects, the large work by P. V. Kane, *History of Dharmaśāstra*, with an enormous wealth of information on all these (and other) topics. Gonda (1980) is a rich compendium of practices and beliefs primarily culled from the Gṛhya literature, though, due to its organization, this book is somewhat difficult to use. Much remains to be done in this area.

References

Apte, V. M. *Social and Religious Life in the Gṛhyasūtras*. Reset ed., Bombay: Bombay Popular Book Depot, 1939.

Gonda, J. *Vedic Ritual: The Non-Solemn Rites*. Leiden-Köln: E. J. Brill, 1980.

Hillebrandt, A. *Ritual-Litteratur. Vedische Opfer und Zauber*. Strassburg: K. J. Trübner, 1897.

Kane, P. V. *History of Dharmaśāstra*. 5 vols. Poona: Bhandarkar Oriental Research Institute, 1930–62; 2nd ed., 1973–90.

Pandey, R. B. *Hindu Saṁskāras*. 1957; 2nd rev. ed., Delhi: Motilal Banarsidass, 1969.

Smith, B. K. "The Unity of Ritual: The Place of the Domestic Sacrifice in Vedic Ritualism." *IIJ* 29 (1986):79–96.

Recent Developments

In India, an increasing interest in Vedic ritual can be observed since Independence. Many public functions and ceremonies and related radio and television broadcasts now include Vedic chanting, and this is actively furthered in South India through the employment at temples of Vedic reciters (*vaidika*), who recite their particular school's texts in its entirety, a "lesson" per day (*vedapārāyaṇa*). Especially at Hoshiarpur and at Poona, many texts, translations, and studies (including such massive undertakings as the Vedic Word Concordance and the Śrautakośa) have appeared. At Poona, again, special attention has also been paid to the actual performance of Vedic rituals. While the more simple forms, such as the Agnihotra and the Dārśapaurṇamāsa, are found performed reasonably often in various parts of India and Nepal (for a list of some 550 Śrauta sacrificers in South Asia during approximately the last hundred years, see Kashikar and Parpola, in Staal 1983, 2: 199–251), the more complicated rituals are quite rare. The Soma ritual, for example, is regularly performed only in certain districts of Andhra, Tamil Nadu, and Kerala. At Poona, a large Vājapeya rite was performed in 1955 (see report, Vājapeya Anuṣṭhāna Samiti, 1956). This was followed by a Pravargya (see van Buitenen 1968, cited earlier). Due to the interest stirred by these rites among the—mainly—Dutch ritualists, J. F. Staal was able to to help organize and film a large Agnicayana in Kerala in 1975 (and again in 1990). The first resulted in a feature film, some thirty video tapes and a large two-volume book production with many photos (Staal 1983). Vedic recitation has increasingly been studied during the past few decades (e.g., by Staal 1961, Howard 1977, 1986, 1988a, b.).

References

Howard, W. *Samavedic Chant*. New Haven: Yale University Press, 1977.

———. *Veda Recitation in Varanasi*. Delhi: Motilal Banarsidass, 1986.

———. *The Decipherment of the Sāmavedic Notation of the Jaiminiyas*. Helsinki: Finnish Oriental Society, 1988[a].

———. *Mantralakshanam: Text, Translation, Extracts from the Commentary, and Notes Including References to Two Oral Traditions of South India*. Delhi: 1988[b].

Staal, J. F. *Nambudiri Veda Recitation. Gravenhage: Disputationes Rheno-Trajectinae, 1961.*

———. *Agni: The Vedic Ritual of the Fire Altar*. 2 vols. Berkeley: Asian Humanities Press, 1983.

Vājapeya Anuṣṭhāna Samiti. Karyacā Vṛttānta. Pune: 1956.

Vedic Mythology

Vedic mythology has attracted at least as much scholarly attention as Vedic ritual. The late nineteenth and early twentieth centuries saw a number of comprehensive treatments, notably Bergaigne's *La religion védique* (1878–83) mentioned above, Macdonell's *The Vedic mythology* (1897), and Hillebrandt's *Vedische Mythologie* (1927–29), as well as the extensive surveys in Oldenberg (1917), Keith (1925), and studies confined primarily to a single text, like that of Hopkins (1908). Though still indispensable for their detailed and stimulating engagement with the text (especially Bergaigne and Hillebrandt), these treatments suffer from overschematization and reliance on the nature-mythology paradigm then current.

The same overly schematic tendency marks a more recent approach toward Vedic mythology, the trifunctionalism associated especially with the French scholar G. Dumézil. For many decades, Vedic material has furnished much of the evidence for the "trifunctional" analysis of Indo-European ideology, a theory that sees all aspects of the culture of the Indo-Europeans (and its daughter cultures) as reflecting a social and ideological division into three major classes, or "functions": priest (1st function), warrior (2nd function), and, roughly, agriculturist (3rd function). This division matches neatly the division of Aryan society in India into Brāhmaṇa, Kṣatriya (or Rājanya), and Vaiśya. In terms of mythology, most gods will be associated primarily with one function, and mythological events will represent aspects of the function(s) of their participants (e.g., strained or harmonious relations between the functions). The body of scholarly work on this subject is quite extensive; a sample might include Dumézil (1940, 1949, 1958).

This approach has yielded a number of important insights into Vedic religion, but to use it as the sole interpretive paradigm requires serious distortion of the material. Though some gods and their exploits fit neatly into one of the three functions, others, including some of the most important (e.g., Agni and Soma), take an uneasy place or must be left totally out of account. The approach also risks an overly simple equating of sociopolitical and religious schemata.

Indeed, what is striking about the Vedic pantheon is its lack of overarching organization. Some gods are transparently "natural"—their names merely common nouns, with little or no characterization or action beyond their "natural" appearance and behavior (e.g., Vāta, deified "Wind"). Others are deified abstractions, again with little character beyond the nouns that name them (e.g., Bhaga: "Portion"). Others belong especially to the ethical and conceptual sphere (e.g., Varuṇa, Mitra), others to ritual practice (Soma, the deified libation). Despite their disparate affiliations, the divinities do not remain compartmentalized; gods of apparently different "origins" are often invoked together and can participate together in mythic activity. Whatever the history and sources of this complex pantheon, it cannot be reduced to a single organizational principle, nor can certain members that might not conform to such a principle be defined as outsiders and latecomers, given that gods of various types have counterparts outside of Vedic. It is well to remember Kuiper's structural(ist) statement (1962–1983, 43) on "the fundamental difficulty of Vedic mythology, viz. the impossibility of understanding a single mythological figure isolated from the context of the mythological system."

Without cataloging every mythic episode and its treatment in the secondary literature, we will make global reference to several scholars who collected and annotated a number of myths from a variety of texts; namely, M. Bloomfield (primarily in his series "Contributions to the Interpretation of the Veda"), H. Oertel (primarily in his series "Contributions from the Jaiminīya Brāhmaṇa to the History of the Brāhmaṇa Literature"), and also E. W. Hopkins (1908). Again, however, more is needed, particularly in confronting the fragments of mythology in the Mantra texts and the prose texts, in an effort to produce a coherent story; see, Sieg (1902) and Jamison (1991).

This brings us to our next question: to what extent do the mythologies of the RV, the Mantra texts, and the Brāhmaṇa texts form a unity, partly obscured by the distorting effects of literary genre and religious purpose—and to what extent has there been a real change in the conception of the deities and their exploits? This question is, of course, parallel to the one we asked about ritual in the two text-types, and it is equally difficult to answer. Given the obvious differences in content, in genre, and in purpose between mythology as presented in the Mantra texts and in the Brāhmaṇa texts, some investigators have on principle excluded the later, prose material from comparison with the poetic evidence, while others (e.g., Sieg 1902, Jamison 1991) attempt to construct a unified picture from these different types of evidence, when they seem to reflect a similar underlying phenomenon.

On the one hand, most of the same gods are mentioned in both types of texts, and many of their characteristics and deeds are at least superficially the same. However, there are some important differences. In the general religious picture, the power of the ritual, the sacrifice, seems to have usurped some of the gods' power. Even in early Vedic, men could use the ritual to manipulate or at least influence the gods' behavior, as we will see; in the middle and late Vedic period, the sacrifice is almost coercive and the gods subject to it—though it does not seem to be the case that the gods are imprisoned by the sacrifice and completely controlled by it, as is sometimes claimed.

This leads to another important question that remains to be thoroughly explored; namely, the relation between myth and ritual in Vedic. Although in the early period of Vedic studies, their intimate connection was not questioned, the sheer mass of material to be surveyed in each area generally guaranteed that in practice each was pursued independently. Hillebrandt's *Vedische Mythologie* (and, to a lesser extent, Bergaigne's *La religion védique*) is exceptional in this regard, as it relies heavily on ritual materials. The perceived excesses of the "ritualistic school" of mythology may have propelled this de facto separation into a matter of principle, and many recent students of one or the other explicitly see the myth/ritual mixture of the texts as tainting the purity of each strain. (Cf. e.g., O'Flaherty 1985, especially 12*ff*).

Nonetheless, the intimacy of the two within this tradition (and not only the Vedic one) cannot be denied: the existence of figures that are at once functioning parts of the ritual and divinities with a developed mythology (e.g., Agni, Soma); the recital of mythic episode in liturgical context; the use of mythology to explain details of the ritual or the ritual itself; the embedding of ritual activity in mythological narrative—all these point to a deep connection felt by the composers of the text (Hoffmann 1968). It seems time now to reexamine this connection without preconceptions in order to distinguish true cases of secondary influence from organic and historica connections. Recent scholars who have worked on this problem, directly or obliquely, include Jamison (1991). For details see:

Bergaigne, A. *La religion védique*. 3 vols. Paris: Bibliothèque de l'Ecole des Hautes Etudes (1878–83), 36, 53–54; into English by V. G. Paranjpe, Poona.

Bloomfield, M. "Contributions to the Interpretation of the Veda, First Series." *AJP* 7 (1886):466*ff*.

———. "Contributions to the Interpretation of the Veda, Second Series." *AJP* 12 (1890):319*ff*.

———. "Contributions to the Interpretation of the Veda, Third Series." *JAOS* 15 (1891):143–182.
———. "Contributions to the Interpretation of the Veda, Fourth Series." *AJP* 12 (1891):414*ff*.
———. "Contributions to the Interpretation of the Veda, Fifth Series." *JAOS* 16 (1894):1*ff*.
———. "Contributions to the Interpretation of the Veda, Sixth Series." *ZDMG* 48 (1894):541*ff*.
———. "Contributions to the Interpretation of the Veda, Seventh Series." *AJP* 17 (1896):399*ff*.
Dumézil, G. *Mitra-Varuṇa*. Paris, 1940; 2nd ed. 1948.
———. *Le troisième souverain*. Paris: G. P. Maisonneuve, 1949.
———. *L'idéologie tripartite des indo-européens*. Bruxelles: Latomus, 1958.
Hillebrandt, A. *Vedische Mythologie*. 2 vols. Breslau: H. H. Marcus, 1927–29.
Hoffmann, K. "Zur Komposition eines Brāhmaṇa-Abschnittes (MS 1 10, 14–16)." In *Mélanges d'indianisme à la mémoire de L. Renou*, 367–80. Paris: Editions E. de Boccard, 1968.
Hopkins, E. W. "Gods and Saints of the Great Brāhmaṇa." *Transactions of the Connecticut Academy of Arts and Sciences* 15 (1908):19–69.
Jamison, S. *The Ravenous Hyenas and the Wounded Sun: Myth and Ritual in Ancient India*. Ithaca and London: Cornell University Press, 1991.
Keith, A. B. *The Religion and Philosophy of the Vedas and the Upanishads*. 2 vols. Cambridge: Harvard Oriental Series 31, 32, 1925.
Kuiper, F. B. J. "The Three Strides of Viṣṇu." In *Festschrift N. Brown*, ed. E. Bender, 137–51. New Haven: 1962.
———. *Ancient Indian Cosmogony*. Ed. J. Irwin. Delhi: Vikas, 1983.
Macdonell, A. A. *The Vedic Mythology*. Strassburg: J. P. Trübner, 1897.
Oertel, H. "Contributions from the Jaiminīya Brāhmaṇa to the History of the Brāhmaṇa Literature, First Series." *JAOS* 18 (1897):15–48.
———. "Contributions from the Jaiminīya Brāhmaṇa to the History of the Brāhmaṇa Literature, Second Series". *JAOS* 19 (1898):97–125.
———. "The Jaiminīya Brāhmaṇa Version of the Dīrghajihvī Legend," *Actes du Onzième Congrés International des Orientalistes, Paris 1897*, vol. I, *Langues et archéologie des pays ariens*, 225–39. Paris, 1899.
———. "Contributions from the Jaiminīya Brāhmaṇa to the History of the Brāhmaṇa Literature, Fourth Series." *JAOS* 23 (1902):325–49.
———. "Contributions from the Jaiminīya Brāhmaṇa to the History of the Brāhmaṇa Literature, Fifth Series." *JAOS* 26 (1905):176–96, 306–14.
———. "Contributions from the Jaiminīya Brāhmaṇa to the History of the Brāhmaṇa Literature, Sixth Series." *JAOS* 28 (1907):81–98.

———. "Contributions from the Jaiminīya Brāhmaṇa to the History of the Brāhmaṇa Literature, Seventh Series." *Translations of the Connecticut Academy* 16 (1909):153–216.

O'Flaherty, W. D. *Tales of Sex and Violence: Folklore, Sacrifice, and Danger in the Jaiminīya Brāhmaṇa*. Chicago: University of Chicago Press, 1985.

Oldenberg, H. *Die Religion des Veda*. 2nd ed. Stuttgart: G. Cotta, 1917; English trans. *The Religion of the Vedas*, 1896, from the 1st ed., Berlin: W. Hertz, 1894.

Sieg, E. *Die Sagenstoffe des Ṛgveda und die indische Itihāsatradition, 1* (*Itihāsa zum Ṛg Veda*). Stuttgart: Kohlhammer, 1902.

The "Philosophy" of Vedic Religion

Early Vedic

Perhaps the most obvious of the motivating ideas of Vedic religion is the Roman principle of "dō ut dēs" ("I give so that you will give"), or in Vedic terms, "give me, I give you" *dehi me dadāmi te:* TS 1.8.4.1, VS 3.50 (Mylius 1973, 476)—that is: reciprocity. The ritual oblations and the hymns of praise that accompany them are not offered to the gods out of sheer celebratory exuberance. Rather, these verbal and alimentary gifts are one token in an endless cycle of exchanges—thanks for previous divine gifts, but also a trigger for such gifts and favors in the future. Most Ṛgvedic hymns contain explicit prayers for the goods of this world and for aid in particular situations, along with generalized praise of the gods' generosity. This principle is so pervasive and so obvious in Vedic literature that it had seldom been explicitly discussed in the secondary literature (cf. now Malamoud 1980, Weber-Brosamer 1988, Wilden 1992), and Heesterman's denial of the principle for Vedic times (1985, 83 and passim) is rather unconvincing. But this comparative dearth of secondary literature should not conceal its importance—or its application to other domains of Vedic thought. For details see:

Heesterman, J. C. *The Inner Conflict of Tradition: Essays in Indian Ritual, Kingship and Society*. Chicago: University of Chicago Press, 1985.

Malamoud, Ch. "La theologie de la dette dans le Brahmanisme", *Puruṣārtha* 4:39–60 (1980) = "The Theory of debt in Brahmanism," in C. Malamoud, *Debt and Debtors*. Delhi, 1983.

Mylius, K. "Die gesellschaftliche Entwicklung Indiens in jungvedischer Zeit nach den Sanskritquellen." *Ethnologisch-Archäologische Zeitschrift* 14 (1973): 425–99.

Weber-Brosamer, B. *Annam: Untersuchungen zur Bedeutung des Essens und der Speise im vedischen Ritual*. Religionswissenschaft und Theologien 3. Freiburg: Schäuble Verlag, 1988.

Wilden, E. *Das Opfer als Bindeglied in der Beziehung zwischen Göttern und Menschen gemäss den Brāhmaṇas*. M.A. thesis, University of Hamburg, 1992.

The extraordinary power and prestige accorded to verbal behavior is another important aspect of Vedic thought that is visible from the earliest times. The very existence of the RV is a tribute to this notion—the multitude of elaborate hymns directed to the same divinity, composed by a variety of bardic families, results from the belief that the gods were most pleased by "the newest hymn," as the text often tells us. The gods of the early Vedic period were not the mere dutiful receivers of a set liturgy that they became in the middle Vedic period, but—as guests at their solemn ritual reception on the offering ground—critical connoisseurs of poetic craftsmanship and virtuosity, just as the modern Hindu gods savor the *stutis* and *stotras* addressed to them in *pūjā* and other rituals. The better the hymn, the greater the reward—to the poet from the patron, to the latter from the god.

But what is most prized is not elegant verbal trickery but rather the putting into words of a cosmic truth. This aspect of Vedic religion has been much discussed—and much disputed—especially in the last fifty years or so. The discussions have centered around two terms, *bráhman-* and *ṛta*. The neuter noun *bráhman-* is the derivational base to which the masculine noun *brahmán* "*possessor of bráhman-*" and ultimately *Brāhmaṇa-*, the name both of the priestly class and of the exegetical ritual texts, are related. Brahman has been the subject of several searching studies by eminent twentieth-century Vedicists (e.g., Renou and Silburn 1949, Gonda 1950, Thieme 1952). Philological examination of the Ṛgvedic passages seems especially to support the view of Thieme that *bráhman* refers originally to a "formulation" (*Formulierung*), the capturing in words of a significant and non-self-evident truth. The ability to formulate such truths gives the formulator (*brahmán*) special powers, which can be exercised even on cosmic forces (see Jamison, 1991, on Atri). This power attributed to a correctly stated truth is found in the (later) "*satyakriyā*" or "act of truth", seminally discussed by W. N. Brown (1940, 1963, 1968), which is in fact already found in the RV and has counterparts in other Indo-European cultures (see, e.g., Watkins 1979). Such formulated speech (*bráhman*) must be recited correctly, otherwise there is danger of losing one's head (as explained in the *indraśatru* legend TS 2.4.12.1, ŚB 1.6.3.8), and it must be recited with its author's name. For details see:

Brown, W. N. "The Basis of the Hindu Act of Truth." *Review of Religions* 5 (1940):36–45.

———. "Ṛgveda 10, 34 as an Act of Truth." *Bharatīya Vidyā* 20–21 (1963): 8–10.

———. "The Metaphysics of the Truth Act (Satya Kriyā)." In *Mélanges d'Indianisme à la mémoire de L.Renou*, 171–77. Paris: E. de Boccard, 1968.

Gonda, J. *Notes on Brahman*. Utrecht: J. L. Beyers, 1950.

Jamison, S. W. *The Ravenous Hyenas and the Wounded Sun: Myth and Ritual in Ancient India*. Ithaca and London: Cornell University Press, 1991.

Renou, L., and L. Silburn. "Sur la notion de Brahman." *Journal Asiatique* (1949): 7–46.

Thieme, P. "Brahman." *ZDMG* 102 (1952):91–129 = Kleine Schriften, 100–38. Wiesbaden: Steiner 1984.

Watkins, C. "Is tre fir flathemon: Marginalia to Audacht Morainn." *Eriu* 30 (1979):181–98.

In the prose texts, the emphasis has shifted slightly from this correct formulation, as freely composed poetry has been replaced by rote recitation in the liturgy. But its influence is still to be discerned in the great stress laid on correct pronunciation of the ancient verses and especially on correct knowledge. "He who knows thus" (*ya evaṃ veda*) about the hidden meanings of the ritual or the homologies it encodes has access to greater power and greater success than one who simply has the ritual performed without this knowledge. The power attributed to esoteric knowledge leads directly to the speculations found in the later parts of the Āraṇyakas and in the Upaniṣads.

The notion of *brahman* is closely allied in early Vedic thought with the term *ṛta*, which is a very difficult and controversial word. Continually celebrated in the RV and invested with the power to keep the cosmos functioning correctly, *ṛta* has been approached in two different ways. On the one hand, it is quite commonly translated "cosmic order" or "cosmic harmony." This interpretation works rather well with its apparent etymology to the Proto-Indo-European root *h_2er "fit together," but it requires that in the negated compound *an-ṛta* "untruth," and in the Avetan cognate *aša* (usually rendered as truth), the word has undergone serious semantic narrowing. On the other hand, it has been strenuously argued (esp. by

Lüders 1951, 1959) that *ṛta* means only "truth," as in *anṛta* and *aša*, and that its cosmic ordering properties are indeed the province of an abstract "truth," as conceived by Vedic culture. Insisting on a single translation for a cultural complex of such importance is no doubt a mistake; nonetheless, it is clear that an abstract yet active Truth is credited with power on the human (cf. *satya-kriyā*), divine, and cosmic planes. Indeed, *ṛta* may be considered an active realization of truth, a vital force that can underlie human or divine action.

Within the well-ordered and creative realm of *ṛta*, the various forces are functioning according to the reciprocal exchange mentioned above. Its basis is the concept of *ṛṇa*, the "debt," or better "obligation" that exists between men on this side and gods, ancestors, and ancient poets on the other side (cf. Malamoud, 1980, cited earlier). This "primordial" obligation is based on the simple fact that human beings are the somatic descendants of the gods (via the eighth Āditya Vivasvant Mārtāṇḍa and his son Manu, the ancestor of mankind). Therefore, they have to take care of their ultimate ancestors, just as they indeed offer food (*śrāddha*, *piṇḍa*) to their direct somatic ancestors, the three immediate predecessors and a vague group of less immediate *pitṛs*. In this scheme, the primordial sages appear more like an afterthought. For the Brahmins, however, they represent both (some of) their direct somatic ancestors and their spiritual ones: they are the creators of their spiritual knowledge, formulated in Vedic verse. All these groups (men, ancestors, seers, gods) therefore are tied together by a close net of obligational relationships, expressed by the term *ṛṇa* "obligation."

The restitution of *ṛṇa* is primarily accomplished in ritual (*yajña*) in which both "food" offerings (*anna*) as well as spiritual offerings (*bráhman*) are made in the form of speech (*vāc*), which must necessarily be true (*satya*) and only in this way can have an effect, that is success in ritual. The whole procedure represents an eternal cycle that functions within the bounds of *ṛta*. In this process, various abstract and less abstract notions take part (e.g., *vāc*, *bráhman*, *śraddhā*, *anna*, *ucchiṣṭa*, *śrāddha*). These seemingly disparate concepts are dealt with in some of the so-called speculative hymns of the RV and AV. All of them, however, have their fixed place in the system of relationships, based on "obligation" (*ṛṇa*), within the all-embracing realm of *ṛta*.

Indeed, the notion of reciprocity is not confined to sentient beings but also informs the Vedic conception of the phenomenal world, in a system we might term *natural economy*. In this schema, natural phenomena originating in heaven come to earth and nourish and are even transformed into other phenomena that ultimately make their way to heaven again, thus participating in a cycle in which nothing is wasted or lost (see Frauwallner 1953, 49, Schneider 1961, Bodewitz 1973, 243*ff.*) For instance, heavenly water falls as rain to earth, produces plants (which are eaten by animals); both plant and animal products are offered at the ritual and thus ascend to heaven in the smoke of the offering fire, to become rain again. The system of identifications and transformations this cycle sets up contributed largely to the middle Vedic system of homologies we will discuss below. For the details of the discussion above see:

Bodewitz, H. W. *Jaiminīya Brāhmaṇa I, 1–65. Translation and Commentary with a Study of the Agnihotra and Prāṇāgnihotra*. Leiden: Brill, 1973.

Frauwallner, E. *Geschichte der indischen Philosophie I*. Salzburg: O. Müller, 1953.

Lüders, H. *Varuṇa*. Ed. L. Alsdorf. Göttingen: Vandenhoeck & Ruprecht, 1951, 1959).

Schneider, U. "Die altindische Lehre vom Kreislauf des Wassers." *Saeculum* 12 (1961):1–11.

The importance of reciprocity and the power of the word are ideas difficult to escape in early Vedic texts and appear in a variety of guises. However, more traditionally "philosophical" issues are harder to approach in the RV. For example, Vedic cosmology and cosmogony have been intensively investigated, but it is difficult to produce a clear and consistent picture of either.

Certain elementary notions are clear. For example, the universe is divided in the first instance into three worlds: earth, the "intermediate space" (*antarikṣa*, some now say "interspace"), and heaven; the gods dwell in heaven (and are etymologically connected to it); certain gods (e.g. Indra) are credited with cosmogonic activities—finding the sun, separating heaven and earth, spreading out the earth, and so forth. Other notions are alluded to frequently but not particularly clearly—features like the heavenly ocean, or events like divine incest (usually, but not always, between heaven and earth). There is no dearth of other such references in the RV, but this is perhaps our problem: there is an embarassment of cosmological and cosmogonic riches, and constructing one picture from it requires rejecting another, often equally plausible, one. The detailed and elaborate schemas of, for example, Lüders 1959, Varenne 1982, Kuiper, and earlier essays, collected in Kuiper 1983 all demonstrate skilled and suggestive use of the available Ṛgvedic hints, but all seem to be required, on the one hand, to ignore large amounts of evidence that does not support their picture and, on the other, to be far more explicit about physical details than the RV seems to allow. For details see:

Kuiper, F. B. J. *Ancient Indian Cosmogony*. Ed. J. Irwin. Delhi: Vikas, 1983.
Lüders, H. *Varuṇa*. Ed. L. Alsdorf. 2 vols. Göttingen: Vandenhoeck & Ruprecht, 1951, 1959.
Varenne, J. *Cosmogonies védiques*. Milan and Paris: Société Edition "Les Belles Lettres," 1982.

It might be that the early Vedic period was a time of ferment, with competing cosmological/-gonic paradigms from various sources. (Note the apt plural in Varenne's title *Cosmogonies védiques*, 1982.) It is even more likely that, beyond the straightforward "facts" on which there was agreement (like the three "worlds"), this intellectual area was a legitimate forum for speculation, and that the speculation was not aimed at producing a precise picture—the exact number of the divisions of heaven or the exact location of the heavenly ocean—for this most unvisual of people, or to produce a precise "history"—who created the earth, when, and how—for this (as we like to think) most unhistorical of people. The purpose of Ṛgvedic speculation was rather to signal in metaphorical and poetic terms the abstract relations among things. That these signals are sometimes contradictory is not surprising: the Vedic poets love paradox (of the type "the son begot the father", etc.), as Bergaigne long ago pointed out, and so do their listeners, the gods, who are often said, in middle Vedic texts, to love the hidden (*parokṣapriyā hi devāḥ*).

It has often been noted that the so-called "speculative hymns," linguistically among the latest of the RV, are in great part cosmogonic, but the import of this has not been entirely grasped. If early Vedic religion had possessed a detailed, agreed upon cosmogony, speculation would not have been necessary—or rather the speculation would have been based upon, or have disputed—the facts of this shared vision. Moreover, the speculations are often framed as questions ("who? what?") or as contradictions (the famed "in the beginning there was neither being nor nonbeing"), which would suggest that the composers had passed beyond what was commonly accepted into the realm of the genuine unknown.

Middle Vedic: The power of ritual

The system of reciprocity identified for early Vedic remained in force in the middle Vedic period, notwithstanding a large amount of political and social change. At the beginning of the so-called Mantra period (see the chapter opening) when the Kuru and Pañcāla tribes develop, in the Kurukṣetra-Haryana and Uttar Pradesh area, the ritual, too, was undergoing the restructuring described above. Nevertheless, the gods are still regarded as nourished by sacrifice carried out by men, and they themselves have to offer (in Kurukṣetra, the *devayajana* "offering place of the gods") to sustain their ancestors, the *pūrve devāḥ*, as well as to support, just like humans, their own position.

Indeed, the ritual, which had been one step in the cyclic exchange of favors between men and gods, has become the compelling mainspring, to which even the gods are in some sense subordinate. When the ritual was restructured from its Ṛgvedic to its classical form and the earlier freely composed verse gave way to a set ritual liturgy of RV verses and other formulae, the verbal form most prized became ritual speech, specifically the triple division into *ṛc*, *sāman*, and *yajuṣ*, and the silence that is, in some ways, its divine counterpart (for silence, see Renou 1949, Brereton 1988).

The elevation of the ritual in the middle Vedic period has affected every aspect of the religious realm, and a large section of the social. In turn, the new power of the ritual derives from the strengthening of the system of identifications we discussed briefly above. The ritual ground is the mesocosm in which the macrocosm can be controlled. Objects and positions in the ritual ground have exact counterparts in both the human (i.e., microcosmic) realm and the cosmic realm; for example, a piece of gold can stand for wealth among men, and the sun in the divine world. The recognition of these bonds of identification—many of which are far less obvious than the example just given—is a central intellectual and theological enterprise, the continuation of the "formulation of mythical truths" discussed above. The universe can be viewed as a rich and often esoteric system of homologies, and the assemblage, manipulation, and apostrophizing of homologues in the delimited ritual arena allows men to exert control over their apparently unruly correspondents outside it. This "ritual science" is based on the strictly logical application of the rule of cause and effect, even though the initial proposition in an argument of this sort ("the sun is gold") may be empirically false. Ritual science received a seminal discussion by Oldenberg (1919) and also by Schayer (1925) and has frequently been treated since (e.g., in the most recent extensive treatment by B. K. Smith 1989; for references to other literature, see Smith 1986: 95, n. 44). For details of the discussion above see:

Brereton, J. P. "Unsounded Speech: Problems in the interpretation of BU(M) I.5:10—BU(K) 1.5.3." *IIJ* 31(1998):1–10.

Oldenberg, H. *Vorwissenschaftliche Wissenschaft: Die Weltanschauung der Brāhmaṇa-Texte*. Göttingen, 1919.

Renou, L. "La valeur du silence dans le culte védique." *JAOS* 69 (1949):11–18.

Schayer, S. "Die Struktur der magischen Weltanschauung nach dem Atharvaveda und den Brāhmaṇa-Texten." *Zeitschrift für Buddhismus* 6 (1925):259–310.

Smith, B. K. "The Unity of Ritual: The Place of the Domestic Sacrifice in Vedic Ritualism." *IIJ* 29 (1986):79–96.

———. *Reflections on Resemblance, Ritual, and Religion*. New York and Oxford: Oxford University Press, 1989.

Speculation in the Āraṇyakas and Upaniṣads

The speculation of the Āraṇyakas and also of the Upaniṣads follows in a natural and systematic development from what has been said above about the middle Vedic period of the Brāhmaṇas and YV Saṁhitās.

First of all, as has been pointed out above, there is no inherent difference in content and style between Brāhmaṇa and Āraṇyaka texts; both deal with rituals, though the Āraṇyakas deal with the more secret rituals such as the Mahāvrata (in the RV) and the Pravargya (in the YV Āraṇyakas). Both rituals indeed are explained in the usual Brāhmaṇa style, which is perhaps most evident in Śatapatha Brāhmaṇa 14, which not only is part of the Brāhmana itself but even is a text already referred to in ŚB 4; see M. Witzel 1987.

If we can indeed trace a development in "philosophy," then it is the gradual increase in importance of the idea of a second death and of retribution for one's action in this world. These ideas occur only in late Brāhmaṇa passages (and mostly in the eastern parts of North India, e.g., *punarmṛtyu*, see M. Witzel 1989). While ritual was believed to provide enough power to eliminate the evil incurred by killing (a fear noticeable already in the Ṛgvedic horse sacrifice), this concern now becomes more of a problem: every action has its automatic consequence, and thus the killing of an animal produces "evil" (*guilt* is not appropriate, as it is a later, moral term, applicable only to karmic concerns). Indeed, in the late Brāhmaṇas the concept of a reversal of fortune in the other world occurs several times. This may indicate that ideas of second birth (and recurrent rebirth), even of *karma*, are nothing but the gradual, but logical, outcome of Brahmanical thought (H.-P. Schmidt, 1968).

It is from such a background that the thinking of the Upaniṣads emerges. The authors of these texts furthered thought that, if not radically new, still involved a thorough rethinking of the existing premises. This can be observed in the development of the texts themselves: It is in the eastern territories of North India, referred to above, that we notice, for the first time, a thorough reorganization of the Brāhmaṇa-style texts (especially in ŚB), including a rethinking of many of the earlier "theological" positions; this region also saw the development of Sūtra style (with the very systematic, but still very elaborate Baudhāyana Śrauta Sūtra, still composed largely in Brāhmaṇa language), while in the Aitareya school the first shorter Sūtra is developed (dealing with the Mahāvrata).

The Upaniṣads are often treated as the beginning of a tradition, the founding texts of Vedānta philosophy (and, to much lesser degree, as the necessary precursor to early Buddhist and Jain thought). But it is at least as accurate to view them as the almost inevitable outcome of the intellectual development we have been discussing. The system of homologies, the mystical identifications, remain the intellectual underpinning of these new texts—the identifications simply become more esoteric and more all-encompassing. Such questioning had been going on during the whole YV Saṁhitā and the Brāhmaṇa period, only it was more hidden (e.g., behind the statement "some say . . ."). In fact, intellectual exchange was going on inside the schools and between them all the time, as the frequent quotation of divergent views in the Brāhmaṇa-type texts clearly indicates. ŚB, especially, bears witness to this by habitually discussing various "solutions" to a problem.

Moreover, the ritual itself, though its actual performance seems less a concern, increasingly becomes the subject of similar identifications. On the one hand, the ritual becomes interiorized: nonphysical counterparts are suggested for ritual actions and objects, so that the ritual can be performed entirely mentally. Moreover, not only the simple objects used in ritual but also whole sections of the ritual, particular recitations, and finally even complete rituals, come to have cosmic counterparts (e.g., the horse of the horse sacrifice in BĀUK 1.1). This is accompanied by an increasing use of multiple identifications (A. Benke 1976). So, as the actual physical performance of the elaborate Vedic rituals seems to decline —at least with some part of the (Brahmanical) population—the concept and structure of ritual spawn intense intellectual activity (including also among some Kṣatriyas and women (cf. Oldenberg 1915, Renou 1953, Horsch 1966, etc.)).

The Upaniṣads, then, do not represent a break with the intellectual tradition that precedes them, but rather a heightened continuation of it, using as raw material the religious practices then current (Renou 1953). What makes the Upaniṣads seem more different than they actually are from the Brāhmaṇas and even from the Āraṇyakas, which contain similar speculative and "mystical" material, is their style. The Brāhmaṇas and the Āraṇyakas are authoritative in presentation; even the most advanced and esoteric speculation is positively stated as an exegetical truism. The early Upaniṣads, with their dialogue form, the personal imprint of the teacher, the questioning and admissions of ignorance—or claims of knowledge—from the students, seem to reintroduce some of the uncertainties of the late RV, give the sense that the ideas are indeed speculation, different attempts to frame solutions to real puzzles. For details see:

Horsch, P. *Die vedische Gāthā- und Ślokalitteratur*. Bern: Francke Verlag, 1966.

Oldenberg, H. *Die Lehre der Upanishaden und die Anfänge des Buddhismus*. Göttingen: Vandenhoeck & Ruprecht, 1915.

Renou, R. "Le Passage des Brāhmaṇas aux Upaniṣad." *JAOS* 73 (1953):138–44.

Schmidt, H.-P. "The Origins of Ahiṃsā. In *Mélanges d'Indianisme à la mémoire de L. Renou*, 625–55. Paris: E. de Boccard, 1968.

Witzel, M. "On the Origin of the Literary Device of the 'Frame Story' in Old Indian Literature." In H. Falk, ed., *Hinduismus und Buddhismus, Festschrift für U. Schneider*, 363–415. Freiburg, 1987.

———. "Tracing the Vedic Dialects." In Colette Caillat, ed., *Dialectes dans les litteratures Indo-Aryennes*, 97–264. Paris, 1989.

The Religious Life: Personal and Popular Religious Experience

As should be clear from the foregoing, we have fairly ample evidence from the whole Vedic period about religious institutions—rituals, mythology, and widely held belief systems (such as *dō ut dēs* or the developoing ideas about rebirth). But we have hardly touched on how these religious institutions affected or were experienced by individuals, or what noninstitutional, "popular" beliefs and practices were mixed, in the religious lives and consciousnesses of individuals, with those "official" ones we have discussed. The evidence for these questions is very scant and, for the most part, indirect, given as always the nature of our texts and their means of preservation.

Even for daily life, outside the narrow sphere of solemn (and Brahmanized house) ritual, material can only be discovered accidentally, so to speak, between the lines. This has been done by Zimmer (1879) for the RV and the other Saṁhitās and has been continued by Rau (1957) and Mylius (1971–74) for the post-RV texts. A shorter treatment of the Brāhmaṇa period is that of Basu (1969), and Ram Gopal (1959) treats the Sūtras. For details see:

Basu, J. *India in the Age of the Brāhmaṇas*. Calcutta: Sanskrit Pustak Bhandar, 1969.

Mylius, K. "Die gesellschaftliche Entwicklung Indiens in jungvedischer Zeit nach den Sanskritquellen." *Ethnologisch-Archäologische Zeitschrift* 12 (1971): 171–97; 13 (1972):321–65; 14 (1973):425–99; 15 (1974):385–432.

Ram Gopal. *India of Vedic Kalpasūtras*. Delhi: National Publishing House, 1959.

Rau, W. *Staat und Gesellschaft im alten Indien nach den Brāhmaṇa-Texten dargestellt*. Wiesbaden: Otto Harrassowitz, 1957.

Zimmer, H. *Altindisches Leben*. Berlin: Weidmannsche Buchhandlung, 1879.

Popular Religion

There is a certain circularity in identifying particular elements embedded in Vedic religion as "popular," since the texts in which they appear are uniformly Brahmanical products. Such identifications may rather reflect our own notions of what is suitably serious and "high," rather than any real stratification in our sources. Nonetheless, there are some checks on these sources.

On the one hand, one can collect the statements in Brāhmaṇa-type texts introduced by "they say." Many of them are popular maxims. Other common beliefs are hidden in the secondary clauses, the *tasmād* sentences of these texts. Examples are: of someone who has died, people say: "it (the *prajātantu*, the line of progeny) has been cut off for him" (*achedy asya*, ŚB 10.45.2.13); or a popular saying has it that one cannot present people with silver as this would produce tears and bad luck (TS 1.5.1); or that termite mounds were regarded as the "ears of the earth" in whose presence one had to speak softly (JB 1.126).

On the other hand, we can utilize texts that lie somewhat outside the Vedic frame. In addition to the Gṛhya and Dharma texts, wherever possible the Vedic materials should be compared with the slightly later evidence of the Pāli canon, which has many conceptual overlaps with the late Brāhmaṇas and the early Upaniṣads. In addition, the evidence of the older strata of the Mahābhārata, which are perhaps more easily accessible now through the work of M. C. Smith (1992), should be taken into account. According to Smith the older strata of the Mahābhārata reflect an early *kṣatriya dharma* based on alliances and keeping one's social obligations—that is, incidentally, still reflected in the beginning sections of the Gītā with the concern for *kuladharma*. Brahmins and Brahminical concerns play, according to Smith, only a very minor role in the ca. 2000 irregular *triṣṭubh* stanzas excised by her as the core of the epic. However, the role of truth, keeping one's oaths and so on, accords well with the Ṛgvedic concepts discussed by Lüders and Thieme.

Such a comparison across the Vedic, Pāli, and Epic texts is something that has, during the past decades, receded more and more from the horizon of scholars, due to the increasing specialization and compartmentalization of Indian studies. However, with regard to religion and culture in general this approach has to be revived so as to arrive at a comprehensive picture of Vedic religion.

Finally, we come to the problem of true heterodoxy in the Vedic period. It is, of course, obvious that by 400 BCE several heterodox systems had developed, notably that of the Buddha and that of Mahāvīra. The two founders of Buddhism and Jainism, however, were not the only prominent teachers of the time. Dīghanikāya 2 gives a good idea of the diversity of competing views. It is certainly surprising that all these movements are recorded from the eastern part of North India only. This may be due to the nature of our sources (the late Brāhmaṇa text and most of the Upaniṣads come from this area). Nevertheless, one would expect some inkling of new ideas in more Western texts such as PB or ChU. For their connections with the Upaniṣad literature, see Horsch (1966).

The problem has been briefly alluded to above; however, as has been stated, the cultural situation in the "homeland" of heterodoxy, the Vedic East (Kosala, Videha) has not been understood well enough. The area was one with a constantly changing ferment of older and new tribes, various social systems, emerging great powers, and so forth. By the time of the Buddha (ca. 400 BCE by recent dating), wandering teachers of all sorts were normal appearances in the towns and villages of the East. We get a glimpse of the earlier stages of this phenomenon when Yājñavalkya leaves home (BĀU 4.5.15). This procedure takes up an older tradition of wandering about as a Veda student and Vrātya, as indeed the structure of the Buddhist saṅgha takes up some *vrātya* features: a rather amorphous group of (not always young) men with a leader, special dress—but not their bloody rituals. Both types of men traveled far away from their homelands, and if we may trust the BĀU and ŚB accounts of Yājñavalkya's travels in the Panjab, such traveling did indeed reach both the western and the eastern ends of Vedic India.

That the east indeed was different from the more central and western sections of northern India can easily be noticed in the simple fact that, in the east, graves were built that differed from what is described in the Vedic texts. While the Kurus and Pañcālas built small, square grave mounds about a yard high, the "easterners and others"(!) are reported by ŚB 12.8.1.5 to have round graves, which the text interestingly calls *asurya*, "demonic." Such mounds have indeed been found at such places as Lauriya on the Nepalese border. These graves have a great similarity, or are virtually the same as, the later *stūpa* of the Buddhists (and the *kurgan* type grave mounds in South Russia). There are a number of other indications of differences in language and customs, such as dialects (Witzel 1989) and social structure (e.g., the oligarchical states of the East, called "republics" by Rhys-Davies (1911), and, following him, by all historians).

Little can be said about the religion of the aboriginal tribes that survived in northern India before merging into the lower Hindu castes. The process of Sanskritization (Srinivas 1952) had been going on at that time, as we witness already in the RV, where some kings with clearly non-Indo-Aryan names were praised as performing proper Aryan rituals (cf. Kuiper 1991). This continues throughout the Mantra and Brāhmaṇa periods, for example by making the leader (*niṣādasthapati*, MS 2.2.4) of a local aboriginal tribe, the Niṣādas ("those residing at their proper place" instead of wandering about like the Āryas), eligible to perform the solemn Śrauta ritual. Even clearer is the evidence from the later (and eastern) section of AB: at 7.18, the Ṛgvedic(!) Ṛṣi Viśvāmitra, assisting the (eastern) Ikṣvāku king Hariścandra, expels his older sons but makes them the ancestors of the local eastern tribes (*dasyu*), the Andhra, Puṇḍra, Śabara, Pulinda, and Mūtiba "who live in large numbers beyond the borders" (*udantya*, just like the Vrātyas, JB 74:1.197): *ta ete 'ndhrāḥ . . . ity udantyā bahavo bhavanti Vaiśvāmitrā dasyūnām bhūyiṣṭhāḥ*). Adoption has been a favorite type of inclusion since the RV.

Apart from this we get tantalizing glimpses of what may have been aberrant behavior, perhaps early Tantra, in the AB 7.13 (cf. also the notions about the Gosava ritual). Compare, finally RV *śiśnadeva, mūradeva.* There is, however, no connection with the so-called Śiva on some Harappa seals. Nothing much for a connection with Vedic beliefs can be deduced from the few seemingly religious objects found in the Indus civilization. Notably, the remnants of so-called fire rituals at Kalibangan may represent nothing more than a community kitchen. For details see:

Horsch, P. *Die vedische Gāthā- und Ślokaliteratur*. Bern: Francke Verlag, 1966.

Kuiper, F. B. J. *Aryans in the Rigveda*. Amsterdam and Atlanta: Rodopi, 1991.

Rhys Davies, T. W. *Buddhist India*. London: T. Fischer Unwin, 1911.

Smith, M. C. *The Warrior Code of India's Sacred Song*. New York: Garland, 1992.

Srinivas, M. N. *Religion and Society among the Coorgs in South India*. Oxford: Clarendon, 1952.

Witzel, M. "Tracing the Vedic Dialects." In Colette Caillat, ed., *Dialectes dans les littératures Indo-Aryennes*, 97–264. Paris, 1989.

Research Tools

There are several critical research tools that pertain to all (or most) of Vedic literature. Bloomfield's *Vedic Concordance* (1906) indexes every Vedic mantra found in editions at the time, and the passage(s) in which it occurs, allowing the researcher to trace the ritual usage of and commentary on virtually every liturgical utterance in the corpus. Bloomfield, Edgerton, and Emeneau's *Vedic Variants* (1930–34), based on the collections of this *Concordance*, allows the development and variation of the language to be traced and the authenticity and relative chronology of particular mantras to be evaluated. The monumental concordances of Vishva Bandhu (1935–65) list every occurrence of every word in the Vedas and Brāhmaṇas, with less complete coverage of the Upaniṣads and Śrauta, Gṛhya, and Dharma Sūtras. This allows lexical, grammatical, and a large variety of philological and cultural studies to be carried out on the whole Vedic corpus with far greater ease than before. In addition, a number of individual texts have concordances or partial concordances as part of their text editions (e.g., R. Simon's Index verborum to the KS 1912). For cross-references one can compare, with great profit, Caland's notes as in Caland-Henry (1906–7) Keith, TS trans., and so forth.

The *Vedic Index* of Macdonell and Keith (1912) is a compendium of the information that can be extracted from Vedic texts on daily life, customs, technology, and personal and geographical names—though it specifically excludes mythological and ritual names and terminology from consideration. Finally, there are some special dictionaries of Vedic ritual terminology (Renou 1954, Sen 1978), a word list of rare words and of those not listed in the dictionary of Monier Williams (i.e., in the two *Petersburg Dictionaries*) by Renou (1934–35), a list and discussion of words of the Mantra language by A. Sharma (1959/60), and a useful if somewhat limited *Vedic Dictionary* by Surya Kanta (1981). The persevering Vishva Bandhu has published two little-known collections of quotations from the Brāhmaṇa and Upaniṣad type literature, Brahmanic quotations (Brāhmaṇoddhārakośa, 1966), and Upaniṣadic citations (Upaniṣaduddhārakośa, 1972), the consistent use of which allows one, to a large measure, to argue from within the Brahmanical system of thought. The only handbook of both the solemn (*Śrauta*) and domestic (*Gṛhya*) rituals has been compiled by Hillebrandt (1897), and the Śrautasūtra texts as such have been described by Kashikar (1968).

The amount of space in this work devoted to text editions, translations, and purely philological research tools may seem excessive, but it should not be forgotten that a major barrier to the understanding of Vedic religion has always been the difficulty of Vedic language and expression. In fact, by no means have all Vedic texts been edited, and even fewer have been translated. It is perhaps no wonder that, because many of the untranslated texts, such as MS, KS, JB, BŚS, have been neglected, often enough even by Sanskrit scholars, comprehensive research into Hindu and Vedic religion has suffered, and many interesting points, such as the only clear mentioning of the Indo-Aryan migration (BŚS) or the later fate of the Kuru tribe (JB), have escaped general notice.

Before concluding this section, two other books that might prove useful may also be mentioned: (1) *The Vedic Age*, edited by R. C. Majumdar, the first volume of the monumental History and Culture of the Indian People, a project of the Bharatiya Vidya Bhavan, Bombay, and (2) *Vedic Bibliography* by R. N. Dandekar, which continues the work initiated by L. Renou.

References

Bloomfield, M. *A Vedic Concordance*. Cambridge: Harvard University Press, 1906.

———. F. Edgerton, and M. B. Emeneau. *Vedic Variants: A Study of the Variant Readings in the Repeated Mantras of the Veda*. 3 vols. Philadelphia, 1930–34. Reprint, Delhi: Motilal Banarsidass, n.d.

Caland, W., and V. Henry. *L'Agniṣṭoma: Description complète de la forme normale du sacrifice de Soma dans le culte védique*. Paris, 1906–7.

Dandekar, R. N. *Vedic Bibliography*. Vol. 1., Bombay: Karnatak Publishing House, 1946; vol. 1, Poona: University of Poona, 1961; vol. 3, Poona: Bhandarkar Oriental Research Intitute, 1973; vol. 4, Poona; Bhandarkar Oriental Research Institute, 1985.

Hillebrandt, A. *Ritual-Literatur. Vedische Opfer und Zauber*. Strassburg: K. J. Trübner, 1897.

Kashikar, C. G. "A Survey of the Śrautasūtras." *Journal of Bombay University* 35, pt. 2, no. 41(1968):vi + 188.

Macdonell, A. A. and A. B. Keith. *Vedic Index of Names and Subjects*. 2 vols. London, 1912. Reprint, Delhi: Motilal Banarsidass, 1958, 1967.

Majumdar, R. C. ed. *The Vedic Age*. London: Allen & Unwin, 1952.

Renou, L. "Index védique." *Journal of Vedic Studies* 1 (1934–35):169–208, 257–320; 2:1–59.

———. *Bibliographie védique*. Paris, 1931.

———. *Vocabulaire du rituel védique*. Paris: Librarie C. Klincksieck, 1954.

Sen, Chitrabhanu. *A Dictionary of the Vedic Rituals Based on the Śrauta and Gṛhya Sūtras*. Delhi: Concept Publishing, 1978.

Sharma, Aryendra. *Beiträge zur vedischen Lexikographie: neue Wörter in M. Bloomfield's Vedic Concordance*. Munich. *PHMA* 5/6 (1959–60).

Simon R. *Index verborum zu L. v. Schroeders Kāṭhakam-Ausgabe*. Leipzig: F. A. Brockhaus, 1912.

Surya Kanta. *A Practical Vedic Dictionary*. Delhi: Oxford University Press, 1981.

Vishva Bandhu, in collaboration with R. Bhim Dev and A. Nath. *A Vedic Word*

Concordance. Lahore and Hoshiarpur: Vishveshvarananda Vedic Research Institute, 1935–65. Consists of five sections in sixteen parts: Section 1.: Saṁhitās (6 parts), 1942–63; 2nd rev. and enlarged ed., 1976. Section 2: Brāhmaṇas (2 parts), 1935–36. 2nd revised and enlarged edition, 1973. Section 3: Upaniṣads (2 parts), 1945. 2nd edition 1977. Section 4: Vedāṅga-Sūtras. (4 parts). 1958–61. Section 5: Consolidated indices to vols. (2 parts), 1964–65.

———. *Brāhmaṇic Quotations* (*Brāhmaṇoddhārakośa*). Hoshiarpur: Vishveshvarananda Vedic Research Institute, 1966.

———. *Upaniṣadic citations* (*Upaniṣaduddhārakośa*). Hoshiarpur: Vishveshvaranandа Vedic Research Institute, 1972.

Editor's Note on Vedic Studies in India in Modern Times

1.

Vedic studies during the modern period in India bifurcate into those that are neo-Hindu in character and follow a course more or less independent of modern scholarship and those that follow the lead provided by such scholarship or at least can be brought into recognizable relationship with it.

2.

The chief representative figures of the former trend are Svāmī Dayānanda Sarasvatī (1824–83), and Śrī Aurobindo Ghose (1872–1950).

Svāmī Dayānanda Sarasvatī, one of the leading figures of modern Hinduism, stands apart from them in his commitment to the Vedas, belief in whose authority was the cornerstone of the Arya Samaj, a reformist Hindu organization that he founded in 1875. The following books provide an adequate account of his life: J. T. F. Jordens, *Dayānanda Sarasvatī: His Life and Ideas* (Delhi: Oxford University Press, 1978); for an autobiographical account, see K. C. Yadav, ed., *Autobiography of Swami Dayānanda Sarasvatī* (New Delhi: Manohar, 1976).

In terms of Vedic Study, Dayānanda's attitude is as follows: (1) he prefers to identify the term *Veda* with only the *Saṁhitā* portion of the Vedic corpus, and (2) he conceives it more as a written than an oral text. For details, see John E. Llewellyn, "From Interpretation to Reform: Dayānanda's Reading of the Vedas," in Laurie L. Patton, ed., *Authority, Anxiety, and Canon* (Albany: State University of New York Press, 1994), 235–51.

In contrast with mainstream Hinduism, however, Dayānanda based Vedic authority not on the nature of the Vedic texts themselves but on their being the word of God; for details see Arvind Sharma, "Swāmī Dayānanda Sarasvatī and Vedic Authority," in Robert Baird, ed., *Religion in Modern India* (New Delhi: Manohar, 1981), 179–96.

The main features of Dayānanda's interpretation of the Vedas is his emphasis on their monotheistic character and his willingness to read anticipations of modern science in them. Curiously, in this, he is supported in general by Śrī Aurobindo, who was educated almost entirely in the West, unlike Dayānanda, who never left the shores of India, although Śrī Aurobindo himself offers a highly spiritual and metaphysical interpretation of the Vedas; see Śrī Aurobindo, *Hymns to The Mystic Fire* (*Hymns to Agni in the Rig Veda translated in their esoteric sense*) (Pondicherry: Śrí Aurobindo Ashram, 1952), and *On the Veda* (Pondicherry: Śrī Aurobindo Ashram, 1956). His interpretation is too individualistic for him to be placed squarely in either the traditional or modern category.

The main representatives of the modern academic trend in the twentieth-century tradition of studying the Vedas in India are C. Kunhan Raja, T. G. Mainkar, and Ram Gopal. Raja examines the Vedas largely from a philosophical perspective, while the perspective of Mainkar is more concerned with aesthetics and poetics; Ram Gopal, on the other hand, tries to stay close to traditional exegetical perspectives while casting a critical glance on modern Western scholarship. For a comparative study, see Laurie L. Patton, "Poets and Fishes: Modern Indian Interpretations of the Vedic Rishi," in Laurie L. Patton, ed., *Authority, Anxiety, and Canon* (Albany: State University of New York Press, 1994), 281–307. Two other scholars also belong here: R. N. Dandekar, for his contribution to the ongoing Vedic bibliography and to Vedic studies in general; and H. D. Velankar, for his English translation of the Seventh Book of the *ṚgVeda*.

A hitherto uncounted scholar is K. Satchidananda Murty, an eminent philosopher; see his Vedic Hermeneutics (Delhi: Motilal Banarsidass, 1993). Murty, Ram Gopal, and K. Satchidananda are innovative in suggesting that both traditional Indian and modern Western approaches to Vedic studies may be amenable to a common taxonomy (see *Vedic Hermeneutics*, 9–13, and Laurie L. Patton, "Poets and Fishes," 291–92).

Two other scholars deserve mention in connection with Vedic studies in India in modern times. One of them is Kapali Sastri, who contributed to the tradition of indigenous interpretation in India; see Prem Nanda Kumar, "T. V. Kapali Sastri's Contribution to Vedic Studies," *Journal of the Indian Council of Philosophic Research* (16 Sept./Dec., 1998): 109–24. The other is A. K. Coomaraswamy (1877–1974), who, stationed in the West, offered perspectives on the Vedas from the standpoint of the "Perennial Philosophy" school, whose prominent members also include René Guénon, Frithjof Schuon, and S. H. Nasr. See *New Approach to the Vedas: An Essay in Translation and Exegesis* (London: Luzac, 1933).

Note

1. The following abbreviations are used:

AĀ	Aitareya Āraṇyaka
AB	Aitareya Brāhmaṇa
AO	Acta Orientalia
AVŚ, ŚS	Atharva Veda, Śaunaka Recension
AVP, PS	Atharva Veda, Paippalāda Recension
BĀU	Bṛhadāraṇyaka Upaniṣad
BŚS	Baudhāyana Śrauta Sūtra
BYV	Black (Kṛṣṇa) YajurVeda
ChU	Chāndogya Upaniṣad
ERE	Encyclopedia of Religion and Ethics
GB	Gopatha Brāhmaṇa
HR	History of Religions
IIJ	Indo-Iranian Journal
JA	Journal Asiatique
JAOS	Journal of the American Oriental Society
JB	Jaiminīya Brāhmaṇa
KB	Kauṣītaki Brāhmaṇa
KpS	Kapiṣṭhala Saṁhitā
KauṣUp	Kauṣītaki Upaniṣad
KS	Kaṭha Saṁhitā or Kāṭhakam
MS	Maitrāyaṇī Saṁhitā
PAPS	Proceedings of the American Philosophical Society
PB	Pañcaviṃśa Brāhmaṇa
RV	Ṛgveda
ŚB	Śatapatha Brāhmaṇa
ŚBM	Śatapatha Brāhmaṇa, Mādhyandina recension
ŚBK	Śatapatha Brāhmaṇa, Kāṇva recension
TB	Taittirīya Brāhmaṇa

TS	Taittirīya Saṁhitā
VS	Vājasaneyī Saṁhitā
VSK	Vājasaneyī Saṁhitā, Kāṇva recension
WYV	White (Śukla) YajurVeda
WZKS	Wiener Zeitschrift für die Kunde Süd-Asiens und Archiv für indische Philosophie (or WZKSOA)
YV	Yajur Veda
ZDMG	Zeitschrift der Deutschen Morgenländischen Gesellschaft

[Written in 1992/95, only partially updated]

FIVE India's Epics

Writing, Orality, and Divinity

ALF HILTEBEITEL

India has two great Sanskrit epics and many oral regional folk epics. This chapter will highlight scholarly work of the last few years as it bears on written, oral, and religious dimensions of these classical and folk texts.[1] It will not attempt to address all oral epics, but rather those that have some close intertwinement with the Sanskrit epics, even though scholars differ as to the degree and kind of the intertwinement. A pervasive issue is the relation between the Sanskrit versions and other Indian "tellings," which are in both Sanskrit and the vernacular languages. The debate in Rāmāyaṇa studies, but also applicable to *Mahābhārata* scholarship, is well defined by Paula Richman as a question of whether one should privilege the classics (1991, 8–9). While Richman wants to see all Rāmāyaṇa variants as equal tellings, Robert P. Goldman argues that it is still reasonable to regard the Sanskrit text as the ultimate source of all versions of the tale in existence (1984, 39). A range of questions about oral and written texts is crucial at all points, as are the parallels between the body of scholarly literature on these topics and the development of Western hermeneutics on the Bible and Homer. The work of two scholars, Ruth C. Katz and Stuart H. Blackburn, one a Mahābhārata specialist and the other a scholar of South Asian oral epics, will figure centrally, both for the similarities I will note between them and for the clarity that their positions open for debate.

Level, Development, Text, Sect, Oral, Written

Katz's *Arjuna in the Mahābhārata* (1989) develops a hermeneutic stance instructive both for what it recapitulates and what it opposes. Her understanding of the Mahābhārata is organized around a theory of levels. She begins with a "heroic" level and ends with a "devotional" one and identifies a mediating function for a "human" level. Katz takes pains to argue that Arjuna's character complications do not arise from the historical superimposition of one layer on another (271). But there are many points where she speaks not of a dialectic interior to the text but of a stratified chronology such as the possibility of "Krishna [being] either absent or not yet fully divinized" in the earliest heroic core (11–12, 23 n. 28). Katz's views parallel those of Blackburn on epic development (discussed below).

Katz seeks to show how "the devotional level of Arjuna's character relates to its heroic level through the mediation of its human level; that is, how devotion restores Arjuna's heroism, which is threatened by his "humanity" (14). Yet it looks like it should be the devotional level that mediates in this formation, as in her more summarial claim that she has shown how Arjuna is a hero and a human being "at the same time"—one who, "in addition . . . plays a third role, which totally reverses the meaning of the other two: he is the religious devotee par excellence. . . . In a dialectic, his heroism and humanity play against one another, being resolved by bhakti (devotion)" (271).

The heroic level is unified around Arjuna as sacrificer: "The metaphor of Kurukshetra as a sacrifice captures the central meaning of the epic at the heroic level" (115, 117–18). It also takes in the link between dharma and victory, which is felt as automatic on the heroic level (243), and a harmony between fate and effort (226). This level of pure heroism, where heroes win justly and do not doubt their prowess, emerges from comparing Arjuna with other figures of "Indo-European/Semitic heroism." Katz draws here on the monomythic hero type of Joseph Campbell (1956) and F. R. S. Raglan (1936) and on Georges Dumézil's concept of a bipartite Indo-European warrior function that opposes refined chivalric Arjuna-Indra-Achilles-type heroes to brutal robust ones of the Bhīma-Vāyu-Heracles type (Dumézil 1969, xi, 59, 82–83, 90). Katz finds Arjuna in the latter, more purely heroic mode, at points where the hero forgets his nobler self and fights in crude, triumphal rages (139, 142, 145, 161), acting out a "berserker ideal of martial ecstasy [that] . . . represents a way of thinking anterior to the extant epic" (73). Katz's notion of a dialectic between the heroic and the human levels speaks from this developmental standpoint: "Sooner or later traditional heroism (that idealization of joyful, conquering masculinity) will betray its weakness toward real life" (272).

The priority of the heroic level raises questions of historicity, as when Katz views Arjuna's role in the cataclysmic burning of the Khāṇḍava Forest as originating from "a historical burning of forests for the purpose of conquest or land-clearing, the animals killed representing the local tribes wiped out during the expansion" (78). Katz favors ethnographic reconstruction of the history of the text, viewing it as what Goldman chidingly calls an "ethnological *roman à clef*" (1984, 27). But she does not argue for the historicity of the main epic story, as have some who take the notion of a heroic age to imply historically identifiable narrative kernels for the two epics. Although she says the main narrative's historicity ultimately does not matter (1989, 32–33, 48 n. 18), she repeatedly argues for historicity, but only of selective figures, processes, and events. Most persistent is her case for the historicity of Arjuna's grandson Pariksit and great-grandson Janamejaya: "Behind the symbolism of Parikshit as a remnant surely stands his historical role" (225; cf. 179).

Since the publication of Katz's book, the notion that Parikṣit and Janamejaya would be historical figures gains some support from Michael Witzel, who views the two as consolidators of the first Indian state, the Kuru state in the region of Kurukṣetra (1997, 260–66, 278). But as Katz correctly sees, even if these two are historical, this would not guarantee the historicity of the stories the epic tells about them or their forebears. From here, however, reasonable speculation turns into a typical narrative fabrication from wayward bits and pieces: this royal family may have been a late invading people "from the north" who "legitimized" themselves through their claim of a connection with Arjuna (13, 30, 94) and probably gave the epic its "historical devotional leaning" as "a family of Vishnu devotees" whose god was Kṛṣṇa (256–57). The "original intent" of the epic, as "reflected in the character of Arjuna," is thus "to report the establishment of Parikshit's effective kingship on the basis of the religious devotion of his ancestors" (268). Katz finds it tempting to connect this royal family's piety with the

Vaiṣṇava Pañcarātra sect, but finds it more likely that it "participated in a pre-Pancharatra form of Vaishnavism" and that what she regards as Pañcarātra material "entered the epic only later, adhering to sectarian devotional material already there" (256–57). The pre-epic literature that mentions Parikṣit and Janamejaya, however, offers nothing about sects, their coming from the north, or their devotion to Viṣṇu or Kṛṣṇa. Katz is reiterating, without acknowledging them, some of the ideas that have come down from the historicizing, not to mention racializing, theories of some of the founding figures of epic scholarship, who worked from "Indo-Germanic," Euro-American Protestant, and Indian nationalist perspectives that all too easily dovetailed on these issues.[2]

One other feature of the heroic level needs mention: its connection with a bardic oral tradition. Katz turns the concept to advantage by invoking the thesis of Albert Lord, so influential in Homeric studies, that oral epic bards make use of stock metric formulae to fill out verses without substantially altering or enriching their meaning (21 n. 6, citing Lord 1960). This ties in with Katz's notion of a loose oral core, with its complement, the priority of oral to written versions. According to Katz, Arjuna's actions in the war books are sometimes heroic, sometimes human, and at other times a devotee's: "The building up of contradictions and repetitions that one finds here is in part a result of expansion of the text through the centuries on the basis of a loose oral core." The use of these constructs becomes clear only in relation to the two expansionist levels.

The human level is occasionally contrasted directly with the heroic. "Where they become fully caught up in human issues, the epic poets accept the moral ambiguity of the Kurukshetra War and understand it, even as they mourn it, by way of a pessimistic view of dharma which is precisely opposite that emphasized at the heroic level" (175). The notion that the king creates the age is heroic; notions of realism and practicality, requiring the king to adapt to his age by *nīti*, or policy, are human (185–86). But the human level is identified not so much through this dialectic as through a kind of empathy: perhaps *Verstehen*, though the term is not used. The human emerges wherever "one may truly identify with Arjuna's human emotions" (186). Most human traits are said to be typical of the human condition (129, 136). But distinctions are unstable. At one point, "His humanity having been established . . . Arjuna returns to his heroic role during his search for revenge" (138). At another, the night-raid sequence "caps the battle books and puts an end to the heroic and human cycle of revenge" (249). Revenge starts out as heroic but, being also ambiguous, turns out to also be human.

Ultimately, however, the defining trait of the human is mortality. We shall note a similar emphasis in Blackburn's notion of the death event as the generative point in the development of oral epics, but for Katz the issue is not how epics start developmentally, but how they mature spiritually. The hero-human transformation is said to transpire in the *Bhagavadgītā*: Arjuna is unprecedented among Indo-European epic heroes for his refusal to fight "out of disgust with war . . . a protest against the endeavor of war itself" (127). It is Arjuna's capacity for reason that "prepares him for a humanizing shift from a purely martial man to a man sensitive to the human condition" (133). Instructed to abandon desire for the fruits of his actions, Arjuna can move from the heroic level to "lowered expectations characteristic of the human condition" (133). One could, of course, read the *Bhagavadgītā* rather differently: does not Kṛṣṇa teach Arjuna to abandon lower expectations (the desire for fruits) by subordinating them to higher ones? Katz modernizes Arjuna into a war protestor, a likeable rethinker of the Indo-European heritage, and personalizes his humanity.

Katz positions herself against Dumézil and Madeleine Biardeau, who "ignore Arjuna's humanity entirely" (18). Biardeau, who idealizes the hero, is the worst offender (19). My work, in particular *The Ritual of Battle* ([1976] 1990), is taken as straddling the two camps (18–19). It is, however, one thing to say that epic characters reveal human depth, or, as A. K. Ramanujan charges, even that divine/human connections should not be overemphasized at the expense of "the architechtonic complexity of the *human* action of the epic" (1991, 434 n. 4); it is another to distinguish a human level from heroic and devotional ones. If one is going to talk about the humanity of Indian epic characters, one needs not only empathy but an anthropology of Indian categories and contexts. Devotion is no less human than heroism; bhakti requires more than a Westernized reader response.

This brings us to the devotional level. Rather than an Indian anthropology, Katz supplies a Christian one that begins with a contrast of Arjuna with Kṛṣṇa and Rāma. Following the euhemeristic model of divinization so influential in Indian epic studies (both classical and folk), Katz says that in the cases of Kṛṣṇa and Rāma, "the hero has become a god, and the human element, although present under the surface, is submerged. In this sense, Arjuna is special, for more than any other Indian hero he is both fully human and fully related to divinity" (1989, 272–73). This christological formulation is made explicit: "One may say, then, that Arjuna plays a Jesus-like role in the Indian epic context insofar as he unites humanity and divinity; thus it is not surprising that Arjuna and Jesus share a common name": "Nara ('Man') for Arjuna and the Son of Man for Jesus" (274; cf. 275 n. 6). Aware that Arjuna is an incarnation of Nara/"Man," Katz views the epic's strand of Nara-Nārāyaṇa mythology as originally independent of any link with Arjuna and Kṛṣṇa or Indra and Viṣṇu (215–16, 218, 240) and suggests that "the identification of Arjuna and Krishna with Nara and Narayana appears to be connected with the worship of Narayana by the Pancharatrins (or some related group)" (220). Although the identification of Viṣṇu as Nārāyaṇa "is reiterated throughout the extant *Mahābhārata*" (215), the Nara/Nārāyaṇa connection thus derives from a late level of sectarian reworking.

Katz thus understands the formation of the *Mahābhārata*'s devotional level as the historical product of sectarian (and other groups') textual interpolations. Since "there was no interdiction on interpolations, poets of various schools of thought could add what they wished to it, and they did so in huge amounts" (11). This was done by "various special interest groups" (149). This approach is bold in taking what Katz calls Viṣṇu-Śiva opposition as the result of sectarian influence. Katz argues that there is no Viṣṇu-Śiva opposition at the heroic level; that is, between heroes who incarnate these gods or represent their opposition. Katz conceives of this opposition only in terms of what she supposes to be sectarian oppositions in the form of rivalry between gods. Thus Aśvatthāman, who incarnates a portion of Śiva, "is more than just a human rejector of Krishna devotion; he seems, rather, to have become an arch-rival god" (1991, 42). Katz does not credit persistent structural rapports between Viṣṇu and Śiva found throughout the Mahābhārata that register a mythologically and theologically significant "opposition of complementarity": one that is arguably rooted in the epic's bhakti rereading of the Vedic sacrifice and has nothing originally to do with sects (Biardeau 1976, 114, 187, 211–12).

The nature of such oppositions brings us back to the question of formulae, which becomes important for Katz's treatment of the night raid in the Mahābhārata's *Sauptika Parvan*. Aśvatthāman incarnates Śiva's destructive role and Kṛṣṇa incarnates Viṣṇu's "beneficent role of preserver and re-creator" in a "division of labor [that] reflects the standard mythology" of the *pralaya*, the eschatological cosmic dissolution (1989, 252). Katz argues that the *Sauptika Parvan* thematizes this opposition "in a form particularly appropriate for Vishnu's devotees: the Shaivic sacrifice that is pralaya . . . is considered horrible and is condemned; later Vishnu rights it" (ibid.). An obvious question arises: if it "reflects the standard mythology," why attribute it to a sect? Katz's answer is to reiterate her polarizing view of the destructive role of Śiva: "Ashvatthaman's role here, that of Shiva at pralaya, is viewed negatively, from the perspective of the Pancharatrins, Vishnu devotees, whose god opposes Shiva/Ashvatthaman and saves the universe in this sequence" (253). Katz says that the *Sauptika Parvan* presents the pralayic Śiva in a manner that is paralleled "nowhere else in the central epic narrative" (252). But she supports this by a long note that tries to dismiss numerous passages where Śiva's connection is expressed by conventional formulae (259–60 n. 13), as if such formulae somehow don't count.

Formula, Interpolation

Katz draws two more familiar supports to her project of stratifying the "extant epic," a term that she shares with James W. Laine (1989, 25–26) and that was recently used for both epics by John Brockington (1998, 20, 34, 44, etc.). It should now be clear, however, that use of this term relies on the free hand of scholars to think degradingly of the haphazard by-products of textual accumulation and to imagine their favorite variety of prior stages in which there would have once been something more originally and authentically "epic" (for Brockington, "the epic proper"; 33), something that would have undergone adulteration before it became "extant." For Katz, one support is Lord's aforementioned thesis about stock metric formulae in oral epic, which has had its greatest influence in Homeric studies but has also widely influenced scholars of the classical Sanskrit epics (notably Brockington 1998) and Indian oral epics as well (notably Smith 1991). The other, drawn from the higher criticism of nineteenth-century scholarship on sources, strata, and interpolations, has prevailed as critical orthodoxy in modern biblical studies (Rowley 1963, 9–10). It may be said that they grew organically from within scholarly traditions that were addressed to questions raised about distinctive features of Homer and the Bible, but not of Indian epics. Yet they have become virtually axiomatic in scholarship on Indian epics and have served as vehicles for imagining them in terms that globalize the methods without addressing the distinctiveness of the texts. They also carry evolutionistic and theological baggage with them.

Drawing on Lord's thesis, Katz takes up the notion of a loose oral core as a means to demythologize the Mahābhārata's heroic level. It is necessary, she says, to distinguish between "mythic associations from purely literary associations, the latter being qualities that are attributed to the character or situation formulaically only" (106). Here we have a text of five thousand pages whose literary character is of no more than secondary interest. Formulae that mention mythic themes in this fashion would appear to be a more or less random stock of available meter-fillers. For a phrase to be formulaic in this way is for it to be the opposite of being chosen deliberately by an astute and innovate Lordian oral poet (112). Such reflex formulae would thus be accounted for as *merely* formulaic on the heroic and human level (242). Especially targeted as *mere* are formulae evoking the pralaya and associations between Arjuna and Śiva.

Katz here is dismissing arguments that Biardeau and I have made (78, 110, and 120 n. 22). I am charged with having overestimated Arjuna's associations with Śiva, which are "essentially formulaic," "either this or an interpolation" (119–20 n. 17). For Katz, pralayic allusions and affinities are significant for heroes (and only for Aśvatthāman, not for Arjuna) only at the "devotional level" of the *Sauptika Parvan*. But if Katz's sectarian detachment of this parvan and her notion of a supervening devotional level are not convincing, then there is nothing left to distinguish such literary "mere formulae" from significant ones.

Katz speaks of a "building up of contradictions and repetitions" resulting from the "expansion of the text through the centuries on the basis of a loose oral core" (271). Even by this admission, most of the "extant" Mahābhārata would result from written composition. As James L. Fitzgerald says, it may seem highly probable that the Sanskrit text of the Mahābhārata was extracted from an improvisational oral tradition" (1991, 154). But the Poona Critical Edition of the Mahābhārata—that is, more or less, Katz's "extant epic"—has convinced Fitzgerald that a "single Sanskrit version of the '*Mahābhārata*,' fixed in writing, was at the base of the entire manuscript tradition" (152). Franklin Edgerton argued the point even more strongly: "But this text was nothing 'fluid'! To be sure we must at present, and doubtless for ever, remain ignorant about many of its details. But we should not confuse our ignorance with 'fluidity.' . . . It is not an indefinite 'literature' that we are dealing with, but a definite literary composition" (1944, xxxvi–xxxvii). Fitzgerald suggests a date for this archetype's composition between 100 B.C.E. and 350 C.E., "undertaken by some royal house for important symbolic and propogandistic purposes"; and he views the *Bhagavadgītā* as the "center and heart of our text," not an interpolation into a prior text (154), as does Katz, who sees it as the product of another sect, the *Bhāgavatas* (1989, 226). These dates would seem to be a little late, and are under review by several scholars, Fitzgerald included. But the important point is that new questions have been broached around the subject of writing, requiring new answers from those who want to maintain a prior oral tradition while acknowledging literary effects and the encompassment of the oral into the written (see Brockington 1998, 59, 115–17, 396; Vassilkov 1999). If, however, we do have a composition of written art in its entirety, it would be impossible to distinguish significant from insignificant formulae on the basis Katz seems to be proposing.

But what kind of text do we have? If methods generated in scholarship on bardic poetry, Homer, and the Bible begin to distort the Mahābhārata, one does well to look at texts closer to it. The Mahābhārata is a text of mixed genres that many have called "encyclopedic." While making reference to numerous genres, Veda, Upaniṣad, Saṃvāda ("dialogue"), Śāstra, Purāṇa, and so forth, it also *is* each of those genres. As comparable with Purāṇa, one can go a certain way with Velcheru Narayana Rao, for whom purānas have an originally oral character distinctive for being "a kind of oral literacy" or "literate orality," with the composition done by "scholars . . . proud of their knowledge of grammar and their ability to possess a written text of what they perform orally" (1993, 95). But what would such a "literate orality" mean before there was writing? To be sure, Veda and Purāṇa are oral genres before they become "mixed" ones in the Mahābhārata. It is this mixture of genres that is "fixed" in the written archetype. Indeed, an interpolated northern passage tells us a story of how this happened, imagining Vyāsa (reputed author of both the Mahābhārata and the post-epic Purāṇas) not only as a composer and arranger but a poet who stumps his amanuensis Gaṇeśa with enigma verses to catch his breath in the heat of his composition, which is also a dictation.

As a poem, however, the Mahābhārata is most like the Rāmāyaṇa. In each of the Sanskrit epics, a Brahman author is among the first heroes of his own composition. While creating his new poem, he tells "old stories" (*purāṇā*) and "just so stories" (*itihāsa*) along the way, and in each case bards (*kuśālavas*, *sūtas*) are among those who disseminate the poem. Thus Rāma's sons Kuśa and Lava are the first *kuśīlavas*; and Ugraśravas, after he has heard the Brahman Vaiśampāyana, one of Vyāsa's five direct disciples, recite the *Mahābhārata* at king Janamejaya's snake sacrifice, relays it to the Ṛṣis of the Naimiṣa Forest. Each of the Mahābhārata's overlapping narrations is said to be of Vyāsa's "entire thought" (*Mbh* 1.55.2; 1.1.23), which we are never there to hear Vyāsa impart himself, neither to these narrators nor anyone else. Similarly, we never hear Vālmīki impart the Rāmāyaṇa to Kuśa and Lava. Whereas Vālmīki is inspired to compose by the god Brahmā and the divine minstrel Nārada, the *Mahābhārata* poets construct Vyāsa's authorship still more daringly in relation to overlapping functions of the deity: like Kṛṣṇa, Vyāsa is an incarnation of a portion of Nārāyaṇa (Mbh 12.337.4 and 55); in the *Bhagavadgītā*, Kṛṣṇa tells us he himself "is Time" (Kāla), while Vyāsa is a kālavādin, "one who preaches Time" (Vassilkov 1999, 18–19). But Vyāsa's authorship is also related to a disciplic function and a bardic function. However these epics were composed, we may say that even if the authors and bards were real individuals known by the names just mentioned, which is highly doubtful, both are fictional characters within the texts themselves.

Yet it may be that those who did compose the epics gave hints of that process in describing the relations between poets, bards, other transmitters, and audiences. Both epics portray their poets, unlike their bards, as being concerned with the longevity of their poems. The epics give us no reason to think of the stories going through a prior "bardic" transmission such as many scholars like to imagine, most notably Brockington (1998, 19, 394–95). The transmission is in each case the reverse: from Brahmans to bards. Unlike their Brahman authors, the bards also do not get much chance to intervene in the stories. Yet the authors can change the course of events.

Current Rāmāyaṇa scholarship is led by the Princeton translation project, headed by Goldman and Sally Sutherland, and with major contributions from Sheldon I. Pollock. From Pollock, we meet another arresting term for what becomes accessible through a critical edition: not an *extant epic* but a *monumental poem*: "When we speak of 'Vālmīki,' we are using the name as a convenient shorthand way of referring to the composer of the monumental *Rāmāyaṇa*, which we have before us in the critically edited text" (Pollock 1986, 25). The Baroda Critical Edition provides us, says Pollock, with "the most uniform, intelligible, and archaic recension of the *Vālmīki Rāmāyaṇa*" (1984b, 92). Pollock sees a prior oral Rāmāyaṇa, but agrees with Fitzgerald about the Mahābhārata: critical editorial choices of the "best" version are more necessary for the Rāmāyaṇa than the Mahābhārata, since for the latter, "a written archetype must have existed" (1984b, 89 n. 20).

Although Pollock builds on Lord's theory of oral formulaic poetry (1984b, 83, 88; 1991, 22 n. 36), he observes that Lord's model of oral transmission cannot account for "the type and quality of manuscript congruence in important sections of the *Rāmāyaṇa*," and that "broad arguments from the nature of oral poetry in general should not be applied uncritically to the Indian evidence" (1984b, 87 n. 13). At this point, apparently prior to his writings on the divinity of Rāma (1984a, 1991), Pollock still refers to the presumed prior oral Rāmāyaṇa as "secular heroic poetry" influenced by "the mnemonic tradition of vedic transmission" (1984b, 87 n. 13). Once he has taken up the theme of Rāma's divinity, however, the problem shifts. In this context, he makes the noteworthy observation that in passages where the divine king is said to be like a number of different gods, "these are not to be thought of simply as shared characteristics, much less as figures of speech, but as equivalences or, better, substantival identities" (1991, 64–65; cf. ibid., 300 n to 3.38.12). This is a start toward reformulating the question of formulae in the textual context. Ultimately, however, once Pollock shows how carefully the theme of Rāma's divinity is tacitly structured into the poem, he gives us very little reason to see the Rāmāyaṇa's archetype as more inherently oral than that of the Mahābhārata.

As to interpolation theory, the most biblically influenced support for Katz's stratification project, Pollock's Rāmāyaṇa scholarship is more decisive. Pollock has adroitly taken on the tyranny of interpolation theory, which in Rāmāyaṇa studies has had its greatest champions in Jacobi (1893; trans. Ghosal 1960) and Brockington (1984). These two have applied their full energies to stratifying the stages of Rāma's divinization,[3] and Brockington continues to present a theory of "growth and development" in which the word *late*, often qualified by *relatively*, becomes a refrain in his treatment of both epics (1998, 130–58, 377–97, and passim). Pollock's response centers on Rāma's divinity, but has wider ramifications. Pollock says that no indigenous critique exists doubting Rāma's divinity as a feature of the poem's "fundamental 'organic' unity" (1991, 15), yet such "were the arguments and suspicions of Western scholars from their earliest acquaintance with the poem": in particular, "the suspicion . . . that those portions of the epic explicitly positing Rāma's status as an incarnation of Viṣṇu were deliberate, and unassimilable, sectarian interpolations" (ibid.). Pollock traces interpolators' guides to the Rāmāyaṇa from the 1840s to the present that can be closely paralleled in Mahābhārata scholarship on Kṛṣṇa (1991, 29 n. 28; cf. Hiltebeitel 1979; 2001, 1–3). As he says, drawing on Hans-Georg Gadamer (1993, 300–307), "It is a notion of peculiar tenacity and prevalence, which now, through the operations of what is referred to rather darkly as *wirkungsgeschichtliches Bewusstsein* (that interpretive consciousness shaped by past interpretations) conditions the response many readers will have to the text" (1991, 17).

Pollock insists that "higher criticism" has only given unsatisfactory reasons for assessing passages as interpolations that bear on Rāma's alleged deification. Rather, he sees that Rāma's *not knowing* that he is divine until he has killed Rāvaṇa is carefully structured into the poem by the narrative necessity of Rāvaṇa's boon that he can only be killed by a man, or someone who at least *thinks* that he is a man. Ironically, this feature of the Rāmāyaṇa has allowed its textual critics to divide passages into "divinizing" versus "human" ones only by misunderstanding the poem—Brockington, for instance, by seeing the key passages as "second stage" ones (1998, 444, 471, 476). Their argument, says Pollock, "has a sense of the 'divine' that is unthinkingly ethnocentric. What is 'contradictory' in the behavior of 'human incarnations' . . . may be so only according to a narrow theological rationalism" (1991, 19). Texts raise questions about "contradiction" that provide "the source of religious mystery and the object of theological reflection" and "make promptings and suggestions" that we should "listen to," rather than "drowning [them] out with our own querulous presuppositions" (20, 21). Indeed, "we must rethink our own sense of what constitutes contradiction" (20) as well as our concept of interpolation (18), which, he says,

> often serves, not to introduce altogether new narrative material, but instead to expand or make manifest the elliptical or latent; . . . Why should it have proved so perfectly easy to "transform" fundamentally a "heroic epic" according to a later theological program, and to do this without a trace of resistance? Perhaps it has not been transformed at all. (19)

All this is quite remarkable and may even have begun as counterintuitive considering that it comes from a scholar whose Marxist theoretical grounding is well known.

In directing attention to "the poem's 'structured' message residing in certain higher-order narrative features," to meanings "inscribed . . . in the logic of the story" (1991, 19), Pollock also shows that "a substantial number of passages long under suspicion" as sectarian interpolations "have received text-historical vindication from the critical edition" (17). This applies not only to book 1, with its many "digressions," seeming contradictions, and "Vaiṣṇava interlude[s]" (Goldman 1984, 76) that have supplied so much grist for the interpolators' mill, but to books 2–6, which have generally been viewed as less stratified and in which text-critically-demonstrable interpolations exist, but "are still strikingly rare" (Pollock 1991, 17–18). I would add that these arguments also apply, mutatis mutandis, to the Mahābhārata.

Yet here Pollock makes a move that must be scrutinized. Both he and Goldman (1984, 58–59) recognize that it is impossible, textually, to reconstruct an originally undivine Rāma, but both see a prior order of exaltation to the religious one. For Goldman, the first exaltation is psychological in origin: rooted in "powerful fantasies . . . central to the formation of the Indian personality, family, and society" (59) that precede Rāma's divinization (43). For Pollock, it is political. The epics address a political problem "effectively" through family imagery, "perhaps even more effectively than [through] the ascription of divine status to the king" (1986, 21). Between politicization of the family and divinization of Rāma, the former is thus the better means, "perhaps," to achieve the above-mentioned political ends, but both are part of the same underlying "ideology" (ibid.). This "political theology" provides Pollock's key to the Rāmāyaṇa's "meaningful unity," which he discerns through a "'mythic' reading of the narrative" that "derives largely from the Indian tradition itself, from the political theology of pre-modern India, and from more general ideological functions of literary production" (43). As he says in a 1993 article, the Rāmāyaṇa is thus "read mythopolitically" (1993, 262).

Pollock views the Rāmāyaṇa as "an imaginative inquiry into the nature of kingship and the peculiar, transcendent nature of the king" (1991, 63). He shows convincingly how the text's portrayal of Rāma reflects, and is in turn an articulation of, classical Indian formulations concerning the divinity of kings. In the Rāmāyaṇa's political theology, the king "is functionally a god because like a god he saves and protects; he is existentially or ontologically a god because he incorporates the divine essence" (47). He has further the godlike power to chastise and to liberate at the same time (50–51, cf. 71–74). These points are all carefully supported by textual references. But the political reading has afforded a hasty assessment of pre-modern Indian religion via strategies of postmodern criticism, literary theory, and political subtexts. The claim that the monumental Rāmāyaṇa promotes a unique political theology is made by detaching that theology, however tenuously, from the bhakti theology of avatars. Having observed that, according to Rāma himself, "Kings are gods who walk the earth in the form of men" (1991, 46), Pollock attempts to trace a further development of this political theology: "Gradually, however, the conception of the divine king basic to the story of Rāma was influenced by two factors already mentioned." First, Viṣṇu came to be associated with the king "perhaps initially as a result of their functional identity"; second, "in Vaiṣṇava theological circles there developed the theory of the avatara, a doctrine of vast absorptive, syncretistic force, which views every manifestation of divine power as testimony to the omnipotence and immanence of Viṣṇu" (52). It is this "gradually" that serves Pollock to posit a secondary consolidation of the monumental Rāmāyaṇa's political theology around such devotional concepts. But as Pollock himself shows, such a gradual process is purely hypothetical: the identification with Viṣṇu and the theology of divine descent "have so fundamentally conditioned the transmission of the poem that it cannot be proved on textual grounds that the composer of the monumental *Rāmāyaṇa*, from which all versions and recensions of the work derive, was ignorant of or indifferent to the equation of Rāma and Viṣṇu" (52). In other words, we may just as well regard this identification, and the mythology of divine descent as well, as secure features of the Critical Edition, and thus of the monumental Rāmāyaṇa.

Yet Pollock pursues these mythic morphemes only in the direction of Rāma the king, and not that of Rāma the avatar. The latter concept is grafted onto a prior political theology. It may be true sociopolitically to say that only a king can be the "extraordinary new creature" to protect the Brahmanical world order; but, mythologically, it is hardly the case that "only" the king does this (42). It is also a function of the avatāra. And not all avatāras are kings. Indeed, Rāma is unique among Viṣṇu's major avataras in being a king. This is a key point in reflecting on the two epics. One cannot fruitfully contrast their portrayals of the ideal king without factoring in their portrayals of the avatāra, which are far more complex than Pollock has indicated. Unlike the Rāmāyaṇa, in which the ideal king is the avatar who cannot know himself to be such until he has slain Rāvaṇa at the war's end, the Mahābhārata splits the ideal king (Arjuna) and the avatar (Kṛṣṇa) as reincarnations of the pair Nara-Nārāyaṇa, leaving the one to learn of the other's divinity before the war (cf. Peterson 1986).

Pollock's king-avatar formulation is precisely the opposite of Biardeau's, who writes of the avatāra as the "divine model of the king" (1976, 171). For Biardeau, the ideal king, under the universalization of bhakti, must act, especially as a warrior, for the welfare of the world (or the rescue of the earth), subordinating his dharma to that of the Brahmans and incorporating within himself the avatar's triple complementary rapports between his brahman and kṣatra (or Brahman and Kṣatriya) powers or dimensions, his affinities with Viṣṇu and Rudra-Śiva, and his cosmogonic and pralayic functions (1976, 171–203, esp. 182–84).

Oral Epics, Deification

How, then, have the connections between Sanskrit classical epics and oral epics been interpreted? I restrict myself to scholarly debates about regional martial epics that make their own connections with the classical epics through traditions that their heroes and heroines reincarnate characters and traits from either the Mahābhārata or the Rāmāyaṇa, or both, as in the case of *Devnārāyaṃ* (Malik 1998, 148, 215–21). The scholarship under discussion was first brought into focus in Blackburn et al's 1989 *Oral Epics in India* and has been discussed elsewhere by Aditya Malik (1998) and myself (1999).

Blackburn himself (1989, 16) proposes a "'nucleus' model of development" that distinguishes two developmental patterns, both of which work by "adding motifs to the core story," "either by grafting independent stories onto the core or by accumulating motifs" (21, 16). The first pattern, which covers most martial epics in his schema, goes through three stages: 1. Death and deification; 2. Supernatural birth; 3. Pan-Indian identity. The second pattern, which concerns mainly romantic epics not under discussion here, skips stage 1 and has only stages 2 and 3, which converge to tell how the hero becomes the stuff of an epic.

Like Katz, Blackburn begins with mortality and a corresponding a priori definition of the "human" as the source of epic. The "overall effect" of the three-phase process in the first pattern is to "obscure the human origins of the hero/god with a prior divine existence" (1989, 22). As with so many Sanskrit-epic scholars, a Western notion of the human thus becomes the basis for a theory of deification, a term that for Blackburn covers three variations: local worship of a deceased hero, divine birth, and pan-Indian identity. With the latter, we are again open to a theory like Katz's of sectarian capture of epic portions: the further that ritual-based oral epics develop beyond local community bonds to become linked with pan-Indian deities, says Blackburn, "the greater the chance that they will be swallowed whole by some form of Vaiṣṇava, Śaiva, or Śākta worship" (27).

Blackburn cites Jan de Vries (1963, 243) and C. M. Bowra (1952, 9–27) on the death lament as "a kind of 'pre-epic' poetry" (1989, 22 n. 13) for local, violently slain heroes. Epical or ballad songs and stories about such figures are found in India and elsewhere. Our problem lies in imagining the transition required by Blackburn's theory to account for the "development" from such stage-1 songs to stage-2/stage-3 epics. He draws from others (Kamal Kothari 1989; John D. Smith 1989) in treating Rajasthani epics from this perspective, but explains the *Elder Brothers Story* (Beck 1982) and *The Epic of Palnāḍu* (Roghair 1982) largely on his own.

These two South Indian oral epics supply examples of "grafting" to the core: they "grew by adding events from the political history of adjacent regions and by absorbing shorter folk narratives" (1989, 17). In *Elder Brothers*, "the episode involving the heroes' births follows the standard sequence of motifs until evil threatens at the moment of their births. Then the supernatural element appears," when Viṣṇu rescues them. Accordingly, the heroes' "human origins . . . disappear when their story spreads and they become gods" (23–24). In *The Epic of Palnāḍu*, the prenatal miracles and avatāric themes at the birth of Brahma Nāyuḍu are evidence that "geographical spread of a story opens it up to supernatural elements, especially in the birth episode" (24). This supernatural connection is secondary: "although Brahma Nāyuḍu is sometimes made an avatar of Viṣṇu in the Palnāḍu epic, this only occurs in those variants with the greatest geographical diffusion, that is, the literate retellings" (25). Blackburn cites Gene H. Roghair (1982, 109–10) on this point, but Roghair, despite straining to argue for the historicity of Brahma Nāyuḍu as a social reformer, does not say that Brahma Nāyuḍu's avatar status derives from literate retellings. In fact, Brahma Nāyuḍu is Viṣṇu's avatar in the *oral* version he has collected. Blackburn's theory creates further problems for him in trying to identify this epic's "real hero." Having problematized Brahma Nāyuḍu's candidacy, he turns to the impetuous Bāluḍu as "perhaps the real hero of the epic" (1989, 24). The phrase registers that Bāluḍu fits most closely Blackburn's death-and-deification model. The "real hero" construct is reminiscent of Katz's primary "heroic level" and the aforementioned monomyth theories of Campbell.

My position is that "deification" covers too many variations in divine/human interaction and generalizes from euhemerist principles. Clearly, deaths are nodal points in epics, especially martial ones. But it is fruitless to single out one death in a "multideath" epic as the "real" one, and unsound to posit that oral epics are *generally* or *necessarily* about heroes who actually lived. Blackburn's theory underemphasizes the complexity of the interrelation *between* heroes. Epics deal with all kinds of heroes, male and female, and with the rapports not only between them but between them and other beings, including deities.

At the further ends of Blackburn's developmental process, then, having gone through stages 2 and 3, are complex oral epics in which heroes and heroines have been "divinized." Among these are a number of regional martial epics whose stories link the heroes, through reincarnations, with the heroes of the classical epics. How has this linkage been understood? According to Blackburn and Joyce B. Flueckiger, links through reincarnations are "not necessarily evidence of a common history for the Sanskrit and folk epics, nor do the resemblances always represent an imitation. . . . Rather, references to the *Rāmāyaṇa* and the *Mahābhārata* or their heroes are often simply a means of legitimizing the folk epics" (1989, 8). This recalls Katz's notion that the "historical" family of Janamejaya "legitimized" itself by claiming descent form the Pāṇḍavas. Blackburn and Flueckiger cite

The Epic of Pābūjī as an example of "legitimization," and the testimony of John D. Smith, who says that when northern oral epics explain how classical heroes come to figure in a story, "in most cases it amounts to no more than the taking up of a loose end" (1989, 182). Determined to argue that oral epics have an integrity independent of the Sanskrit epics, Blackburn and Flueckiger find that "character-based commonalities between folk and Sanskrit epics are admittedly superficial." Thus, "even where there are extensive borrowings from the Sanskrit epics, folk epics carry new meanings because they live in new social settings" (1989, 8). Now the closing point should win universal agreement. But the dismissive generalizations about classical and oral-epic linkages discourage reflection on the "superficial" "borrowing" process. As Jonathan Z. Smith has shown, notions of "borrowing" and "dependency" are simply negative comparative strategies (1990, 47).

Ironically, one thus finds that rather than examining more closely the trivialized links between Sanskrit and oral epics, this branch of oral-epic scholarship links itself with the generalizations of scholars who have written about the Sanskrit epics. The same "historically effected consciousness" (*wirkungsgeschichtliches Bewusstsein*) that drives and permeates the interpretation of classical epics also affects scholarship on India's oral epics. Smith, for example, supports his "loose ends" explanation by treating what he calls "doubtful" aspects of *Pābūjī*'s connections with the Rāmāyaṇa as essentially "metaphoric" or non-"literal" formulae and accretative interpolations that do not help him in his quest for the historical Pābūjī (1991, 83–84, 91–94). For him, beneath the "loose ends" that oral epics pick up from the Sanskrit epics lies a deeper unity on the level of "ideology"—as with Pollock, a usage of the term *ideology* to disclose a dark underside to the ostensibly religious.

Smith's "picture" is of a "remarkably consistent" ideology that "differs radically from conventional *bhakti* theology" (1989, 176), and it is especially "found in the Sanskrit and martial epics" (193, 178), which attribute human suffering to the gods, "who pass evil into the world in order that they should be free from it in heaven" (176). "Epic heroes, and by extension we ourselves, are the gods' scapegoats" (193). This ideology is "in essentials a single, coherent" one that "varies remarkably little from time to time and place to place" (ibid.). Smith claims to uncover this stark and covert ideology as something "far-removed from Kṛṣṇa's celebrated explanation of his own presence on earth" (176) in *Bhagavadgītā* 4.8 as restorer of dharma from age to age and, implicitly, as avatar. When Kṛṣṇa tells Arjuna to act without desire for the fruits of his actions, he has base desires of his own in championing the self-interest of the gods. By lumping all gods together in this charge and ignoring bhakti hierarchies, Smith ignores the very bhakti structures that he attempts to expose as hypocritical.

As with the scholarship on classical epics, there is thus a general failure in work on oral epics, or at least these regional, martial oral epics, to get beyond linear models and come to grips with certain complexities of the texts. I will address two of these: straitjacketing notions of the "epic" genre, and peripheralization of the significance of bhakti and avatāra.[4]

Clearly, "epic" is for India an etic or "outsider" category, no less for oral epics than for classical ones. More than this, as Malik observes, while no Indian Sanskrit or vernacular terms correspond to *epic*, oral epics are themselves, like classical epics, multi-genred: in the case of *Devnārāyaṇ*, the "oral narrative structure of the text . . . is composed of epistemological categories such as 'remembrance,' on the one hand, and aspects of 'speech genres' such as 'repetition,' 'dialogue,' and 'reported speech,' on the other." Further, there is the category of "divine testimony" (*parcyo*), and a visual narrative (*paṛ*), as well as the oral one (1998, 10–11; cf. 100–108). Indeed, oral performances are called "reading the paṛ" (*paṛ vācṇo*); that is, simultaneously "decoding" its iconic images and "reconstructing" their meaning, so that one may even speak of "reading" the "writing of the *paṛ*" (*paṛā kā lekh*) (ibid., 16–11), a "reading" and "writing" that provides "*literary* design" to the "divine testimony," and "extends into the realm of *presencing* the divine" (16–21, 109).

Such considerations raise the question of how deep the difference is between verbal "written" manuscripts and a pictorial scroll. As with the free ride given to the notion that the Sanskrit epics have a prior oral core, too much has been made, beginning with Albert Lord himself, of the notion that authentic oral epics and the oral poets who produce and transmit them must be free of the contamination of writing (Lord 1960, 23–25, 79, 109). Neither Indian nor Yugoslav oral bards, such as we know them, have composed oral epics in cultures free of writing. Indeed, virtually all the oral epics that Lord describes in *The Singer of Tales* have, as major turning points, the delivery of letters and other written documents (35–95,

224–33), something Lord fails to theorize other than to identify it as a "theme" (68–98).

As to bhakti and avatāra, the complexity of India's regional oral martial epics lies not just in their links with the classical epics through reincarnations and divine-human incarnations (like that of Viṣṇu in Brahma Nāyuḍu, mentioned above), but with a larger "grammar" or "intertextuality" in which these concepts are played out in relation to other texts, both oral and written, including but not limited to devotional texts, and in both Sanskrit and the vernaculars (Malik 1998, 102–14). Temporal and spatial dislocations also make way for these linkages to be reenplotted into regionally defined terms. My contention is that the linkages and the dislocations must be understood together. On this matter, I limit myself to a discussion of how the goddess figures in these inter-epic complexities, and how, until only recently, this scholarship has addressed her.

Work on martial oral epics is virtually unanimous on one point: females are the primary instigators of destruction. No matter how many forces are at work driving the heroes toward their doom, central among them are the motivations of goddesses and heroines (Beck 1982, 182; Kothari 1989, 114; Roghair 1982, 135; Schomer 1989, 147; Smith 1986, 59; 1989, 182, 190; 1991, 96–98; Malik 1993, 280). Most explanations have focused on gender relations and sexual fantasies, although Brenda E. F. Beck and Karine Schomer go beyond this. Part of the problem is that these formulations isolate gender, sexuality, goddesses, and heroines as if they pose a set of problems unique to themselves, but secondary, in the "developmental" sense, to the primary martial epic world, which, again echoing Katz's primary "heroic level," is thought to be about males and death. Thus Blackburn, and the others who share his vision on this point, situate the goddess, and heroines linked with her, as one of the primary contributors to the secondary and tertiary processes of deification. For Kothari, stating the matter most baldly, the heroine-goddess's great importance lies in placing "the epic on a different plane than the historical reality of the male heroes" (1989, 115). In other words, heroines and goddesses mythicize historically real men (cf. Beck 1982, 32; Roghair 1982, 125–26; Schomer 1989, 146). Smith, for whom Viṣṇu, Śiva, and the goddess all come into Indian epics as belated explanations for the dumping of "celestial garbage" (1989, 176), also transposes this schema back on the classical epics. Whereas Viṣṇu and Śiva remain pretty much their same selves from classical to oral epics, "Goddesses are relatively unimportant in the *Mahābhārata* and *Rāmāyaṇa*, but they play a major role in many vernacular epics" (1989, 182).

This position is untenable. As Dumézil recognized, the *Mahābhārata* unfolds from Viṣṇu's response to the plea of the goddess Earth (Bhūdevī) to lift from her, lest she sink back into the ocean, the burden of demons who have incarnated themselves upon her as kings (1968, 33–257, esp. 168–69). The same goddess Earth gives birth to Sītā from a furrow, and opens a pit to reclaim her when she leaves the world in the Rāmāyaṇa. Draupadī, incarnation of the goddess Śrī in the *Mahābhārata*, is born from an earthen fire altar (*vedi*). At her birth, a heavenly voice announces that she will be the cause of the destruction of the warrior class. More classical epic examples could be cited. The point, however, is not just to disagree with Smith and others who view the goddess as unimportant in the classical epics, but to move on from her evident importance to understand the ways in which she figures in relation to Śiva, Viṣṇu, and the theology of divine incarnations, not only in the classical epics but in oral regional martial epics that reenplot these paradigms in dislocated "shatter zones," where the focus turns to relations between virgin goddesses and heroines and the region's land (see Hiltebeitel 1999, 37–43; Malik 1998, 87, 114, 119–30). By moving goddesses and heroines to secondary and tertiary levels of a presumed order of development, scholars of India's oral epics, like scholars of her classical epics, have bewilderingly treated both oral and classical epics as if they originally did without them.

Notes

1. This chapter revises and expands upon Hiltebeitel 1995, somewhat redefining its focus around the three issues of the subtitle.

2. See Hiltebeitel 1979, 67–83; and 1998, especially on the intriguing scholarship of C. V. Vaidya.

3. Katz's great predecessor in Mahābhārata interpolation "analysis" is Hopkins, who finds the same route to explaining the "deification" of Kṛṣṇa in his epic studies ([1901] 1969), which he later reinforced for both Kṛṣṇa and Rāma in his comparative studies (1918, 209–17; 1923, 310–12).

4. Prior to his 1998 study, Malik was the only near-exception. He stated in 1993 his intention to examine the oral epic hero and incarnation of Viṣṇu, Devnārāyaṇ's "association with the '*avatāra*' sequence, within the larger context

of classical and folk-religious patterns found in Hinduism" (1993, 392). But he ends up endorsing Blackburn by arguing for two prior "co-terminous" perceptions about society (organized around a king/deity) and divinity (deified hero), from which the avatar complex is detached as a purāṇic "feature" that "may well be of marginal importance to members of the cult" (400). Malik supplies no argument to support this would-be marginality and seems to have richly revised these views in his 1998 study (cited in the references).

References

Beck, Brenda E. F. 1982. *The Three Twins: The Telling of a South Indian Folk Epic*. Bloomington: Indiana University Press.

Biardeau, Madeleine. 1976. "Etudes de mythologie hindoue: 4. *Bhakti* et *avatāra*." *Bulletin de l'Ecole Pratique des Hautes Etudes* 63: 87–237.

Blackburn, Stuart H. 1989. "Patterns of Development for Indian Oral Epics." In Blackburn et al, *Oral Epics in India*, 15–32.

Blackburn, Stuart H., and Joyce B. Flueckiger, eds. 1989. Introduction to Blackburn et al, *Oral Epics in India*, 1–14.

Blackburn, Stuart H., Peter J. Claus, Joyce B. Fleuckger, and Susan S. Wadley, eds. 1989. *Oral Epics in India*. University of California Press.

Bowra, C. M. 1952. *Heroic Poetry*. New York: Macmillan.

Brockington, John L. 1984. *Righteous Rāma: The Evolution of an Epic*. Oxford: Oxford University Press.

———. 1998. *The Sanskrit Epics*. Leiden: E. J. Brill.

Campbell, Joseph. 1956. *The Hero with a Thousand Faces*. Meridian.

De Vries, Jan. 1963. *Heroic Song and Heroic Legend*. Trans. B. J. Timmer. Oxford: Oxford University Press.

Dumézil, Georges. 1968. *Mythe et épopée: L'idéologie des trois fonctions dans les épopées des peuples indo-européens*. Paris: Gallimard.

———. 1969. *The Destiny of the Warrior*. Trans. Alf Hiltebeitel. Chicago: University of Chicago Press.

Edgerton, Franklin, ed. 1944. *The Sabhāparvan, Being the Second Book of the Mahābhārata*. In Vishnu S. Sukthankar and S. K. Belvalkar, gen. eds., *The Mahābhārata for the First Time Critically Edited*. Poona: Bhandarkar Oriental Research Institute.

Fitzgerald, James L. 1991. "India's Fifth Veda: The *Mahābhārata*'s Presentation of Itself." In Sharma, *Essays on the Mahābhārata*, 150–70.

Gadamer, Hans-Georg. 1993. *Truth and Method*. Second rev. ed., trans. J. Weinsheimer and D. G. Marshall. New York: Continuum.

Goldman, Robert P., ed. and trans. 1984. *The Rāmāyaṇa of Vālmīki: An Epic of India*, vol. 1: *Bālakāṇḍa*. Princeton: Princeton University Press.

Hiltebeitel, Alf. 1979. "Kṛṣṇa in the *Mahābhārata* (A Bibliographical Essay)." *Annals of the Bhandarkar Oriental Institute* 60: 65–107.

———. [1976] 1990. *The Ritual of Battle: Krishna in the Mahābhārata*. Albany: State University of New York Press.

———. 1993. "Epic Studies: Classical Hinduism in the *Mahābhārata* and the *Rāmāyaṇa*." Annals of the Bhandarkar Oriental Research Institute 74: 1–62.

———. 1995. "Religious Studies and Indian Epic Texts." *Religious Studies Review* 21, 1: 26–32.

———. 1999. *Rethinking India's Oral and Classical Epics: Draupadī among Rajputs, Muslims, and Dalits*. Chicago: University of Chicago Press.

———. 1998. "Empire, Invasion, and India's National Epics." *International Journal of Hindu Studies* 2, 3: 387–421.

———. 2001. *Rethinking the Mahābhārata: A Readers's Guide to the Education of the Dharma King*. Chicago: University of Chicago Press.

Hopkins, Edward Washburn. [1901] 1969. *The Great Epic of India: Its Character and Origin*. Calcutta: Punthi Pustak.

———. 1918. *The History of Religions*. New York: Macmillan.

———. 1923. *Origin and Evolution of Religion*. New Haven: Yale University Press.

Jacobi, Hermann. 1960. *The Rāmāyaṇa: Das Rāmāyaṇa of Dr. Hermann Jacobi*. Trans. S. N. Ghosal. Original German version 1893. Baroda: Oriental Institute.

Katz, Ruth C. 1989. *Arjuna in the Mahabharata: Where Krishna Is, There Is Victory*. Columbia: University of South Carolina Press.

———. 1991. "The *Sauptika* Episode in the Structure of the *Mahābhārata*." In Sharma, *Essays on the Mahābhārata*, 130–49.

Kothari, Kamal. 1989. "Performers, Gods, and Heroes in the Oral Epics of Rajasthan." In Blackburn et al., *Oral Epics in India*, 102–17.

Laine, James W. 1989. *Visions of God: Narratives of Theophany in the Mahābhārata*. Vienna: Gerold.

Lord, Albert. 1960. *The Singer of Tales*. Cambridge: Harvard University Press.

Malik, Aditya. 1993. "Avatāra, Avenger, and King: Narrative Themes in the Rājasthānī Oral Epic of Devnārāyaṇ." In Heidrun Brückner, Lothar Lutz, and A. Malik, eds., *Flags of Flame: Studies in South Asian Folk Culture*, 375–410. New Delhi: Manohar.

———. 1998. "Divine Testimony: The Rajasthani Oral Narrative of Devnārāyaṇ," vol. 1: "Study." Professional dissertation, University of Heidelberg. Personal communication.

Narayana Rao, Velcheru. 1993. "Purāṇa as Brahmanical Ideology." In Wendy

Doniger, ed., *Purāṇa Perennis: Reciprocity and Transformation in Hindu and Jaina Texts*, 85–100. Albany: State University of New York Press.

Peterson, Indira V. 1986. Review of Pollock, trans., *The Rāmāyaṇa of Vālmīki: An Epic of Ancient India*, vol. 2, *Ayodhyākāṇḍa*. *Religious Studies Review* 12: 97–102.

Pollock, Sheldon I. 1984a. "Ātmānaṃ mānuṣaṃ manye: *Dharmākūtam* on the Divinity of Rāma." *Journal of the Oriental Institute of Baroda* 33: 505–28.

———. 1984b. "The Rāmāyaṇa Text and the Critical Edition." In Goldman, *The Rāmāyaṇa of Vālmīki: An Epic of India*, vol. 1: *Bālakāṇḍa*, 82–93.

———. 1993. "Rāmāyaṇa and Political Imagination in India." *Journal of Asian Studies* 52: 261–97.

———, trans. 1986. *The Rāmāyaṇa of Vālmīki: An Epic of Ancient India*, vol. 2: *Ayodhyākāṇḍa*, ed. Robert P. Goldman. Princeton: Princeton University Press.

———, trans. 1991. *The Rāmāyaṇa of Vālmīki: An Epic of Ancient India*, vol. 3: *Araṇyakāṇḍa*, ed. Robert P. Goldman. Princeton: Princeton University Press.

Raglan, F. R. S. 1936. *The Hero: A Study in Myth, Tradition, and Drama*. Oxford University Press.

Ramanujan, A. K. 1991. "Repetition in the *Mahābhārata*." In Sharma, *Essays on the Mahābhārata*, 419–43.

Richman, Paula. 1991. "The Diversity of the *Rāmāyaṇa* Tradition." Introduction to Richman, ed., *Many Rāmāyaṇas: The Diversity of a Narrative Tradition in South Asia*, 3–21. Berkeley: University of California Press.

Roghair, G. H. 1982. *The Epic of Palnāḍu: A Study and Translation of Palnāḍi Vīrula Katha*. Oxford: Clarendon Press.

Rowley, H. H. 1963. *The Growth of the Old Testament*. New York: Harper Torchbooks.

Schomer, Karine K. 1989. "Paradigms for the Kali Yuga: The Heroes of the Ālhā Epic and Their Fate." In Blackburn et al., *Oral Epics in India*, 140–54.

Sharma, Arvind, ed. 1991. *Essays on the Mahābhārata*. Leiden: E. J. Brill.

Smith, John D. 1986. "Where the Plot Thickens: 'Epic Moments' in Pābūjī." *South Asian Studies* 2: 53–64.

———. 1989. "Scapegoats of the Gods: The Ideology of the Indian Epics." In Blackburn et al., *Oral Epics in India*, 176–94.

———. 1991. *The Epic of Pābūjī: A Study, Transcription, and Translation*. Cambridge: Cambridge University Press.

Smith, Jonathan Z. 1990. *Drudgery Divine: On the Comparison of Early Christianities and the Religions of Late Antiquity*. Chicago: University of Chicago Press.

Sukthankar, Vishnu S. [1942] 1957. *On the Meaning of the Mahābhārata*. Bombay: Asiatic Society of Bombay.

Vassilkov, Yaroslav. 1999. "*Kālavāda* (the Doctrine of Cyclical Time) in the *Mahābhārata* and the Concept of Heroic Didactics." In Mary Brockington and Peter Schreiner, eds., *Composing a Tradition: Concepts, Techniques, and Relationships*. Proceedings of the First Dubrovnik International Conference on the Sanskrit Epics and Purāṇas, August 1997, 17–34. Zagreb: Croatian Academy of Sciences and the Arts.

Witzel, Michael. 1997. "The Development of the Vedic Canon and its Schools: The Social and Political Milieu." In Witzel, ed., *Inside the Texts Beyond the Texts*. Harvard Oriental Series, Opera Minora, vol. 2, 257–345. Cambridge: Harvard University Press.

SIX The Purāṇas

A Study in the Development of Hinduism

GREGORY BAILEY

The Purāṇas are a huge body of literature composed principally in the Sanskrit and Tamil languages but also represented in vernacular forms through translations and reworkings of older versions originally composed in Sanskrit or Tamil. Individual Purāṇas are bulky, unwieldy, and sometimes stylistically inelegant, but for all that they contain picaresque myths and legends replete with sex, humor, color, and drama; they include extensive details of rituals, customs, and lifestyle information and multitudes of case studies that reveal how the normative teachings of the culture that the Purāṇas reflect should be applied in practice. As with all literary documents in India, the dating of the Purāṇas is notoriously difficult, and this has been a source of exasperation for the many scholars who have shown an inclination to work on them. It is generally accepted that the earliest Sanskrit Purāṇas may date as far back as the fourth century A.C.E., but the various schools of scholarship out of which recent Purāṇic studies have formed have been extremely reluctant to posit an original datable form to any given Purāṇa, preferring instead to focus on each individual Purāṇa as an evolving text and attempting to discover some of the compositional principles that give shape to this evolution.

When reading the Purāṇas, what we find is a collection of texts filled with symbols of the past mixed easily with startlingly new literary and cultural material. Whether any tension was felt by reciters and audience about what is, in truth, a juxtaposition of the traditional and the new seems unlikely, yet the presence of such a juxtaposition compels us to interpret the Purāṇas as a textual process successful in transforming whatever was new, and potentially radical, into a form acceptable to the present. This corresponds to a very ancient indigenous perception of the Purāṇas in which they are defined as preserving the old while constantly coming to terms with the new. Never should they be seen as static relics of a past frozen into the present. If they are anything they are signs of an ongoing process of cultural adaptation and transformation. One of the many conclusions drawn from this understanding of the Purāṇas is that we are entitled to read them as a mirror of the changes occurring in Hinduism during the first two millennia of the Christian era—that is, given the production of new Purāṇas, virtually up until the present.

In this survey I provide a systematic coverage of scholarly work on Purāṇic production, covering editions and translations, attempts at defining the genre, interpretations of the contents of individual Purāṇas, and the Purāṇas as sources for history. Unlike some other branches of Indian studies, the study of the Purāṇas has been relatively neglected in both Western and Indian scholarship. Three stages of research can be isolated, each illustrative of the principal discursive features of Purāṇic scholarship over the past century and a half. The first covers the period from the publication of H. H. Wilson's translation of the *Viṣṇu Purāṇa* in 1840 until the appearance of W. Kirfel's *Das Purāṇa Pañcalakṣaṇa* in 1927. Wilson's work was instrumental in limiting the definition of what could be considered a Purāṇa and, as such, took a clear prescriptive view on the nature of the genre. Kirfel's book marks the beginning of the second period and owes its fame to its influence on the development of a new methodology of epic/Purāṇic research, a methodology epitomized in the ongoing work of the so-called German "text-historical school." This period continues to the present, although a new period of Purāṇic research began with the appearance of L. Rocher's important synoptic work *The Purāṇas*, published in 1986. An ambitious work, this volume succeeds not only in giving a very accurate summary of all previous work carried out on the Purāṇas, but also provides a coverage of all available Sanskrit Purāṇas. At the least it seriously attempts to define the limits of the entire field of Purāṇic research.

More recently (1993) this third period has witnessed the publication of *Purāṇa Perrenis*, a collection of essays by scholars who have sought to apply to Purāṇic analysis the methods of literary criticism associated with structural analysis in conjunction with a strong appreciation of the broader sociocultural context that has produced and nurtured the Purāṇic process and that has in turn been effected by it.

This chapter is restricted mainly to the second half of the second period and to the third period. While the focus is primarily on monographs, I have also made reference to journal articles and edited collections of articles. Some of the most important recent advances in Purāṇic research have been made in these publications.

Number and Extent of Purāṇas

A very comprehensive survey (Rocher 1986) of the Sanskrit Purāṇas lists approximately seventy-five titles. Cort (1993, 185) suggests that the total number of Jain Purāṇas is about seven hundred, even if, generically, not all correspond with the model of the Hindu Purāṇas. Shulman (1980) cites an estimate by Zvelebil that there may be as many as two thousand Tamil Purāṇas. Irrespective of whether all of these should be classified as belonging to an identical genre, the number is huge. Nor should it be forgotten that there are many other texts calling themselves Purāṇas, in a variety of Indian vernaculars, that if only for this reason alone must be included in the genre. Of the Purāṇas, only the eighteen so-called *mahāpurāṇas* have received much attention from scholars, leading to the supposition that the sheer bulk of Purāṇas is probably considerably greater than contemporary estimates. The total number of verses of the *mahāpurāṇas* has been estimated at approximately four hundred thousand, making them about four times the size of the *Mahābhārata*. Nor does this include the much larger number of *upapurāṇas*, the so-called lesser Purāṇas, determined by the Purāṇic tradition as worthy of the name Purāṇa, even if not belonging to the *mahāpurāṇa* category.

Besides the multitudes of individual titles, we also need to be aware of the even larger numbers of manuscripts of individual Purāṇas found in public and private collections all over India. Such manuscripts are important not just because of the sheer bulk of their number. Equally significant are the widespread variations between manuscripts of the same Purāṇa, especially those originating in different regions of India, confirming the belief that a single Purāṇa is not restricted to a fixed content, though possibly a fixed form, and that one of the principal characteristics of the genre is the status of Purāṇas as what Doniger calls "fluid texts" (Doniger 1991, 31). The mixture of fixed form and seemingly endless variety of content has enabled the Purāṇas to be communicative vehicles for a range of cultural positions. Scholars have sometimes reacted to this multiplicity of content and their apparent capacity to deal with every possible topic by describing them as encyclopedic texts (Kane 1962, 925), a title suggestive of bulk as well as of comprehensive coverage of data.

On a practical level, these features make the Purāṇas very difficult to work with. No one scholar could ever hope to have a chance of mastering their entire contents, though the likelihood of machine-readable texts make this goal an eventual probability. No scholar has been able to offer a programmatic study of this literature on the basis of a reading of all instances of the entire genre, something more easily undertaken for the epics or the Dharmaśāstra texts, for example. However, this is not the stumbling block it might seem. Its principle disadvantage is in preventing us from determining what might be an exact inventory of the contents of the Purāṇas. At the best we only have rough summaries of their contents.

Despite this, scholars have been able to make a number of programmatic statements about the Purāṇas on the basis of ongoing studies of the principal *mahāpurāṇas*, though such statements have usually not been designed to outline the formal features of the genre. Stylistically there is substantial uniformity between the Purāṇas, and there is a significant overlap of content between various Purāṇas. It is, however, an outstanding feature of the Purāṇas as a common genre that each one possesses an individuality in its relation to all others. Of course, this is a feature of any body of literature constitutive of an individual genre, and the originality of a given author who is identified as placing himself self-consciously within that genre is measured by his ability to demonstrate idiosyncratic creativity within a set of compositional restrictions. However, this idea of originality is primarily Western and belies the fact that in the kind of oral genres of which the Purāṇas continue to form a part, such originality is neither promoted nor recognized. Like most forms of cultural creation in India, the function of the Purāṇas was to reprocess and comment upon old knowledge—somehow to anchor the present back into the timeless past of an artificially reconstructed and remotely remembered Vedic culture.

What we are confronted with in reading the Purāṇas is a juxtaposition of Vedic symbols, communicated through mythic material foregrounded in the Vedas, but especially the two Sanskrit epics, and ritual, devotional, and śāstric material deriving from many different sources, both oral and written. For a number of reasons, we automatically equate what is traditional in ancient India with the Vedas, but we must accept the two epics, rather than the Vedas, as a more important source of content and style for the Purāṇas (Doniger 1993). This recognition should lead us to give a more sophisticated classification of levels of traditionality in these texts than a bland distinction between Vedic and non-Vedic allows to us.

References

Cort, J. "An Overview of the Jain Purāṇas." In W. Doniger, ed., *Purāṇa Perennis: Reciprocity and Transformation in Hindu and Jaina Texts*. Albany: State University of New York Press, 1993, 185–206.

Doniger, W. "Echoes of the Mahābhārata: Why Is a Parrot the Narrator of the *Bhāgavata Purāṇa* and the *Devībhāgavata Purāṇa?*" In *Purāṇa Perennis*, 31–57.

———. "Fluid and Fixed Texts in India." In J. B. Flueckiger and L. J. Sears, eds., *Boundaries of the Text: Epic Performances in South and Southeast Asia*, 31–41. Ann Arbor: Center for South and Southeast Asian Studies, University of Michigan, 1991.

Hazra, R. C. *Studies in the Upapurāṇas:* vol. 1, *Saura and Vaiṣṇava Upapurāṇas*. Calcutta: Sanskrit College, 1958.

———. *Studies in the Upapurāṇas:* vol. 2, *Śākta and Non-Sectarian Upapurāṇas*. Calcutta: Sanskrit College, 1963.

Kane, P. V. *History of Dharmaśāstra*. Vol. 5/2. Poona: Bhandarkar Oriental Research Institute, 1962.

Rocher, L. *The Purāṇas*. Wiesbaden: Otto Harrassowitz, 1986.

Shulman, D. *Tamil Temple Myths*. Princeton: Princeton University Press, 1980.

Primary Sources

Texts and Translations

Purāṇic Studies have not received a spectacular fillip of the kind enjoyed by the two epics, where the production of critical editions has been such an important causal influence in new translations and other interpretative work. Indeed, the first complete survey of the Sanskrit Purāṇas was published only in 1986, under the pen of Ludo Rocher. This has become an invaluable reference work. It is true, however, that the Kashi Raj Trust has, since 1968, produced critical editions of three Purāṇas—the *Kūrma* (1967), *Vāmana* (1967), and *Vāraha* (1981), with an edition of the *Garuḍa* currently being printed—and that Nag Publishers in Delhi have recently reprinted many of the editions of the Purāṇas published around the turn of the century by the Veṅkaṭeśvara Steam Press in Bombay. Individual Purāṇas do not present us with a unitary narrative plot akin to that of the epics: they seem to defy a generic unity, despite the attempts by some Western scholars to establish the *pañcalakṣaṇa* as the basis of an imperious generic classification. Because of these two factors and in reflection of the huge differences between individual Purāṇas and their often very different temporal origins, it is difficult to see how Purāṇic studies could be stimulated by the production of critical editions or some other literary exemplar facilitating their analysis as one of a piece. Even where individual Purāṇas, such as those edited by the Kashi Raj Trust, have been published with something resembling a critical apparatus, their appearance has not prompted the kind of scholarly disagreement on textual readings that has happened in the case of the two Sanskrit epics. I suspect this is because the Purāṇas are regarded quite differently by scholars, as if they were less worthy of close reading than the epics because they do not offer a clear narrative plot that can initially provide the basis for a cohesive interpretation.

A 1994 article announcing a new edition of the *Skandapurāṇa* (only the first volume of ten projected volumes having yet appeared) is helpful in attempting to clarify some of the issues in the editing of Purāṇas following the lead given by the critical editing of the two epics and the Purāṇic work of the Kashirāj trust. R. Adriaensen et al. write, "The editing of Purāṇas is however a somewhat controversial activity. . . . Several distinguished scholars have indeed expressed serious doubts about the possibility of value of critical editions of Purāṇas." (328) While they do not withdraw from the idea of the critical edition, they are careful to illuminate exactly what they expect from it:

> All the manuscripts [of the *Skandapurāṇa*] have in our opinion suffered to a fairly large extent from purely involuntary scribal errors. We thus attempt a "critical" edition, in the sense that we try to identify readings

> which have arisen as a result of such scribal errors and to correct them as far as possible. On the other hand, we are equally aware of the fact that many of the divergences of the manuscripts are the result of deliberate change, a process that elsewhere[1] has been described as "composition in transmission" and an editor must realize that such processes were probably already at work in a stage of the transmission of the text which predates all our manuscript witnesses. Given that a Puranic text has a certain inherent fluidity, it may be unwise to be solely intent on the reconstruction of the original. Furthermore, we are in basic agreement with those who emphasize that all versions of a (Puranic) text should ideally be taken into account, rather than concentrating solely on a single version which can never be anything but a hypothetical reconstruction. (Adriaensen, Bakker, and Isaacson, 1994, 29)

The question arising from this and demanding a response from both methodologies, implied in the above statement, can be coined in these words: Where does the Purāṇa lie in all of this and how should we analyze this Purāṇa when it is located? Of course, this begs the question of the nature of the genre, but at the least it requires us to accept that the Purāṇa must surely be *whatever it is* that allows the various recitational traditions to operate with a "composition in transmission," to use their words, and that allows the text to be regarded as hanging together as some kind of coherent whole by those who "possess" it as reciters, hearers, or commentators.

What I have just written does not mean significant developments have been lacking in this area of Purāṇic studies over the last twenty years or so. Since 1969 many of the *mahāpurāṇas* have been translated by different scholars and published by Motilal Banarsidass in an ongoing series under the general title of Ancient Indian Tradition and Mythology. These translations are often extensively annotated and contain lengthy introductions aiming to date the particular Purāṇa and set its geographical and theological context. Significantly, the quality of the translations has scarcely been commented upon in scholarly journals, and while many of them may not reach the exact level of literal precision favored by many Western translators, they do capture in many ways what the Sanskrit versions of the Purāṇas are about. The attempt to produce an exact literal translation reflects the implicit impulse to transfix one text as the privileged version somehow more genuine than all the others. In contrast, the generally "controlled looseness" of these translations facilitates the replication of the loose texture of Purāṇic narrative, almost as if the resulting English translation was simply another version of the given Purāṇa, a mixture of translation, paraphrase and composition. What has resulted is a successful transposition of Purāṇic narrative into English in a way accurately communicating Purāṇic style. In sum, this series has made available in translation (sixty-four volumes to date) texts that otherwise may not have been translated for many years.

Other than this, translation of the Purāṇas has been restricted to parts of Purāṇas, summaries, and collections of Purāṇic texts. Of the latter, two stand out in particular. One by O'Flaherty (1975) focuses on Hindu mythology, divided primarily in terms of the myth cycles associated with particular gods, the other is Dimmitt and van Buitenen (1978), which has the principal themes of the Sanskrit Purāṇas as a genre. A good translation and analysis of the commentaries of the celebrated *Devīmāhātmya* of the *Mārkaṇḍeya Purāṇa* was published by Coburn in 1991. Mention here could also be made of two other works by O'Flaherty (1973, 1976) that deal with the mythology of Śiva and the theme of evil in Hindu mythology since they make available translated summaries of many Purāṇic myths. Similar is a book by David Shulman (1980) on South Indian temple myths. Shulman uses summaries of myths taken from Tamil *Talapurāṇas*. A complete English summary of the *Brahma Purāṇa* is given by Söhnen and Schreiner (1989).

References

Adriaensen, R., H. T. Bakker, and H. Isaacson. "Towards a Critical Edition of the Skandapurāṇa." *Indo-Iranian Journal* 37 (1994): 324–31.

———. *The Skandapurāṇa:* Vol. 1, *Adhyāyas 1–25: Critically Edited with a Prolegomena and English Synopsis*. Groningen: Forsten, 1998.

Coburn, Thomas B. *Encountering the Goddess: A Translation of the Devī-māhātmya and a Study of Its Interpretation*. Albany: State University of New York Press, 1991.

Dimmitt, C., and J. A. B. van Buitenen. *Classical Hindu Mythology: A Reader in the Sanskrit Purāṇas*. Philadelphia: Temple University Press, 1978.

Gupta, A. S., ed. *The Kūrma Purāṇa*. Varanasi: All-India Kashiraj Trust, 1967.

———. *The Vāmana Purāṇa*. Varanasi: All-India Kashiraj Trust, 1967.

———. *The Vāraha Purāṇa*. 2 vols. Varanasi: All-India Kashiraj Trust, 1981.

O'Flaherty, W. D. *Asceticism and Eroticism in the Mythology of Śiva*. London: Oxford University Press, 1973.
———. *The Origins of Evil in Hindu Mythology*, Berkeley: University of California Press, 1976.
———. *Hindu Mythology*. Harmondsworth: Penguin, 1975.
Shastri, J. L. *The Śiva-Mahāpurāṇa*. 4 vols. New Delhi: Motilal Banarsidass, 1970–.
Tagare, G. V. *The Skanda-Purāṇa*. Part xix, 1997 (64 vols. So far).
Shulman, D. *Tamil Temple Myths*. Princeton: Princeton University Press, 1980.
Söhnen, R., and P. Schreiner. *Brahmapurāṇa: Summary of Contents, with Index of Names and Motifs*. Wiesbaden: Harrassowitz, 1989.

Aids to Purāṇic Studies

In recent years, several books have appeared that fit the category of neither text nor translation. They make a contribution of a different kind, one that will become apparent only over the next generation of Purāṇic scholarship. The first consists of bibliographical work. One of the great merits of Rocher's (1986) book on the Purāṇas is the extremely comprehensive bibliography it offers on all the Sanskrit Purāṇas. Published six years later was the massive *Epic and Purāṇic Bibliography* (1992), including exhaustive listings of works on the epics and Purāṇas in a range of languages virtually since Indology began. It provides short summaries of all monographs.

This bibliography is part of a new series of books on the Purāṇas, now more than a decade old, being published in the series Purāṇa Research Publications, under the editorship of Heinrich von Stietencron of the University of Tübingen. The series was launched with the publication by P. Schreiner and R. Söhnen of *Sanskrit Indices and Text of the Brahmapurāṇa* (1987), a path-breaking work to the extent that it provides the first computerized indices of a Purāṇa. Although it can be used as a concordance, it is really a synoptic text edition and an exhaustive index of every word of that edition. When all Purāṇas have indexes of the same quality as this one, the field of study will be revolutionized. The second volume in the series (R. Söhnen and P. Schreiner 1989) gives a complete summary of the contents of the Purāṇa plus a very comprehensive index of names and motifs. A similar kind of information—lists of *tīrthas* and meters and *sandhi*—is contained in part in *A Study of the Nīlamata* (1994), which deals with the *Nīlamata Purāṇa*.

References

Ikari, Y., ed. *A Study of the Nīlamata—Aspects of Hinduism in Ancient Kashmir*. Kyoto: Institute for Research in the Humanities, 1994.

Schreiner, P., and R. Söhnen. *Sanskrit Indices and Text of the Brahmapurāṇa*. Wiesbaden: Harrassowitz, 1987.

Söhnen, R., and P. Schreiner. *Brahmapurāṇa: Summary of Contents, with Index of Names and Motifs*. Wiesbaden: Harrassowitz, 1989.

Stietencron, H., K. P. Gietz, A. Malinar, et al. *Epic and Purāṇic Bibliography (up to 1985), Annotated and with Indexes*. 2 vols. Wiesbaden: Harrassowitz, 1992.

Interpretation

Definition of the Genre

Interpretative work on Purāṇic narrative has been bedevilled by the precedent set by H. H. Wilson in the lengthy introduction to his translation of the *Viṣṇu Purāṇa* (1840). Wilson saw Purāṇic studies as consisting in the process of differentiating authentic from inauthentic textual portions on the basis of a somewhat arbitrary view of what constituted a Purāṇa. Implicitly he was setting up prescriptive rules for the definition of the Purāṇa genre, rules that subsequently came to form an important interpretative frame for the Purāṇa. Wilson's procedure for denominating what text generally belonged to the genre was based on one of the tradition's own definitions—that of the *pañcalakṣaṇa*. Accordingly, the real Purāṇa was one whose contents conformed most closely to what was specified by the *pañcalakṣaṇa* definition, a definition centered on content but not narrative structure (although a certain narrative sequence is certainly implied by the cosmogonic configuration of the *pañcalakṣaṇa*). However, the contents of the extant Purāṇas are ample testimony to the narrowness of this choice, many texts that call themselves Purāṇas containing very little *pañcalakṣaṇa* material. That it is so narrow calls its precise relevance into question without, for all that, requiring its total abandonment as one criterion for a text being a Purāṇa. A more judicious use of this concept is to argue that the genre presupposes the *pañcalakṣaṇa* scheme, such that any text calling itself a Purāṇa will be considered by an audience as bringing to life a "fictional world" grounded in the *pañcalakṣaṇa* narratives (Narayana Rao 1993; Bailey 1995). It does not matter whether or not the actual text contains any *pañcalakṣaṇa* material because the audience will assume that the "fictional world" is where the action of the narrative occurs, irrespective of whether the audience has anything more than a passing knowledge of the five *lakṣaṇas*.

Detailed analysis of the *pañcalakṣaṇa* from the perspective of content has been undertaken primarily by M. Biardeau, who has made a major contribution to Purāṇic analysis in the first three of her *Études de mythologie Hindoue*, articles often erroneously seen as simply subordinate to, or preparatory for, her more sustained analysis of the Mbh. She is the first Western scholar to undertake a rigorous structural analysis of a body of Purāṇic mythology, attempting to isolate a mythic logic and to define principles of coherence in the face of what previous scholars had dismissed as a mass of inconsistencies deriving from mythic and didactic material dating from different time periods, randomly and crudely juxtaposed. Her analysis of the Purāṇic cosmogony—including primary creation, recreation, and cosmic destruction—reveals the shaping influence of a distinct set of social values, most crudely represented as the opposition between *pravṛtti* and *nivṛtti* and the incorporation of the former by the latter under the influence of a bhakti ideology and its corresponding poetics. In addition to delineating a coherent conceptual structure for the Purāṇic cosmogonic narratives Biardeau also finds a historical dimension in these same narratives.

For Biardeau, this consists of a set of texts associated with the *Taittirīya* school of the *Black Yajur Veda*. A broad indication of the direction of the integration is confirmed when she writes, "It remains the case that the structures put in place by the Purāṇic cosmogonic and eschatological myths had integrated dharma and the sacrificial religion, under their most classical brahmanical form, with new perspectives on salvation" (Biardeau 1976, 117). Biardeau locates two different synchronic layers of myth, derived from different time periods, and traces the way in which one has been transformed into the other, while leaving traces of the original source. It is an argument for locating in specific texts reflections of deep changes in culture and ideology. The strength of such an analysis is that it is able convincingly to demonstrate how the Purāṇic cosmogony is firmly anchored into an older cultural bedrock, against which it could be seen both as a reaction and a reinterpretation.[2] When the Vedic bedrock emerges, as it so often does, in the *Mahābhārata* and the Purāṇas, it gives both sets of texts a depth of tradition they otherwise may not have had, such that, although the text might be legitimately regarded as standing within a post-Vedic temporal and cultural frame, it preserves the basis that this culture has in a Vedic past that must increasingly have become an abstraction in the memory of audiences of Purāṇic recitations.

More recently, Giorgio Bonnazzoli, in many articles in the periodical *Purāṇa*, has attempted to provide a different kind of theoretical base to Purāṇic studies, though one can still perceive the historicism of the European philologist in it. He has concentrated on what one might call "emic" factors in his study of particular Purāṇas, attempting to see how Purāṇas categorize themselves, or what the interpretative significance of a Purāṇic *anukramaṇikā*, or list of contents, might be. In addition, through his work with the Kashiraj Trust he has reflected long on the applicability of the idea of the critical edition in the field of the editing of Purāṇas.

Of the little analytic work undertaken on the generic qualities of the Purāṇa, most has been based on the Sanskrit Purāṇas. However, several of the contributions in a recent publication, *Purāṇa Perrenis*, dealing with Telegu and Kannada texts, inform us in a strongly revisionary manner about the apparent built-in process of transformation and innovation that has caused so many problems of interpretation for philologically minded scholars. The value of non-Sanskritic forms whose origin lies in vernacular compositions in the widest possible sense, not just imitations of Sanskrit forms, reveals the range of potentialities for development and transformation the genre shows.

Sthalapurāṇas, widespread in Sanskrit, Tamil, and vernacular languages, must also be considered here. Most of the Tamil *Talapurāṇas* date from the sixteenth century and hence are quite late, but they still retain most of the generic features we find in the Sanskrit Purāṇas and *māhātmyas*, themselves normally embedded in the Purāṇic narrative. Above all they relate to a particular location and provide a "mythic history" of that location, a history blending together well-known myths centered on a particular god, usually Viṣṇu, Śiva, or Gaṇeśa, a description of rituals appropriate to the god and location. As Shulman tells us,

> The format of the works is conventionalized: beginning with invocations to the deities of the shrine, the author proceeds to pay obeisance to Naṭarāja-Śiva, the sixty-three Śiva saints (*nāyaṉmār*) as a group, . . . and the servants of Śiva generally . . . inevitably there will be one or more

> cantos singing highly conventionalized descriptions of the beauties of the town or village in which the shrine is located (*tirunakaraccarukkam*), the river that flows through it or the sacred tank within the walls of the shrine (*tīrttavicetam*), the region as a whole (*tirunāṭṭuccarukkam*), and perhaps a central image worshipped in the temple (*mūrttivicetam*). . . . The actual myths are often introduced by the story of the creation of the Naimiṣāraṇya . . . or simply by an account of the arrival there of the narrator, Sūta. . . . The Sūta then proceeds to narrate the Purāṇa. (Shulman, 1980, 30–31)

Finally, mention should be made of another group—the so-called caste, or *Jātipurāṇas*. Rocher (1986, 72) lists several of these that come from Gujarat, and Veena Das has studied two as the basis for her book *Structure and Cognition* (1977). More recently, J. Bapat (1998) has studied two such Purāṇas, composed in Marathi, deriving from Maharashtra and detailing the "mythological history" of the Gurav *jāti*, a caste of non-Brāhmaṇical priests.

If we are going to take seriously, by contrast, the occurrence of Purāṇas outside of the Hindu *mahāpurāṇas*, we should also examine the Jain Purāṇas in order to investigate the possibility that Purāṇic composition, understood as a particular kind of process of transmission of cultural values, operates within other spheres of South Asian culture besides the purely Hindu sphere. To the Jain and Hindu Purāṇas could be added the Buddhist *avadāna* literature, as it contains many similarities with the Jain Purāṇas, generically conceived. Cort argues that the distinctive feature of the Jain Purāṇas is the elaboration they give of the so-called *śalākā puruṣas*, great men, divided into four categories (Tirthaṅkaras, Cakravartins, Baladevas, and Vāsudevas), an elaboration framed within the Jain notion of "universal history": "This universal history provided the contextual framework within which the Jain Purāṇic tradition was located. Therefore, we can define a Jaina Purāṇa as a text dealing with the life story of one or more of the sixty-three Jaina heroes, and a Mahāpurāṇa as a text dealing with the entire universal history" (195). If content is a point of difference between the Jain and the Hindu Purāṇas, another crucial difference concerns the authorship. As Cort writes, "The Jaina Purāṇas are works in which the hand of the author is ever present, shaping his material in the light of his own purposes and beliefs. The Jaina authors were interested in communicating to their audience an argument for Jaina religion and morality" (202). Jaina Purāṇas have authors who have been historically identified, whereas the Hindu Purāṇas have no identifiable author except for Vyāsa, whose compositional activity, while it belongs in the realm of myths, is designed to anchor the origin of those texts he disseminates within the transcendent, of which he is a symbol.

While acknowledging the considerable differences between the Hindu *mahāpurāṇas* and the Jaina Purāṇas, it is still worthwhile to search for common features, if only to discover some element of the Purāṇic genre that lies beyond its individual expressions in different religious traditions and, perhaps, goes back to a deeper formative element of South Asian culture. This common feature is the focus found in both sets of Purāṇas on the construction of a comprehensive history for their imputed audiences. History in these genres does not denote that discipline (or worldview) aiming to give shape to the causal development of empirical events and their intellectual explanation, as it is in the West. In contrast, the Purāṇas offer a chronicle of political, religious, and cosmological events, narrated with such detail that a broad context is produced in which a range of meanings can be accessed. The Hindu *mahāpurāṇas* provide a complete view of all those types of religious possibilities that have been canvassed outside of the Purāṇas themselves. Specific models of behavior are offered with respect to the principal constellations—devotion, ritual, and asceticism—around which all Indian religions group themselves. In the combination of cosmic, social, and individual, these histories find their open-ended and ongoing relevance. They are always complete, while always open because of their breadth. In the sense of providing an "historical" origin for the sanctity of a particular location or the divine origins of a particular caste, a clear historical frame also occurs in all of the *Sthala-* and *Jātipurāṇas* as well.

Nor should certain specimens of Buddhist literature be omitted here. Hardy (1993) has already noted the *Mahāvastu* as being illustrative of what he calls a "Purāṇic process," since "its bulk deals with a partial life-story of the Buddha. Various incidents in his life aroused the curiosity of the disciples of the Buddha, and he narrated 'past stories' (*jātakas*) to demonstrate how the present circumstances make perfect sense in view of former events." This insight would surely be extended if a deeper study was made of the extensive Buddhist *avadāna/apadāna* literature, centered on episodes of the life of the Buddha portrayed in mythological narrative. Of course, to be fully convincing, some evidence of an "historical" perspective would need to be located in the *avadānas*, even if this history was primarily confined to a biography of the Buddha and the modeling opportunities that this delivers. Beyond those *avadānas* centered on *karmavipāka* and events in the Buddha's life, mention can be made of the "*Vratāvadānamālā* 'Garland of *Avadānas*' on (the origin of) festivals or rites' [which] is a collection of legends which were invented to explain the origin of some feasts or rites." (Nakamura 1980, 138). Clearly, the "mythical history" created in any Purāṇa must be considered a central element of the genre.

References

Bailey, G. *The Gaṇeśa Purāṇa:* vol. 1, *The Upāsanākhaṇḍa*. Wiesbaden: Harrassowitz, 1995.

Bapat, J. "A Jātipurīṇa (Clan-history myth) of the Gurav Temple Priests of Maharashtra." *Asian Studies Review* 22, no. 1 (1998): 63–78.

Biardeau, M. *Études De Mythologie Hindoue:* vol. 1, *Cosmogonies Purāṇiques*. Paris: École Française D'Extrême Orient, 1981. First published in *Bulletin de l'École Française d'Extrême Orient* 54 (1968): 19–45; 55 (1969): 59–105; 58 (1971): 17–89.

———. "Études De Mythologie Hindoue IV." *Bulletin de l'École Française d'Extrême Orient* 63 (1976): 111–263.

Bonazzoli, G. "The Dynamic Canon of the Purāṇas." *Purāṇa* 21 (1979): 116–66.

———. "Purāṇic Paramparā." *Purāna* 22 (1980): 33–60.

———. "Schemes in the Purāṇas." *Purāṇa* 24 (1982): 146–89.

———. "Remarks on the Nature of the Purāṇas." *Purāṇa* 25 (1983): 77–113.

Das, V. *Structure and Cognition: Aspects of Hindu Caste and Ritual*. Delhi: Oxford University Press, 1977.

Gangadharan, N. "Sthala Purāṇas." *Purāna* 40, no. 1 (1998): 45–64.

Hardy, F. "Information and Transformation: Two Faces of the Purāṇas." In *Purāṇa Perennis*. 159–82.

Kulke, Hermann. *Cidambaramāhātmya: Eine Untersuchung der religionsgeschichtlichen und historischen Hintergrunde fur die Entstehung der Tradition einer sudindischen Tempelstadt*. Wiesbaden: Harrassowitz, 1970.

Nakamura, H, *Indian Buddhism. A Survey with Bibliographical Notes*. Ogura: Kansai University of Foreign Studies Publications, 1980.

Narayana Rao, V. "Purāṇa as brahminic Ideology." In *Purāṇa Perennis*, 85–100.

Shulman, D. *Tamil Temple Myths*. Princeton University Press, 1980.

Wilson, H. H. *The Vishṇu Purāṇa, a System of Hindu Mythology and Tradition, Translated from the Original Sanscrit and Illustrated by Notes Derived Chiefly from Other Purāṇas*. London: Oriental Translation Fund Committee, 1840. Reprinted with an introduction by R. C. Hazra, Calcutta: Punthi Pustak, 1961.

History of Purāṇic Texts

The methodological implications of Wilson's introduction have been profound. While his extreme position concerning the definition of the genre is no longer accepted uncritically, it has succeeded, at least during the second period of Purāṇic studies, in substantially confining the scope of Purāṇic research to the delineation of texts pertaining to different chronological periods. This has manifested itself in two principal applications. The first is exemplified in all those studies owing their initial inspiration to the pioneering efforts of W. Kirfel, *Das Purāṇa Pañcalakṣaṇa: Versuch einer Textgeschichte* (1927) to develop "text histories" of the Purāṇic cosmogonic myths on the basis of close philological analysis of printed editions and manuscripts. The five books Kirfel published using this methodology inspired a whole generation of German and German-trained scholars, and it still maintains a powerful influence (for summary and criticisms, see Bailey 1987, 1995).

The most recent study in which this method is utilized is that of A. Mertens, *Der Dakṣamythus in der episch-puranischen Literatur* (1998). Others are A. Bock, *Der Sāgara-Gaṅgāvataraṅa-Mythus in Der Episch-Purāṇischen Literatur* (1984), A. Gail, *Paraśurāma, Brahmane und Krieger* (1977), G. C. Tripathi, *Der Ursprung und die Entwicklung der Vāmana-Legende in der indischen Literatur*, (1968), and P. Hacker, *Prahlāda* (1960). The intention of these studies is to explore a particular theme or mythologeme and to catalog its versions, where it is a question of a complete myth or a particular role within a myth, in terms of their relative positions within a Purāṇic chronology determined by the analyst. Once the versions—taken mostly from the Purāṇas, but for historical context also from Vedic literature and the epics—have been organized chronologically, they can be compared and contrasted. Evidence for historical change, especially in the area of religion, is derived from the changes charted in specific alterations noted in the chronological sequence of texts. In Hacker's words, "The aim is to reach beyond the history of texts to a knowledge of individual events concerning the religious history of Hinduism. . . . However, after one has found a primary form, that is, after one has initially glanced backwards, the view must be turned forwards onto the course of development. Only in this way will the individual processes in the history of the complex spiritual structure, which we name Hinduism, become generally perceptible" (1960, 341, 344). Besides Kirfel's pioneering work, the methodological principles Kirfel put to use in his early work on the *pañcalakṣaṇa* texts of the *mahāpurāṇas* were refined more explicitly and with considerable subtlety in a series of articles and monographs by Hacker.

A second, different, attempt to define a history of Purāṇic texts is almost exclusively associated with the name of R. C. Hazra and his book *Studies in the Purāṇic Records on Hindu Rites and Customs* (1940), plus many articles, where he sought to describe forms of Purāṇas that are earlier than those extant in current printed editions. The medieval law digests (*Nibandhas*) contain extensive quotes from individual Purāṇas and statements about the sizes of the *mahāpurāṇas* (e.g., as found in the first chapter of the *Dānasāgara* of Ballālasena). By searching these texts and comparing the quotes with those found in printed editions and manuscripts of extant Purāṇas, Hazra made informed guesses about the likely changes in dimensions and contents these Purāṇas had undergone. Whether or not one accepts the results presented by Hazra (see 1–189), his publications give empirical proof—as if any more is needed—to the continually transforming text of individual Purāṇas. Besides this rather trivial result, his research demonstrates two other more significant theses: firstly, the *mahāpurāṇas* as a body of literature were centrally involved in the Brāhmaṇical syntheses of religion and culture being undertaken in medieval India, especially during the Mughal period; secondly, that the *Nibandhas* deserve much more study that they have hitherto been given. Not only do they throw clear light on the function—albeit, a highly intellectual one—of Purāṇas in establishing a kind of cultural authority, they may also provide signposts for a more specific delineation of the Purāṇic genre, one focusing more on the dharmaśāstric and devotional components of the text, in contrast to the *pañcalakṣaṇa* material.

The emphasis placed in both methods on describing the history of Purāṇic texts is a necessary corollary of the strong desire to develop textual histories within individual Purāṇas and across the Purāṇic literary stock as a whole. Indeed, the two approaches dovetail: Hazra analyzes chronological levels within individual Purāṇas, whereas the German scholars, working across the entire range of Purāṇic literature, have concentrated their efforts on the chronological differentiation of text passages of identical or similar working, of which there are many examples within the Purāṇas. "The methodological priority of examination of individual pieces, justified by the insight into the secondary character of the transmitted textual wholes, necessitates that some methods, which in the older research were customary and are still today applied now and then without reflection, should be abandoned as unproductive or misleading" (Hacker, 1961, 486). Both methodologies derive their distinctiveness from a diachronic approach to the Purāṇic recitational tradition (whether this applies to the recitational tradition of the individual Purāṇa or to the tradition as a whole), the effect of which is to make a portion of the Purāṇa (i.e., its paradigmatic axis) the basic unit of analysis, not the Purāṇa as a whole. Leaving aside the methodological problems involved in not taking full account of features—anaphora, context, contrast of literary styles and units of content—that arise only on the syntagmatic axis of the text, this procedure tends to underestimate the validity of the indigenous view that a Purāṇa is to be received both as a whole and as a collection of parts.[3]

I have discussed these methodologies because up until the time I take to be the beginning point of the present study—about 1970—they were representative of the principal theoretical approaches to the study of the Purāṇas. This was especially so for the German school, where Kirfel made explicit his methodological principles in the introduction to his *Das Purāṇa Pañcalakṣaṇa*, principles later refined and elaborated by Hacker.

References

Bailey, G. "On The Object of Study in Purāṇic Research: Three Recent Books on the Purāṇas." *Review: Asian Studies Association of Australia* 10 (1987): 106–14.

———. *The Gaṇeśa Purāṇa*. Vol. 1, *The Upāsanākhaṇḍa*. Wiesbaden: Harrassowitz, 1995.

Bock, A. *Der Sāgara-Gaṅgāvataraṇa-Mythus in Der Episch-Purāṇischen Literatur*. Stuttgart: Franz Steiner Verlag, 1984.

———. "Die Madhu-Kaiṭabha-Episode und ihre Bearbeitung in der Anonymliteratur des Pañcarātra." *Zeitschrift der Deutschen Morgenländischen Gesellschaft* 137 (1987): 78–109.

Gail, A. *Paraśurāma, Brahmane und Krieger: Untersuchung über Ursprung und Entwicklung eines Avatāra Viṣṇus und Bhakta Śivas in indischen Literatur*. Wiesbaden: Harrassowitz, 1977.

Hacker, P. "Purāṇen und Geschichte des Hinduismus; Methodologische, programmatische und geistesgeschichliche Bemerkungen." *Orientalistische Literaturzeitung* 55 (1960): 341–54; reprinted in Hacker, *Kleine Śchriften*, L. Schmithausen, ed., 1–7. Wiesbaden: Franz Steiner Verlag, 1978.

———. *Prahlāda: Werden und Wandlung einer Idealgestalt: Beiträge zur Geschichte des Hinduismus*. Wiesbaden: Franz Steiner Verlag, 1960.

———. "Zur Methode der geschichtlichen Erforschung der anonymen Sanskritliteratur des Hinduismus." *Zeitschrift der Deutschen Morgenländischen Gesellschaft* 111 (1961): 483–92; reprinted in Hacker, *Kleine Schriften*, 8–17.

Hazra, R. C. *Studies in the Purāṇic Records on Hindu Rites and Customs*. Dacca University, 1940; reprint, Delhi: Motilal Banarsidass, 1975.

———. *Commemoration Volume*. *Purāṇa* 27, no. 1 (1985).

Kirfel, W. *Das Purāṇa Pañcalakṣaṇa: Versuch einer Textgeschichte*. Bonn: Schroeder, 1927.

Mertens, A. *Der Dakṣamythus in der episch-purāṇischen Literatur: Beobachtungen zur religionsgeschichtlichen Entwicklung des Gottes Rudra-Śiva im Hinduismus*. Wiesbaden: Harrassowitz, 1998.

Tripathi, G. C. *Der Ursprung und die Entwicklung der Vāmana-Legende in der indischen Literature*. Wiesbaden: Harrassowitz, 1968.

Cultural Studies

A complete separate genre of Indological writing on the Purāṇas is represented by a large number of monographs, all coming from the hand of Indian authors, presenting a catalog of the cultural data and realia contained within a specific Purāṇa. While these have the appearance of comprehensive indexes of individual Purāṇas, comprehensive in the sense of providing (apparently) exhaustive repertoire of the cultural data occurring in the text, the adoption of this methodology betrays a dependence upon the view that the Purāṇas, are encyclopedias of Indian culture.[4] Such books deal only with the content of the Purāṇa and so, once more, restrict themselves to the paradigmatic axis of the text. They exhibit no concern in investigating the way this material is combined in the running narrative, though the external context of the text, mainly the Vedas, other Purāṇas, and the epics, are brought into consideration as a means of placing the material within some kind of wider historical frame. Consistent with this, there is always implicit in these studies the view that the Purāṇas reflect a direct extension of Vedic culture and that the Purāṇas are really narrating a kind of history that would be coherent if only the texts were not so committed to their classificatory mode of presentation.

In the end, though, the volumes that embody this method of reading the Purāṇas are really just indexes, and to some extent mimic the cataloging tendency, often recognized as an important component of Purāṇic style. They group together an enormous amount of material and rehearse the richness of the Purāṇic genre as a statement of Indian culture at a particular, imprecisely defined, period. A wholly positivistic method is employed in searching through the Purāṇa, no cognizance being given to the possibility that all material incorporated into a Purāṇa is in some sense encoded and that the meaning of the text (and, therefore, of the material within it) is dependent upon the meaning of this code. The intent of the method is summarized in one of its earliest exemplars: "To the idea that the state plays a preponderant role in the life of peoples, that the acts of governments, the facts of internal policy, of diplomacy and of war constitute the core of history, there has been opposed the thesis that the object of history is civilization, that is, a collection of facts on very different planes among which material and intellectual facts are of prime importance" (D. R. Patil, *Cultural History from the Vāyu Purāṇa*, 1946, 3). "Facts" are the building blocks of these books, but what they offer the scholar is the rewriting of a primary source in a manner implicitly trying to reaffirm its status as a statement of Indian national culture.

This genre of Indological literature was studied in an article published by Klaus Bruhn in 1962. Bruhn classifies the type of scholarly work represented in it into three types, depending on whether their primary source is (1) a single text; (2) a single artistic work; (3) those not restricting themselves to a single source. In summarizing the principle of analysis underlying them, Bruhn points out one of the limitations of this kind of approach: "It has recently often been assumed that the individual text already furnishes a transparent image of the life and thought of its time. This simply awaited, as it were, to be recast into the systematic form of a cultural study, through doing which it is no longer necessary to draw in material from other sources" (Bruhn 1962, 256). Any critical tone is largely absent here, but it does come out in later parts of his article, when he describes the analytical component of these studies as being confined almost to the construction of lists of objects of cultural interest.

One of the principal problems Bruhn points toward is the lack of contextualization offered in many of these studies and the apparent eschewal of parallel sources of information (1962, 258). The ordering principles applied to the primary sources distort the manner in which the material is presented in the primary sources—the problem that must be taken into consideration in any treatment of the occurrence of the "cultural material" in literature or art. What this kind of study ends up delivering is just another template ordered according to analytical principles unable to provide an accurate reflection of what has been found in the primary source and totally cut off from the material and intellectual foundations of the culture that produced them.

References

Awasthi, A. B. L. *Studies in Skanda Purāṇa*. Lucknow: Kailash Prakashan, 1965.

Arora, R. K. *Historical and Cultural Data from the Bhaviṣya Purāṇa*. New Delhi/Jullundur: Sterling, 1972.

Arya, S. *Religion and Philosophy of the Padma-Purāṇa*. Delhi: Nag, 1988.

Bruhn, K. "Cultural Studies." *Indo-Iranian Journal* 5 (1962): 253–70.

Desai, N. Y. "Ancient Indian Society, Religion, and Mythology as Depicted in the Mārkaṇḍeya-Purāṇa: A Critical Study." MS, University of Baroda, 1968.

Gangadharan, N. *Garuḍa Purāṇa: A Study*. Varanasi: All-India Kashiraj Trust, 1972.

———. *LiṅgaPurāṇa: A Study*. Delhi, Ajanta, 1980.

Kantawala, S. G. "Cultural History from the Matsyapurāṇa." Baroda: MS, University of Baroda, 1964.

Pai, G. K. *Cultural History from the Kūrma-Purāṇa*. Cochin: Sukrtindra Oriental Research Institute, 1975.

Patil, D. R. *Cultural History from the Vāyu Purāṇa*. Poona: Deccan College Research Institute, 1946; reprint, Delhi: Motilal Banarsidass 1964.

Seth. S. *Religion and Society in the Brahma Purāṇa*. New Delhi: Sterling, 1979.

Theology

Despite the long-held judgment that Purāṇas are repositories of myths and rituals focused on a small group of gods, principally Viṣṇu, Śiva, Gaṇeśa, Sūrya, and the goddess, the amount of scholarly work on theological subjects within the Purāṇas is less than one might expect. *Theology* is a word perhaps having more relevance to Christianity and Islam than to Hinduism, yet most Purāṇic texts contain much that is directly concerned with the description of the attributes and functions of deities and the methods of their worship. If the body of myths found *in extenso* in the Purāṇas take up the central themes in the culture over a period of two millennia, they also provide the opportunity for more formal statements of the nature of given deities, whose manifestation can be classified as *nirguṇa* and/or *saguṇa*. Where the deity is being described in a manner designed to emphasize its *nirguṇa* aspect, the kinds of statement used will stress the unknowability of the deity and will make much use of Vedāntic terminology. However, when the deity's *saguṇa* aspect is to be stressed, a much more iconic style of description is used, especially where it is expressed in the form of a *stotra*, a hymn of praise.

Most of the books described in the preceding section contain lengthy chapters summarizing myths judged by the authors to be centered on the activities of specific gods, and they also include lists of attributes directly associated with these gods as these attributes are listed in the Purāṇa. However, theological study of complete Purāṇas or parts of Purāṇas considered as a task in itself is less common. Two examples that do tackle this task are the books of T. Coburn and C. MacKenzie Brown. Coburn, *The Crystallization of the Goddess Tradition* (1984) and *Encountering the Goddess* (1991), has exhaustively studied the *Devīmāhātmya*, especially the semantic development of each component (revealed in epithets, hymns, and the three myths of the *Devī-māhātmya*) of the goddess as she is presented in that text and the theological elements in the many extant commentaries on the text. What he succeeds in doing is to expose the conceptual layering behind the *Devī-māhātmya*, one given new semantic resonance because of the specific way it has been combined with more recent material. Altogether it makes an important contribution to the study of Purāṇic eclecticism, one of the principal stylistic features of the genre, yet one that has hardly been discussed in the scholarly literature. Coburn's is a theoretical contribution as well as a detailed textual analysis. The first part of his book offers many methodological insights and makes the plea that the Purāṇic narrative must be studied in both its synchronic and diachronic perspectives.

MacKenzie Brown's two books both deal with the figure of the goddess in two different Purāṇas. The first of these, *God as Mother* (1974), concentrates on the *Brahmavaivarta Purāṇa*. I have not seen it, so I will make no comment about it. His more recent *The Triumph of the Goddess* (1990) presents the teaching about the goddess in the *Devībhāgavata Purāna* and also shows how a distinct theological conception of the goddess—demonstrating the integration in a single image of such antinomies as destructive/

peaceful, maternal/erotic and immanent/transcendent—has provided the means for establishing coherence across the narrative of the Purāṇa. While the book concentrates on the diachronic axis of the text, breaking it up into different chronological layers, it also shows a sensitivity to the received text and the description of narrative and theological structures that hold the text together as a unity.

To this small group of works, the important book of F. Hardy, *Viraha-bhakti* (1983), offers a very extensive treatment of Kṛṣṇa devotion in the *Bhāgavatapurāṇa* and explores the intertextual influences on that text coming especially from the Tamil poetry of the Å̱lvārs. A further treatment of bhakti in this same text is A. Gail's *Bhakti im Bhāgavatapurāṇa* (1969), in which the theology of Viṣṇu is studied extensively as part of the devotional system expressed throughout the text. Theological treatments of Viṣṇu and Śiva are often found incidentally in the books listed in the preceding list of references since one of the consistent results of the text-historical approach is the chronicling of changing theological motivations producing differences in Purāṇic texts that have very close wording. In the first volume of *Prahlāda*, Hacker has given extensive treatments of Viṣṇu's theology in the *Viṣṇu and Bhāgavata Purāṇas*.

References

Coburn, T. *The Crystallization of the Goddess Tradition*. Delhi: Motilal Banarsidass, 1984.

Gail, A. J. *Bhakti im Bhāgavatapurāṇa: Religionsgeschichtliche Studie zur Idee der Gottesliebe in Kult und Mystik des Viṣṇuismus*. Wiesbaden: Harrassowitz, 1969.

———. *Paraśurāma, Brahmane und Krieger: Untersuchung über Ursprung und Entwicklung eines Avatāra Viṣṇus und Bhakta Śivas in indischen Literatur*. Wiesbaden: Harrassowitz, 1977.

Hacker, P. *Prahlāda: Werden und Wandlung einer Idealgestalt: Beiträge zur Geschichte des Hinduismus*. Wiesbaden: Franz Steiner Verlag, 1960.

Hardy, F. *Viraha-bhakti: The Early History of Kṛṣṇa Devotion in South India*, Delhi: Oxford University Press, 1983.

MacKenzie Brown, C. *God as Mother, A Feminine Theology in India: An Historical and Theological Study of the Brahmavaivarta Purāṇa*. Hartford: Stark, 1974.

———. *The Triumph of the Goddess: The Canonical Models and Theological Visions of the Devī-Bhāgavata Purāṇa*. Albany: State University of New York Press, 1990.

Mertens, A. *Der Dakṣamythus in der episch-puranischen Literatur: Beobachtungen zur religionsgeschichtlichen Entwicklung des Gottes Rudra-Śiva im Hinduismus*. Wiesbaden: Harrassowitz, 1998.

The Purāṇas in a Historical Context

In deference to a tendency, often implicit, from all sides of Purāṇic studies to envisage the Purāṇic genre as much as a dynamic process of transmission and synthesis as a collection of specific books, and their accompanying oral recitations, it is necessary at least to review what has become an important emerging trend in contemporary Purāṇic studies.[5] This trend can be understood as a two-sided problem. On the one hand, the problem has been conceptualized as the attempt to come to terms with a distinctive, if not *the* distinctive, feature of Purāṇic composition, in which the process of composition and transmission—by definition encompassing textual growth and perceptible change according to given rules yet to be precisely determined—readily takes data from different chronological periods, such that the genre as a whole becomes a kind of chronological library of events and also a regional mosaic of myths and rituals. This process is considered one of absorption, synthesis, and integration, a consideration given depth by the enormously variegated data—witnessed directly by the *Agni*, *Viṣṇudharmottara*, *Garuḍa*, *Padma*, and *Skanda Purāṇas*, in particular—taken up into the genre. On the other hand, this problem makes sense only if its opposite is posed: What kind of specific historical situation and historical dimension of long durée contains the forces that produce the absorptive process represented in the Purāṇic genre? Defined as a scholarly problem, it would involve analyzing the historical conditions (broadly understood) that may have directly given rise to the creation of the mixed genre of Purāṇa, on the one hand, and variations in conditions productive of the individual Purāṇas. Purāṇic composition then could be regarded as being tied down to the occurrence of quite specific events or historical trends, but also capable of breaking out of any kind of tight historical straitjacket as evidenced by their contemporary survival.

The general principle underlying the first aspect of the problem is laid down clearly, as applied to the *Padmapurāṇa*, in a recent exemplar of the scholarly genre of cultural studies (noted under that heading, above):

> In course of its evolution there were several factors that contributed to the growth of the Padma-Purāṇa which seems to be the work of several

> centuries. With the progress of time, there were changes in the ideas and beliefs, in the modes of living and thinking, and in the environment of different groups of people. There were different sects flourishing in the field of religion and naturally, there were sectarian rivalries too, in the society. The Padma-Purāṇa was utilized by them freely. Accordingly, the Padma-Purāṇa was recast and revised sometimes in a drastic manner, in the wake of new requirements. The Padma-Purāṇa seems to have pointed out its own unstable character when it states that in course of time, the Purāṇa was no longer accepted by the people; Lord Viṣṇu took the form of Vyāsa and re-edited it in every Yuga [citing *Padma. Sṛṣṭi*, 1.49–50; cf. *Matsya-Purāṇa*, 53.8–9; *Devī-bhāgavata-Purāṇa*, 1.3. 19–20]. It may be pointed out here, that tradition demanded its recasts and revisions with the changes in society so that its utility as work [*sic*] of authority might not decrease. (Arya 1988, viii)

A logical extension of this view is to take the Purāṇas as texts whose purpose is to provide a synthesis capable of healing distinctive and potentially disruptive streams of belief and practice within the culture. Note that *it is the text that presents a synthesis*, a synthesis that must also have been manifested elsewhere in the society (though it is not clear where), at the same time coexisting with the individual elements responsible for creating the very need for emphasis. A very recent expression of this tendency comes from a new book on Gaṇapati:

> In the early centuries of the Christian era, as Śiva and Viṣṇu grow in importance, a new body of literature known as the Purāṇas comes into being. These texts reflect a changing material and social milieu. As Brahmanical culture spreads from the madhyadeśa region into the peripheral areas and tries to cope with the challenge of Buddhism and Jainism, it comes in contact with a variety of new ethnic groups and undergoes a process of syncretism. As a result, newer gods take precedence over the Vedic divinities. A variety of new myths or new versions of old myths are created with the purpose of glorifying Śiva and Viṣṇu and, later the Goddess. The rise in stature of these new gods results in the inclusion of several non-Vedic deities as part of their expanding pantheons. (Thapan 1997, 111)

Attractive as this view may be, it rests on several unproven assumptions, the most prominent being that Brahmanism (always an artificial entity) was severely weakened in the early centuries of the Christian era due to the rapacious inroads of Buddhism and Jainism. How would this assumption come to terms with the emergence of a great work of cultural criticism—the *Mahābhārata*—in the early centuries of the pre-Christian era? That text presents a picture of the elites of the culture consistently questioning the theoretical assumptions lying behind the dharmic structure upon which that culture was coming to rest. A second assumption this view makes, one equally in need of historical justification, is that a process of synthesis had not been going on even earlier. Surely some kind of synthesis occurs when any culture comes into contact with another, even where the contribution of one might be much greater than the other because of economic and military superiority.

Hazra also focuses on the synthetic role of the Purāṇas—both as a reflection of sociocultural synthesis and as part of the very process whereby that synthesis occurred—as do many other Indian scholars, in part because it enables them to account for the simultaneous heterogeneity and uniformity (expressed in the strong dharmaśāstric component) of Purāṇic contents. Recognition of the important dharmaśāstric subtext within the Purāṇic genre is a significant part of the synthesis theory in the sense that the body of rules of conduct codified under the name dharmaśāstra makes available one solid and comprehensive standard of behavior in the face of so many variants coming from the different regions of South Asia.

In the volume *Purāṇa Perrenis*, cited several times already, the problem of the historical status of the Purāṇas and of their function as cultural products is taken up in a different way. One perspective argues that the Purāṇas should be seen in some way as transitional texts. Laurie Patton has focused on this problem in a 1997 article centered on the *Bṛhaddevatā*, not a Purāṇic text, but "interactive" in the same way as the Purāṇas, and she suggests that "some texts . . . [The *Jaiminīya Brāhmaṇa*, the *Bṛhaddevatā*, the *Mahābhārata*, and the Purāṇas] reflect such interactions [between different versions of reality] more transparently than others. Such a view opens the way toward reading works other than the Epics with an eye towards the interactions between the Vedic worldview and that which has been deemed the more classically 'Hindu' form of thought" (1993, 4–5).

Still another thematic representation of this integrative function emerges out of the assumption that the Purāṇas effect a working integration of the "great" and "little" traditions. When writing of the *Skanda*

Purāṇa, Doniger says, "Clearly, it has served someone's purpose, perhaps even several conflicting purposes. On the one hand, it has proved a means whereby the Sanskrit tradition could encompass rival traditions, could 'kill by embracing' as the saying goes. Or, to look at it from the other standpoint, it has been a door through which the local, vernacular Purāṇas could enter into the *soi-disant* mainstream tradition. It has enabled the vernacular tradition to legitimate itself by claiming to be part of an infinitely expansible Sanskrit text." (1993, 60). This sets the theoretical imperative, but the task remains for future Purāṇic scholars to fill in the details by investigating the precise mechanics of the integration of non-Sanskritic and regional material into the Sanskrit Purāṇas and by providing an educated guess about the total percentage of this material in relation to that deriving from the so-called great tradition.

A potentially very fruitful way to investigate this second historical aspect of the Purāṇas is to take the important suggestion of V. Narayana Rao in defining a kind of Purāṇic culture in which a distinct set of texts was produced that sum up culture in both a synchronic (i.e., as a set of rules defining traditionally sanctioned conduct at any given time in the Purāṇic universe created within the *pañcalakṣaṇa* frame) and a diachronic sense, insofar as any given Purāṇa demonstrates its heritage as Vedic, or traditional through reference back to an epic lineage, while attempting to maintain a continuity with its recitational present. This produces "a text flexible in content but fixed in its ideological apparatus. Purāṇa and itihāsa . . . are such texts" (1993, 93).

The broad principle on which this is worked out is summarized by Narayana Rao: "What is common to all the three cases I have mentioned above is that all of them begin with what we call 'myth' and move into what we call 'history,' with no dividing line between them. This is one continuous line of events. I intend to show . . . that this continuity is what the Purāṇic worldview promotes, and that it results from the ideological frame of Purāṇas" (1993, 86–87). While these sentences condemn us to the resolution of virtually insuperable problems—especially the attempt within the Indian context to locate the interrelationship between myth and history and their different epistemological bases—they firmly set the direction to be taken in any kind of serious interpretation of the integrative role of the Purāṇas considered historically. Moreover, Narayana Rao's conceptualization of the problem focuses on the dual role of Purāṇas as offering a process of transmission for change and authority and an ideological frame that is itself a product of particular sociohistorical positionings yet to be defined with any accuracy.

A similar position, if deriving from different source materials, is advanced by Hardy, who, in what is almost an aside, asserts that "'Purāṇic Hinduism' ought to be differentiated from other forms of Hinduism." (1993, 170) Hardy's rich theoretical peregrinations cannot be summarized easily; suffice it to say they provide guidelines for investigating the symbiotic relationship the Purāṇic process has with historical context, for refining the generic conditions of the Purāṇic narrative and for defining the limits of Purāṇic intertexuality. Here is how he summarizes this programmatically:

> A program for exploring the Purāṇas has been put forward that envisages a historical process of transmitting and imposing meaning, from the past into the present, through a particular mode of discourse (the Purāṇic) and operating within rational constraints. This process is indirectly documented in a series of texts (themselves of different degrees of solidification and fixation) and, more directly, in the very continuity of the process of producing such works. Behind this dynamic activity lies the acknowledgment of a need simultaneously to make localised concrete environments meaningful and to expand these limited horizons (integration, pan-Indianization). (Hardy, 1993, 181–82)

Hardy notes rightly the applicability of this dual process of text composition as a form of cultural adaptation to non-Hindu traditions in South Asia. Further elaboration of this program will surely be invaluable for discovering how South Asian culture constantly reproduces itself within the context of all the fragmentary pressures contained in any very rich culture.

References

Doniger, W. "The Scrapbook of Undeserved Salvation: The *Kedāra Khaṇḍa* of the *Skanda Purāṇa*." In W. Doniger, ed., *Purāṇa Perennis*, 59–81.

Hardy, F. "Information and Transformation: Two Faces of the Purāṇas." In W. Doniger, ed., *Purāṇa Perennis*, 159–82.

Narayana Rao, V. "Purāṇa as brahminic Ideology." In W. Doniger, ed., *Purāṇa Perennis*, 85–100.

Patton, L. "The Transparent Text: Purāṇic Trends in the Bṛhaddevatā." In W. Doniger, ed., *Purāṇa Perennis*, 3–29.

Thapan, A. R. *Understanding Gaṇapati: Insights into the Dynamics of a Cult*. New Delhi: Manohar, 1997.

The trend to view the Purāṇa as a dynamic process and not just as a textual product can serve to bring together the divergent trends of contemporary Purāṇic studies and can provide a dimension wherein the Purāṇas will be seen as vital sign posts for understanding cultural formation across South Asia historically. This judgment applies even while Purāṇic studies are still in their infancy. Much more work will be done on the production of texts offering the scholar the equipment for determining the influence of different manuscript traditions on the development of a complete recitational tradition. Still more books will be produced interpreting sections of Purāṇas utilizing the "text-historical" approach. And one hopes that the study of Purāṇic intertextuality will be taken up as a new challenge finally to come to terms with the eclectic nature of the Purāṇic text and to locate the genre within all of the other competing genres of South Asian literature. If, though, scholars are insistent upon locating the Purāṇic tradition within a material historical referent, the question of the historicity of "Purāṇic histories" and their success in creating their own historical tradition will have to be approached in a more systematic way than hitherto. Here lies the major future challenge for Purāṇic studies.

Notes

1. The reference is to Hans Bakker, *Deutscher Orientalistentag: Ausgewählte Vorträge*, vol. 22 (Stuttgart: 1989), 331*ff*.

2. How this reaction and reinterpretation actually occurred is not recorded and must be inferred. A study of the commentaries of those Purāṇas that have actually been commented upon may provide signposts for putting some flesh on these inferences.

3. This is also asserted by Pollock in reference to the *Rāmāyaṇa*. "One of our principal critical tasks would then be to ponder how the work functions as a unit, how its parts fit together to establish a large and coherent pattern of signification? A provisional readiness to posit a meaningful unity of the work is at the very least a hermeneutical necessity." S. Pollock. trans. *The Rāmāyāṇa of Vālmīki. An Epic of Ancient India. Vol. III Araṅyakāṇḍa*, Princeton: Princeton University Press, 1991, 5.

4. Perhaps *encyclopedia* is too strong since there is an almost uniform tendency to use the adjective *encyclopedic* rather than the noun when dealing with

the Purāṇas (cf. Rocher 1986, 78–80). But compare Sharda Arya, *Religion and Philosophy of the Padma-Purāṇa* (Delhi: Nag, 1988): "The Padma-Purāṇa is an inexhaustible encyclopaedia of knowledge" (i).

5. I do not include in this section such important works as Y. Ikari, ed., *A Study of the Nīlamata—Aspects of Hinduism in Ancient Kashmir* (Kyoto: Institute for Research in the Humanities, 1994), which use a particular Purāṇa to study the history of a particular region of India.

SEVEN The Bhagavadgītā and Classical Hinduism

A Sketch

MILTON EDER

A milestone year for the *Bhagavadgītā* (or Gītā) recently passed before a Western reading audience, its two hundredth anniversary in English translation. The text's first translation appeared in 1785 through the efforts of Sir Charles Wilkins. Wilkin's *Bhăgvăt-Gēētā or Dialogues of Krēēshană and Ărjōōn; in Eighteen Lectures with Notes*, with its uniquely transliterated title and surfeit of diacritics, suggested the exotic. The text's first century in English was marked by Sir Edwin Arnold's *The Song Celestial* (1885). Arnold's widely read poetic rendition forms the central star in a constellation of Gītā translations that appeared in the 1880s (e.g., M. M. Chatterji 1880, J. Davies 1882, K. T. Telang, blank verse, 1875, prose 1882). Thereafter, English readers would have greater access to the Gītā, and Western scholars would begin to take greater interest in assessing the text's contributions to Indian thought and to Hinduism. A new constellation of scholarly Gītā translations and studies appeared around the bicentennial of Wilkins's publication: K. Bolle (1979), G. Feuerstein (1980), J. A. B. van Buitenen (1981), R. Gotshalk (1985), B. Stoler Miller (1986), R. Minor (1982), E. Sharpe (1985), A. Sharma (1986), P. Sinha (1987). It is at this juncture that we look back to assess the relationship between the Gītā and classical Hinduism.

In the more than two centuries of Western encounter with the Gītā, scholars, religious figures, and lay enthusiasts have produced approximately three hundred English translations and perhaps thousands of interpretive studies. Although it has not proven possible to discuss or even mention many fine monographs, articles, and translations in this sketch of major trends in modern scholarship about the Gītā, I reference a few additional key works from the extensive Gītā archive in the notes for this chapter.[1] Rather than attempt an exhaustive account of scholarship on the Gītā, I address major trends in past scholarship. We begin by reviewing ideological orientations in the Western study of the Gītā and then will entertain new directions for future research and translation.

Early Western Encounters with the Bhagavadgītā

Warren Hastings wrote to Nathaniel Smith recommending that the East India Company undertake publication of the *Bhăgvăt-Gēētā* [*sic*][2] in translation by Sir Charles Wilkins. In that letter, published with the 1785 translation, Hastings pronounced "the *Gēētā* a performance of great originality; of a sublimity of conception, reasoning, and diction, almost unequaled; and a single exception, among all the known religions of mankind, of a theology accurately corresponding with that of the Christian dispensation, and most powerfully illustrating its fundamental doctrines."[3] Hastings's suggested correspondence between the Gītā and Christian theology characterized the major trend in European scholarly inquiry during the first century of modern Gītā studies.

Many scholars during the first century of Western interest in the Gītā and Indian religion assumed history to be a substantiation and fulfillment of the one true religion explained by the Bible.[4] Other scholars followed G. W. F. Hegel, who divorced history from literal readings of the Old Testament. Hegel, however, still situated Hindu religious thought and Indian civilization at an inferior stage of development to that of Christianity and Western civilization.[5] Both perspectives shaped the Western study of India, with the European interpretation of Sanskrit texts, particularly the *Nārāyaṇīya* episode of the *Mahābhārata*, providing evidence to support historical contact and the borrowing of ideas from the West. In the later half of the nineteenth century, many Western scholars considered the Gītā a Brahmanic adaptation of New Testament ideas on Indian soil, and they sought to demonstrate direct Christian influence on the Gītā with its theistic declarations.[6] This interpretive orientation provided the Gītā status as a preeminent Hindu "scripture." The interest in connections between the Gītā and Christian thought is evident in the translation of Mohini M. Chatterji, *The Bhagavad Gītā or the Lord's Lay, with Commentary and Notes, as well as References to the Christian Scriptures*. Chatterji, however, makes no mention of Christian borrowings in his introduction to the translation, where Chatterji remarks that the Gītā is five thousand years old.[7] Claiming such an early date effectively silences all possibility of Christian influence. Indian scholars before and after Chatterji have ascribed great antiquity to texts and events in Indian history.

Claims of direct Christian influence on the Gītā rose and fell during the nineteenth century until, at its end, John Davies wrote of the Gītā's author—although without absolute certainty—that "he was affected, though imperfectly and obscurely, by the influence of a purer system than that which prevailed in his native country."[8] As the Gītā specifically and Indian thought and culture more generally came under closer scrutiny, similarities between Christian religious doctrine and the ideas expressed in the Gītā were no longer so readily evident.

Western claims about Christian influence on the Gītā had been directly challenged by Kashinath Trimbak Telang in the introduction to his 1875 translation. Rather than focus on the similarities or differences between Christian ideas and ideas expressed in the Gītā, Telang marshaled evidence from European scholarship to place the New Testament at a later time than previously claimed by scholars writing about Christian influences on the Gītā. Through his use of European text-critical scholarship, Telang argued convincingly that the New Testament in its present form was not as old as the time of Christ, which was assumed in the debates about borrowing in the Gītā. He went on to show that the text of the Gītā must be older than the New Testament. Establishing a foundation for the interpretation of the Gītā as a text originating within the Indian cultural tradition, Telang's argument epitomizes the major interpretive shift between the first and second centuries of modern Gītā studies.

Kashinath Trimbak Telang published a second Gītā translation in 1882. It appeared in the eminent Clarendon Press *Sacred Books of the East* Series, edited by F. Max Müller. The only non-Western scholar to contribute to this series, Telang began the introduction to his 1882 Gītā translation,

> The student of the Bhagavadgītā must, for the present, go without that reliable historical information touching upon the author of the work, the time at which it was composed, and even the place it occupies in literature, which one naturally desires, when entering upon the study of any work. . . . There is no exaggeration in saying, that it is almost impossible to lay down even a single proposition respecting any important matter connected with the Bhagavadgītā, about which any such consensus can be said to exist.[9]

Telang went on to advance a chronology that situated the origins of the Gītā in the period when the presystematic Upaniṣads and their philosophical speculations were composed. Drawing on ideas in the Gītā itself and comparing those ideas to those of other texts, Telang suggested that the text evolved from the early Upaniṣadic speculations and that it preceded Buddhism. Both internal and external evidence suggested a date no later than the third century B.C.E. As the Gītā's ideas were the product of a presystematic philosophical tradition, Telang considered the Gītā a unified composition in spite of its numerous contradictions in content.[10] By examining the place the Gītā occupies in the Sanskrit textual tradition, Telang initiated the modern scholarly inquiry into the Gītā's relation to ancient Indian textual and religious traditions.[11]

Toward a Scholarly Consensus

Scholarship about the Gītā in its second century of translation into Western languages focused on better understanding the text's historical origins, meanings, and religious and cultural significance. While the discourse on Christian influence was not forgotten immediately, the major scholarly trends in the second century included situating the text within the Sanskrit tradition and reading the text for what it said about Indian society, particularly about caste and *dharma*. Attention was also increasingly focused on understanding the Gītā's extensive commentarial tradition. While no scholarly consensus has as yet been reached about authorship, dating, and the relation of the Gītā to the *Mahābhārata*, the potential answers to these issues became more clearly defined.

Investigation of the Gītā's origins in the latter half of the nineteenth century and the early twentieth century was linked to the philological dissection of the epic *Mahābhārata*. Parallelling the archaeological search for origins, philologists sought the earliest strata of this mammoth epic to distinguish the initial tales of heroism from the later-formulated theological doctrines. Additional philological inquiry sought to identify mythological elaboration from the text's original historical facts. Differences of opinion on the relationship between the Gītā and the *Mahābhārata* abounded in this extremely speculative hermeneutic enterprise. The most prominent opinions asserted that the Gītā existed independently and was incorporated into the epic in toto or that some verses in the Gītā were original to the epic while others were added later. Rarely would it be claimed that the Gītā was part of the original *Mahābhārata* or that the Gītā was entirely constituted by interpolations to the epic. Interpretive consensus on the composition of the *Mahābhārata* would eventually coalesce around the idea that the epic had been composed or compiled between the fourth century B.C.E. and the fourth century C.E. Initially, however, with the priority and preeminence of Christianity shaping the early Western, primarily European, study of Indian religion, the theistic passages in the Gītā were thought to have been Brahmanic interpolations added to the Gītā and the epic toward the latter half of an eight-hundred-year period.

Early in the twentieth century, Richard Garbe's approach to the question of Christian influence on Indian religious thought was indicative of the shift toward a comparativist and early relativist position in scholarly discourse. Garbe wrote: "All identities and similarities in the teachings of these two great world religions, so far as *essential* matters are concerned, originated independently of one another, and therefore are of far greater significance for the science of religion than if they rested upon a loan."[12] Garbe, a German, also noted that Indians thought the Gītā a unified text, and Western Indologists thought it to contain interpolations, debating, however, over what was interpolated. Garbe, and following him a second German scholar, Rudolf Otto, sought to identify the original text of the Gītā.

Garbe's philological analysis of the "original Gītā" builds upon nineteenth-century text-critical studies that read texts for their account of history.[13] In assessing the Gītā, Garbe disagreed with his German predecessors Wilhelm von Humboldt and Adolf Holtzmann, who labeled the Gītā a Brahmanic interpolation. Garbe thought the text to have originated in a non-Brahmanic milieu. For Garbe, the original Gītā combined Bhāgavata theism with *sāṁkhya yoga* philosophical ideas. Contradictions within the Gītā indicated Brahmanic interpolations, starting with the identification of *Kṛṣṇa* and the Vedic deity *Viṣṇu*. During the second stage, *Kṛṣṇa* was identified with *Brahman*, the absolute. Finally, a Brahmanic systematization of *Bhāgavata* ideas akin to Rāmānuja's *Visīṣṭādvaita Vedānta* interpretation came to be incorporated into the text.[14] While Western scholars have applauded Garbe's sensitive reading of individual verses, they have found fault with his theory about the stages of the Gītā's composition.[15]

Rudolf Otto built upon the approach of Garbe while contributing to the early-twentieth-century discourse in the science of religion. Otto—a theologian best known for his *Das Heilige* (1917), translated as *The Idea of the Holy* (1923)—compared culturally specific representations of religious experiences and their interpretations. Like Garbe, Otto rejected the idea of Christian influence through historical contact and borrowing. Otto explained similarities between religions and religious traditions as the result of psychological propensities. In his study of the Gītā, Otto observed a discontinuity between the epic setting and the Gītā's contents. He determined that the conversation between Kṛṣṇa and Arjuna could not have occurred on the battlefield while the two great armies, dressed for war, stood ready to battle. He identified an original strata according to what seemed appropriate to the epic setting. The original text included the introduction of the warriors, verses from chapter 2 and chapter 10, much of the *Viśvarūpa Darśana* (or Arjuna's vision of Kṛṣṇa's transcendent and immanent form) in chapter 11, and finally the return to the battlefield and impending war at the end of chapter 18. Otto theorized that more than three-quarters of the seven hundred verses comprising the Gītā had been added, reversing the proportion of original and interpolated verses that Garbe identified. Without corroboration from a single manuscript nor Indian commentator, Otto identified eight distinct theological doctrines separately composed and inserted into the "ur-text" over a thousand-year period. Following Otto's work of the 1930s, argument about the stratification of the Gītā have largely fallen into disfavor in the West.[16] Otto's writings about Hinduism and the Gītā remain relatively obscure.

Two Indian scholars have recently advanced theories about the original Gītā. According to Gajanan Shripat Khair, *Quest for the Original Gītā* (1969), the changes in terminology throughout the text, the shifts in meanings, the contradictory statements, and the diverse views do not satisfy the logic, reason, and objectivity that modern readers bring to a text. Khair argues that the Gītā was composed in three stages and completed by the third century B.C.E. The first stage developed ideas of *yoga* and *karman* for the elite, refuting the encouragement to renunciation by Buddhist and Jaina proponents. The second stage occurred about a century later with a revision of *karma-yoga* ideas and the incorporation of *sāṁkhya* ideas. The third stage of textual development occurred within the next two centuries, when a devotional theism was added and the entire text reworked. This final revision enabled the text to appeal to a wider array of social classes. While Western scholars have not embraced Khair's origin theory about the Gītā being composed in three stages, by three different authors at three times, Khair's close readings and textual analysis presents valuable insights on the relationship between the Gītā and the Upaniṣads and for interpreting meanings in the Gītā.

Phulgendra Sinha (1986) has more recently advocated a very different origin theory. Sinha claims that around 800 C.E. an original Gītā grew into the *Bhagavadgītā*. Mentioning manuscripts from Bali and Farrukhabad, Sinha attempts to provide a textual basis for his claim that the original Gītā was composed of only eighty-four verses. He does not question the authenticity of these manuscripts or engage questions raised by others.[17] According to Sinha, "when this original Gītā was reworked, and rationalist thought was distorted by changing all the ancient books of philosophy, India as a nation developed a pattern of thought which had its roots not in Indian soil but in another culture. [The original text was not recognized because] all other prominent philosophic and Yoga texts were altered and suppressed. With the rediscovery of the original Gītā, I hope that the people of India will once again come to know their actual treasure and will be inspired to adopt it." For Sinha, a Śaṅkarācārya-inspired Brahmanic revival advocating monotheism produced an "abrupt and intriguing" discontinuity and decline in Indian religious philosophy and Hindu thought. Sinha contends that historians of Indian philosophy "have not dealt with the widespread revision of ancient rational philosophy which signaled the onset of the dark age of Indian culture." *The Gītā As It Was* advances a theory in the service of a contemporary, nationalist-inspired construction of Hinduism. While Sinha's philological claims appear highly suspect, his vision of a once-pure Indian religion distorted by Brahmans tangentially connects classical and modern Hinduism.[18] Sinha's speculative theory weakly challenges the now almost universally accepted idea of the Gītā's textual unity from no later than the second century C.E.

Scholars from Telang onward sought to date the Gītā through a comparison of Sanskrit linguistic forms, phrases and verses between texts. As the Gītā appeared to predate Pāṇini's "grammar," the *Aṣṭādhyāyī*,[19] historical reasoning pointed toward Upaniṣadic origins. Pāṇini forms a watershed between the Sanskrit of the ancient Vedic sacrificial tradition and the classical Sanskrit textual tradition. The epic Sanskrit of the Gītā could not be accommodated comfortably within either tradition. Others interpreted the Gītā's Sanskrit as indicating non-Brahmanic influences. Among Indological scholars of the early twentieth century, the Gītā came to be recognized as an Upaniṣadic text, with many dating the Gītā within the first half of the eight-hundred-year period theorized for the epic's development. The interrelation of the Gītā with the earlier Upaniṣadic texts was formally articulated by Colonel G. A. Jacob.[20]

R. G. Bhandarkar, in his *Vaiṣṇavism, Śaivism, and Minor Religious Systems* (1913), gleans historical information from many sources to explain the Gītā's date and content. Adhering to philological and text-critical practices of Western scholarship, Bhandarkar argues that the Gītā "was composed no later than the beginning of the fourth century before the Christian era." He also asserts that "all the points that constitute the Ekāntika religion [devotional theism] of the Bhagavadgītā are to be found in the older religious literature."[21] Specifically, he encouraged scholarly recognition of the Gītā as a conglomeration of early Upaniṣadic ideas.[22] Bhandarkar derived the Gītā's devotional theism, or *bhakti*, from the Upaniṣadic concept *upāsanā*, a contention that has not found wide acceptance. However, Bhandarkar's scholarship on the Gītā's origins within an Indian cultural historical context has shaped subsequent scholarly discourse.

Franklin Edgerton, writing in 1925, thought the Gītā to contain speculation on three principles introduced in "the Upaniṣads that show us the beginnings of the fundamental principles of later, classical Hinduism": pessimism, which Edgerton glosses as the belief in the evil of all ordinary life; the belief in transmigration and the doctrine of karma; and a belief in salvation from evil, brought about primarily through knowledge. These principles comprise the predominant concerns of later Hindu thinkers and religious sects who have ordered, explained, and interpreted these principles and their interrelationship differently. Edgerton argued that the Gītā augmented these philosophical speculations from the Upaniṣads with ideas about one's devotion to God. This enabled the text to appeal to a popular audience by elevating "the emotional and concrete above the rational and abstract *because* they are 'easier.'"[23] For Edgerton, the Gītā contains an introduction to Hinduism.

The interpretation of the Gītā by W. Douglas P. Hill (1928) illustrates the importance of Garbe's and Bhandarkar's theories on the origins of the Gītā's theism. Extracting historical information available from ancient Sanskrit sources and from modern studies of those sources, Hill concludes that Kṛiṣṇa [*sic*] was not originally a God, but a man, "helping his friends at Kurukṣetra, and . . . [a] student learning that doctrine so unwelcome to the orthodox priests."[24] The advocacy of doctrines unwelcome to the priests is one characteristic of the early Upaniṣads. Hill's work also incorporates the later stages of a late-nineteenth-century European interest in the historicity of the great world religious figures, Christ, Buddha, and Kṛṣṇa of the Gītā. The similarities in their biographies, initially a sign of borrowing, would from now on be adequately explained through discourses on universal truth or the axial age.

Interpretations of the Gītā and its meanings have been influenced by the scholarly construction of the text and its cultural historical origins. Hill provides us a commonly shared point of departure on the text for the first half of the twentieth century:

> The sectarian author wished to insist on the absolute supremacy of Kṛiṣṇa Vāsudeva, and at the same time to conciliate the enemies of his cult. . . . The poet is determined to appease the orthodox; the Veda and its *devas*, the Upaniṣads with the Vedāntic theory of Brahman-Ātman, the conceptions of *puruṣa* and *īśvara*, Sāmkhya knowledge and Yoga practice—none of these are neglected; liberation is won by work, by knowledge, by devotion—by all these three in due proportion; and over all there broods the grace of God that stirs and meets the love of man. The performance of caste-duty is taught; religious privilege is extended beyond the male twice-born to Śūdras and to women.[25]

The Gītā's catholicity proved one reason previous scholars argued about different authors at different times composing parts of the text. Following Bhandarkar, however, Hill also proclaimed the Gītā a unified text. Hill finds a unifying theme in the Gītā's representation of Kṛṣṇa as Supreme. At this time, the discussion of unity meant that a single author was held to have composed the Gītā.

Writing almost a quarter of a century after Hill and Edgerton, Sarvapalli Radhakrishnan recognized the Gītā as originating from the period between the early Upaniṣads and the rise of the philosophical systems. Combining the "living elements of Hindu life and thought into an organic unity," Radhakrishnan still remains aware of diverse perspectives within the text:

> Many apparently conflicting beliefs are worked into a simple unity to meet the needs of the time, in the true Hindu spirit, that over all of them broods the grace of God. The question of whether the Gītā succeeds in reconciling the different tendencies of thought will have to be answered by each reader for himself after he completes study of the book. The Indian tradition has always felt that the apparently incongruous elements were fused together in the mind of the author and that the brilliant synthesis he suggests and illuminates, though he does not argue and prove it in detail, fosters the true life of spirit.[26]

In addition to the Gītā's comprehensive synthesis expressing the foundations of Hinduism, Radhakrishnan also finds within the text a universality representative of perennial philosophy.

A close reading of the Gītā by, primarily, nineteenth-century scholars whose interpretations identified distinct and conflicting ideas led to the conclusion that the text contained contributions by various authors. By the mid-twentieth century, however, Telang's view on the unity of the Gītā had become widely accepted. Consensus had been achieved on some other issues, too, most notably that the text was produced between the fourth century B.C.E. and the second century C.E. Although the text would be considered a unified composition, attempts to identify an author would no longer occupy scholarly attention.

While most scholars accepted the idea of the unity of the Gītā, consensus on its cultural historical significance within ancient India was not so easily achieved. Attempts to identify the Gītā's origins and importance for the development of Hinduism depended upon other texts. About this approach, Nirad Chaudhuri remarked,

> The most surprising part of the methodology of the scholars when dealing with Hindu texts is the monotonous lament about the impossibility of fixing dates of their composition, rounded off by attributions to a definite date or a period of time which is either a century or even many centuries. And this is done without giving any reason whatsoever. . . . In the absence of external evidence, the main reliance on the scholars for establishing the date of texts has been on a comparison of ideas. Now, to try to fix the date of one idea by noting its similarity or dissimilarity to another idea whose date itself has not been established by any kind of evidence, is a procedure whose unsoundness need not be pointed out.[27]

In order to bolster the indeterminate dates of the Sanskrit sources, Chaudhuri identifies two events that scholars use to provide chronological structure: the Aryan migration of ca. 1500–1200 B.C.E., which is only a conventional hypothesis; and the life of the Buddha, from ca. 550 B.C.E. to 480 B.C.E., which possesses a fair degree of certainty. Viewing texts and their ideas in relation to these two events provides speculation with a false sense of certainty that is nowhere more evident than in scholarly attempts to date the Gītā. As Chaudhuri points out, S. Dasgupta claims the Gītā is pre-Buddhistic and so was composed by the fifth century B.C.E.; for R. C. Zaehner, who finds evidence of Buddhist influence, the Gītā becomes a text from the fifth to second centuries B.C.E.; and for K. N. Upadhyaya, who considers the Gītā a Brahmanic response to both Buddhist and Upaniṣadic speculation, the fifth or fourth century B.C.E. is appropriate.[28]

In the second century of modern Gītā studies, the discourse on the cultural historical significance of the Gītā as the foundation of Hinduism can be summarized as follows. Vedic religious practices, or Brahmanism, gives way to Hinduism as the classical Indian religion. The differences between these two religious traditions include a shift from sacrificial ritual (*yajña*) to temple worship (*pūjā*); a shift from the belief in the efficacy of ritual to bring about desired results (*karma*) to a recognition of continual devotion directed toward a particular, personally chosen deity (*bhakti*); a shift from avoiding death to a concern with *mokṣa*, or liberation; and a shift from *ṛta* involving a closed yet ordered universe that subsumed man to *dharma* and man existing within a greater social order.[29] The development of classical Hinduism for most historians of India occurs from the fourth century C.E. Lasting about four centuries, classical Hinduism is coterminous with the reign of the Guptas. After this golden age, Indian civilization declined, with both religious and political disunity, Islamic conquests, and the subsequent European domination of vast areas on the subcontinent completing India's ancient and classical historical legacy.[30]

In reviewing modern scholarship on the Gītā according to prominent themes in the latter half of the second century, scholars focused on the Gītā as a unified text and increasingly as an authoritative text for Hinduism. R. C. Zaehner (1969) considered both the text and the Gītā's contents to be unified. Zaehner explained that he was not "simply trying to read my own interpretation of the mystical phenomenon into the Gītā as critics will doubtless not be slow to assert." Hence, he said, he had "not followed the method of even so impartial and objective a scholar as Edgerton who reduced his notes to a minimum and offered his own 'interpretation' of the Gītā by rearranging it according to topic without unduly obtruding his own views."[31] Similar to Edgerton, Hill and Radhakrishnan wrote introductions that examined the meanings of key concepts without regard for the text's organization. One year prior to the publication of Zaehner's interpretation and translation, Eliot Deutsch (1968) argued that the Gītā's structure was central to understanding its message: "In order to understand the Gītā, let alone to appreciate its artistic and spiritual legacy, one must not take an argument, an appeal, a doctrine, out of its teaching context." Deutsch contends, in the essays accompanying his translation, that the Gītā uses a "progressive teaching" technique, "a step-by-step leading of the self to higher levels of insight and understanding. It [the technique] is founded, psychologically, on the belief that at any given time one is capable of grasping and assimilating only those ideas or arguments that are commensurate with one's achieved level of understanding."[32] Deutsch accepted the Gītā's unity and recognized its roots in the presystematic Upaniṣads. He encouraged readers to explore the text's philosophical unity rather than fault it for possessing inconsistencies.

Two recently published paperback translations oriented toward the classroom also situate the Gītā at the foundations of Hindu culture. Barbara Stoler Miller builds upon Deutsch's approach, claiming that "central concepts are consistently repeated and reinterpreted." She translates to bring out the Gītā's "drama, monumentality, and strong narrative movement, . . . [because] this dimension of the Gītā is usually ignored by scholars, who puzzle over the elliptical philosophical discourse without realizing that much of its meaning lies in its expressive structures."[33] Also depicting the Gītā as "the product of a time of transition," W. J. Johnson writes that the text's purpose is "to reconcile diverging world views." Johnson offers a more nuanced cultural historical contextualization of the Gītā within ancient India in the introduction to this second inexpensive translation. Identifying themes in "what we have come to call the 'Hindu' tradition," Johnson's text would not be appropriate for classes with only one day to devote to the study of ancient India, Hinduism, and the Gītā.[34] While both translators situate the Gītā at the foundations of religious Hinduism, neither translator alludes to the text's origins in presystematic Upaniṣadic thought. What remains common, however, is that the Gītā comprises a site of competing ideas and ideologies. This understanding of the Gītā has been reinforced by an increase in discourse about the text's vastly divergent commentaries.[35] In addition, from the middle of the twentieth century on, Indian civilization began to be interpreted in terms of a dynamic between a "great" tradition and many "little" traditions. The little traditions appear as a fertile source of religious ideas, producing *bhakti* poets and religious cults and movements. The religious contributions of little (including oral) traditions in vernacular languages expanded scholarly inquiry into Indian and Hindu religious texts beyond Sanskrit.[36]

Eliot Deutsch assessed the Gītā's cultural historical significance as an authoritative text for Hinduism by explaining that the Sanskrit textual tradition distinguishes between two kinds of authoritative texts. Vedic texts are designated as *śruti*. Such texts are "heard," or revealed, and originate with creation. Independent of human existence, *śruti* texts are true for all time. In contrast, *smṛti* texts are remembered. Such texts originate within and result from human experience. The separation of *śruti* and *smṛti*, Vedic and Hindu source materials, organizes most sourcebooks and readers of "Sanskrit literature."[37] Although technically *smṛti*, Deutsch states that the Gītā has the status of *śruti:* "It is in fact the most revered and celebrated text in Hinduism. Countless orthodox Hindus recite passages from it daily, and on special occasions the entire work is recited by groups of devotees."[38] J. A. B. van Buitenen had made similar observations in his study of Rāmāuja's *Bhagavadgītā* commentary (1956): "The position of the Gītā as an authoritative text is an ambiguous one. It is called an upaniṣad, but forming part of itihāsa, it is *smṛti*, albeit a *smṛti* which has more prestige than many a *śruti* text."[39] In his subsequent work on the *Mahābhārata* (1981), van Buitenen noted the epic's claim to be the fifth Veda, and he acknowledged that parts of the epic came to be accorded different cultural status. Emphasizing the Gītā's epic context by publishing a translation of the entire *Bhagavadgītāparvan*, the section of the *Mahābhārata* from which the eighteen chapters of the Bhagavadgītā are usually parsed, van Buitenen again remarked that the Gītā has "come to be accepted as a source text with an authority close to that of *śruti*."[40] The Gītā's *śruti*-like status has been reiterated and stamped authoritative by Eliot Deutsch and Lee Siegel in the *Bhagavadgītā* entry to *The Encyclopedia of Religion* (1987). Characteristic of many Indians writing about the Gītā, A. C. Bhaktivedanta Swami Prabhupāda considers the Gītā's devotional, or *bhakti*, religion and the text itself as "the essence of Vedic knowledge and one of the most important Upaniṣads in Vedic literature."[41] These assessments of the Gītā's near-*śruti* status incorporate a reflexive, Indian cultural perspective on the Gītā, but it is far from a consensus opinion.

In addition to the Gītā's status as an authoritative text, Radhakrishnan is among the many prominent voices proclaiming the Gītā's historical and contemporary importance. Dedicating his translation to Mahatma Gandhi, Radhakrishnan says in his introduction that "the *Bhagavadgītā* is more a religious classic than a philosophical treatise. It is not an esoteric work designed for and understood by the specially initiated but a popular poem. . . . Millions of Hindus, for centuries, have found comfort in this great book."[42] Similarly, the *Bhagavadgītā* entry in *The Encyclopedia of Religion* says that "the Bhagavadgītā is perhaps the most widely read and beloved scripture in all Indian religious literature. Its power to counsel and inspire its readers has remained undiminished in the almost two thousand years since its inception. . . . The text is read by all Hindus": Vaiṣṇava and Śaiva, low caste and high, urban and village dwellers "have some familiarity with and/or have been influenced by the Gītā."[43] These claims about the importance of the text for all Hindus are premised on a subtle shift; the philosophical Gītā is now labeled a religious text.

While claims for the Gītā's importance seem reasonable, other scholars claim that the Gītā possesses little or no historical importance for most Indians.[44] According to the respected historian D. D. Kosambi, the Gītā was "powerful in forming the consciousness of upper-class Hindus . . . [but]

the document plays no part in forming the social consciousness of the lower classes."[45] Nirad Chaudhuri observed that the Gītā's "specific doctrines have no place in the practice of Vaishnavaism as it has been ever since it became a popular cult. Although such a statement would sound paradoxical I would say that the more highly regarded a text is in theory the less it is followed in practice."[46] Ursula King, like Romila Thapar, also believes that the Gītā's historical role was limited. King recognizes the text's preeminence for modern, international or global Hinduism,[47] but she argues that the Gītā's absence in the premodern iconographic record is a sign that it lacked cultural historical significance for Hindus.[48] King measures the text's rise to eminent status over the last century through its increasing acceptance as a subject for artistic portrayal in popular culture such as on calendar pictures. By equating an absence of visual artifacts with a lack of importance, however, King ignores the numerous Gītā translations in vernacular languages and the commentarial traditions.[49] Without a more thorough consideration of the vernacular language and regional religious traditions, dismissal of the Gītā's importance during the pre-British period is premature. To the contrary, the absence of the Gītā as a subject for iconographic representations from the pre-British period may reflect the text's elevated, *śruti*-like status.

For the present, we must accept that little solid historical evidence has been uncovered that provides details about the social and/or religious significance of the Gītā and its influence on Indian and/or Hindu daily life, past or present. The lack of evidence may be attributable to the scholarly division of labor between text-oriented scholars in the humanities and social-scientific contextualizers. It may also reflect a scholarly interest in the theological position or positions developed in the Gītā at the expense of its practical and this-worldly applications. While Franklin Edgerton stressed the practicality and this-worldliness of the Upaniṣads and Gītā's teachings, he advanced this minority position between the two world wars (1925). It was a time when comparative cultural discourse represented the West as material and practical while the East was spiritual and otherworldly. Whatever additional reasons may be deduced, claims about the Gītā's historical importance are difficult to substantiate.

In the modern period, the Gītā has been highly esteemed and commented upon by prominent nationalists.[50] Western scholars have criticized interpretations and commentaries by Aurobindo, Tilak, and Gandhi because these moderns appropriate the text to justify religious and/or political agendas at the expense of its (ancient) scriptural and intended meaning.[51] While the Gītā has influenced and inspired modern Indians, ethnographic accounts of contemporary Indian society contain little or nothing about the Gītā's contemporary significance.

Much like the arbitrary approach to dating, scholars must get beyond a reliance on mere labels, where the attribution "philosophical" discursively defines the Gītā as unimportant to the larger population while labeling the text "religious" or "practical" serves to emphasize its influence. Questions about the cultural historical significance of the Gītā need to be posed. Even if such questions are only partially answered, the inquiry would enhance our understanding of Indian religious traditions and of the Gītā's great or little historical significance. There are numerous publications about the Sanskrit commentaries on the Gītā (with *Jñāneshvarī* constituting an exception[52] from the pre-British period). Arvind Sharma's work on Abhinavagupta's *Gītārthasaṅgraha* (1983), interesting as it is, epitomizes the scholarly tendency to stop with only a translation or description of the commentator's positions. The next challenge involves asking questions about a commentary representing the everyday understanding of people. We must also recognize that the scholarly emphasis on the study of the Sanskrit commentaries on the Gītā has resulted in a disregard for the text's history and relevance within vernacular languages. Is it possible to determine in what region or regions Sanskrit and/or vernacular manuscripts were most and least prominent? For which if any communities did the Gītā possess special importance? Can we separate the study of classical Hinduism from the contemporary appropriations of the Gītā to inquire after the text's influence on modern religious practice? These kinds of research questions need to be asked.

The theological questions emphasized within Western Gītā scholarship have pushed the Gītā's ontological significance aside. The divide has been widening since World War I when South Asian scholarly discourse joined the second major wave of disciplinary formation in U.S. higher education. Characterizing the shift from intellectual to academic study in American Indology, McCaughey remarks, "The study of the outside world, particularly its contemporary forms, remained beyond their purview."[53] From that time on, academic inquiry began to exclude certain strands of inquiry. Unlike modern political figures, the work of most modern religious exegetes and spiritual figures such as swamis, sadhus, and gurus who have written commentaries on or interpretations of the Gītā have been marginalized in Western academic discourse.[54] This situation negatively impacts contemporary awareness of how the Gītā may be influential and relevant for modern Indian thought and practice.[55] While the latter half of the twentieth century has witnessed an increased attention shown to the study of texts and their contexts,[56] research to demarcate contemporary and historical contexts of the Gītā would make a valuable contribution to the debate about the centuries-long relevance of the Gītā for millions of Hindus.

Another Translation?

In the two hundred plus years since Wilkins first translated the Gītā, the text has been translated into English more than three hundred times. Rather than focus on the failings or accomplishments of translators in their approach to specific verses or passages, the remainder of this chapter identifies issues commonly addressed by translators and examines those issues in relation to a few recent translations.

Gītā translators tend to keep two vastly different historical contexts in mind as they approach their task. Scholars who translate the Gītā have most often attempted to convey the meaning or spirit of the ancient "original" text, approximating a two-thousand-year-old message. Other translators have attempted to communicate the Gītā's message for modern life, with attention to the spiritual guidance available from the Gītā increasing over the last century. Translators adopting the latter approach have been marginalized as purveyors of Eastern spirituality by Western scholars from about the time of World War I. This is particularly true of translations by Theosophists and Indian religious figures. Alternatively, to represent the Gītā in translation as an ancient Indian text requires the identification of a context, a task we know to be burdened by uncertainty about the Gītā's date, authorship, and its seeming contradictions. As. W. J. Johnson observes:

> The question of the *Gītā's* "real" meaning does, however, raise additional problems for the translator, in so far as all translation inevitably involves interpretation, and any translation which seeks, as this one does, to render most of the Sanskrit technical terminology into English,

> interprets more than others. Where the Sanskrit original may remain open to a variety of readings, the English translation fixes on one, not arbitrarily so in the eyes of the translator, but nevertheless with a greater or lesser degree of compromise.[57]

Whatever the explicit or implicit interpretive approach of the translator, the ideal of representing the ancient meanings of the Gītā is quickly confounded by the reliance upon commentaries that are centuries old. Commentaries by Śaṅkara and Rāmānuja have been most frequently cited, with Śaṅkara's *Advaita Vedānta* interpretations more prominent in philosophically oriented discourse and Rāmānuja's *Viśiṣṭādvaita Vedānta* readings more conspicuous within discourses on religion. This cursory alignment requires clarification. A study on how commentaries have influenced modern Gītā interpretations and shaped translations would prove insightful.[58]

In opposition to the dichotomy of the Gītā's ancient and contemporary significances, the linguistic challenges translators face have led scholars to recognize two fundamental translation strategies. As Callewaert and Hemraj observe, a "formal equivalence" approach seeks to establish a word-for-word translation that "assumes that all languages are sufficiently alike in form. . . . This direct transfer neglects the fact that languages do not have the same 'shape.' No single word in any language corresponds completely in meaning with any word in another language." These and other translation incommensurabilities lead to the conclusion that "this kind of Formal Equivalence (FE) is not a satisfactory method."[59] Translators who use a dynamic-equivalence strategy begin with the "underlying structure. The source form-and-meaning-composite is analyzed. It is decomposed into basic concepts and kernel structures within the source language. Then the equivalent meaning is given all attention and equivalent kernel forms are sought in the receptor language. Finally, these are re-composed in the receptor language at the desired surface level within the cultural world into which one intends to move."[60] A dynamic-equivalence strategy is clearly evident in Van Buitenen's 1981 translation. He departs from the vast majority of Gītā's translations by breaking with "the traditional practice of enshrining each verse in its own paragraph, which thwarts easy reading and often blasts the thrust of the argument. In line with the rest of the [*Mahābhārata*] translation, the *ślokas* have been rendered in prose, the other meters in verse."[61] Van Buitenen also used a dynamic-equivalence strategy when translating individual words. For example, in chapter 3 he translates the Sanskrit terms *buddhi* (v. 1 and 2), *sāṃkhya* (v. 3), and *jñāna* v. 42), with the same English word, *insight*. Van Buitenen considered the Gītā one of "the more technically philosophical portions" of the epic, and the translation of these Sanskrit terms represent an Indian civilizational dialogue about a cultural ideal. While translations combine aspects of fixed strategies and dynamic-equivalence strategies, the latter type, emphasizing meaning over form, is more prevalent.

To resolve the problem of identifying satisfactory semantic correspondences for terms in the Sanskrit original, some translators mark selected technical terms by employing fixed lexical equivalents. For example, F. Max Müller marked *ātman* when he equated it to the English word *Self* for its peculiar ring in the introduction to volume 1 of the *Sacred Books of the East Series* (1875). Telang's 1882 translation made consistent use of this equivalent, and it appears in a majority of subsequent Gītā translations in English. By specifying and explaining selected fixed equivalences between the guest and host languages, translators can highlight specific cultural concepts. Barbara Stoler Miller recognized and accepted the shortcomings of this approach: "Although in many cases no single English term exactly expresses the Sanskrit term, and a case may be made for using alternative translations in different contexts, I have chosen to maintain a consistency of technical terms in translations in order to represent the texture of the original."[62] Miller made the most extensive use of a fixed-equivalence strategy for technical terms in her translation, providing a glossary with definitions and the fixed equivalents for more than thirty concepts. While a formal-equivalence strategy involving the entire text has not proven viable, translators often employ fixed equivalents functioning at the level of words, mimicking and marking particular concepts within a text.

The tension between the fixed and dynamic-equivalence strategies is evident in the scholarly approach to the translation of epithets in the Gītā. Multiple names for deities are handled in two ways, according to A. K. Chakravorty.[63] Those conversant with Indian mythology often find within the multiple names specific details about the complex natures or personalities of those named. To share such details with their readers, Feuerstein (1980),[64] van Buitenen (1981), and Johnson (1994) transliterate the Gītā's epithets. Other translators claim the readers of translations do not posses the cultural knowledge necessary to appreciate the implicit details about a character's personality. As a result, many Western, and even some Indian, scholars ignore the diversity of epithets in the Gītā and the portrait of personality developed through the use of multiple names. Kees Bolle, acknowledging the importance of "proper names and standard epithets," has "not made many attempts at translation" because these names have little meaning for an English reading audience.[65] Similarly, Miller remarked that transliterating the many and varied names often proves "of little significance and [they] are cumbersome."[66] She use the names Kṛṣṇa and Arjuna almost exclusively. Unintended consequences can result from this syncretistic approach, however, as when Bolle remarks that "Kṛṣṇa is none other than God, Viṣṇu himself, and in chapter 11 he reveals himself in his full glory to Arjuna."[67] By ignoring the various epithets as meaningful, the consistent use of the names Kṛṣṇa and Arjuna reinforces the devotional and monotheistic aspects of the Gītā and potentially reinforces assumptions encountered in social-evolutionary theories.

Richard Gotshalk's translation is unusual for his attempt to translate epithets as if they informed a character's personality, emotional condition, or relationship to others. Gotshalk considered the Gītā a "dialogic whole," approaching the text as a literary rather than a theological or philosophical work. His translation includes an "Index of Epithets for Arjuna and Kṛṣṇa."[68] Readers will find that epithets that refer to hair create some interesting connections within the Gītā. Kṛṣṇa is called *Keśava*, or Fair-Hair, when the Gītā begins with Arjuna and Kṛṣṇa surveying the battlefield and armies and when Arjuna resolves not to fight (I.31; II.54; II.1); when Arjuna affirms the authority of Kṛṣṇa's words (X.14); as Saṃjaya reports that Arjuna had heard *Keśava's* instructions to fight (XI.35); and as the dialogue concludes (XVIII.76). In an almost complete parallel to these epithets for Kṛṣṇa, epithets for Arjuna also possess hair imagery. The epithet *Guḍākeśa*, translated as Thick-Hair, occurs when Arjuna refuses to fight (I.24; II.9) and prior to his experience of the *viśvarūpa* form of deity (X.20; XI.7). Gotshalk's translation conveys the hair imagery in the epithets for Arjuna and Kṛṣṇa that appear at the Gītā's quintessential dramatic moments. By translating the epithets, Gotshalk's text subtly relates two incongruous and intense physical experiences (of the terrible as human and divine). Connecting these two moments highlights the often overlooked human uncertainty about heroism and the glorification of war that is part of the Gītā's relation to the *Mahābhārata*.[69]

In addition to the two translation strategies remarked upon above, an additional strategy could be incorporated to the advantage of future Gītā translations. As noted previously, Edgerton found the Gītā "unsystematic—one may fairly say helter-skelter—in its arrangement. It often contradicts itself, or at least it seems to do so."[70] While situating the text within an Upaniṣadic context and the changing religious ideology of ancient India, he identified positions and tensions within the text and he depicted themes in the Gītā as if they were coherent arguments.[71] In my reading, Edgerton's translation develops a compromise between fixed and dynamic equivalence strategies. For some key concepts, Edgerton uses two English equivalents. He translated *yajna* as *sacrifice* in chapter 4 (e.g., IV.25, 28, 30–33). All other instances of the word *yajña* are translated with *worship* (e.g., III.14–15; XVI.1; XVII.7, 11–13). This dual equivalence points to two major sources that Edgerton identifies as informing the Gītā, the Vedic sacrificial tradition and the devotional, or *bhakti*, tradition. Similarly, Edgerton employed two equivalents for the terms *puruṣa* (man and spirit) and *ātman* (soul and self). What appear to be specific equivalents employed by Edgerton illustrates what I call a "context specific" translation strategy. Unfortunately, it is a careful scrutiny of Edgerton's translation rather than his introductory remarks that identifies the potential correspondences between these equivalents and the differing ancient Indian religious traditions. For a translation to prove successful, the translator, rather than the reader, must accept responsibility for articulating the relationship between interpretation and translation.

In the introductions to their translations, Kees Bolle and J. A. B. van Buitenen also delve into the Gītā's Upaniṣadic context, drawing attention to the Gītā's ideas about religious practice, ritual, and *karman*. A brief discussion of these two translations reveals how a context specific translation strategy provides a desirable compromise to the fixed and dynamic-equivalence strategies.

According to Kees Bolle, "Terms bearing on ritual have been the most neglected by the translators of Sanskrit texts."[72] Bolle encourages study of these and other terms in his translation by including two indices: one catalogues Sanskrit equivalents for English words, the other has English equivalents for Sanskrit words. His word choices for translating the word *karman* include ritual, rite, work, action, cultic act, actions and rites, and sacrifice. Bolle even indicates that *karman* was omitted in the translation of a verse (IV.15). Exemplifying a dynamic-equivalence strategy, Bolle's translation fails to explain how equivalents refer to or represent specific Indian cultural traditions. In the future, translations should attempt to make an explicit link between the interpretation contained in the introductory essay and the interpretation that is the translation.

Van Buitenen goes further than many other scholars in connecting his interpretation and his translation. While arguing that the Gītā is an integral part of the *Mahābhārata*, van Buitenen explains the Gītā's cultural historical point of departure.

> It is against this complex background, of the diminished but continuing prestige of the Veda (now almost wholly subservient to ritualism) and the demand for the orthodoxy of *dharma*, of *saṃsāra* of rebirth now assumed to result from acts, of the mystical philosophies among the orthodox that were held superior to the practical philosophy of the act, with the correlated tendencies toward *saṃnyāsa*, and of the total rejection of the Veda and brahmin authority by the heterodox who advocated the asocial pursuit of personal salvation—it is against this background that Kṛṣṇa's doctrine of the act needs to be viewed.[73]

For van Buitenen, previous forms of thought, knowledge, and practice do not become extinct. Rather, religious ideas conflict and coexist. This characterization suggests a more complex and nuanced Upaniṣadic context.

Van Buitenen then goes on to explore how these issues find expression in the Gītā. He expounds in his introduction on such concepts and issues as yoga, *buddhi*, action, nonaction, knowledge, *bhakti* and the idea(s) of God. About these last two, he remarks: "*Bhakti*, then, appears as a form of religiosity specifically Hindu in that it allows a religious man to create out of a social polytheism a personal monotheism."[74] After further clarifying how *bhakti* allows individuals to choose a personal object of supreme devotion, van Buitenen elaborates by moving from a discussion of this idea within a generalized Indian cultural context to a discussion of the expression of this idea within the dialogue of the Gītā. Other concepts are similarly considered as van Buitenen moves from context to text, explaining cultural ideas and ideals and examining their specific representations and elaborations within the Gītā. This translation goes furthest among scholarly attempts to translate the Gītā as an ancient Indian text to connect clearly interpretation and translation. Van Buitenen sets a good example for translators, who should continue to specify how their translations represent their interpretations of both text and context.

Discussions of Gītā translations usually involve issues of accuracy,[75] aesthetics,[76] or personal preference. What I am suggesting is that translators connect their interpretive understanding of the Gītā to their translation more directly than has been the practice up to now. If translators continue their silence about how their own translations represent social and cultural movements and ideas, then new translations will not be very valuable.[77]

Greater specificity is needed in the scholarly interpretation of the Bhagavad-gītā's significance within Indian civilizational or cultural-historical contexts. Without new knowledge or without a translator's explanation of how their work expresses a civilizational context, the scholarly need for additional translations will remain small.

Notes

1. Major works cataloging or describing modern scholarship on the Gītā that do not appear elsewhere in these notes include Jagdish Chander Kapoor, *Bhagavad-Gītā, an International Bibliography of 1785–1979 Imprints* (New York: Garland, 1983); Ram Dular Singh, *Bhagavad Gītā Reference Guide: Bhagavad Gītā Rendered in the Languages of the World* (Calcutta: Bibliographic Society of India, 1984); S. C. Roy, *The Bhagavad-Gîtá and Modern Scholarship* (London: Luzac, 1941); Robert Minor, "The Bhagavadgītā and Modern Scholarship: An Appraisal of Introductory Conclusions," *Journal of Studies in the Bhagavadgītā* (1981), 1:29–60.

2. Bhagavadgītā and Gītā comprise the now standard transliterations of the text's title. In this chapter, I do not alter transliteration schemes in the titles of published works or in quotes.

3. Warren Hastings's letter appeared in Charles Wilkins, trans., *Bhăgvăt-Gēētā or Dialogues of Krĕĕshnă and Ărjōōn; in Eighteen Lectures with Notes*, reprinted with an introduction by George Hendrick (1785; Gainesville, Fla.: Scholars' Facsimile Press, 1959), 10.

4. For examples of a Christian perspective shaping interpretation, see Thomas Maurice, *The History of Hindostan*, 2 vols. (London, 1795); *Brahmanical Fraud Detected; or the Attempts of the Sacerdotal Tribe of India to invest their Fabulous Deities and Heroes with the Honours and attributes of the Christian Messiah, Examined, Exposed, and Defeated* (London, 1812); *Indian Antiquities or Dissertations of Hindostan*, 8 vols. (New Delhi: Concept Publishing, [1812–14] 1984);

and M. E. de Polier, *Mythologie des Indous*, 2 vols. (Roudolstadt: La librarie de la cour; Paris: Schoell, 1809). On the Christian view of Hinduism and the Gītā during this period, see Eric Sharpe, *The Universal Gītā: Western Images of the Bhagavad Gītā: A Bicentenary Survey* (La Salle, Ill.: Open Court, 1985), 32–46.

5. Wilhelm Halbfass, *India and Europe: An Essay in Understanding* (Albany: State University of New York Press, 1988), 84–99. For a detailed account of Hegel's interpretation of the Gītā, see Dorothy M. Figueira, "Scholarly Collusion and the Ethos of Despair: The Initial Reception of the *Bhagavad Gītā*," in *The Exotic: A Decadent Quest* (Albany: State University of New York Press, 1994), 63–89.

6. Most importantly, Franz Lorinser, *Die Bhagavadgita: Übersetzt und Erläutert* (Breslau, 1869); a translation of the introduction is found in "Traces in the Bhagavad-Gîtâ of Christian Writings and Ideas," in *Indian Antiquary* (1873) 2:283–96. An early response is found in John Muir, "On Dr. Lorinser's Bhagavad Ĝtá and Christian Writings," in *Indian Antiquary* (1875) 4:77–81. Some early twentieth-century scholiasts trace the study of Indian *bhakti* back to Lorinser's 1869 publication.

7. Mohini M. Chatterji, *The Bhagavad Gītā or the Lord's Lay, with Commentary and Notes, As Well As Reference to the Christian Scriptures*, with a preface by Ainslee Embree (New York: Causeway Books, 1960).

8. John Davies, *The Bhagavad Gītā: or The Sacred Lay*, 3rd ed. (London: Kegan Paul, Trench, Trübner, 1893), 189.

9. Kashinath Trimbak Telang, *The Bhagavadgītā with the Sanatsujātīya and the Anugītā* (Delhi: Motilal Banarsidass, [1882] 1965), 8:1–2. Surendranath Dasgupta, *A History of Indian Philosophy*, 5 vols. (Cambridge: Cambridge University Press, [1922] 1951), 1:8, situates the Gītā's origins within an Upaniṣadic context.

10. A varied literature exists about contradictions in the Gītā; for example, Betty Heimann, "Terms in Statu Nascendi in the Bhagavadgītā," in *New Indian Antiquary* (1939–40), 2:193–203; P. M. Modi, "Bhagavadgītā: Its Teaching and the Harmony of its Adhyayas," in *Acharya Dhruva Smaraka Grantha*, Acharya Drhuva commemoration volume (Ahmedabad: Gujarat Vidya Sabha, 1946), 51–56; Dr. K. V. Apte, "Contradictions in the Bhagavadgītā," *Journal of the Asiatic Society of Bombay* (1964–65), 39/40 n.s.:105–24; Arvind Sharma, "The Bhagavad Gītā: A Study in Contradiction," in *Thresholds in Hindu-Buddhist Studies* (Calcutta: Minerva, 1979), 112–33, reprinted in *Textual Studies in Hinduism* (New Delhi: Manohar, 1980), 69–102.

11. Robert Minor, *Bhagavad-Gītā: An Exegetical Commentary* (New Delhi: Heritage, 1982), 33–50. Minor summarizes debates over and opinions on authorship and dating of the Gītā. He labels all scholarly conclusions conjectural.

12. Richard Garbe, *India and Christendom: The Historical Connections between Their Religions*, Lydia Gillingham Robinson, trans. (La Salle, Ill: Open Court, 1959), 184–85. This edition contains revised, authorized translations of essays originally published in *The Monist* (1911–14).

13. The relevance of this approach is aptly demonstrated by the contents of S. P. Gupta and K. S. Ramachandran, eds., *Mahābhārata: Myth and Reality, Differing Views* (Delhi: Agam Prakashan, 1976).

14. Richard Garbe, *Die Bhagavadgītā; aus dem Sanskrit übersetzt, mit einer Einleitung über ihre ursprüngliche Gestalt* (Leipzig: Haessel, 1905); see also "Garbe's Introduction to the Bhagavadgītā," trans. N. B. Utgikar, *Indian Antiquary* 47 (1918): supp., 1–36.

15. For general responses to Garbe, see E. Washburn Hopkins, review of *Die Bhagavadgītā*, by Richard Garbe (1905), in *Journal of the Royal Asiatic Society* (1915), 384–89; and Franklin Edgerton, *The Bhagavad Gītā; or Song of the Blessed One, India's Favorite Bible* (London and Chicago: Open Court, 1925), 97–100; see also F. Edgerton, "Review of *The Original Gītā*, by Rudolf Otto," in *Review of Religion* 4 (1940): 447–50. S. K. Belvalkar issues technical responses to Garbe in *Shree Gopal Basu Mallik Fellowship Lectures on Vedanta Philosophy* (Poona: Bilvankunja, 1929), 1:91–101; and to Rudolf Otto in "Miscarriage of Attempted Stratification of the Bhagavadgītā," *Journal of the University of Bombay* (1937): 5/6:63–133.

16. Rudolf Otto, *The Original Gītā, The Song of the Supreme Exalted One*, trans. and ed. J. E. Turner (London: Allen & Unwin, 1939). See also *The Idea of the Holy: An Inquiry into the Non-rational Factor in the Idea of the Divine and Its Relation to the Rational*, trans. John W. Harvey (Oxford: Oxford University Press, 1923), and Hans Rollman, "Rudolf Otto and India," *Religious Studies Review* 5, no. 3 (1979): 199–203.

17. Jan Gonda, "The Javanese Version of the Bhagavadgītā," *Tijdschrift von Indische Taalhand-en Volken-leunde* 75 (1935): 36–82; also S. K. Belvalkar, "A Fake (?) 'Bhagavadgītā' Manuscript," *Journal of the Ganganath Jha Institute* 1 (1943): 21–31.

18. Phulgendra Sinha, *The Gītā As It Was: Rediscovering the Original Bhagavadgītā* (La Salle, Ill.: Open Court, 1987), 95, xvii, and 141, respectively. For a review of scholarly problems with the "text," see K. Kunjunni Raja, "The Bhagavadgītā: The Problems of the Text," in *Gītā Samīkṣā*, ed. E. R. Sreekrishna Sarma (Tirupati: Sri Venkateswara University, 1971), 161–68.

19. B. N. Sarma Krishnamurti, "The Grammar of the Gītā: A Vindication," in *Annals of the Bhandarkar Oriental Research Institute* (1930), 11:284–99, responds to V[aidyanath] K[ashinath] Rajwade, "The Bhagavadgītā from

Grammatical and Literary Points of View," in *Commemorative Essays Presented to Sir Ramakrishna Gopal Bhandarkar* (Poona: Bhandarkar Oriental Research Institute, 1917), 325–38. Rajwade finds the Gītā written in substandard Sanskrit and devoid of poetic qualities.

20. Colonel G. A. Jacob, A *Concordance to the Principal Upanishads and Bhagavadgītā* (Government of India reprint, Delhi: Motilal Banarsidass, [1891] 1963). See also George C. O. Haas, "Recurrent and Parallel Passages in the Principal Upanishads and the Bhagavad-Gītā, with references to other Sanskrit Texts," in *Journal of the American Oriental Society* 42 (1922): 1–43; and Dr. Satya Swarup Misra, "Linguistic Chronology of Śrīmadbhagwadgītā," in *Rtambharā: Studies in Indology, Acharya Udaya Vira Felicitation Volume*, ed. K. C. Varma et al. (Ghaziabad: Society for Indic Studies, 1986), 75–77.

21. R. G. Bhandarkar, *Vaiṣṇavism, Śaivism, and Minor Religious Systems* (Poona: Bhandarkar Oriental Research Institute, [1913] 1982), 18, 40.

22. A study of the manuscripts and translations that include the chapter-ending colophons, containing the phrase *iti śrīmadbhagavadgītāsūpniṣatsu* (within the authoritative Bhagavadgītā Upaniṣad), could prove interesting. These colophons are not included in the critical edition of the *Mahābhārata*, but they are frequently included by Indian translators.

23. Franklin Edgerton, *The Bhagavad Gītā or Song of the Blessed One: India's Favorite Bible* (Chicago: Open Court, 1925), 29 and 96, respectively. Harper Torchbooks (1964) republished Edgerton's 1925 interpretation and 1944 translation.

24. W. Douglas P. Hill, *The Bhagavadgītā*, 2nd ed. (London: Oxford University Press, [1928] 1953), 11.

25. Hill ([1928] 1953), 21–22.

26. S. Radhakrishnan, *The Bhagavadgītā* (New York: Harper Colophon, [1948] 1973), 14–15.

27. Nirad C. Chaudhuri, *Hinduism: A Religion to Live By* (New York: Oxford University Press, 1979), 32–33.

28. See, for example, K. N. Upadhyaya, *Early Buddhism and the Bhagavadgītā* (Delhi: Motilal Banarsidass, 1971).

29. See, for example, two articles by the same title, J. A. B. van Buitenen, "Dharma and Mokṣa," in *Philosophy East and West* 7, nos. 1–2 (1957): 33–40, and Daniel H. H. Ingalls, "Dharma and Mokṣa," in *Philosophy East and West* 7, nos. 1–2 (1957): 41–48.

30. Ronald Inden, *Imagining India* (Oxford: Blackwell, 1990), 109–15.

31. R. C. Zaehner, *The Bhagavad-Gītā* (New York: Oxford University Press, [1969] 1973), 3.

32. Eliot Deutsch, *The Bhagavad Gītā* (New York: Holt, Rinehart & Winston, 1968), 20–22.

33. Barbara Stoler Miller, *The Bhagavad-gītā: Krishna's Counsel in Time of War* (New York: Bantam, 1986), 162, 16.

34. W. J. Johnson, *The Bhagavad Gītā* (Oxford: Oxford University Press, 1994), ix–x.

35. Gerald James Larson, "The *Bhagavad Gītā* as Cross-Cultural Process: Toward an Analysis of the Social Locations of a Religious Text," *Journal of the Academy of Religion* 43 (1975):651–69.

36. On the limitations of the great tradition/little tradition dichotomy, see A. K. Ramanujan, *Folktales from India: A Selection of Oral Tales from Twenty-Two Languages* (New York: Pantheon, 1991), xiii–xx.

37. See, for example, Sarvapalli Radhakrishnan and Charles A. Moore, *A Sourcebook in Indian Philosophy* (Princeton: Princeton University Press, 1957); Ainslie T. Embree, ed., *Sources of Indian Tradition*, vol. 1, 2nd rev. ed. (New York: Columbia University Press, 1988). For a different configuration of classical and popular with a concentration on the concept of *bhakti*, see Cornelia Dimmitt and J. A. B. van Buitenen, eds. and trans., *Classical Hindu Mythology: A Reader in the Sanskrit Purāṇas* (Philadelphia: Temple University Press, 1978), 3–13.

38. Deutsch, *The Bhagavad Gītā* (1968), 3.

39. J. A. B. van Buitenen, *Rāmāuja on the Bhagavadgītā* (Delhi: Motilal Banarsidass, [1956], 1968), 7.

40. J. A. B. van Buitenen, *The Bhagavadgītā in the Mahābhārata: Text and Translation* (Chicago: University of Chicago Press, 1981), 12. See also Eliot Deutsch and J. A. B. van Buitenen, *A Source Book of Advaita Vedānta* (Honolulu: University of Hawaii Press, 1971), 34–36.

41. A. C. Bhaktivedanta Swami Prabhupāda, *The Bhagavadgita As It Is* (Los Angeles: Bhaktivedanta Book Trust [1968] 1972), xix.

42. Radhakrishnan *The Bhagavadgītā* [1948] 1973), 11.

43. *Encyclopedia of Religion* (1987), s.v. "Bhagavadgītā."

44. Prem Nath Bazaz, in *The Role of the Bhagavadgita in Indian History* (New Delhi: Sterling, 1975), suggests how little is known about even its contemporary meanings.

45. D. D. Kosambi, *An Introduction to the Study of Indian History*, 2nd rev. ed. (Bombay: Popular Prakashan, 1975), 128. See also D. D. Kosambi, "The Avatāra Syncretism and Possible Sources of the Bhagavad Gītā," *Journal of the Bombay Branch of the Royal Asiatic Society*, nos. 24/25 (1948–49): 121–34; "Social and Economic Aspects of the Bhagavad Gītā," in *Myth and Reality: Studies in the*

Formation of Indian Culture (Bombay: Popular Prakashan, 1962), 12–41; and, "The Historical Development of Bhagavad Gītā," reprinted from *Enquiry* (1959), in *Studies in the History of Indian Philosophy*, 3 vols., ed. D. Chattopadhyaya (Calcutta: Indian Council of Historical Research, 1978), 1:243–66.

46. Chaudhuri, *Hinduism*, 30.

47. The Gītā's prominence for global Hinduism is demonstrated, in one way, by the International Federation of Geeta Ashrams, founded in 1974 by Swami Hariharji Maharaj. This group also sponsors international conferences with a combination of lay and academic presentations.

48. Ursula King, "Iconographic Reflections on the Religious and Secular Importance of the Bhagavad-Gītā within the Image World of Modern Hinduism," *Journal of Studies in the Bhagavadgītā* 5–7 (1985–87):161–88, reprinted in *New Essays in the Bhagavadgītā: Philosophical, Methodological, and Cultural Approaches*, comp. Arvind Sharma (New Delhi: Books and Books, 1987), 161–88; and Ursula King, "The Iconography of the Bhagavad Gītā," *Journal of Dharma* 7, no. 2 (1982): 146–63. Romila Thapar, *History of India* (Penguin, 1966), 1:133–34. See also Romila Thapar, "Imagined Religious Communities? Ancient History and the Modern Search for a Hindu Identity," in *Interpreting Early India* (Delhi: Oxford University Press, 1992), 60–88.

49. For information on manuscripts and early publications of the Gītā, see Winand M. Callewaert and Shilanand Hemraj, *Bhagavadgītānuvāda: A Study in Transcultural Translation* (Ranchi: Satya Bharati, 1983), 17–38. Callewaert and Hemraj provide brief historical surveys to introduce the bibliographies for the different languages. They also include an essay on the translation of the Gītā.

50. P. M. Thomas, *Twentieth Century Indian Interpretations of Bhagavadgita: Tilak, Gandhi, and Aurobindo* (Bangalore: Christian Institute for the Study of Religion and Society, 1987), offers an exceptional study of the Gītā and Indian nationalism.

51. For example, some of the essays in Robert N. Minor, ed., *Modern Indian Interpreters of the Bhagavadgita* (Albany: State University of New York Press, 1986); also Agehananda Bharati, "Gandhi's Interpretation of the Gītā: An Anthropological Analysis," in Sibnarayan Ray, ed., *Gandhi, India, and the World: An International Symposium* (Philadelphia: Temple University Press, 1970), 57–70; and Agehananda Bharati, "The Hindu Renaissance and Its Apologetic Patterns," *Journal of Asian Studies* 29, no. 2 (1970):267–88. For a different approach, see Arvind Sharma, "The Gandhian Hermeneutical Approach to the Gītā: A Case Study in Ahiṃsā," in *Textual Studies in Hinduism* (New Delhi: Manohar, 1980), 121–33.

52. *Jñāneshvarī: Bhāvārthadīpikā*, 2 vols., translated from the Marathi by V. G. Pradhan ed. H. M. Lambert (London: Allen & Unwin, 1967).

53. Robert A. McCaughey, *International Studies and Academic Enterprise: A Chapter in the Enclosure of American Learning* (New York: Columbia University Press, 1984), 51.

54. McCaughey's historical claim suggests that publications like Ernest Wood, *The Bhagavad Gītā Explained* (Los Angeles: New Century Bookshop, 1954), or Archie J. Bahm, *Yoga: For Business Executives and Professional People* (New York: Citadel, 1965) would be more easily marginalized than earlier works such as Annie Besant, *The Bhagavad Gītā; or The Lord's Song* (Madras: Christian Literature Society, 1895) or possibly William Quan Judge, *The Bhagavad-Gītā; The Book of Devotion, Dialogues Between Krishna, Lord of Devotion, and Arjuna, Prince of India* (New York: The Path; London: Theosophical Society, 1890).

55. Dilip Bose, *Bhagavad-Gītā and Our National Movement* (New Delhi: People's Publishing House, 1981), provides some critical observations on the Gītā in contemporary India. In addition, Nataraj Guru, in *The Bhagavad Gītā* (Bombay: Asia Publishing House, 1961), examines the Gītā's modern philosophical significance. Swami Chidbhavananda, *The Bhagavad Gītā* (Tirupparaitturai: Tapovanam, 1965), and, Swami Chinmayananda, *Sreemad Bhagawad Geeta* (Madras: Chinmaya Publications Trust, 1969), have published translations and commentaries on the text's religious significance that have been ignored in Western scholarly discourse.

56. Milton Singer, "Text and Context in the Study of Contemporary Hinduism," and "Search for a Great Tradition in Cultural Performances," in *When a Great Tradition Modernizes: An Anthropological Approach to Indian Civilization* (Chicago: University of Chicago Press, [1972] 1980), 39–54, 67–80; Philip Lutgendorf, *The Life of a Text: Performing the Rāmcaritmānas of Tulsīdās* (Berkeley and Los Angeles: University of California Press, 1991).

57. Johnson *The Bhagavad Gītā* (1994), xx.

58. T. G. Mainkar, in *A Comparative Study of the Commentaries on the Bhagavadgītā* (Delhi: Motilal Banarsidass, 1969), addresses the accuracies and inaccuracies of primarily Śaṅkara among Gītā commentators.

59. Callewaert and Hemraj, *Bhagavadgītānuvāda* (1983), 72.

60. Ibid., 73.

61. Van Buitenen, *The Bhagavadgītā in the Mahābhārata* (1981), xii.

62. Miller, *The Bhagavad-Gītā*, 16. For Miller's lexicon of key words, see pp. 162–68.

63. A. K. Chakravorty, "Vedic Deities: The Mystery behind Their Multiple Names," *Indian Historical Quarterly* 38, no. 4 (1962): 292–302. For a revised Western scholarly view, see Jan Gonda, "Notes on Names and the Name of God

in Ancient India," in *Verhandelingen der Koninklijke Nederlandse Akademie van Wetenschappen* (Amsterdam) 75, no. 4, n.s.: 47 (1969–70).

64. Georg Feuerstein, *The Bhagavadgītā: Yoga of Contemplation and Action* (New Delhi: Gupta & Sons, for Arnold-Heinemann, 1980).

65. Kees Boole, trans., *The Bhagavadgītā: A new translation* (Berkeley and Los Angeles: University of California Press, 1979), 245.

66. Miller *The Bhagavad-gītā*, 17.

67. Bolle *The Bhagavadgītā*, 219.

68. Richard Gotshalk, *Bhagavad Gītā: Translation and commentary* (Delhi: Motilal Banarsidass, 1985), xiv, 239–40.

69. The vast literature on the moral and ethical dimensions of the Gītā includes Robert Hume, "Hinduism and War," *American Journal of Theology* 20 (1916): 32–44; Edgerton, *The Bhagavad Gītā* (1925), 85–88; Paul Weiss, "The Gītā: East and West," *Philosophy East and West* 4 (1954): 253–58, along with the comment and discussion by Haridas Chaudhuri, "The Gītā and Its Message for Humanity," *Philosophy East and West* 5 (1955–56): 245–53; G. W. Kaveeshwar, *The Ethics of the Gītā* (Delhi: Motilal Banarsidass, 1971); T. M. P. Mahadevan, "Philosophia Perennis in the Bhagavad-Gītā," in Satya Deva Misra, ed., *Modern Researches in Sanskrit: Dr. Veermani Pd. Upadhyaya Felicitation Volume* (Patna: Indira Prakashan, 1987), 31–60; Milton Singer, ed., *Nuclear Policy, Culture, and History*, 1987 colloquium report, University of Chicago (Chicago: Center for International Studies, 1988), 73–102, and the rejoinder by Parasu Balakrishnan, *The Bhagavad Gītā and Nuclear Policy: The Chicago Colloquium* (Bombay: Bharatiya Vidya Bhavan, 1993).

70. Edgerton, *The Bhagavad Gītā* (1925), ii. Edgerton edited volume 2 of the Mahābhārata critical text during the 1930s. The sixth book of the epic contains the *Bhagavadgita* and was published by the Bhandarkar Oriental Research Institute of Poona, under the general editorship of S. K. Belvalkar, 1943–45. Edgerton's own Gītā translation appeared in the Harvard Oriental Series, 1944; one volume contains the Sanskrit text and his own translation; a second volume contains his 1925 interpretation with emended mentalistic phraseology and Sir Edwin Arnold's 1885 translation.

71. Echoing Edgerton, Feuerstein (1980) proclaimed a synthesis of the Gītā's ideas less than desirable but a "convenient device" all the same. Feuerstein, however, organizes an interpretation into Western philosophical categories (i.e., ontology, epistemology, theology, and anthropology, without elaborating on any assumptions or problems involved in using categories originating from within Western philosophical discourse).

72. Bolle, *The Bhagavadgītā* (1979), 250.

73. Van Buitenen, *The Bhagavadgītā in the Mahābhārata* (1981), 16.

74. Ibid., 25.

75. Juan Mascaro, *The Bhagavad Gītā* (New York: Penguin, 1962), has been criticized for an emphasis on the Vedic sacrificial tradition.

76. For one of the few extended discussions of specific Gītā translations, see Gerald Larson, "The Song Celestial: Two Centuries of the Bhagavadgītā in English," *Journal of Studies in the Bhagavadgita* 3 (1983):1–55; see also Callewaert and Hemraj *Bhagavadgītānuvāda* (1983).

77. On contemporary theological and philosophical issues, see R. C. Zaehner (1969). On questions of the Gītā as an ancient text, see G. S. Khair (1969). For examples of questions translators could expand upon, see M. B. Emeneau, "Bhagavadgītā Notes," in *Mélanges D'Indianisme a la Mémoire* (Paris: Publications De L'Institute De Civilisation Indienne, 1968), 269–78; Robert Minor, "Religious Experience in Bhagavadgītā Eleven and the Text's Interpretation," *Journal of Studies in the Bhagavadgītā* (1985–87); reprinted in *New Essays in the Bhagavadgītā Philosophical, Methodological, and Cultural Approaches*, comp. Arvind Sharma (New Delhi: Books and Books, 1987), 138–50.

EIGHT Medieval Devotional Traditions

An Annotated Survey of Recent Scholarship

PHILIP LUTGENDORF

> Between the ancient and the modern lies the *bhakti* movement, the spread of a personal devotional faith. Its roots are in the far past, its flowering is still apparent today, its place in history is puzzling and fascinating.
>
> Eleanor Zelliot (1976, 143)

The aim of this chapter is to explore recent trends in the scholarly study of South Asian religious movements that flourished during the period commonly styled *medieval*. Like the term *Hindu*, this chronological designation derives from a model created by outsiders—a historical model, but one that is not unlike the religious model of "world religions" or *-isms* that is applied to the South Asian situation only with difficulty. There are unfortunate connotations associated, in Western historiography, with a period positioned between an idealized "classical" antiquity and a "renaissance" of art and learning that led directly to our "modern" era of intellectual and scientific progress. Indeed, these connotations were intended by those who first applied the term *medieval* to India, since Indologists of the last century tended to conceptualize a classical, Sanskritic past and a modern, Western-dominated age of progress, and to regard intervening centuries as an era of superstitious faith, political stagnation, and derivative culture.

The chronology of *medieval* is also problematic. A common assumption that medieval India commenced with the decline of the Gupta Empire in the mid-sixth century C.E., or roughly a century later with the death of King Harṣa, seems to have been based on the overemphasis of earlier historians on the northern part of the subcontinent, as well as on their conviction that large, centrally administered empires represented the hallmark of "classical" culture. The recent blossoming of Dravidian studies offers a corrective to the first assumption, while the second has also begun to be addressed by historical studies of regional dynasties and kingdoms. Other historians commence the medieval period with the establishment of Islamic rule over much of northern India at the close of the twelfth century; this view, too, ignores developments to the south, the complexities of Hindu-Muslim interaction, and the overall continuity of Hindu religious forms and practices. Likewise, the fixing of the terminus ad quem of the period with the consolidation of British power over much of the region at the close of the eighteenth century assumes an epochal impact for Western hegemony that some now dispute and tends to obscure the fact that many religious and cultural trends of preceding centuries continued to flourish in India's changed political climate, displaying a vitality that in some cases has continued to this day.

Yet the term *medieval India* has been widely used for so long that one can scarcely avoid it. Like many another term laden with foreign conceptual baggage, it has been translated into South Asian languages and is now widely used in Indian academic and popular writing (e.g., the Hindi adjective *madhyakālīn*). However, from the standpoint of cultural historians and scholars of religion, the period extending roughly from the decline of the Guptas to the rise of the British does have certain salient features, though these have little to do with patterns of polity and cannot be uniformly observed throughout the subcontinent. One may broadly generalize that although Vedic rites continued to be observed in many parts of India and Vedic tradition still enjoyed enormous prestige, and though the Sanskrit language continued to flourish and to produce copious literature, the "medieval" period, by any definition, must be associated with the rise of regional languages and their literatures, and the latter in nearly every case were dominated by devotional poetry characterized by a set of religious attitudes generally subsumed under the term *bhakti*. It is the literature of bhakti in its regional proliferation, and the religious practices and institutions to which it was linked, that will determine the organizing framework for this chapter, although some attention will also be given to religious writings in Sanskrit as well as to the continuity of traditions (such as Tantra) that predate the rise of modern languages.

Although the interconnectedness of many devotional traditions has long been recognized within India, the broad concept of a "bhakti movement" seems to have been another product of nineteenth-century Western scholarship, and the appropriateness of the label is a subject of ongoing debate. Apart from providing an annotated bibliography, this chapter will aim briefly to consider something of the historiography of bhakti; to note the changing ideological positions and motives of scholars who seek to represent Hindu devotional traditions in their writings.

Other limitations must be stated. Despite a number of lacunae that will be identified in due course, the available literature on medieval Hinduism is already vast and includes important works in all Indic and European languages as well as in Japanese. It also includes large amounts of English-language material published within India in recent years, much of which (thanks to the acquisition program of the Library of Congress) is available in major U.S. university libraries, but a good deal of which rehashes older scholarship or propounds sectarian positions. The present survey will be restricted to materials in English that, in my opinion, represent a substantial or original contribution to medieval studies, and it will prefer monographs and edited volumes to journal articles or individual essays, unless the latter represent unique contributions unavailable elsewhere. It will also emphasize works published by major scholarly presses since these are likely to be most available to those who may want to use this survey to guide their own or their students' reading. It is thus offered more as a sampler of exemplary research than as a comprehensive annotated bibliography—for the latter would far exceed the spatial limitations of this chapter. Undoubtedly, and despite my best efforts, there are major omissions that will be readily apparent to specialists in given regional traditions.

With a few exceptions, my survey will restrict itself to works published during the past three decades. It is appropriate to focus on this time period for several reasons. One is that the scholarship it encompasses has indeed been characterized by identifiable trends, which will be discussed shortly. Another is simply to avoid reiterating what has already been said elsewhere—specifically by Eleanor Zelliot in her comprehensive bibliographical essay "The Medieval Bhakti Movement in History," which established the regional linguistic framework I largely adhere to below.[1] The short bibliographies that follow each section of that essay—another useful feature that I will emulate—represent most of the major source materials on the vernacular traditions published in English up to the mid-1970s, and include many groundbreaking translations prepared in the late-nineteenth and early-twentieth centuries, some of which today appear dated in style or substance, but others of which remain quite useful; for all of these I refer readers to Zelliot's 1976 article. In a few instances, I will depart from Zelliot's geographical schema (e.g., to create sections on "Sūrdās and the Braj Poetic Tradition," on "Jain Traditions," and on "Goddesses"), and I will also consider works dealing with sectarian theology and ritual, or based on source materials in Sanskrit.

Apart from bibliographies, Zelliot offers a comprehensive outline of the bhakti phenomenon, which as a social historian she views as a sociocultural "movement" rather than as simply a "concept of devotional worship" (143). Whether or not one agrees with her approach, one will find her brief sketches of saint-poets and their traditions a useful précis of medieval Hindu culture, and again I will refrain from reiterating what she has already stated. Zelliot's essay also identifies a number of neglected topics that she hoped to see future research address; it is, of course, interesting to note to what extent these topics have been taken up in the last quarter of a century. Before I begin my discussion of regional traditions, however, I will offer some general observations on changing approaches to the study of medieval Hinduism.

From Pioneers to Participants

Whereas nineteenth-century Indologists tended to focus on the Sanskrit and Prakrit literatures of ancient South Asia, regarding it (on the model of Greek and Latin) as the classical foundation of an often-romanticized Aryan culture, scholars who were more actively involved in the life of the region—generally as colonial administrators or missionaries—were often attracted to medieval vernacular literature. From their ongoing contact with local people, these scholars realized that such literature represented not simply signal and often foundational works in regional languages, but also usually living traditions that continued to exercise a profound influence on everyday life. The songs and sayings of medieval saint-poets were the aphorisms of folk speech, the liturgies of popular religious practice, and the scripts of cultural festivals and pageants; to understand their content was an essential means to the ends of both efficient colonial administration and Christian proselytization. Additionally, many of these scholars were attracted to bhakti materials for another reason that had more to do with European intellectual history than with that of South Asia: in the fervent devotion expressed by Hindu saint-poets, they saw vindication for Western concepts of a monotheistic "natural religion," and the triumph of a personal deity who, however distantly and imperfectly, reflected the God of Christianity—and incidentally, challenged the concept of an impersonal absolute favored by some post-Enlightenment philosophers.[2]

Euro-American presuppositions about religion established certain models and assumptions that have continued to influence later generations of scholars, both in India and the West, and affect the course and outcome of research. When we read the learned George Grierson's (now thoroughly discredited) speculations on the Nestorian Christian "influence" on early Vaiṣṇavism or the Reverend Ernest Trumpp's patronizing dismissal of the songs of the Sikh gurus (in the preface to his 1877 translation of the *Ādi Granth*), we confront only some of the more obvious manifestations of cultural prejudice. More subtle ones have proven more intractable—for example, the tendency to separately analyze Hindu "religion" and "philosophy" (rigidly divided along post-Enlightenment Western lines) or to discuss the bhakti "reformation" using Protestant Christian categories and assumptions (such as the notion that elaborate temple ritual, codified spiritual practice, or priestly mediation necessarily herald the corruption of a more pristine or "spontaneous" religious experience).

A further limitation on early scholarship was less ideological than technological: scholars reared in a text-oriented environment tended to seek written documents for study and often displayed little sensitivity to the broader context of South Asia's vibrant oral culture. Thus they associated bhakti primarily with foundational texts and gave less attention to the sectarian practices that arose from them (but that in some cases helped to generate them) or to the texts' interaction with their audience through ongoing traditions of performance and commentary.

By the mid-twentieth century, developments both within and beyond South Asia had begun to alter scholarly approaches to the study of medieval Hinduism. The independence struggle encouraged the rise of a new indigenous scholarship, trained in Western academic disciplines of history and text-criticism but imbued with a sense of nationalism, that sought to reexamine the early literatures of the modern languages. The research of Tamil scholars like U. V. Swaminatha Aiyar and of Hindi scholars like Mataprasad Gupta and Pitambardatt Barathval led to important discoveries—such as the richness and sophistication of the long-neglected Tamil *Cañkam* literature and the connection between late-Buddhist and Nāth yogic traditions and the sectarian philosophy of the Vīraśaivas and the Sants. During succeeding decades, these insights were incorporated into the writings of Western scholars, who increasingly availed themselves of modern Indian scholarship in regional languages.

The post–World War II period witnessed a growing recognition, especially in the United States, of the importance of interdisciplinary regional studies—a scholarly agenda underwritten, in part, by the strategic concerns of the cold war and that led to the establishment of a network of National Resource Centers (NRCs) for South Asian studies. During the 1960s, NRCs at such institutions as the Universities of Chicago and Pennsylvania, Columbia University, and the University of California at Berkeley experienced significant growth in faculty numbers and greatly expanded their library holdings and other resources. Besides encouraging the study of previously neglected languages—for example, Tamil, Telugu, Bengali, and Marathi—the creation of centers led to a more holistic approach to the study of Indic culture. The impact of both these trends will be clear in the sections that follow—for example, in the striking progress in South Indian studies and in the growing number of works that straddle the disciplinary boundaries between religion, history, and anthropology or that pursue "medieval" traditions into the "modern" period.

Other concurrent factors that deserve mention include the rise of the history of religions as an academic discipline and the growing interest in fieldwork and performance studies. The altered perspective of, in Zelliot's words, "the scholar who is also participant-observer" (146) was already becoming apparent at the time of her essay; in the intervening years it has become more the rule than the exception that scholars of medieval Hinduism carry out fieldwork among communities whose religious practice is influenced by the songs of saint-poets.

If colonial scholars were constrained to view Hindu devotional traditions from the perspective of a largely unchallenged assumption of the superiority of the Christian worldview, the generations of Euro-American scholars writing since the 1960s have come of age in a, so to speak, altered state of consciousness, characterized by a new willingness to take inner experience seriously and by an enhanced appreciation—sometimes accompanied by a degree of personal commitment—for the religious inspiration of South Asian culture. Although this perspective has not been without excesses of its own, the best scholarship of recent years has been characterized by an ecumenism (in the broadest sense) that would have been unthinkable half a century ago and by a sympathetic effort at cross-cultural translation of religious ideals. Other significant trends of the recent past have included renewed interest in Śaivism, both Tamil and Kashmiri, in the Rāma devotional tradition (both relatively neglected in the first wave of post-1960s research), and in the role of women and goddesses in medieval Hinduism. Each of these developments will be referred to again when I consider specific regional traditions below.

Medieval Hinduism in Regional Perspective

Tamil Vaiṣṇavism and Śaivism

In a well-known allegory in the ca. sixteenth-century *Bhāgavata māhtāmya* (a glorification of the *Bhāgavata purāṇa*), bhakti appears as a woman who begins her life story with the statement, "I was born in the Dravidian country."[3] The remark reflects the apparent belief of North Indian devotees of that period, particularly Vaiṣṇavas, that they participated in a tradition that had originated in the south. Early scholars of bhakti generally accepted this belief, which was sometimes attributed to the influence of the four *ācāryas* associated with major Vaiṣṇava sects, all of whom had been southerners. Similarly, it was widely assumed that the *Bhāgavata purāṇa* itself—the most influential Vaiṣṇava text in Sanskrit—had been composed in South India and that it incorporated many themes first expressed in Tamil, which, alone among the medieval vernacular languages, possessed a classical literature largely independent of that of Sanskrit. But a more precise understanding of the nature of the southern influence had to await a new generation of scholars trained in Dravidian languages.

Indeed, recent scholarship has convincingly demonstrated that the origins of the bhakti orientation cannot be understood without reference to the earliest literature of Tamil—which, incidentally, predates the "medieval" period as it is usually understood. This literature was first introduced to a Western audience through A. K. Ramanujan's *The Interior Landscape* (1967). A second, much-expanded anthology of translations, with an afterword containing additional discussion of literary conventions and the oral nature of Tamil poetry, appeared in 1985 as *Poems of Love and War*. Apart from presenting elegant translations, Ramanujan introduced the system of *aintiṇai*, or "five landscapes," developed by Tamil aestheticians to represent the moods of love. But since ancient Tamil poetry was largely "secular" in its themes (and for this reason was virtually ignored in Tamil Nadu during the late-medieval period) its relevance to later bhakti poetry was not readily apparent in Ramanujan's pioneering work (hence *The Interior Landscape* was not cited by Zelliot). Two works published in 1975, however—K. V. Zvelebil's *Tamil Literature* and George L. Hart's *The Poems of Ancient Tamil*—posit continuities between classical and medieval Tamil. Hart questions the "secular" label for *cañkam* poetry, arguing that it was precisely the Tamil concept of sacred power localized in specific places and persons—especially in women, kings, and in certain sites and stones—that made possible the sensitivity to landscape and emotion manifested both in the *akam/puram* poetic system and in the religious perspective characteristic of early bhakti. A further statement of Hart's theory, with special reference to the role of the king and the Tamil concept of sin, appears in his 1979 essay "The Nature of Tamil Devotion."

Friedhelm Hardy's ambitious study, *Viraha-Bhakti* (1983), provides more detailed evidence of the influence of both *cañkam* literary conventions and of Tamil folk traditions (especially of ecstatic emotionalism and possession) on the early Āḻvārs—the line of Vaiṣṇava singers active between roughly the sixth and tenth centuries—as well as on the author of the *Bhāgavata* and, through it, on northern traditions of Kṛṣṇa bhakti, most notably on Caitanya and the Bengal school. Hardy's scholarship is meticulous, and his insights are far-reaching—I must still echo his observation on the need for research into the neglected pāñcarātra and āgamic traditions in order better to understand the relationship between temple religion and early bhakti and into the complex interaction of early Tamil Śaiva and Vaiṣṇava traditions; his prose renderings of Āḻvār hymns, however, are intended more to illustrate his arguments than to stand on their own as poetry.

Expressive translations of poems from the *Tiruvāymoḻi* of Nammāḻvār (a.k.a. Śaṭakōpaṉ, ca. 880–930)—the most revered song-cycle of Tamil Vaiṣṇavism—appear in A. K. Ramanujan's *Hymns for the Drowning* (1981), accompanied by an illuminating afterword relating them to broader themes in bhakti traditions. R. D. Kaylor and K. K. A. Venkatachari's *God Far, God Near* (1981) presents an analysis of Nammāḻvār's religious outlook and practice as derived from the *Tiruvāymoḻi*. Additional poems by Nammāḻvār, together with selections from three other Vaiṣṇava and two early Śaiva saint-poets, are offered in Norman Cutler's *Songs of Experience* (1987). A notable feature of Cutler's work is his effort to apply the insights of contemporary literary criticism to the analysis of a "poetics of Tamil devotion"—an approach rarely applied to bhakti texts. Āṇṭāḷ (ca. ninth century), the only woman among the twelve major Āḻvārs, is the subject of an admirable study and translation by Vidya Dehejia (1991) that includes an introductory essay and translations of the thirty short songs of the *Tiruppāvai* and of fourteen longer poems. Dehejia also authored a more comprehensive study of early Tamil bhakti, *Slaves of the Lord, the Path of the Tamil Saints* (1988); it offers a solid introduction to both the Śaiva and Vaiṣṇava saint-poets, a modest anthology of translations, and excellent illustrations of the later iconography of the saint-poets.

The earliest major rendering of the Rāmāyaṇa story in a regional language was also composed in Tamil. The massive epic *Irāmāvatāram*, by Kampaṉ, created during the height of Cola dynastic power in the late-twelfth century, is regarded by many as the supreme masterpiece of medieval Tamil literature. A single but pivotal book of this epic is available through George Hart and Hank Heifetz's translation *The Forest Book of the* Rāmāyaṇa *of Kampaṉ* (1988), which strives to convey something of the baroque and incandescent quality of its language and imagery and includes an essay introducing Kampaṉ and his age. A serviceable complete rendering of *Irāmāvatāram* is available in six volumes translated by P. S. Sundaram under the auspices of the government of Tamil Nadu (1989–94). A fascinating glimpse into a modern performance tradition based on Kampaṉ's text is provided by Stuart Blackburn's study of puppeteer-exegetes in Kerala, *Inside the Drama House* (1996).

A major contribution to the study of the Śaiva Nāyaṉmār tradition is Indira Viswanathan Peterson's *Poems to Śiva: The Hymns of the Tamil Saints* (1989). Besides offering highly readable translations of several hundred songs from the anthologies collectively known as *Tēvāram*—which constitute the first seven books of the Tamil Śaiva canon—Peterson provides stimulating literary and contextual analysis, including a study of contemporary traditions of liturgical chanting in Śaiva temples. The seventh book of the *Tēvāram*, and its poet, the eccentric ca. ninth-century Cuntarar, is the subject of David Shulman's comprehensive study *Songs of the Harsh Devotee* (1990), which includes translations of one hundred *patikams*, or lyric poems. A visceral legend of another early Śaiva saint, Cekkiḻār, is featured in Shulman's study of "filicide and devotion," *The Hungry God* (1993). Māṇikkavācakar (also ninth century), an influential saint-poet considered antecedent to the Nāyaṉmārs, receives extended treatment in Glenn Yocum's *Hymns to the Dancing Śiva* (1982), a theological and contextual study of the poet's celebrated *Tiruvācakam* that offers many translated excerpts from that work; hymns from the *Tiruvācakam* also appear in Cutler's *Songs of Experience*.

The songs of the early Tamil saint-poets display passionate attachment to specific images and religious sites and often allude to regular ceremonial worship. In time, both groups of singers became canonized by sectarian traditions that incorporated their emotional bhakti into theological and ritual systems, generally encoded in Sanskrit manuals. To Dhavamony's important study of the Śaiva Siddhānta system (cited by Zelliot) has been added K. Sivaraman's *Śaivism in Philosophical Perspective* (1983), while the importance of the city of Chidambaram (a.k.a. Citamparam) and its great temple to Śiva in medieval Tamil culture is the subject of B. Natarajan's *The City of the Cosmic Dance: Chidambaram* (1974). A focused study of this temple and its unique priestly lineage, based on textual and iconographic sources and on extensive fieldwork, is presented in Paul Younger's *The Home of the Dancing Śivaṉ* (1995). In addition, several essays in Fred Clothey and J. Bruce Long's *Experiencing Śiva* (1983) reflect on various aspects of the context of Tamil Śaiva tradition. Shulman's richly detailed study *Tamil Temple Myths* (1980) explores the manner in which the conventions of *caṅkam* poetry, the emotionalism of bhakti singers, and the intermingling of Aryan and Dravidian legend all coalesced in the mature temple culture of the medieval south. The historical studies of Burton Stein, such as his 1973 essay "Devi Shrines and Folk Hinduism in Medieval Tamilnadu" and his earlier article "The Economic Function of a Medieval Hindu Temple" (1960) represent a valuable resource for scholars interested in the changing role of the temple.

Richard Davis's *Ritual in an Oscillating Universe* (1991) is based on analysis of Sanskrit Śaivāgama manuals; it examines both their philosophy and their utilization in the great, royally endowed temples of Kanchipuram; and on a more theoretical level it shows the limitations of the academic distinction between "theology" and "ritual." C. J. Fuller's anthropological research on the Śaiva goddess temple of Mīnākṣī at Madurai is presented in *Servants of the Goddess* (1984); though primarily concerned with the modern period, it provides some historical information. Also notable is Fred Clothey's 1978 study of one of the important "minor" deities of South Indian Śaivism, *The Many Faces of Murukan*. Finally, Karen Pechilis Prentiss, in *The Embodiment of Bhakti* (1999), provides an unusually ambitious diachronic study of Tamil Śaiva bhakti traditions spanning the seventh to fourteenth centuries. Tracing the rise of Śaiva bhakti through the songs of itinerant saint-poets, the iconography of royally patronized temples, and the crystallization and exegesis of a sectarian canon she argues for a shared meaning of bhakti as "a theology of embodiment" (9), using this notion to critique prevailing academic assumptions.

Though rooted in the devotionalism of the Āḻvārs and indeed canonizing their songs as a "Tamil Veda," the influential Śrīvaiṣṇava sect is more characteristically represented by theological writings in Sanskrit and by a vast commentarial literature in Maṇipravāḷa—a hybrid literary dialect of Tamil and Sanskrit. Neither of these genres was discussed by Zelliot, but both have received major treatments in recent years. Important sources for the study of the most influential expounder of this tradition remain J. A. B. van Buitenen's *Rāmānuja on the Bhagavadgītā* (1968), which contains a condensed rendering of the *Gītābhāṣya* commentary; John B. Carman's study of the polarity of the immanence and transcendence of Viṣṇu, *The Theology of Rāmānuja* (1974), and Robert C. Lester's *Rāmānuja on the Yoga* (1976), which examines the great *ācārya*'s views on the means to *mokṣa* or liberation. An attempt to reconstruct the teachings of Rāmānuja's venerated precursor Yāmuna (early-eleventh century) may be found in Walter

G. Neevel's *Yāmuna's Vedānta and Pāñcarātra* (1977), which examines the synthesis of Vedic tradition with popular temple ritual in early Śrīvaiṣṇavism. Rāmānuja's metaphysics are the subject of Julius Lipner's study *The Face of Truth* (1986). Vasudha Narayanan's *The Way and the Goal* (1987) examines early Śrīvaiṣṇava understandings of the nature of bhakti and the importance of *prapatti* ("reliance on grace").

A central concept of Śrīvaiṣṇavism is that of *ubhayavedānta*, a "dual vedanta" woven of Sanskrit and Tamil strands; this was particularly elaborated in the commentarial literature of the twelfth to fifteenth centuries, which sought to reconcile the ecstatic mysticism of the Āḻvārs with the Vedic philosophical and ritual tradition. Two important studies of this literature are K. K. A. Venkatachari's *The Maṇipravāḷa Literature of the Śrīvaiṣṇava Ācāryas* (1978), which focuses on Periyavāccāṉpiḷḷai, the "emperor of commentators," and John Carman and Vasudha Narayanan's *The Tamil Veda* (1989), which examines the commentary of Pillan (ca. 1150), cousin and disciple of Rāmānuja, on the *Tiruvāymoḻi* of Nammāḻvār. The latter work includes some sixty pages of translations of *Tiruvāymoḻi* verses, with Pillan's exegesis, and is a welcome addition to the scant scholarly literature that seriously examines the indigenous analysis of bhakti poetry. Also notable in this regard are Francis X. Clooney's two sensitive studies of Śrīvaiṣṇava exegesis, *The Art and Theology of Śrīvaiṣṇava Thinkers* (1994) and *Seeing Through Texts* (1996)—the latter combining an examination of twelfth-to-fourteenth-century sectarian exegetes with a contemporary dialogue between Roman Catholic and Śrīvaiṣṇava theologians. Another volume by Narayanan, *The Vernacular Veda* (1994), adds more data on the tradition's subsequent performative and ritual elaboration of the Āḻvars's songs, together with some forty pages of liturgical texts translated by Carmen, Clooney, Narayanan, and Ramanujan. Śrīvaiṣṇava temple culture was also the subject of a 1977 article by Friedhelm Hardy, "Ideology and Cultural Contexts of the Śrīvaiṣṇava Temple."

Classical Tamil

Hart, George L. "The Nature of Tamil Devotion." In *Aryan and Non-Aryan in India*. Madhav M. Deshpande and Peter E. Hook, eds., 11–33. Michigan Papers on South and Southeast Asia, no. 14. Ann Arbor: Center for South and South East Asian Studies, 1979.

———. *The Poems of Ancient Tamil: Their Milieu and Their Sanskrit Counterparts*. Berkeley and Los Angeles: University of California Press, 1975.

Ramanujan, A. K. *The Interior Landscape: Love Poems from a Classical Tamil Anthology*. Bloomington and London: Indiana University Press, 1967.

———. *Poems of Love and War: From the Eight Anthologies and the Ten Long Poems of Classical Tamil*. New York: Columbia University Press, UNESCO, 1985.

Zvelebil, Kamil V. *Tamil Literature*. Leiden: E. J. Brill, 1975.

Tamil Vaiṣṇavism

Blackburn, Stuart W. *Inside the Drama House: Rāma Stories and Shadow Puppets in South India*. Berkeley and Los Angeles: University of California Press, 1996.

Carman, John B. *The Theology of Rāmānuja: An Essay in Interreligious Understanding*. New Haven and London: Yale University Press, 1974.

Carman, John B., and Vasudha Narayanan. *The Tamil Veda: Pillan's Interpretation of the* Tiruvāymoḻi. Chicago: University of Chicago Press, 1989.

Clooney, Francis Xavier. *The Art and Theology of Śrīvaiṣṇava Thinkers*. Madras: T. R. Publications, 1994.

———. *Seeing through Texts: Doing Theology among the Śrīvaiṣṇavas of South India*. Albany: State University of New York Press, 1996.

Cutler, Norman. *Songs of Experience: The Poetics of Tamil Devotion*. Bloomington and Indianapolis: Indiana University Press, 1987. [Also contains Śaiva poetry of the Nāyaṉmārs.]

Dehejia, Vidya. *Āṇṭāl and Her Path of Love: Poems of a Woman Saint from South India*. Albany: State University of New York Press, 1991.

———. *Slaves of the Lord: The Path of the Tamil Saints*. New Delhi: Munshiram Manoharlal, 1988.

Hardy, Friedhelm. "Ideology and Cultural Contexts of the Śrīvaiṣṇava Temple." *Indian Economic and Social History Review* 14 (1977): 119–51.

———. *Viraha-Bhakti: The Early History of Kṛṣṇa Devotionalism in South India*. Delhi: Oxford University Press, 1983.

Hart, George L., and Hank Heifetz, trans. *The Forest Book of the* Rāmāyaṇa *of Kampaṉ*. Berkeley and Los Angeles: University of California Press, 1988.

Kaylor, R. D., and K. K. A. Venkatachari. *God Far, God Near: An Interpretation of the Thought of Nammāḻvār*. Bombay: Ananthacharya Indological Research Institute Series No. 5 (supplement), 1981.

Lester, Robert C. *Rāmānuja on the Yoga*. Madras: Adyar Library and Research Center, 1976.

Lipner, Julius. *The Face of Truth: A Study of Meaning and Metaphysics in the Vedantic Theology of Rāmānuja*. Albany: State University of New York Press, 1986.

Narayanan, Vasudha. *The Way and the Goal: Expressions of Devotion in the Early Śrī Vaiṣṇava Tradition*. Washington, D.C.: Institute for Vaiṣṇava Studies, 1987.

———. *The Vernacular Veda: Revelation, Recitation, and Ritual*. Columbia: University of South Carolina Press, 1994.

Neevel, Walter G. *Yāmuna's Vedānta and Pāñcarātra: Integrating the Classical with the Popular*. Harvard Dissertations in Religion, 10. Missoula, Mont.: Scholars Press, 1977.

Ramanujan, A. K. *Hymns for the Drowning*. Princeton: Princeton University Press, 1981.

Sundaram, P. S. *Kamba Ramayanam*. 6 vols. Madras: Government of Tamil Nadu, 1989–94.

van Buitenen, J. A. B. *Rāmānuja on the Bhagavadgītā*. Delhi: Motilal Banarsidass, 1968.

Venkatachari, K. K. A. *The Maṇipravāla Literature of the Śrīvaiṣṇava Ācāryas*. Bombay: Ananthacarya Research Institute Series, No. 3, 1978.

Tamil Śaivism and Śaiva Siddhānta

Clothey, Fred W. *The Many Faces of Murukan: The History and Meaning of a South Indian God*. The Hague: Mouton, 1978.

Clothey, Fred W., and J. Bruce Long, eds. *Experiencing Śiva*. Columbia, Mo.: South Asia Books, 1983.

Davis, Richard. *Ritual in an Oscillating Universe: Worshipping Śiva in Medieval South India*. Princeton: Princeton University Press, 1991.

Fuller, C. J. *Servants of the Goddess: The Priests of a South Indian Temple*. Cambridge: Cambridge University Press, 1984.

Natarajan B. *The City of the Cosmic Dance: Chidambaram*. Delhi: Orient Longman, 1974.

Peterson, Indira Viswanathan. *Poems to Śiva: The Hymns of the Tamil Saints*. Princeton: Princeton University Press, 1989.

Prentiss, Karen Pechilis. *The Embodiment of Bhakti*. New York: Oxford University Press, 1999.

Shulman, David Dean. *Tamil Temple Myths: Sacrifice and Divine Marriage in the South Indian Śaiva Tradition*. Princeton: Princeton University Press, 1980.

———. *Songs of the Harsh Devotee: the Tēvāram of Cuntaramūrttināyaṉār*. Philadelphia: Department of South Asia Regional Studies, University of Pennsylvania, 1990.

———. *The Hungry God: Hindu Tales of Filicide and Devotion*. Chicago: University of Chicago Press, 1993.

Sivaraman, K. *Śaivism in Philosophical Perspective: A Study of the Formative Concepts, Problems, and Methods of Śaiva Siddhānta*. Delhi: Motilal Banarsidass, 1983.

Stein, Burton. "Devi Shrines and Folk Hinduism in Medieval Tamilnadu." In *Studies in the Language and Culture of South Asia*, ed. Edwin Gerow and Margery D. Lang, 75–90. Seattle: University of Washington Press, 1973.

———. "The Economic Function of a Medieval Hindu Temple." *Journal of Asian Studies* 19 (1960):163–76.

Yocum, Glenn E. *Hymns to the Dancing Śiva: A Study of Māṇikkavācakar's* Tiruvācakam. New Delhi: Heritage, 1982.

Younger, Paul. *The Home of the Dancing Śivaṉ*: The Traditions of the Hindu Temple in Citamparam. New York: Oxford University Press, 1995.

The Vīraśaivas and Mādhva Vaiṣṇavas of Karnataka

The poetry of the "heroic" Śaiva devotees of Karnataka (tenth to twelfth century), whose followers are also known as Liṅgāyats for the Śaiva emblem they wear, was introduced to Western readers through the powerful renderings of A. K. Ramanujan's *Speaking of Śiva* (1973), which also contains an introduction to the teachings of the sect. This widely circulated translation promoted further academic study of the tradition, as did the concern among some Liṅgāyats in India to assert a formal religious identity distinct from the Hindu mainstream. Among the major translations to appear subsequently is Zvelebil's *The Lord of the Meeting Rivers* (1984), which includes additional *vacanas* of Basavaṇṇa (1105–67), an early and influential Vīraśaiva leader. He is also the focus of a playfully titled study by sociologist Karigonder Ishwaran, *Speaking of Basava* (1992), which uses him as a lens for a thoughtful reexamination of the Liṅgāyats that questions their incorporation within the framework of bhakti and indeed of Hinduism. A substantial appendix offers additional translated *vacanas* "of sociological significance." Ishwaran's earlier study, *Religion and Society among the Lingayats of South India* (1983) made a solid attempt at a brief but comprehensive survey of the tradition, from its origins to the present day.

R. Blake Michael's textual and historical research is reflected in *The Origins of Vīraśaiva Sects* (1992), an in-depth study of the *Śūnyasampādane* (which Michael translates as "the graduated attainment of the void"), a collection of *vacanas* that represent, Michael argues, the theological debates of the coalescing sectarian tradition, operating within the cosmopolitan religious environment of the early Vijayanagara Empire. Twenty poems from that same anthology also appeared in elegant translations by Judith Kroll and U. R. Anandtha Murthy (1988). The teachings of Tontada Siddhaliṅgeśvara (ca. 1400), who is credited with having developed, in a cycle of 701 poems, a systematic metaphysics for the sect, are available in awkward translations by Armando Menezes and S. M. Angadi in *Siddhaliṅga, Essence of Ṣaṭsthala* (1978). R. C. Hiremath's study of *Sri Channabasavesvara* (1978), a nephew of Basavaṇṇa, who flourished ca. 1160 and became a prominent poet-theologian, is comprehensive, though marred by sectarian platitudes.

Recent research has also examined the role of women in the Liṅgāyat tradition: despite its sweeping title, Leela Mullatti's *The Bhakti Movement and the Status of Women* (1989) is primarily a focused sociological study of the contemporary Liṅgāyat community of Dharwar, Karnataka, although it includes information on the historical position of women in the sect. Vijaya Ramaswamy's provocatively titled *Walking Naked* (1997) is more historical and much broader in scope, with chapters on early Tamil traditions, the Vīraśaivas, and the Vārkarī sect of Maharashtra.

Although the Vīraśaiva tradition originated in what is now Karnataka and much of its *vacana* literature was composed in Kannada, the Liṅgāyat sect spread into adjoining regions of Andhra Pradesh, and it was in Telugu that Pālkuriki Somanātha (ca. thirteenth century) composed its great hagiographic work, the *Basava purāṇa*. This has appeared in an annotated translation by Velcheru Narayana Rao and Gene H. Roghair as *Śiva's Warriors* (1990). Apart from presenting the legendary life of Basavaṇṇa, this text glorifies a number of other sectarian figures, emphasizing their radical devotion to Śiva and their anti-Brahman ideology.

Like Rāmānuja in the Tamil country, the great Vaiṣṇava theologian of Karnataka, Madhva (a.k.a. Ānandatīrtha, ca. 1238–1317), wrote in Sanskrit and expounded a modified system of Vedānta that became the basis for an influential sect. Though not associated with a line of early poet-singers (and omitted by Zelliot), Madhva's frankly dualistic philosophy reflected fervent devotion to Viṣṇu and became an influential school during the Vijayanagar period. Useful introductions to Madhva's thought may be found in *Viṣṇu, the Ever Free* (1985), by Ignatius Puthiadam, and in T. P. Ramachandran's *Dvaita Vedānta* (1976).

Eric J. Lott's *Vedantic Approaches to God* (1980) is an illuminating comparative study of the thought of Śaṇkara, Rāmānuja, and Madhva. Much useful material can also be found in B. N. Krishnamurti Sharma's massive *History of the Dvaita School of Vedānta and Its Literature* (1981); the same author's *Śrī Madhva's Teachings in His Own Words* (1961) is another useful compendium; it contains an appendix devoted to the later Haridāsa tradition of saint-poets, who flourished during the late Vijayanagara period. Some were initiated into the Mādhva tradition but were devotees of the god Viṭṭhala at Pandharpur (in present-day Maharashtra) or of Venkaṭeśvara at Tirupati (in modern Andhra). An inelegant translation of 175 songs of Purandaradāsa (ca. 1480–1564), who is said to have been the founder of this tradition, was published by D. Seshagiri Rao in 1978 as *Anthology of Saint-Singer Shri Purandara Dasa*. William J. Jackson's *Songs of Three Great South Indian Saints* (1998) offers brief studies and more polished translations of the hymns of the Mādhva Kannada singers Purandaradāsa and Kanakadāsa (ca. 1509–1607), as well as selections from the thousands of Telugu songs that the Śrīvaiṣṇava saint-poet Tallapaka Annamācārya (ca. 1408–1503) composed for the patron deity of Tirupati hill.

The renewal of interest in the Vijayanagar Empire following excavations at the ruins of its capital city at present-day Hampi has led to a number of publications containing material relevant to religious scholars. The articulation of South Indian notions of divine kingship in this greatest of medieval Hindu empires is briefly touched on in a largely descriptive but richly illustrated "preliminary report" by Fritz et al., *The Royal Centre at Vijayanagara* (1984), while much data on the sectarian orientations of the court and on popular practice within the empire may be found in Konduri Devi's *Religion in Vijayanagara Empire* (1990) and in Anila Verghese's *Religious Traditions at Vijayanagara as Revealed Through Its Monuments* (1995). The most comprehensive historical treatment is Burton Stein's *Vijayanagara* (1989). An early account of the empire containing much legendary and religious material is provided in Phillip Wagoner's *Tidings of the King* (1993), a study and translation of the early-seventeenth-century Telugu text *Rāyavācakamu*.

Vīraśaivism

Hiremath, R. C. *Sri Channabasavesvara: Life and Philosophy*. Dharwad: Karnatak University, 1978.

Ishwaran, K. *Religion and Society among the Liṅgāyats of South India*. Leiden, E. J. Brill, 1983.

———. *Speaking of Basava: Lingayat Religion and Culture in South Asia*. Boulder: Westview, 1992.

Kroll, Judith, and U. R. Anantha Murthy, trans. "Twenty Vacanas from *Śūnya Sampādane*." *Poetry World*, no. 2 (1988): 55–67 (special issue edited by Daniel Weissbort).

Menezes, Armando, and S. M. Angadi, eds. and trans. *Siddhaliṅga, Essence of Ṣaṭsthala: Vacanas of Tontada Siddhaliṅgeśvara*. Dharwad: Karnatak University, 1978.

Michael, R. Blake. *The Origins of Vīraśaiva Sects*. Delhi: Motilal Banarsidass, 1992.

Mulatti, Leela. *The Bhakti Movement and the Status of Women: A Case Study of Vīraśaivism*. New Delhi: Abhinav, 1989.

Narayana Rao, Velcheru, and Gene H. Roghair. *Śiva's Warriors: The Basava Purāṇa of Pālkuriki Somanātha*. Princeton: Princeton University Press, 1990.

Ramanujan, A. K. *Speaking of Śiva*. Harmondsworth, Eng.: Penguin Books, 1973.

Ramaswamy, Vijaya. *Walking Naked: Women, Society, and Spirituality in South India*. Shimla: Indian Institute of Advanced Study, 1997.

Zvelebil, Kamil V. *The Lord of the Meeting Rivers: Devotional Poems of Basavaṇṇa*. Delhi and Paris: Motilal Banarsidass/UNESCO, 1984.

Vaiṣṇavism

Jackson, William J. *Songs of Three Great South Indian Saints*. Delhi: Oxford University Press, 1998.

Lott, Eric J. *Vedantic Approaches to God*. New York: Barnes & Noble, 1980.

Puthiadam, Ignatius. *Viṣṇu, the Ever Free*. Madurai: Dialogue Series, 1985.

Ramachandran, T. P. *Dvaita Vedānta*. New Delhi: Arnold Heinemann, 1976.

Seshagiri Rao, D. *Anthology of Saint-Singer Shri Purandara Dasa*. Bangalore: Parijatha Publications, 1978.

Sharma, B. N. Krishnamurti. *History of the Dvaita School of Vedānta and Its Literature: From the Earliest Beginnings to Our Own Time*. 2nd rev. ed. Delhi: Motilal Banarsidass, 1981.

———. *Śrī Madhva's Teachings in His Own Words*. 1961; reprint, Bombay: Bharatiya Vidya Bhavan, 1978.

Vijayanagara

Devi, Konduri Sarojini. *Religion in Vijayanagara Empire*. New Delhi: Sterling, 1990.

Fritz, John M., George Michell, and M. S. Nagaraja Rao. *The Royal Centre at Vijayanagara: A Preliminary Report*. Melbourne: University of Melbourne, Department of Architecture and Building, 1984.

Stein, Burton. *Vijayanagara*. Cambridge: Cambridge University Press, 1989.

Verghese, Anila. *Religious Traditions at Vijayanagara as Revealed through Its Monuments*. New Delhi: Manohar, 1995.

Wagoner, Phillip. *Tidings of the King: A Translation and Ethnohistorical Analysis of the* Rāyavācakamu. Honolulu: University of Hawaii Press, 1993.

Telugu Traditions

At its height, the Vijayanagara Empire included portions of the Telugu-speaking region, and the popular Telugu Śaiva poet Dhūrjaṭi (mid-to-late-sixteenth century), is traditionally said to have been patronized by one of its kings. The collaboration of poet Hank Heifetz and translator Velcheru Narayana Rao has produced an anthology of his songs praising the deity enshrined in the Kāḷahasti temple, *For the Lord of the Animals* (1987). This highly readable translation includes an afterword by Narayana Rao that constitutes a major contribution to the neglected area of Telugu studies.

The continued activity of saint-poets and theologians in the post-Vijayanagara period is documented in *The Power of the Sacred Name* (1994), which assembles V. Raghavan's scholarly writings on what he terms the *nāmasiddhānta* tradition of the Kaveri delta region, ca. 1650–1850. Presented with two introductory essays by editor William J. Jackson, the collection treats of the sectarian leaders Āyyāvāl, Bodhendra, Sadāśiva, Brahmendra, Nārāyaṇa Tīrtha, and Sadguru Svāmī, as well as the renowned Telugu singer and composer Tyāgarāja (1767–1847; Raghavan's study of the latter originally appeared as a separate volume in 1983). Telugu poetry of a very different sort is made available through well-crafted and witty translations in the anthology *When God Is a Customer* (1994), compiled by Narayana Rao, A. K. Ramanujan, and David Shulman, which offers seventeenth and eighteenth-century erotic-devotional songs composed by male poets who assumed the literary personae of courtesans.

Although Gene H. Roghair's *The Epic of Palnāḍu* (1982) is primarily concerned with the subject matter and performance of a contemporary Telugu oral tradition, it deserves citation here since certain aspects of its tale cast light on the interaction of Vaiṣṇavism and Śaivism (especially Vīraśaivism) in medieval Andhra.

Heifetz, Hank, and Velcheru Narayana Rao. *For the Lord of the Animals—Poems from the Telugu: The* Kāḷahastīśvara Śatakamu *of Dhūrjaṭi*. Berkeley and Los Angeles: University of California Press, 1987.

Jackson, William J., ed. *The Power of the Sacred Name: V. Raghavan's Studies in Nāmasiddhānta and Indian Culture*. Delhi: Sri Satguru Publications, 1994.

Narayana Rao, Velcheru, A. K. Ramanujan, and David Shulman. *When God Is a Customer: Telugu Courtesan Songs by Kṣetrayya and Others*. Berkeley: University of California Press, 1994.

Raghavan, V. *Tyāgarāja*. New Delhi: Sahitya Akademi, 1983.

Roghair, Gene H. *The Epic of Palnāḍu: A Study and Translation of Palnāṭi Vīrula Katha, a Telugu Oral Tradition from Andhra Pradesh*. New York: Oxford University Press, 1982.

Maharashtrian Vaiṣṇavism

The considerable literature produced in English on the saint-poets of Maharashtra during the 1920s and 1930s—much of it the labor of the prolific U.S. missionary Justin E. Abbott of Poona—remains a standard source for research on this tradition, which flourished in a region that historically served as a bridge between northern and southern India. The foundational classic of the Marathi language, the *Bhāvārthadīpikā* of Jñānadeva (a.k.a. Jñāneśvar, ca. 1275–96), better known as the *Jñāneśvarī*, an epic-length commentary on the *Bhagavadgītā* in the style of an oral storyteller, is available in a competent but somewhat turgid translation prepared by V. G. Pradhan during the 1940s and reissued by State University of New York Press in 1987. The same translation, more readably rewritten by an American devotee, Swami Kripananda, was published by the same press in 1989 as *Jnaneshwar's Gītā*. Apart from these efforts, however, Jñānadeva's masterpiece—which combines fervent devotion to Kṛṣṇa with an advaitin philosophical stance—remains little studied outside of India.

It has long been known that Jñānadeva was influenced by the Nāth yogic tradition, and his second major work, now available in a sensitive translation by the Marathi poet Dilip Chitre as *Anubhavamrut: The Immortal Experience of Being* (1996), indeed confirms this link, as well as the influence of the Kashmiri Śaivism of Abhinavagupta. Chitre feels that its eight hundred verses provide a bridge between these traditions and the later Vārkarī tradition of Vaiṣṇava bhakti.

With the exception of Nāmdev, who will be considered below in my discussion of literature on the Sants, the works of the poets in this tradition—especially those who, like Eknāth (1548–1600), were devoted to the regional cult center of Viṭṭhala (a.k.a. Viṭhobā) at Pandharpur—remain accessible primarily in the translations cited by Zelliot. Another exception is Tukārām (ca. 1608–49), the last and most popular of the major Vārkarī saint-poets, whose songs, known as *abhaṅgas*, have been translated in Prabhakar Machwe's short anthology, *Tukārām's Poems* (1977), and in a larger and very effective translation by Chitre, *Says Tukā* (1991). Several have been powerfully rendered—along with songs by the women poets Muktābāi and Janābāi—by Arun Kolatkar in "Translations from Tukaram and Other Saint-Poets" (1981). A brief biography and assessment of Tukaram is provided in Bhalchandra Nemade's *Tukaram* (1980).

Eknāth's prolific output included an imaginary debate between a Hindu and a Muslim—a rare treatment of such interaction in premodern literature—that has been the subject of an article by Zelliot (1982); another of Zelliot's essays is devoted to this Brahman poet's *bhāruḍs*, songs put into the mouths of a remarkably broad cast of street characters in the old city of Paithan ("Eknath's *Bhāruḍs*," 1987). The untouchable saint Cokhāmela (ca. fourteenth century), to whom are attributed some three hundred songs, has been the subject of articles by Zelliot (1981) and by Charlotte Vaudeville (1977), and is featured in the translation, *On the Threshold: Songs of Chokhamela*, by Rohini Mokashi-Punekar (2002). Other significant contributions to the secondary literature on this tradition include portions of Shankar Gopal Tulpule's surveys *Classical Marathi Literature* (1979) and *Mysticism in Medieval India* (1984). To Deleury's important monograph on the Viṭṭhala cult (cited by Zelliot), has been added Gunther Sontheimer's *Pastoral Deities in Western India* (1989), an illuminating study of the worship of the folk deities Birobā, Mhaskobā, and Khandobā.

An anthology of essays on *Religion and Society in Maharashtra*, edited by Milton Israel and N. K. Wagle (1987), contains much additional material on the medieval saint-poets and their enduring influence. The militant seventeenth-century Rāma devotee Samarth Rāmdās, who is credited with having inspired Shivājī and promoted the worship of Hanumān in Maharashtra, awaits serious study in English; he is the subject of several piously uncritical monographs, such as V. P. Bokil, *Rajguru Ramdas* (1979). Rāmdās's most famous work, the didactic and mystical *Dāsbodh*, has been made accessible through an unannotated but serviceable translation by W. G. Tambwekar (1992).

The cult of Dattātreya in medieval Maharashtra and beyond warrants further investigation. Antonio Rigopoulos's *Dattātreya* (1998) makes a start, citing much of the relevant literature and offering some interesting speculation about this composite deity. The once-secret sect of the Mahānubhāvas, dating from the thirteenth century, which claims Dattātreya as part of its spiritual lineage, has been the subject of two fine monographs by Anne Feldhaus. *The Religious System of the Mahānubhāva Sect* (1983) outlines the Mahānubhāva cosmology and translates a major (if enigmatic) sectarian treatise; *The Deeds of God in Ṛddhipur* (1984) presents the biography of the playful and irreverent Guṇḍam Rāu̱l (thirteenth century), whom Mahānubhāvas revere as a divine incarnation; it also offers a vivid picture of life in a medieval village in central Maharashtra. A third book by Feldhaus, coauthored with the venerable Marathi scholar S. G. Tulpule, *In the Absence of God* (1992) offers an annotated translation of the sectarian treatise *Smṛtisthal*. Another Mahānubhāva poet, Hayagrīvācārya (ca. 1265–1324), composed (in Ian Raeside's words) "the first account in a modern Indian language of the 'Western tradition' of the Kṛṣṇa legend" (emphasizing Kṛṣṇa as savior-hero rather than pastoral lover); it has been translated and analyzed by Raeside, in *Gadyarāja* (1989).

Bokil, Vinayak Pandurang. *Rajguru Ramdas*. Poona: Kamalesh P. Bokil, 1979.

Chitre, Dilip, trans. *Anubhavamrut: The Immortal Experience of Being*. New Delhi: Sahitya Akademi, 1996.

———, trans. *Says Tukā*. New York: Penguin, 1991.

Feldhaus, Anne. *The Deeds of God in Ṛddhipur*. New York: Oxford University Press, 1984.

———, ed. and trans. *The Religious System of the Mahānubhāva Sect: The Mahānubhāva Sūtrapāṭha*. New Delhi: Manohar, 1983.

Feldhaus, Anne, and S. G. Tulpule. *In the Absence of God*. Honolulu: University of Hawaii Press, 1992.

Israel, Milton, and N. K. Wagle, eds. *Religion and Society in Maharashtra*. Toronto: University of Toronto Centre for South Asian Studies, 1987.

Kolatkar, Arun, trans. "Translations from Tukaram and Other Saint-Poets." *Journal of South Asian Literature* 27, no. 1 (1982):109–14.

Kripananda, Swami. *Jnaneshwar's Gītā: A Rendering of the Jnaneshwari*. Albany: State University of New York Press, 1989.

Machwe, Prabhakar. *Tukaram's Poems*. Calcutta: United Writers/Firma KLM, 1977.

Mokashi-Punekar, Rohini. *On the Threshold: Songs of Chokhamela*. New Delhi: Book Review Literary Trust, 2002.

Nemade, Bhalchandra. *Tukaram*. New Delhi: Sahitya Akademi, 1980.

Pradhan, V. G., trans. *Jñāneśvarī*. Ed. H. M. Lambert. 1948; Albany: State University of New York Press, 1987.

Raeside, Ian. *Gadyarāja: A Fourteenth Century Marathi Version of the Kṛṣṇa Legend*. Bombay: Popular Prakashan, 1989.

Rigopoulos, Antonio. *Dattātreya: The Immortal Guru, Yogin, and Avatāra*. Albany: State University of New York Press, 1998.

Sontheimer, Gunther Dietz. *Pastoral Deities in Western India*. Translated by Anne Feldhaus. New York: Oxford University Press, 1989.

Tambwekar, W. G., trans. *Dasbodh, an English Version*. Bombay: Shri Samarth Ramdas Swami Krupa Trust, 1992.

Tulpule, Shankar Gopal. *Classical Marathi Literature: From the Beginning to A.D. 1818*. A History of Indian Literature 9:4. Wiesbaden: Harrassowitz, 1979.

———. *Mysticism in Medieval India*. Wiesbaden: Harrassowitz, 1984.

Vaudeville, Charlotte. "Cokhāmela, an Untouchable Saint of Maharashtra." *South Asian Digest of Regional Writing* 6 (1977):60–79.

Zelliot, Eleanor. "Chokhāmela and Eknāth: Two *Bhakti* Modes of Legitimacy for Modern Change." In *Tradition and Modernity in Bhakti Movements*, ed. Jayant Lele. Leiden: E. J. Brill, 1981.

———. "Eknath's *Bhāruḍs*: The Sant as Link between Cultures." In *The Sants: Studies in a Devotional Tradition of India*, ed. Karine Schomer and W. H. McLeod. Delhi: Motilal Banarsidass, 1987.

———. "A Medieval Encounter between Hindu and Muslim: Eknāth's Drama-poem *Hindu Turk Samvād*. In *Images of Man: Religion and Historical Process in South Asia*," ed. Fred Clothey. Madras: New Era, 1982.

Tantra, Yoga, and Kashmir Śaivism

The medieval period witnessed a great proliferation of esoteric schools oriented toward the worship of Śiva and various attendant deities, and/or one or another goddess, and utilizing complex ritual and psychophysical techniques to produce experiences of transcendence. Much of the lore of these Tantric traditions was communicated orally, but their written teachings were generally in Sanskrit, and this category of literature is excluded from Zelliot's survey of bhakti. This need not be the case, however, for the Tantric schools influenced bhakti movements in significant ways and were in turn influenced by them. A Nāth yogi influence on the Vīraśaivas and Sants has long been assumed; the Kashmiri Trika school of Tantric Śaivism produced not only a complex metaphysics but also fervent devotional songs to Śiva, and its religio-aesthetic theories would eventually find echoes in late-medieval Vaiṣṇava practices. It should also be noted that Tantric ritual played a prominent role in many devī cults and influenced prominent śākta texts such as the *Devī māhātmya* and the *Devī bhāgavata purāṇa* (the latter also betrays Vaiṣṇava influence); hence, there is some overlap in subject matter between the materials considered here and those treated below in the section on goddesses.[4]

Research on Tantra has been frustrated by the extreme difficulty and indeed deliberate obscurity of some of its texts, but recent years have seen significant contributions to the disentangling of the tradition's enigmas. Among general works, one may cite Teun Goudriaan and Sanjukta Gupta's comprehensive survey *Hindu Tāntric and Śākta Literature* (1981) and Andre Padoux's *Vāc* (1990)—the latter a pioneering study of Hindu concepts of the word and their ramifications for Tantric practices based on mantra. Alexis Sanderson's work, primarily published in articles, includes insightful research on Kashmir Śaivism and early Buddhist Tantra; an example of his approach may be found in "Meaning and Tantric Ritual" (1995). Mark S. G. Dyczkowski's *The Canon of the Śaivāgama and the Kubjikā Tantras of the Western Kaula Tradition* (1988) draws heavily on Kashmiri Śaiva sources in sketching canonical literature and also introduces the widespread cult of the goddess Kubjikā. Introductory material on the South Indian Śākta tradition may be found in Douglas R. Brooks's *The Secret of the Three Cities* (1990), which includes a translation of the *Tripura upaniṣad* and its eighteenth-century commentary by Bhāskararāya of the Śrīvidyā school. This school is the subject of Brooks's second book, *Auspicious Wisdom* (1992), which focuses on the highly developed cult of the goddess Lalita Tripurasundarī among South Indian Brahmans.

Other significant studies devoted to individual texts include Teun Goudriaan's *The Vīṇāśikhatantra* (1985), which introduces and translates an early northern Tantra that worships Śiva in the awesome form of the royal deity Tumburu, and J. A. Schoterman's *The Yonitantra* (1980), a text concerned with the famous Kāmākhya Devī shrine in Kamarupa, Assam, but showing a distinct Vaiṣṇava influence; Schoterman's introduction includes a fascinating treatment of the historic relationship between Viṣṇu/Kṛṣṇa and the cult of the *yoni*. A single work of the Kubjikā school, the ca. twelfth-century *Ṣaṭsāhasra saṃhitā*, has appeared in a partial translation by J. A. Schoterman (1982). Sanjukta Gupta's annotated translation of the

Lakṣmī Tantra (1972) makes available a major Vaiṣṇava pāñcarātra text. A work deserving special mention is David G. White's monumental study of the interaction of Ayurvedic, yogic, Tantric, and alchemical systems in medieval South Asia, *The Alchemical Body* (1996). White's work sheds much new light on the theories and practices of the influential Nāth tradition and includes accounts of historic and modern exponents of *siddha* practices intended to produce transcendent experiences and physical immortality (and gold).

Trika metaphysics and cultic practice have attracted wide interest in recent decades, in part due to the inspiration of Swami Lakshman Joo, a modern exponent of the tradition, and of the Maharashtrian guru Muktananda, who looked to it for inspiration; important studies have been published both in India and in the United States, where a major series of new works and reprints has been sponsored by State University of New York Press. In *The Doctrine of Vibration* (1987), Mark S. G. Dyczkowski outlines the doctrines and practices of the Trika school; Paul Eduardo Muller-Ortega's *The Triadic Heart of Śiva* (1989) emphasizes the symbolism of the heart in the writings of Abhinavagupta (Muller-Ortega's study also includes a concise review of previous scholarship). The mystical practices and goals of the tradition are further discussed in Deba Brata Sen Sharma's *The Philosophy of Sādhana* (1991).

An ambitious series of translations of key Trika texts has been undertaken by Jaideva Singh, a student of Swami Lakshman Joo: it includes the *Vijñānabhairava*, an early treatise on yoga (1979); the ca. ninth-century *Śiva Sūtras*, with their commentary, *Vimarśinī*, by Kṣemarāja, a pupil of Abhinavagupta (1979); the *Spanda-kārikās*, another set of commentaries on the *Śiva Sūtras*, focusing on the doctrine of vibration (1980); and the *Pratyabhijñāhṛdayaṃ*, a ca. eleventh-century digest of the Pratyabhijñā system of philosophy, attributed to Kṣemarāja (1982)—reissued by State University of New York Press in 1990 as *The Doctrine of Recognition*. Singh's translation of a major work by Abhinavagupta, *Parātrīśikā-vivaraṇa*, appeared as *A Trident of Wisdom* (1989).

Though the Trika school is best known for its rigorous philosophy, the tradition also produced emotional poetry characterized by many of the themes and concerns found in other devotional movements. The moving Sanskrit hymns to Śiva of Utpaladeva (ca. 900–950), *Śivastotrāvalī*, which are still chanted daily by some Kashmiri Hindus, serve to remind us that not all bhakti poetry is in vernacular languages. These hymns are featured in a highly accessible translation by Constantina Rhodes Bailly, *Shaiva Devotional Songs of Kashmir* (1987). An earlier rendering by N. K. Kotru appeared in 1985.

Devotional songs to Śiva in the Kashmiri language were composed by the ca. fourteenth-century woman ecstatic Lal Ded (or Lallā Ded); early translations of her songs (noted by Zelliot) have been supplemented by B. N. Parimoo's *The Ascent of Self* (1978). The same author's *Lalleshwari* (1987) presents the traditional biography of the poet, with some additional translations.

Tantra and Yoga

Brooks, Douglas Renfrew. *Auspicious Wisdom: The Texts and Traditions of Śrīvidyā Śākta Tantrism in South India*. Albany: State University of New York Press, 1992.

———. *The Secret of the Three Cities: An Introduction to Hindu Śākta Tantrism*. Chicago and London: University of Chicago Press, 1990.

Dyczkowski, Mark S. G. *The Canon of the Śaivāgama and the Kubjikā Tantras of the Western Kaula Tradition*. Albany: State University of New York Press, 1988.

Goudriaan, Teun. *The Vīṇāśikhatantra: A Śaiva Tantra of the Left Current*. Delhi: Motilal Banarsidass, 1985.

Goudriaan, Teun, and Sanjukta Gupta. *Hindu Tāntric and Śākta Literature*. Wiesbaden: Harrasowitz, 1981.

Gupta, Sanjukta, trans. *Lakṣmī Tantra: A Pāñcarātra Text*. Leiden: E. J. Brill, 1972.

Padoux, Andre. *Vāc: The Concept of the Word in Selected Hindu Tantras*. Trans. Jacques Gontier. Albany: State University of New York Press, 1990.

Sanderson, Alexis. "Meaning and Tantric Ritual." In *Essais sur le rituel*, ed. Anne-Marie Blondeau and Kristofer Schipper, 15–95. Louvain and Paris: Peeters, 1995.

Schoterman, J. A. *The Yonitantra*. New Delhi: Manohar, 1980.

———, ed. and trans. *The Ṣaṭsāhasra Saṃhitā*, chapters 1–5. Leiden: E. J. Brill, 1982.

White, David Gordon. *The Alchemical Body: Siddha Traditions in Medieval India*. Chicago: University of Chicago Press, 1996.

Kashmir Śaivism

Bailly, Constantina Rhodes. *Shaiva Devotional Songs of Kashmir: A Translation and Study of Utpaladeva's* Shivastotrāvalī. Albany: State University of New York Press, 1987.

Dyczkowski, Mark S. G.. *The Doctrine of Vibration: An Analysis of the Doctrines and Practices of Kashmir Shaivism*. Albany: State University of New York Press, 1987.

Kotru, N. K., trans. *Śivastotravalī of Utpaladeva*. Delhi: Motilal Banarsidass, 1985.

Muller-Ortega, Paul Eduardo. *The Triadic Heart of Śiva: Kaula Tantricism of Abhinavagupta in the Non-Dual Śaivism of Kashmir*. Albany: State University of New York Press, 1989.

Parimoo, B. N., trans. *The Ascent of Self: A Re-interpretation of the Mystical Poetry of Lalla Ded*. Delhi: Motilal Banarsidass, 1978.

Sen Sharma, Deba Brata. *The Philosophy of Sādhana, with Special Reference to the Trika Philosophy of Kashmir*. Karnal, Haryana: Natraj Publishing House, 1983; reprint, Albany: State University of New York Press, 1991.

Singh, Jaideva, trans. *Pratyabhijñāhṛdayaṃ, the Secret of Self-Recognition*. 1963; rev., Delhi: Motilal Banarsidass, 1982; reissued as *The Doctrine of Recognition: A Translation of the Pratyabhijñāhṛdayaṃ*, Albany: State University of New York Press, 1990.

———. *Śiva Sūtras: The Yoga of Supreme Identity*. Delhi: Motilal Banarsidass, 1979.

———. *Spanda-Kārikās, the Divine Creative Pulsation: The Kārikās and the Spandanīrṇaya*. Delhi: Motilal Banarsidass, 1980.

———. *A Trident of Wisdom*. Albany: State University of New York Press, 1989.

———. *Vijñānabhairava; or, Divine Consciousness: A Treasury of 112 Types of Yoga*. Delhi: Motilal Banarsidass, 1979.

North Indian Traditions

When we turn to the late-medieval traditions of India north of the Vindhyas, it becomes more difficult to arrange poets and movements according to regional or linguistic criteria. This is partly due to the fluidity of dialects during the period and to the use by saint-poets of composite literary *bolīs* in order to reach wider audiences. The sectarian movements these poets inspired were similarly geographically diffused. The *Ādi Granth*, the sacred scripture of Sikhism, for example, is generally thought to be written in "Punjabi," but much of its poetry is in composite dialects of Western Hindi, and it includes songs by the Maharashtrian tailor Nāmdev and the Banarsi weaver Kabīr. The latter's songs and sayings are found in virtually all North Indian languages, and the weaver-saint has been claimed by both Muslim Sufis and Rāmānandī Vaiṣṇava sectarians. In view of such problems, the Indian scholars who authored pioneering studies of bhakti literature earlier in this century frequently relied on a schema that cut across regional and linguistic lines by dividing devotees into *nirguṇa* and *saguṇa* traditions—those devoted to an "attributeless" Absolute and those who revered a personal deity "with attributes" of iconography and mythology. Although based on indigenous categories dating back to at least the time of the *Bhagavadgītā*, this schema, too, has proven problematic since many saint-poets, on closer examination, elude assignment to either camp.

In surveying the North Indian material, I find some of Zelliot's divisions obsolete; for example, she places Kabīr with the "Rāmānandīs"—alluding to a now-questioned Vaiṣṇava claim that he was a disciple of the shadowy Rāmānanda—and isolates Tulsīdās as a "solitary, influential figure" (he was the latter but not the former, although the subsequent Rāma bhakti tradition remains relatively unstudied). Instead, I will discuss Kabīr together with the later Sant traditions that looked to him for inspiration and will separately examine the Sikhs and the sectarian traditions of Kṛṣṇa and Rāma bhakti.

Kabīr and the Sants

An important insight of twentieth-century Indian scholarship has been the recognition of the link between certain North Indian exponents of primarily *nirguṇa* bhakti and worship of the divine Name—collectively known as Sants—and earlier traditions of *haṭha yoga* taught by the wandering mendicants known as Nāths, whose influence extended southward into Maharashtra and Karnataka. Nāth imagery is common in the utterances attributed to Kabīr, who is believed to have lived in Banaras during the late-fifteenth to the early-sixteenth century. Though something of Kabīr's fame was communicated to Western readers through Tagore's famous 1915 translation of Bengali songs (nearly all of which are now thought to represent later voices in the pan–North Indian Kabīr tradition), the critical study of Kabīr in English had made little progress by the time of Zelliot's 1976 essay. The past quarter of a century, however, has seen significant contributions to the understanding of Kabīr's life and work. Charlotte Vaudeville's *Kabīr* (1974) was the first volume of a projected two-volume translation of the *Kabīr granthāvalī*—one of three major recensions of what are thought to be the oldest and most authentic Kabīr poems. It offered the poet's aphorisms in the form of couplets (*sākhīs*), in conscientious if not compelling translations. More important, a magisterial opening essay synthesized the best of Indian and European research on Kabīr and his milieu. The projected second volume was to comprise the longer lyric poems from the *granthāvalī*, but Vaudeville eventually became convinced that this collection was itself far too inclusive and inauthentic. She instead culminated her Kabīr research with *A Weaver Named Kabīr* (1993), a large volume comprising a complete revision of her introductory essay and translations of the poems (from all three recensions) that she had concluded were most likely to have been composed by Kabīr.

Selections from a second major recension—that preserved by the Kabīr Panth sect in eastern Uttar Pradesh—appeared in translation as *The Bījak of Kabīr* by Linda Hess and Shukdev Singh (1983). Terse, impassioned, and at times vulgar, these lucid translations effectively communicate the poet's iconoclastic perspective to a modern Western audience; useful appendices include an essay by Hess on Kabīr's use of paradoxical "upside-down" language. The third major recension of Kabīr's poems—more than a hundred compositions contained in the Sikh scripture as collected in ca. 1604—likewise appear in a commendable translation by Nirmal Dass, *Songs of Kabīr from the Ādi Granth* (1991). An illuminating introduction examines the relationship of Kabīr to the early Sikh gurus and offers critical evaluation of the work of Hess, Singh, and Vaudeville. Also recommended, especially for college courses, is the brief but lucid section on Kabīr in John Stratton Hawley and Mark Juergensmeyer's anthology *Songs of the Saints of India* (1988).

To the earlier studies that trace Kabīr's legend and the subsequent elaboration of sects claiming inspiration from him have been added works that take a more critical look at the development of Kabīr hagiography: David C. Scott's *Kabīr's Mythology* (1985) and David N. Lorenzen's *Kabīr Legends and Anantadās's Kabīr Parachāi* (1991). The latter includes a critical edition and translation of the earliest known collection of Kabīr legends and an introductory essay that attempts to establish Kabīr's probable chronology. Additional material on Kabīr, together with Lorenzen's essays on other *nirguṇa* saint-poets, appear in his *Praises to a Formless God* (1996).

Other figures and branches of the Sant tradition have also received notable study, especially by the prolific Belgian scholar Winand Callewaert. His extensive work on the poetry and sectarian following of Dādū Dayāl (ca. 1544–1603), a Gujarati cotton-carder widely revered in northwest India whose followers assembled important manuscript anthologies of

Sant poetry, is discussed in the 1978 monograph *The Sārvāṅgī of the Dādūpanthī Rajab* and in his subsequent study *The Hindi Biography of Dādū Dayāl* (1988). In collaboration with Mukund Lath of Rajasthan, Callewaert offered a critical edition and partial English translation of *The Hindi Padāvalī of Nāmdev* (1989), containing songs of the influential Maharashtrian saint (ca. 1270–1350), who traveled widely in the North. The result of exhaustive research in Rajasthani archives, this study includes copious notes on topics ranging from sectarian and musical traditions to variations in scribal orthography and the utility of computers in editing medieval manuscripts; the translations are spare and effective. Nāmdev is also the subject of a thoughtful introductory study by Nirbhai Singh, *Bhagata Nāmadeva in the Guru Grantha* (1981), which utilizes both Marathi and Sikh sources. The Banarsi cobbler Raidās (a.k.a. Ravidās, ca. 1450–1520), whose fervent poetry remains a major source of religious inspiration to many North Indian Dalits, is the subject of a study and translation by Callewaert and Peter Friedlander, *The Life and Works of Raidās* (1992).

The problem of the religious identity of the Sants, their morphological kinship to Nāths and Sufis, and their characteristic mode of reverence for a living guru who serves as a channel for and personification of the Absolute, is investigated at length in Daniel Gold's *The Lord as Guru* (1987). Gold also traces the history of the Rādhāsoāmī branches of the tradition, several of which have continued to flourish in the modern period. Further discussion of these traditions is found in Mark Juergensmeyer's *Radhasoami Reality* (1991). The later Sant poet Garīb Dās of Rohtak in modern Haryana (ca. 1717–74) is the subject of a study by K. C. Gupta (1976) that includes texts of numerous *dohās* and songs accompanied by serviceable translations. Additional writings by Callewaert, Gold, Hess, Juergensmeyer, Vaudeville, Zelliot, and other scholars of the *nirguṇa* tradition appear in *The Sants* (1987), a comprehensive anthology edited by Karine Schomer and W. H. McLeod. Also relevant is Hawley and Juergensmeyer's *Songs of the Saints of India*, which includes brief but informative essays on Raidās and Guru Nānak, together with elegant translations of their selected songs.

Kabīr

Dass, Nirmal, trans. *Songs of Kabīr from the Ādi Granth*. Albany: State University of New York Press, 1991.

Hawley, John Stratton, and Mark Juergensmeyer. *Songs of the Saints of India*. New York: Oxford University Press, 1988.

Hess, Linda, and Shukdev Singh, trans. *The Bījak of Kabīr*. San Francisco: North Point Press, 1983.

Lorenzen, David N. *Kabīr Legends and Anantadās's* Kabīr Parachāi. Albany: State University of New York Press, 1991.

———. *Praises to a Formless God: Nirguṇī Texts from North India* Albany: State University of New York Press, 1996.

Scott, David C. *Kabīr's Mythology: The Religious Perceptions, Doctrines, and Practices of a Medieval Indian Sant*. Delhi: Bharatiya Vidya Prakashan, 1985.

Vaudeville, Charlotte, trans. *Kabīr*. Oxford: Clarendon Press, 1974.

———. *A Weaver Named Kabīr*. New Delhi: Oxford University Press, 1993.

Other Sant Traditions

Callewaert, Winand M. *The Hindi Biography of Dādū Dayāl*. Delhi: Motilal Banarsidass, 1988.

———. *The Sārvāṅgī of the Dādūpanthī Rajab*. Leuven: Departement Orientalistiek, Katholieke Universiteit, 1978.

Callewaert, Winand M., and Mukund Lath. *The Hindi Padāvalī of Nāmdev*. Delhi: Motilal Banarsidass, 1989.

Callewaert, Winand M., and Peter Friedlander. *The Life and Works of Raidās*. New Delhi: Manohar. 1992.

Gold, Daniel. *The Lord as Guru: Hindi Sants in the Northern Indian Tradition*. New York: Oxford University Press, 1987.

Gupta, K. C. *Sri Garib Das: Haryana's Saint of Humanity*. New Delhi: Impex India, 1976.

Juergensmeyer, Mark. *Radhasoami Reality: The Logic of a Modern Faith*. Princeton: Princeton University Press, 1991.

Schomer, Karine, and W. H. McLeod, *The Sants: Studies in a Devotional Tradition of India*. Berkeley: Berkeley Religious Studies Series; Delhi: Motilal Banarsidass, 1987.

Singh, Nirbhai. *Bhagata Nāmadeva in the Guru Grantha*. Patiala: Punjabi University, 1981.

The Sikhs

The origin and history of the Sikh faith—which many scholars have treated as an offshoot of the broad Sant tradition—has come under intense scrutiny in recent decades, in part due to political events in North India and concerns over community identity shared by many Sikhs worldwide.

The result has been not simply a flood of publications (which include both copious polemic and sectarian material as well as more objective scholarship) but a politically charged climate in which it has become increasingly difficult—even dangerous—to pursue historical research. Although there has been much criticism (some quite justified) of "orientalist" scholarship and its lingering effects, and resentment at the study of the tradition by non-Sikhs (see, e.g., the relatively balanced 1991 study by Darshan Singh, *Western Perspective on the Sikh Religion*), the most vitriolic criticism, and in some cases, threats of violence, have been directed against Sikh scholars teaching in Canadian and U.S. universities.

The work of W. Owen Cole, especially *Sikhism and Its Indian Context, 1469–1708* (1984), examines the religious milieu of Guru Nānak and attempts to reconstruct his authentic teachings. By clarifying Nānak's debt to the Sants and essential accord with their worldview, Cole seeks to counter an earlier view of Sikhism as a synthesis of Hinduism and Islam (a view abhorrent to modern Sikhs), and finds little evidence of Islamic influence on early Sikh teachings. Also useful is Cole's brief study *The Guru in Sikhism* (1982). In collaboration with Piara Singh Sambhi, Cole also produced an accessible introductory study, *The Sikhs* (1978). The many contributions to Sikh studies of W. H. McLeod have likewise been supplemented by a comprehensive introductory volume, *The Sikhs, History, Religion, and Society* (1989), as well as five essays on *The Evolution of the Sikh Community* (1975), which trace the development of sectarian identity. McLeod's research on hagiographic sources has also produced a major study, *Early Sikh Tradition* (1980), and an annotated translation, *The B40 Janam Sākhī* (1980), a text on the early life of Guru Nanak, compiled in 1733.

Such historical research, little noticed outside of academic circles in the 1970s and early 1980s, has since come under attack in sectarian publications. The lives of Gurus Nānak, Arjan, and Gobind Singh are the focus of Anil Chandra Banerjee's historical study, *The Sikh Gurus and the Sikh Religion* (1983). A more sectarian perspective is in Dalbir Singh Dhillon's *Sikhism, Origin and Development* (1988), which disputes McLeod on a number of points. Many of the scholars cited here are also contributors to Mark Juergensmeyer and N. Gerald Barrier's anthology *Sikh Studies* (1979).

The most controversial research emerged in the 1990s. It includes Pashaura Singh's unpublished University of Toronto dissertation on the evolution of the Sikh scriptures (the very suggestion of "evolution" as opposed to revelation being increasingly anathema to some Sikhs), "The Text and Meaning of the *Ādi Granth*" (1991), which quickly generated a response anthology with the strident title *Planned Attack on Aad Sri Guru Granth Sahib: Academics or Blasphemy* [*sic*] (1994). Harjot Oberoi's study of popular religion in the Punjab in the nineteenth century, *The Construction of Religious Boundaries* (1994), documents a relatively pluralistic and fluid folk-Sikhism that was, in Oberoi's view, increasingly standardized by urban intellectual "reformers," influenced in part by British concepts of homogenous religious identity. It, too, provoked a firestorm of criticism (e.g., the vitriolic 1995 anthology *Invasion of Religious Boundaries*) and led eventually to Oberoi's resignation from a chair in Sikh Studies at the University of British Columbia. In such a climate, Gurinder Singh Man's meticulous critical study of *The Goindval Pothis* (1996)—three early manuscripts related to the *Ādi Granth*—includes a cautious disclaimer separating the study of concrete documents from a valid faith in a homogeneous and revealed holy book.

The great *Ādi Granth* itself, containing nearly six thousand poems, is available to English-language readers (including, nowadays, many Sikhs outside of India) in two four-volume complete translations—both, alas, stylistically awkward: Gopal Singh's *Sri Guru Granth Sahib: English Version* (1978) and Gurbachan Singh Talib's *Sri Guru Granth Sahib* (1984–90). The former has also been condensed into an eleven-hundred-page *Anthology* (1989), attractively printed but with its inelegancies intact. Despite a New Age title and an introduction larded with pious inaccuracies, a U.S. devotee, Sardarni Premka Kaur, offers in *Peace Lagoon* (1971) surprisingly effective translations of selected hymns of five of the gurus, and Hawley and Juergensmeyer's anthology *Songs of the Saints of India*, cited earlier, contains spare and elegant renderings of eighteen selections by Nānak. A variety of early Sikh writings are also available through McLeod's translations in his anthology and survey *Textual Sources for the Study of Sikhism* (1984). Aspiring students of the original texts can consult Christopher Shackle's grammar, *An Introduction to the Sacred Language of the Sikhs* (1983).

Probably the most effective introduction to the power of Sikh liturgy for college students and general readers, however, is Nikky-Guninder Kaur Singh's *The Name of My Beloved* (1995), which offers lovely renderings of numerous songs from the *Ādi Granth* and the *Dasam granth* that are recited in daily devotions and life-cycle rituals by devout Sikhs. Singh is also the author of a unique study of Sikh tradition from a feminist perspective, *The Feminine Principle in the Sikh Vision of the Transcendent* (1993), that offers a thoughtful reappraisal of sectarian literature from the songs of the earliest gurus to a twentieth-century mystical epic.

Banerjee, Anil Chandra. *The Sikh Gurus and the Sikh Religion*. New Delhi: Munshiram Manoharlal, 1983.

Banerjee, Anil Chandra, and Piara Singh Sambhi. *The Sikhs: Their Religious Beliefs and Practices*. London: Routledge & Kegan Paul, 1978.

Cole, W. Owen. *The Guru in Sikhism*. London: Darton, Longman & Todd, 1982.

———. *Sikhism and Its Indian Context, 1469–1708*. London: Darton, Longman & Todd, 1984.

Dhillon, Dalbir Singh. *Sikhism: Origin and Development*. New Delhi: Atlantic Publishers, 1988.

Giani, Bachiter Singh, ed. *Planned Attack on Aad Sri Guru Granth Sahib: Academics or Blasphemy*. Chandigarh: International Centre of Sikh Studies, 1994.

Juergensmeyer, Mark, and N. Gerald Barrier, eds. *Sikh Studies: Comparative Perspectives on a Changing Tradition*. Berkeley: Berkeley Religious Studies Series, 1979.

Kaur, Sardarni Premka, comp. and trans. *Peace Lagoon: The Songs of Guru Nanak, Guru Amar Das, Guru Ram Das, Guru Arjun, and Guru Gobind Singh*. San Rafael, Calif.: Spiritual Community, 1971.

Man, Gurinder Singh. *The Goindval Pothis: The Earliest Extant Source of the Sikh Canon*. Cambridge: Harvard University, Department of Sanskrit and Indian Studies, 1996.

Mann, Jasbir Singh, Surinder Singh Sodhi, and Gurbaksh Singh Gill, eds. *Invasion of Religious Boundaries: A Critique of Harjot Oberoi's Work*. Vancouver: Canadian Sikh Study and Teaching Society, 1995.

McLeod, W. H. *Early Sikh Tradition: A Study of the Janam-sākhīs*. Oxford: Clarendon Press, 1980.

———. *The Evolution of the Sikh Community: Five Essays*. Delhi: Oxford University Press, 1975.

———. *The Sikhs: History, Religion, and Society*. New York: Columbia University Press, 1989.

———, ed. and trans. *The B40 Janam Sākhī*. Amritsar: Guru Nanak Dev University, 1980.

———. *Textual Sources for the Study of Sikhism*. Manchester: Manchester University Press, 1984.

Oberoi, Harjot. *The Construction of Religious Boundaries: Culture, Identity, and Diversity in the Sikh Tradition*. Chicago: University of Chicago Press, 1994.

Shackle, Christopher. *An Introduction to the Sacred Language of the Sikhs*. London: School of Oriental and African Studies, University of London, 1983.

Singh, Darshan. *Western Perspective on the Sikh Religion*. New Delhi: Sehgal Publishers Service, 1991.

Singh, Gopal, trans. *Sri Guru Granth Sahib: English Version*. 4 vols. Chandigarh: World Sikh University Press, 1978.

———. *Sri Guru Granth Sahib: An Anthology*. Calcutta: M. P. Birla Foundation, 1989.

Singh, Nikky-Guninder Kaur. *The Feminine Principle in the Sikh Vision of the Transcendent*. Cambridge: Cambridge University Press, 1993.

———, trans. *The Name of My Beloved: Verses of the Sikh Gurus*. San Francisco: Harper, 1995.

Singh, Pashaura. "The Text and Meaning of the *Ādi Granth*." Ph.D. diss., University of Toronto, 1991.

Talib, Gurbachan Singh, trans. *Sri Guru Granth Sahib in English Translation*. 4 vols. Patiala: Punjabi University, 1984–90.

Early Kṛṣṇa Bhakti in Northeast India

The spread of Vaiṣṇavism in Bengal and Orissa during the twelfth century, probably spurred on by the missionary activities of South Indian teachers like Rāmānuja and promoted by certain kings of the Sena and Gaṅgā dynasties, produced a cultural efflorescence whose manifestations included the elevation of Lord Jagannātha of Puri to the role of a state deity and the composition of mystico-erotic songs to Kṛṣṇa, the most famous example of which is the Sanskrit cycle attributed to Jayadeva, *Gītagovinda* (late-twelfth century). Yet it has long been recognized that the history of Buddhist and Tantric activity in this region formed an important background to the Vaiṣṇava movement, and a key group of popular Buddhist texts, the *Caryāgīti*, is treated in Per Kvaerne's *An Anthology of Buddhist Tantric Songs* (1977). Kvaerne's comprehensive introduction includes analysis of the meaning of *sandhyābhāṣā* (the metaphorical language of Tantrism) and of the key concept of *sahaja* ("spontaneousness"); unfortunately, the translated texts themselves sink beneath the weight of scholarly apparatus and bracketed explication.

The *Gītagovinda* is available in Barbara Miller's translation as *Love Song of the Dark Lord* (1977), which includes an introductory essay summarizing recent scholarship on Jayadeva and his milieu and analyzing the theology and artistry of the cycle. Lee Siegel's study of the same text, *Sacred and Profane Dimensions of Love in Indian Traditions* (1978), includes another translation as well as additional analysis of Jayadeva's erotic mysticism, which was to exert a profound influence on later Vaiṣṇavism. Another early song-cycle of Kṛṣṇa bhakti in Sanskrit that was popular in Northeast India (although it was probably composed by a Mādhva poet in the southern Deccan in the thirteenth century) was the *Kṛṣṇakarṇāmṛta*, attributed to Līlāśuka Bilvamaṅgala; it is available through a critical edition and translation by Frances Wilson, *The Love of Krishna* (1975).

The deity said to have inspired Jayadeva's songs, and in whose worship the *Gītagovinda* became an important liturgical text, was the subject of a groundbreaking study by Kanhu Charan Mishra, *The Cult of Jagannātha* (1971); this was followed in 1978 by the anthology *The Cult of Jagannātha and the Regional Tradition of Orissa*, edited by Eschmann et al., which presented the fruits of an Indo-German interdisciplinary study of the holy city of Puri that combined the insights of anthropologists and historians with those of religious scholars. The essays reveal the dynamic that synthesized regional folk elements with Brahmanized Vaiṣṇavism and a royal cult at the most important surviving medieval temple of North India. Additional research on this tradition is reflected in Gopinath Mohapatra's *Jagannātha in History and Religious Traditions of Orissa* (1982) and in the same author's *The Land of Viṣṇu* (1979). The latter work includes a complete translation of the *Puruṣottamakṣetra māhātmyaṃ*, a eulogy of the city of Puri belonging to the important but little-studied genre of purāṇic *māhātmya* texts. A unique work on the Jagannātha cult is Frédérique Marglin's *Wives of the God-King* (1985), which uses both ethnographic and historical methods to examine the tradition of female temple dancers known as *devadāsīs*. A useful overview of regional developments is provided by A. K. Deb's *The Bhakti Movement in Orissa* (1984).

Jagannātha became a major inspiration for Caitanya and the later Bengali Vaiṣṇavas, who will be discussed below; the study of pre-Caitanya Vaiṣṇavism in Bengal has been enriched by a commendable translation of its earliest extant Bengali-language text, the earthy and erotic *Śrīkṛṣṇakīrtana* of Baṛu Caṇḍīdāsa (ca. fourteenth century) in M. H. Klaiman's *Singing the Glory of Lord Krishna* (1984). Klaiman's introduction sheds fresh light on the early social history of the Vaiṣṇava movement and challenges some of the later sectarian views that have been accepted by other scholars.[5]

Deb, Achintya Kumar. *The Bhakti Movement in Orissa: A Comprehensive History*. Calcutta: Kalyani Devi, 1984.

Eschmann, Anncharlott, Hermann Kulke, and Gaya Charan Tripathi, eds. *The Cult of Jagannātha and the Regional Tradition of Orissa*. New Delhi: Manohar, 1978.

Klaiman, M. H., trans. *Singing the Glory of Lord Krishna: The* Śrīkṛṣṇakīrtana *of Baṛu Caṇḍīdāsa*. American Academy of Religion Classics in Religious Studies, no. 5. Chico, Calif.: Scholars Press, 1984.

Kvaerne, Per. *An Anthology of Buddhist Tantric Songs: A Study of the* Caryāgīti. Oslo, Norway: Universitetsforlaget, 1977; New York: Columbia University Press, 1977.

Miller, Barbara Stoler, ed. and trans. *Love Song of the Dark Lord: Jayadeva's* Gītagovinda. New York: Columbia University Press, 1977.

Mishra, Kanhu Charan. *The Cult of Jagannātha*. Calcutta: Firma K. L. Mukhopadhyay, 1971.

Mohapatra, Gopinath. *Jagannātha in History and Religious Traditions of Orissa*. Calcutta: Punthi Pustak, 1982.

———. *The Land of Viṣṇu: A Study on Jagannātha Cult*. Delhi: B. R. Publishing, 1979.

Siegel, Lee. *Sacred and Profane Dimensions of Love in Indian Traditions as Exemplified in the* Gītagovinda *of Jayadeva*. New York: Oxford University Press, 1978.

Wilson, Frances, ed. and trans. *The Love of Krishna: The Kṛṣṇakarṇāmṛta of Līlāśuka Bilvamaṅgala*. Philadelphia: University of Pennsylvania Press, 1975.

Caitanya and Bengal Vaiṣṇavism

The ecstatic and charismatic Śrīkṛṣṇa Caitanya (ca. 1486–1533), who spent much of his life in Puri, inspired a great flowering of Kṛṣṇa devotion in Bengal that spread across much of northern India and—through the twentieth-century Hare Kṛṣṇa/ISKCON movement—indeed far beyond. To the earlier studies of his life and teachings cited by Zelliot may be added Deb Narayan Acharyya's *The Life and Times of Śrīkṛṣṇacaitanya* (1984), which focuses on the saint's early life as portrayed by leading sectarian biographers.

An essential reference for the study of the first and second generations of the Caitanya tradition is Ramakanta Chakravarti's *Vaiṣṇavism in Bengal:*

1486–1900 (1985), a comprehensive study that extends the pioneering research of S. K. De. The twelve major biographies of Caitanya are the subject of a monograph in preparation by Tony K. Stewart, whose comparative approach is reflected in "One Text from Many: The *Caitanyacaritāmṛta* as 'Classic' and 'Commentary'" (1994) in *According to Tradition*, cited in the final section below. The monumental and (for later Gauḍīya devotees) definitive biography of the great mystic is available in Edward C. Dimock's translation *The Caitanyacaritāmṛta of Kṛṣṇadāsa Kavirāja*, edited and annotated by Stewart (1999). Kavirāja's opus provides not only a vivid portrait of Caitanya as his contemporaries remembered him and an interpretation of his life as a dual incarnation of Rādhā and Kṛṣṇa, but also a summum of the complex theological system developed by the Vrindavan Gosvāmins, Caitanya's intellectual heirs.

That theology and its related ritual practice has inspired a considerable literature in English, notable examples of which are Sudhindra Chandra Chakravarti's *Philosophical Foundation of Bengal Vaiṣṇavism* (1969), which includes a treatment of Gosvāmin epistemology and ethics, and Janardan Chakravarti's *Bengal Vaiṣṇavism and Śrī Chaitanya* (1975), which contains useful synopses of the major writings of the six Gosvāmins and of the hagiographic literature of the sect. A. K. Majumdar's *Gauḍīya Vaiṣṇava Studies* (1978) supplements his earlier important contributions by relating the Bengali school to older pāñcarātra Vaiṣṇava traditions. Jagannath Sinha's *The Philosophy and Religion of Chaitanya and His Followers* (1976) is a philosophically oriented survey of sectarian leaders from Śrīdhara Gosvāmi to Baladeva Vidyābhūṣaṇa, while Mahanamabrata Brahmachari focuses on one of the most important Gauḍīya thinkers in *Vaiṣṇava Vedānta: The Philosophy of Śrī Jīva Gosvāmī* (1974). Jīva's writings also form the basis for Stuart Mark Elkman's *Jīva Gosvāmin's Tattvasandarbha* (1986), which utilizes eighteenth-century commentaries on one of Jīva's writings by Baladeva Vidyābhūṣaṇa and Rādhāmohana to illustrate the evolution of the Gauḍīya tradition.

The centrality of drama in the Gauḍīya tradition is explored from different perspectives in works by Donna M. Wulff and David Haberman. Wulff's *Drama as a Mode of Religious Realization* (1984) is a study and partial translation of *Vidagdhamādhava*, a play by Rūpa Gosvāmī, in the context of the aesthetics of devotion developed by sectarian teachers. In *Acting as a Way of Salvation* (1988), Haberman focuses on the application of that aesthetic theory to the religious practice of historic and contemporary devotees. Significantly, Haberman seeks to redress the tendency of earlier scholars to emphasize the (alleged) emotional spontaneity of bhakti poetry and practice by showing how Rūpa Gosvāmī's highly formalized discipline of *rāgānugā sādhana*, incorporating role-playing and visualization, sought to make the experience of mystical love accessible to wider circles of initiated devotees. The effects of such role playing, and its coexistence with a spontaneity bordering on aberration, are vividly evoked in June McDaniel's study of religious ecstasy in Bengal, *The Madness of the Saints* (1989), which includes accounts of both Vaiṣṇava and Śākta devotees. The impact of Gauḍīya Vaiṣṇavism on neighboring Orissa is the subject of Prabhat Mukherjee's *History of the Caitanya Faith in Orissa* (1979).

Maheshvara Neog's 1965 study of Śaṅkaradeva and Assamese Vaiṣṇavism has appeared in a revised edition as *Early History of the Vaiṣṇava Faith and Movement in Assam* (1985); this is supplemented by Neog's edition of *The Bhakti-ratnākara of Śaṅkaradeva* (1982), which includes an English summary of this Sanskrit text. A valuable 1930 study of unorthodox Vaiṣṇavism available in reprint is Manindra Mohan Bose's *The Post-Caitanya Sahajiyā Cult* (1986), which includes lengthy translations from Bengali Tantric sources. Both Sahajiyā and Caitanyite influence is evident in the songs of the wandering singers known as Bauls; ethnomusicologist Charles Capwell's study *The Music of the Bauls of Bengal* (1986) includes both illuminating introductory essays and a modest number of translations of Baul songs.

Acharyya, Deb Narayan. *The Life and Times of Śrīkṛṣṇacaitanya*. Calcutta: Firm K. L. Mukhopadhyaya, 1984.

Bose, Manindra Mohan. *The Post-Caitanya Sahajiyā Cult*. Calcutta: Calcutta University, 1930; New Delhi: Gian Publishing House, 1986.

Brahmachari, Mahanamabrata. *Vaiṣṇava Vedānta: The Philosophy of Śrī Jīva Gosvāmī*. Calcutta: Das Gupta, 1974.

Capwell, Charles. *The Music of the Bauls of Bengal*. Kent, Ohio: Kent State University Press, 1986.

Chakravarti, Janardan. *Bengal Vaiṣṇavism and Śrī Chaitanya*. Calcutta: Asiatic Society, 1975.

Chakravarti, Ramakanta. *Vaiṣṇavism in Bengal: 1486–1900*. Calcutta: Sanskrit Pustak Bhandar, 1985.

Chakravarti, Sudhindra Chandra. *Philosophical Foundation of Bengal Vaiṣṇavism: A Critical Exposition*. Calcutta: Academic, 1969.

Dimock, Edward C., trans. *The Caitanyacaritāmṛta of Kṛṣṇadāsa Kavirāja*. Ed. Tony K. Stewart. Cambridge: Harvard University, Department of Sanskrit and Indian Studies, 1999.

Elkman, Stuart Mark. *Jīva Gosvāmin's Tattvasandarbha: A Study of the Philosophical and Sectarian Development of the Gauḍīya Vaiṣṇava Movement*. Delhi: Motilal Banarsidass, 1986.

Haberman, David L. *Acting as a Way of Salvation: A Study of Rāgānugā Bhakti Sādhana*. New York: Oxford University Press, 1988.

Majumdar, Ashoke Kumar. *Gauḍīya Vaiṣṇava Studies*. Calcutta: Jijnasa/Best Books, 1978.

McDaniel, June. *The Madness of the Saints: Ecstatic Religion in Bengal*. Chicago: University of Chicago Press, 1989.

Mukherkee, Prabhat. *History of the Chaitanya Faith in Orissa*. New Delhi: Manohar, 1979.

Neog, Maheshvara. *The Bhakti-ratnākara of Śaṅkaradeva: Critically Edited Sanskrit Text, with a Resume in English and History of the Concept of Bhakti in a Critical Introduction*. Patiala: Punjab University, 1982.

———. *Early History of the Vaiṣṇava Faith and Movement in Assam*. Delhi: Motilal Banarsidass, 1980; rev. ed. of *Śaṅkaradeva and His Times*, Gauhati: Gauhati University, 1965.

Sinha, Jagannath. *The Philosophy and Religion of Chaitanya and His Followers*. Calcutta: Sinha Publishing House, 1976.

Wulff, Donna M. *Drama as a Mode of Religious Realization: The* Vidaghdamādhava *of Rūpa Gosvāmin*. Chico, Calif.: Scholars Press, 1984.

Sūrdās and the Braj Poetic Tradition

The worship of Kṛṣṇa Gopāl—the divine child and adolescent cowherd of Vrindavan—experienced a significant revival in North and Central India during the late-Sultanate and Mughal periods, producing a brilliant literature in several dialects of Hindi and a proliferation of sects and practices. The scholarly study of this tradition, which often celebrated the loves of its lord in imagery of frank eroticism, emerged during the twentieth century from the shadow of disrepute to which Victorian scholarship had relegated it, and the past twenty-five years have seen major contributions to scholarly literature.

The towering figure of Hindi poetry associated with Kṛṣṇa is Sūrdās, a sixteenth-century singer of Vrindavan who is popularly held to have been blind from birth. The Sūrdās songs continue to be widely performed. John

Stratton Hawley's *Sūrdās: Poet, Singer, Saint* (1984) gives the best introduction to date, incorporating the insights of modern Indian scholarship and the results of the author's manuscript research to offer a plausible portrait of the saint in the context of his age—a portrait that challenges many popular and sectarian interpretations of Sūrdās's life and attitudes. Bryant's *Poems to the Child-God* (1978) includes beautiful translations of some of the poems for which Sūrdās is most famous—his evocations of Kṛṣṇa's infancy and childhood. Moreover, the author's lucid analysis of the poet's "structures and strategies" remains a signal contribution to bhakti research, utilizing modern critical tools to highlight the intent and craft underlying a bhakti poet's apparent "simplicity" and "conventionality."

Hawley and Juergensmeyer's *Songs of the Saints of India* (cited earlier) contains an informative chapter on Sūrdās with additional fine translations. Further discussion of the poet appears in Hawley's *Krishna: The Butter Thief* (1983), which utilizes both iconographic and textual materials spanning two millennia to trace the evolution of a single motif in Kṛṣṇa bhakti. The culmination of Bryant and Hawley's research on Sūrdās is yet to appear: a projected two-volume *Sūrpadāvalī*, which will offer the Devanāgarī text with critical apparatus as well as translations of some four hundred songs that these researchers have concluded represent the oldest and most authentic of the many thousands attributed to the poet. Usha Nilsson's *Surdas* (1982), offers a more traditional view of the saint's life, with translations of some of the most popular songs attributed to him. Other recent research on Sūrdās and his age may be found in two anthologies published in India, Nagendra's *Sūradāsa, a Reevaluation* (1979) and Nagendra and K. D. Sharma's *Sūradāsa: His Mind and Art* (1978).

Popular tradition regards Sūrdās as one of a group of eight poets (*aṣṭachāp*) who composed under the inspiration of the great Vaiṣṇava teacher Vallabhācārya—an attribution Hawley disputes in the case of Sūrdās. In any case, it is clear that the latter stood near the beginning of a great outpouring of Braj poetry inspired by the Rādhā-Kṛṣṇa theme, and that the songs of many later poets were adopted for liturgical purposes by a number of prominent sects. The second-best-known poet of the *aṣṭachāp*, Nanddās, who was active during the mid–sixteenth century and was indeed a follower of Vallabha's son Viṭṭhalnāth, is the subject of R. S. McGregor's *The Round Dance of Krishna and Uddhav's Message* (1973): the title refers to the poet's two most celebrated works, which are presented here in rhythmic though somewhat florid English verse.

Another mid-sixteenth-century Braj poet inspired by the "round dance," or *rāsa līlā*, of Rādhā and Kṛṣṇa was Harirām Vyās (born ca. 1510), whose sectarian affiliation is a matter of controversy. His major work *Rās-pañcādhyāyī* has been critically edited and translated in Heidi Pauwels's *Kṛṣṇa's Round Dance Reconsidered* (1996). A contemporary and friend of Harirām was Svāmī Haridās, who became revered as the founder of the Haridāsī sect. His major anthology of 128 devotional songs, painstakingly edited with the aid of computer analysis of manuscripts, is presented together with translations and a discussion of the songs' musical performance tradition in Ludmila Rosenstein's *The Devotional Poetry of Svāmī Haridās* (1997). Another sectarian founder-figure was Hit Harivaṃś (1502–52), who followed the tradition of the *Gītagovinda* in emphasizing the importance of Rādhā, Kṛṣṇa's beloved, elevating her, in time, to supreme status. Charles S. J. White's *The Caurāsī Pad of Śrī Hit Harivaṁś* (1977) offers the original text and translation of this poet's most famous work, as well as a critical introduction to his school, the Rādhā-vallabha *sampradāya*. A second translation of these songs, incorporating a critical edition of the original, was published by Rupert Snell as *The Eighty-Four Hymns of Hita Harivaṃśa* (1991).

The Puṣṭi mārg sect founded by Vallabhācārya (ca. 1479–1531) flourished under the patronage of mercantile classes in Rajasthan and Gujarat; by the late-nineteenth century the opulence of its temples and allegedly sybaritic lifestyle of some of its preceptors led to an infamous court case, in consequence of which the sect was branded as licentious, a stigma that contributed to its neglect by later scholars. Several recent studies have returned to the roots of the tradition: James D. Reddington examines the application of the theology of *śuddhādvaita* ("pure non-dualism") to the mythical scenarios of the *Bhāgavata purāṇa* in *Vallabhācārya on the Love Games of Kṛṣṇa* (1983), which includes a translation of Vallabha's commentary on six chapters of the purāṇa's tenth book. A useful earlier study not cited by Zelliot is Mrudula I. Marfatia's *The Philosophy of Vallabhācārya* (1967). Richard K. Barz discusses the early activities of Vallabha's followers in *The Bhakti Sect of Vallabhācārya* (1976), which includes translations of four hagiographies of special relevance to the coalescence of the sect. The complete *Caurāsī vaiṣṇavān kī vārtā* by Vallabha's grandson Gokulnāth (ca.

1552–1641), from which these four accounts are drawn, is available in English as *Eighty-four Vaishnavas* (1985), translated by Shyam Das, an American-born devotee of Puṣṭi mārg. As in many Indian versions, the basic text is here interwoven with the commentary *Bhāvprakāś* of Harirāy and is based on the 1948 Dwarkadas Parikh edition. Two other useful translations by Shyam Das—well-written, though from a devout sectarian perspective—are *Ashta Chaap* (1985), an anthology of the eight poets, and *Chaurasi Baithak* (1985), a translation of another work by Gokulnāth that describes his grandfather's pilgrimage to sites associated with Kṛṣṇa.

A sample of later Vallabhite teaching is provided by Shyam Das's *Ocean of Jewels* (1986), which translates a seventeenth-century treatise by Bālakṛṣṇa Bhaṭṭ and is written in the style of a *śāstrārth*, or theological debate. Although seven branches of the Puṣṭi mārg are fairly well documented, an eighth (located in what is now Pakistani Sind) has been little studied; the major work of its founder Kevalarām (born 1617) is the subject of Alan Entwistle's critical edition and translation *The Rāsa Māna ke Pada of Kevalarāma* (1993). The most comprehensive work on the contemporary Puṣṭi mārg, based on fieldwork in Ujjain, Madhya Pradesh, in the late-1970s, is Peter Bennett's *The Path of Grace* (1993), an appreciative anthropological and sociological study that examines the tradition through its own categories, stressing bhakti ideals such as *sevā* ("service") as an alternative to hierarchical social theory.

The inspiration of the Kṛṣṇaite saints of the sixteenth and seventeenth centuries bore fruit not only in poetry and theology but also in sacred geography, architecture, and cultural performance, as the Braj region became a center for pilgrimage and ritual drama. Charlotte Vaudeville's influential article "Braj, Lost and Found" (1976) helped spark additional investigation into the process whereby the landscape of Mughal-period Mathura was symbolically and tangibly reimagined by Hindu devotees as the lost paradise of Kṛṣṇa. Much documentation of this phenomenon may be found in Alan Entwistle's comprehensive sourcebook *Braj, Centre of Krishna Pilgrimage* (1987), a rich compendium of information on diverse aspects of the Kṛṣṇa cult and its literature, which updates and expands on the information provided in F. S. Growse's classic *Mathurā, a District Memoir* (1882; reissued in a 1979 reprint).

The ancient connection of the North Indian Vaiṣṇava tradition with theater was convincingly demonstrated by Norvin Hein's *The Miracle Plays of Mathurā* (1971), a comprehensive study spanning the classical, medieval, and modern periods. In addition to vivid description of *rās* and *Rāmlīlā* performances, this work includes painstaking textual archaeology aimed at uncovering the roots of Vaiṣṇava dramatic genres, and its publication sparked new interest in these performance traditions. Among the works influenced by Hein's pioneering efforts, John Stratton Hawley's *At Play with Krishna* (1981), though primarily concerned with contemporary *rāslīlā* productions, contains information on the bhakti literature from which they draw inspiration. David Haberman's adventurous study, *Journey through the Twelve Forests* (1994) combines a vivid personal narrative of a pilgrimage in Braj with descriptions of traditional performances, a précis of key sectarian myths, and an accessible yet scholarly history of Kṛṣṇa worship; it might provide an ideal introduction to the tradition for college classes. Another accessible work is David Kinsley's *The Divine Player* (1979), which examines the development of the Kṛṣṇa cult and its doctrine of *līlā*.

Barz, Richard K. *The Bhakti Sect of Vallabhācārya*. Faridabad: Thomson, 1976.

Bennett, Peter. *The Path of Grace: Social Organization and Temple Worship in a Vaishnava Sect*. Delhi: Hindustan Publishing, 1993.

Bryant, Kenneth E. *Poems to the Child-God: Structures and Strategies in the Poetry of Sūrdās*. Berkeley and Los Angeles: University of California Press, 1978.

Bryant, Kenneth E., ed., and John Stratton Hawley, trans. *Sūrpadāvalī: The Poems Attributed to Sūrdās in the Early Manuscript Traditions*. 2 vols. Cambridge: Harvard Oriental Series, forthcoming.

Entwistle, Alan W. *Braj, Centre of Krishna Pilgrimage*. Groningen: Egbert Forsten, 1987.

———. *The Rāsa Māna ke Pada of Kevalarāma: Introduction, Critical Edition, and Translation*. Groningen: Egbert Forsten: 1993.

Growse, Frederick Salmon. *Mathurā: A District Memoir*. 1882; reprint, New Delhi: Asian Educational Services, 1979.

Haberman, David. *Journey through the Twelve Forests: An Encounter with Krishna*. New York: Oxford University Press, 1994.

Hawley, John Stratton. *Krishna, the Butter Thief*. Princeton: Princeton University Press, 1983.

———. *Sūrdās: Poet, Singer, Saint*. Seattle: University of Washington Press, 1984.

Hein, Norvin. *The Miracle Plays of Mathurā*. New Haven: Yale University Press, 1972.

Kinsley, David R. *The Divine Player: A Study of Kṛṣṇa Līlā*. Delhi: Motilal Banarsidass, 1979.

Marfatia, Mrudula I. *The Philosophy of Vallabhācārya*. Delhi: Munshiram Manoharlal, 1967.

McGregor, Ronald Stuart. *Nanddās: The Round Dance of Krishna and Uddhav's Message*. London: Luzac, 1973.

Nagendra, ed. *Sūradāsa: A Reevaluation*. New Delhi: National Publishing House, 1979.

Nagendra, and K. D. Sharma, eds. *Sūradāsa, His Mind and Art*. Chandigarh: Bahri, 1978.

Nilsson, Usha. *Surdas*. New Delhi: Sahitya Akademi, 1982.

Pauwels, Heidi Rika Maria. *Kṛṣṇa's Round Dance Reconsidered: Harirām Vyās's Hindi* Rās-pañcādhyāyī. Richmond, Surrey, Eng.: Curzon, 1996.

Reddington, James D., S. J. *Vallabhācārya on the Love Games of Kṛṣṇa*. Delhi: Motilal Banarsidass, 1983.

Rosenstein, Ludmila L. *The Devotional Poetry of Svāmī Haridās*. Groningen: Egbert Forsten, 1997.

Shyam Das, trans. *Ashta Chaap: Lord Krishna's Eight Poet Friends*. Baroda: Shri Vallabha, 1985.

———. *Chaurasi Baithak: Eighty-Four Seats of Shri Vallabhāchārya*. Baroda: Shri Vallabha, 1985.

———. *Eighty-four Vaishnavas*. Baroda: Shri Vallabha, 1985.

———. *Ocean of Jewels: Prameyaratnārṇava of Lallu Bhaṭṭa*. Baroda: Shri Vallabha, 1986.

Snell, Rupert, ed. and trans. *The Eighty-Four Hymns of Hita Harivaṃśa: An Edition of the* Caurāsī Pada. Delhi: Motilal Banarsidass, 1991.

Vaudeville, Charlotte. "Braj, Lost and Found." *Indo-Iranian Journal* 18, nos. 3–4 (1976):195–213.

White, Charles S. J., trans. *The "Caurasi Pad" of Śrī Hit Harivams*. Honolulu: University Press of Hawaii, 1977.

Mīrābāī and Narsiṃha Mehta

In the absence of historical evidence concerning her life and of early manuscript sources for her songs, the Rajasthani princess Mīrābāī (ca. 1516–46?) appears, for scholars, the most problematic of the major Hindi saint-poets, even as she remains, for devotees, one of the most popular. A good introductory treatment of her legend together with fine translations of her songs appears in Hawley and Juergensmeyer's *Songs of the Saints of India*. A. J. Alston's longer study *The Devotional Poems of Mīrābāī* (1980) includes introductory essays that draw effectively on the past few decades of Indian scholarship, as well as translations of some two hundred of her songs from Paraśurām Caturvedī's Hindi anthology: these are best described (to quote the book jacket) as "sober"; they convey the subject matter but not the fervent flavor that makes Mīrābāī so beloved among Indian audiences. A more accessible source is Shama Futehally's *In the Dark of the Heart* (1994), which offers the Devanāgarī text and lovely translations of thirty songs from standard modern collections.

Two long essays by Kumkum Sangari appeared under the title "Mirabai and the Spiritual Economy of Bhakti" in the *Economic and Political Weekly* (1990); they represent a notable attempt—albeit dense with trendy social-science jargon—to analyze Mira's songs from a feminist and subalternist perspective and to raise larger issues concerning the social impact of bhakti. More successful efforts in this direction may be found in two recent studies that deal primarily (and refreshingly) with the reception of devotional poetry—its use by such diverse audiences as (in Mīrābāī's case) women and low-class devotees, traditional elites, academic scholars, Indian nationalists, and progressive activists. Parita Mukta's *Upholding the Common Life* (1994) reveals Mīrābāī's enduring meaning for women, tribals, and oppressed communities in Gujarat and Rajasthan. Nancy M. Martin's *Mirabai: Woman Saint of India* (2002) offers a comprehensive study of the "multiple representations" of Mīrābāī.

The most popular bhakti poet of Gujarat, Narsiṃha Mehta (ca. 1414–81), is represented by a translated collection, *Devotional Songs of Narsi Mehta* (1985), by Swami Mahadevananda.

Alston, A. J. *The Devotional Poems of Mīrābāī*. Delhi: Motilal Banarsidass, 1980.

Futehally, Shama. *In the Dark of the Heart: Songs of Meera*. San Francisco: HarperCollins, 1994.

Mahadevananda, Swami, trans. *Devotional Songs of Narsi Mehta*. Delhi: Motilal Banarsidass, 1985.

Martin, Nancy M. *Mirabai: Woman Saint of India*. New York: Oxford University Press, 2002.

Mukta, Parita. *Upholding the Common Life: The Community of Mirabai*. New Delhi: Oxford University Press, 1994.

Sangari, Kumkum. "Mirabai and the Spiritual Economy of *Bhakti*." *Economic and Political Weekly*, July 7, 1990, 1464–75; July 14, 1990, 1537–52.

Jain Traditions

The pan-Indian Jain tradition is especially prominent in contemporary Gujarat and Rajasthan, yet as a non-Hindu tradition with a literature dating to before the beginning of the common era and later extending into most of the regional languages it entirely eluded the categories of Zelliot's essay and has indeed long been neglected by Western scholars of Indian religion. Several notable recent studies—by giving serious study to Jain laypeople and their practices, which sometimes parallel the expressions of Hindu bhakti—have begun to address this lacuna and to challenge the stereotype of Jainism as purely austere and scholastic. John Cort's *Open Boundaries* (1998) explores Jain identity in historical and transregional perspective. The same author's more recent *Jains in the World* (2001) offers a comprehensive portrait of Jainism as a lived religious practice. Anthropologist Lawrence Babb's *Absent Lord* (1996), based on fieldwork in Gujarat and Rajasthan, explores the complex ritual culture of image-worshipping Śvetāmbar Jains. Kendall Folkert's *Scripture and Community* (1993), edited by Cort, assembles the research of a promising young U.S. scholar of Jain traditions whose life was cut tragically short.

Babb, Lawrence A. *Absent Lord: Ascetics and Kings in a Jain Ritual Culture*. Berkeley: University of California Press, 1996.

Cort, John E. *Jains in the World: Religious Values and Ideology in India*. New York: Oxford University Press, 2001.

Cort, John E. *Open Boundaries: Jain Communities and Cultures in Indian History*. Albany: State University of New York Press, 1998.

Folkert, Kendall W. *Scripture and Community: Collected Essays on the Jains*. Ed. John E. Cort. Atlanta: Scholars Press, 1993.

The Rāma Tradition

A phenomenon particularly associated with the medieval period was the rise of the devotional cult of Rāma, the hero of the Rāmāyaṇa epic. The relative dearth of classical religious texts associated with this tradition—apart from the Sanskrit epic itself and literary retellings—led early Indologists to characterize it as a "late" and "derivative" phenomenon, resulting in its comparative neglect. Recent decades have brought new publications that examine the emergence of the cult and help explain its phenomenal popularity in recent centuries. Here mention must be made of the new, seven-volume translation *The Rāmāyaṇa of Vālmki,* edited by Robert P. Goldman and based on the Baroda critical edition, five volumes of which have appeared to date. Although the main text is a product of a period earlier than we are concerned with here, the translators have drawn extensively on medieval commentaries, to which they make reference in their detailed notes. In addition, each volume includes introductory essays that represent substantial contributions to research.

Frank Whaling's *The Rise of the Religious Significance of Rāma* (1980) is a circumscribed but useful study of the characterization of the protagonist in three major texts: the Sanskrit *Rāmāyaṇa* of Vālmīki, the *Adyātma,* or "metaphysical" *Rāmāyaṇa* (ca. fifteenth century), and the Hindi *Rāmcaritmānas* of Tulsīdās (ca. 1574). Whaling argues against the standard Indological theory of the gradual divinization of an originally "secular" hero and suggests that Rāma's transcendent status, already evident in the earliest versions of his story, was variously interpreted through the theological lenses of succeeding periods. The influential *Adhyātma Rāmayāṇa,* which attempted a synthesis of the Rāma narrative and *advaita* metaphysics and strongly influenced Tulsīdās and other vernacular poets, is now available in no less than four translations (by Lala Baij Nath, 1913; Chandan Lal Dhody, 1995; Ramjung Bahadur Singh, 1997; and Swami Tapasyananda, 1985).

The city most closely associated with Rāma and his epic is the subject of Hans Bakker's *Ayodhyā* (1986), a monumental study incorporating archaeological, numismatic, and textual evidence. Bakker concludes that a Gupta king may have first identified the Buddhist center of Saket with the legendary capital of the Raghu dynasty, but that devotional worship of Rāma at the site probably does not predate the eleventh century. The second half of his study offers a translation and interpretation of portions of the ca. twelfth-century *Agastya saṃhitā,* in which pāñcarātra metaphysics are reinterpreted in the light of a new understanding of Viṣṇu as Rāma, and of the *Ayodhyā māhātmya,* a late-purāṇic text magnifying the greatness of the city as a pilgrimage center. Bakker's historical study is carried into the late-medieval and modern periods in anthropologist Peter van der Veer's richly detailed study of pilgrimage functionaries in Ayodhya, *Gods on Earth* (1988). Taken together, Bakker's and van der Veer's writings deliver, in effect, what Whaling's overambitious title promised—a panorama of the emergence of Rāma worship in North India. Van der Veer's study includes substantial documentation of the activities of sadhus of the influential Rāmānandī order, who also figure prominently in Robert Gross's anthropological survey *The Sādhus of India* (1992) and in historian William Pinch's *Peasants and Monks in British India* (1996); the latter work includes material on both the early history and emerging hagiography of the sect.

Some additional insights on Rāmaite traditions can be found in two conference volumes published by India's state Sahitya Akademi: *The Ramayana Tradition in Asia*, edited by V. Raghavan (1980) and *Asian Variations in Ramayana*, edited by K. R. Srinivasa Iyengar (1983). Also deserving of note is William L. Smith's *Rāmāyaṇa Traditions in Eastern India* (1994), which surveys a large number of medieval devotional and folk retellings from Assam, Bengal, and Orissa, and the collection *Rama-Katha in Tribal and Folk Traditions of India* (1993), edited by K. S. Singh and Birendranath Datta, which contains a score of seminar papers. In addition, a pair of anthologies edited by Paula Richman, *Many Rāmāyaṇas* (1992) and *Questioning Ramayanas* (2000), focus on folk, regional, and sectarian variations and contested interpretations of the narrative, through essays that span the medieval and modern periods. Prolific sociologist G. S. Ghurye provides valuable data on the historical and sociopolitical impact of the Rāma story in *The Legacy of the Ramayana* (1979), although his interpretations are heavily colored by modern Hindu nationalism.

The writings of the most influential Rāmaite saint-poet Tulsīdās (ca. 1543–1623) remain available in English principally through the translations by Growse, Hill, and Allchin, cited by Zelliot. Due to his use of alliteration, rhyme, and ellipsis, Tulsīdās presents formidable obstacles to a translator who wishes to convey any more than the (often redundant) narrative content; the *Rāmcaritmānas*, his most beloved work and the cultural epic of the Hindi belt, has fared especially badly in translation, and a newer English rendering by Ram Chandra Prasad (1990), though graced by the Devanāgarī text, a Hindi prose gloss, and lavish nineteenth-century illustrations, adds nothing to the ploddingly prosaic version of W. D. P. Hill. To my ear, the terse and rhythmic prose of Growse's 1891 translation *The Rāmāyaṇa of Tulasīdāsa* (reissued in 1978), though based on a slightly corrupted bazaar edition, gives a better flavor of the original to the non-Hindi reader than any subsequent rendering. A recent translation of a single sub-book of the epic, the *Sundar Kāṇḍ*, attempts a less prosaic approach using blank verse and modern American diction (Lutgendorf, 2001).

Scholarly studies of Tulsidas abound, especially from Indian presses; most are close textual or comparative analyses of the poet's major works. Examples of this type of research may in found in a volume edited by Nagendra, *Tulasīdāsa, His Mind and Art* (1977). A study by Edmour Babineau, *Love of God and Social Duty in the Rāmcaritmānas* (1979), contrasts the epic's teachings with those of saint-poets of the Sant tradition, especially Kabīr. To Hein's earlier work on the *Rāmcaritmānas* performance tradition has been added Lutgendorf's *The Life of a Text* (1991), which traces the rise of several important genres of performance—ritual recitation, oral exegesis, and folk drama—into modern times (cf. Blackburn's *Inside the Drama House*, cited earlier). The enthusiastic adoption and reinterpretation of Tulsīdās's "conservative" epic in the nineteenth and twentieth centuries by members of the untouchable leatherworker caste in Central India is the subject of Ramdas Lamb's unique study *Rapt in the Name* (2002).

Bakker, Hans. *Ayodhyā*. Groningen: Egbert Forsten, 1986.

Baij Nath, Lala, trans. *The Adhyātma Rāmāyaṇa*. Panini Office ed., 1913; reprint, New York: AMS Press, 1974.

Dhody, Chandan Lal, trans. *The Adhyatma Ramayana: Concise English Version*. New Delhi: M. D. Publications, 1995.

Goldman, Robert P., general ed. *The Rāmāyaṇa of Vālmīki: An Epic of Ancient India*. 7 vols.: vol. 1: *Bālakāṇḍa*, trans. Robert P. Goldman, 1984; vol. 2: *Ayodhyākāṇḍa*, trans. Sheldon I. Pollock, 1986; vol. 3: *Araṇyakāṇḍa*, trans. Sheldon I. Pollock, 1991. vol. 4: *Kiṣkindhākāṇḍa*, trans. Rosalind Lefeber, 1994; vol. 5: *Sundarakāṇḍa*, trans. Robert P. Goldman and Sally J. Sutherland Goldman, 1996. Princeton: Princeton University Press.

Ghurye, G. S. *The Legacy of the Ramayana*. Bombay: Popular Prakashan, 1979.

Gross, Robert Lewis. *The Sādhus of India: A Study of Hindu Asceticism*. Jaipur: Rawat, 1992.

Growse, Frederic Salmon, trans. *The Rāmāyaṇa of Tulasī Dāsa*. Cawnpore: E. Samuel, 1891; reprint, Delhi: Motilal Banarsidass, 1978.

Iyengar, K. R. Srinivasa, ed. *Asian Variations in Ramayana*. New Delhi: Sahitya Akademi, 1983.

Lamb, Ramdas. *Rapt in the Name: The Ramnamis, Ramnam, and Untouchable Religion in Central India*. Albany: State University of New York Press, 2002.

Lutgendorf, Philip. *The Life of a Text: Performing the* Rāmcaritmānas *of Tulsidas*. Berkeley and Los Angeles: University of California Press, 1991.

———, trans. "From the Ramcaritmanas of Tulsidas, Book 5: Sundar Kand." *Indian Literature* 45: 3, no. 203 (2001): 143–81.

Pinch, William. *Peasants and Monks in British India*. Berkeley: University of California Press, 1996.

Prasad, Ram Chandra, trans. *Tulasidasa's Shriramacharitamanasa*. Delhi: Motilal Banarsidass, 1990.

Raghavan, V., ed. *The Ramayana Tradition in Asia*. New Delhi: Sahitya Akademi, 1980.

Richman, Paula, ed. *Many Rāmāyaṇas: The Diversity of a Narrative Tradition in South Asia*. Berkeley and Los Angeles: University of California Press, 1992.

———, ed. *Questioning Ramayanas: A South Asian Tradition*. New Delhi: Oxford University Press, 2000.

Singh, K. S., and Birendranath Datta, eds. *Rama-Katha in Tribal and Folk Traditions of India: Proceedings of a Seminar*. Calcutta: Seagull, 1993.

Singh, Ramjung Bahadur, trans. *Adhyatma Ramayana*. Delhi: Bharatiya Kala Prakashan, 1997.

Smith, William L. *Rāmāyaṇa Traditions in Eastern India: Assam, Bengal, Orissa*. 2nd rev. ed. New Delhi: Munshiram Manoharlal, 1994.

Tapasyananda, Swami, trans. *Adhyātma Rāmāyaṇa, The Spiritual Version of the Rama Saga*. Mylapore, Madras: Sri Ramakrishna Matha, 1985.

Van der Veer, Peter. *Gods on Earth: The Management of Religious Experience and Identity in a North Indian Pilgrimage Centre*. London: Athlone, 1988.

Whaling, Frank. *The Rise of the Religious Significance of Rāma*. Delhi: Motilal Banarsidass, 1980.

Goddesses

Another tradition that was long neglected by scholars is the worship of a great variety of female divinities, ranging from nurturing and auspicious "mother goddesses" to ferocious and/or protective goddesses who are most often virginal, independent figures. Such traditions reflect a religious experience probably rooted in the earliest strata of South Asian culture, but significantly elaborated on during the medieval period due to the popularity of Tantric and Śākta practices. These were branded "primitive" and "degenerate" during the nineteenth century by British scholars and elite Hindu reformers, though the pan-Indian popularity of devīs was little affected by such critiques.

An overview of goddess traditions, primarily focused on mythology but with some attention to sectarian practice, is provided by David Kinsley's accessible compendium, *Hindu Goddesses* (1986)—a good starting point for a student seeking to investigate this aspect of Hinduism. Kinsley's second book on goddess traditions, *Tantric Visions of the Divine Feminine* (1997), is a more specialized study of the theology of the ten goddesses known as *mahāvidyās*. Tracy Pintchman's *The Rise of the Goddess in the Hindu Tradition* (1994) offers an attempt to locate historical roots of devī worship in Vedic and purāṇic sources, arguing that Brahmanical influence played a key role in shaping the medieval theology of the great goddess. One of the most influential mythological texts of the Śākta tradition, the *Devī bhāgavata purāṇa*, receives prominent treatment in two works by C. Mackenzie Brown, *God as Mother* (1974) and *The Triumph of the Goddess* (1991); the latter shows how the author(s) of the purāṇa reinterpreted older theological models to assert the supremacy of the goddess over male deities and to transform her into a figure of broad devotional appeal. The most widely recited Sanskrit invocation of a goddess, the *Devī māhātmya*, or *Durgā saptaśatī*—a catalog of epithets and mythological references that is regarded as a potent ritual text, especially for the two annual "nine nights" festivals of goddess worship—is likewise the subject of two studies by Thomas Coburn, *Devī Māhātmya: The Crystallization of the Goddess Tradition* (1985) and *Encountering the Goddess* (1991). The former reconstructs the religiohistorical developments that led to the composition of the *Māhātmya*; the latter offers a translation of its nearly seven hundred verses and a study of its later interpretation and ritual use. In contrast to these studies that examine pan-Indian traditions encoded in Sanskrit texts, William L. Smith's *The One-Eyed Goddess* (1980) presents a focused study of the cult of the snake goddess Manasā, who is celebrated in a series of Middle Bengali *maṅgala* praise-poems.

A variety of perspectives on later traditions of goddess worship, including many that relate to non-Śākta sectarian orientations, are provided by the essays in *The Divine Consort* (1982), edited by John Stratton Hawley and Donna M. Wulff (1982). Lynn Gatwood's *Devi and the Spouse Goddess* (1985) argues for "two distinct versions of the female principle in India, one of which is free from divine male control, and the other necessarily defined by such control": although Gatwood's binary division may be overstated and has since been critiqued by other scholars, it seems to have been part of a paradigm shift in Hindu goddess studies—reflected, for example, in the complete revision of Hawley and Wulff's anthology as *Devī: Goddesses of India* (1996), to incorporate more essays on "independent goddesses and goddesses who dominate their male partners"; Wendell Charles Beane's *Myth, Cult, and Symbols in Śākta Hinduism* (1977) is primarily a study of the theology and ritual that developed around the figure of Durgā-Kālī, the prototypical fierce goddess of the śaktī cult.

As in the case of other devotional traditions, recent research on goddess worship has often been enriched by ethnographic work. Two fine examples, both centered on the Himalayan foothills, are Kathleen Erndl's *Victory to the Mother* (1993), a comprehensive study of the cult of the "seven sisters" of the Punjab hills, and William Sax's *Mountain Goddess* (1991), which examines the worship of Nandā Devī in the Kumaon region. The river goddesses of Maharashtra are the subject of a unique study by Anne Feldhaus, *Water and Womanhood* (1995), which draws on rich textual, iconographic, and oral sources. A South Indian example is provided by William P. Harman's *The Sacred Marriage of a Hindu Goddess* (1989), a study of the cult of Mīnākṣī in Madurai, which includes a translation of a seventeenth-century Tamil account of her wedding to Sundareśvara, a local form of Śiva. Also notable is Alf Hiltebeitel's wide-ranging research on the Tamil folk worship of Draupadī, heroine of the Sanskrit *Mahābhārata* epic, reflected in his two-volume study, *The Cult of Draupadī* (1988, 1991).

Beane, Wendell Charles. *Myth, Cult, and Symbols in Śākta Hinduism*. Leiden: E. J. Brill, 1977.

Brown, C. Mackenzie. *God as Mother: A Feminine Theology in India*. Hartford, Vt.: Claude Stark, 1974.

———. *The Triumph of the Goddess: The Canonical Models and Theological Issues of the* Devī-Bhāgavata Purāṇa. Albany: State University of New York Press, 1990.

Coburn, Thomas B. *Devī Māhātmya: The Crystallization of the Goddess Tradition*. Columbia, Mo.: South Asia Books, 1985.

———. *Encountering the Goddess: A Translation of the* Devī-Māhātmya *and a Study of Its Interpretation*. Albany: State University of New York Press, 1991.

Erndl, Kathleen. *Victory to the Mother: The Hindu Goddess of Northwest India in Myth, Ritual, and Symbol*. New York: Oxford University Press, 1993.

Feldhaus, Anne. *Water and Womanhood: Religious Meanings of Rivers in Maharashtra*. New York: Oxford University Press, 1995.

Gatwood, Lynn E. *Devi and the Spouse Goddess*. Riverdale, Md: Riverdale, 1985.
Harman, William P. *The Sacred Marriage of a Hindu Goddess*. Bloomington and Indianapolis: Indiana University Press, 1989.
Hawley, John Stratton, and Donna Marie Wulff, eds. *The Divine Consort: Rādhā and the Goddesses of India*. Berkeley: Berkeley Religious Studies Series, 1982.
———, eds. *Devī: Goddesses of India*. Berkeley: University of California Press, 1996.
Hiltebeitel, Alf. *The Cult of Draupadī*: Vol. 1, *Mythologies: From Gingee to Kurukṣetra*. Chicago: University of Chicago Press, 1988.
———. *The Cult of Draupadī*: Vol. 2, *On Hindu Ritual and the Goddess*. Chicago: University of Chicago Press, 1991.
Kinsley, David. *Hindu Goddesses: Visions of the Divine Feminine in the Hindu Religious Tradition*. Berkeley and Los Angeles: University of California Press, 1986.
———. *Tantric Visions of the Divine Feminine: The Ten Mahāvidyās*. Berkeley: University of California Press.
Pintchman, Tracy. *The Rise of the Goddess in the Hindu Tradition*. Albany: State University of New York Press, 1994.
Sax, William: *Mountain Goddess: Gender and Politics in a Himalayan Pilgrimage*. New York: Oxford University Press, 1991.
Smith, William L. *The One-Eyed Goddess: A Study of the Manasā Maṅgal*. Stockholm: Almquist & Wiksell, 1980.

Anthologies and General Studies

A resource of particular value for the study of medieval traditions is Jan Gonda's comprehensive survey volume *Medieval Religious Literature in Sanskrit* (1977), which includes nearly a hundred pages on pāñcarātra literature as well as detailed treatments of the āgamic tradition and of such ubiquitous genres as *stotra* and *māhātmya*, revealing that medieval Sanskrit authors, no less than those who composed in vernacular languages, were largely preoccupied with "devotion, sacrificial cult, pilgrimage and adoration of images and symbols and a belief in Divine grace" (1).

Since 1979 a series of international conferences on "Devotional Literature in New Indo-Aryan Languages" have been held triannually in Europe and England. Each conference is intended to produce a volume offering a representative sample of research conducted over the three-year period; five have appeared to date—edited by Callewaert (1980), Thiel-Horstmann (1983), McGregor (1992), Mallison (1994), and Entwistle (1999).

Topics addressed are broader than the conference title suggests and essentially embrace all bhakti-related phenomena. Thus these publications offer a sampling of recent research on the medieval period, especially that done by British and European scholars. Another significant collection appeared in 1981 as *Tradition and Modernity in Bhakti Movements*, edited by Jayant Lele. Its essays cover a range of regional traditions and give special emphasis to the unorthodox social message of many devotional teachers. Pioneering French bhakti scholar Charlotte Vaudeville, the author of important studies of Tulsīdās, Kabīr, and the Vrindavan Kṛṣṇa tradition, was honored in a 1991 festschrift edited by Diana Eck and Françoise Mallison, *Devotion Divine*, which includes some fine essays. The similarly titled collection *Love Divine* (1993), edited by Karel Werner, features the work of scholars based in the United Kingdom and includes two essays on devotional traditions in South and Southeast Asian Buddhism.

Several other anthologies offer interdisciplinary perspectives on popular Hinduism since medieval times, emphasizing folk or heterodox traditions often neglected in text-based studies. A volume edited by Alf Hiltebeitel, *Criminal Gods and Demon Devotees* (1989), examines the Hindu fascination with what one essay terms "transgressive sacrality" and the almost ubiquitous presence of popular (and sometimes ferocious) guardian deities. Joanne Waghorn and Norman Cutler's edited volume *Gods of Flesh, Gods of Stone* (1985) explores the religious phenomenon of embodiment across a spectrum of activities that include possession, ritual drama, and the construction and worship of divine images. *The Gods at Play* (1995), edited by William Sax, examines the concept and performative expressions of *līlā* in traditions as diverse as Kashmir Śaivism, Bengal Śāktism, and Vaiṣṇava and folk contexts. Contributions to the study of the still relatively neglected literature of bhakti hagiography appear in Vaudeville's *Myths, Saints, and Legends in Medieval India* (1996) and in *According to Tradition* (1994), edited by Winand Callewaert and Rupert Snell. The social implications of devotional ideologies is the special focus of *Bhakti Religion in North India* (1995), edited by David Lorenzen, which includes an introduction in which he expounds a typology of *nirguṇa* and *saguṇa* traditions along sociopolitical lines. Another comparatively neglected topic is addressed in a collection edited by Jeffrey Timm, *Texts in Context* (1992), which explores the interpretive methods and insights of traditional sectarian commentators.

The broad phenomenon of bhakti and the problem of satisfactorily defining it is the topic of Krishna Sharma's study *Bhakti and the Bhakti Movement* (1987), which I referenced above (see notes 2 and 3). In seeking to offer "a new perspective" on the nature of bhakti, Sharma attacks what she terms its "current accepted academic definition," which she characterizes as emphasizing (1) belief in a personal god; (2) a nonmonistic view of reality; and (3) negation of the efficacy of the vedāntic notion of *jñāna* (6–7). Her most valuable insights stem from her critique of the intellectual agenda of early Western Indologists, for whom the categories of "religion" and "philosophy" were definitively separated and who equated "natural religion" with monotheistic belief in a personal god. Scholars like H. H. Wilson and George Grierson were also influenced, Sharma argues, by the extreme but somewhat atypical theism of the Gauḍīya Vaiṣṇava school. Through their writings, Gauḍīya doctrines—particularly those that seemed in accord with Christian positions—were projected as normative for bhakti as a whole and became part of a definition of "the bhakti religion" fully articulated in an influential 1909 article by Grierson in *The Encyclopedia of Religion and Ethics*. Sharma points out that this definition, based on Western categories, overlooks the ongoing interaction between advaitin and devotional perspectives reflected in such texts as the *Bhakti sūtras* of Nārada and Śāṇḍilya. Thus when Westerners ponder how a learned advaitin like Madhusūdana Sarasvatī (seventeenth century) could have composed, in addition to commentaries on the writings of Śaṅkarācārya, fervent devotional songs to Kṛṣṇa, they are struggling with categories of their own creation and pondering a "problem" that, for most Hindus, implies simply a matter of context. The weakest element in Sharma's study, apart from its redundant style, is her failure to cite later examples of scholarly use of the "definition" that she alleges they uphold. Many of the studies already cited in this chapter offer a treatment of bhakti and its varieties that is considerably more nuanced and more sensitive to Indian categories than Sharma's argument would suggest. Nevertheless, her book is a worthy investigation into the historiography of bhakti in the context of the Indo-British encounter and its intellectual legacy.

Callewaert, Winand M., ed. *Early Hindī Devotional Literature in Current Research*. Leuven: Department Orientalistiek, Katholieke Universiteit, 1980.

Callewaert, Winand M., and Rupert Snell, eds. *According to Tradition: Hagiographical Writing in India*. Wiesbaden: Harrassowitz Verlag, 1994.

Eck, Diana L., and Françoise Mallison, eds. *Devotion Divine—Bhakti Traditions from the Regions of India; Studies in Honor of Charlotte Vaudeville*. Groningen: Egbert Forsten, 1991.

Entwistle, Alan W., Carol Salomon, with Heidi Pauwels, and Michael C. Shapiro. *Studies in Early Modern Indo-Aryan Languages, Literature, and Culture: Research Papers, 1992–1994, presented at the Sixth Conference on Devotional Literature in New Indo-Aryan Languages*. New Delhi: Manohar, 1999.

Gonda, Jan. *Medieval Religious Literature in Sanskrit*. Wiesbaden: Otto Harrassowitz, 1977.

Hiltebeitel, Alf, ed. *Criminal Gods and Demon Devotees: Essays on the Guardians of Popular Hinduism*. Albany: State University of New York Press, 1989.

Lele, Jayant, ed. *Tradition and Modernity in Bhakti Movements*. Leiden: E. J. Brill, 1981.

Lorenzen, David N., ed. *Bhakti Religion in North India: Community Identity and Political Action*. Albany: State University of New York Press, 1995.

Mallison, Françoise, ed. *Studies in South Asian Devotional Literature, 1988–1991*. Paris: École Française d'Extréme-Orient; New Delhi: Manohar, 1994.

McGregor, Ronald Stuart, ed. *Devotional Literature in South Asia: Current Research, 1985–1988*. Cambridge: Cambridge University Press, 1992.

Sax, William S., ed. *The Gods at Play: Līlā in South Asia*. New York: Oxford University Press, 1995.

Sharma, Krishna. *Bhakti and the Bhakti Movement: A New Perspective*. New Delhi: Munshiram Manoharlal, 1987.

Thiel-Horstmann, Monika, ed. *Bhakti in Current Research, 1979–1982*. Berlin: Dietrich Reimer Verlag, 1983.

Timm, Jeffrey, ed. *Texts in Context: Traditional Hermeneutics in South Asia*. Albany: State University of New York Press, 1992.

Vaudeville, Charlotte. *Myths, Saints, and Legends in Medieval India*. Comp. Vasudha Dalmia. New Delhi: Oxford University Press, 1996.

Waghorne, Joanne Punzo, and Norman Cutler, eds. *Gods of Flesh, Gods of Stone*. Chambersburg, Pa.: Anima, 1985.

Werner, Karel, ed. *Love Divine, Studies in* Bhakti *and Devotional* Mysticism. Richmond, Surrey, Eng.: Curzon, 1993.

Having identified some recent trends and individual achievements in the study of medieval Hinduism and its regional traditions, I will briefly underscore several themes that I believe merit the attention of future scholars. Among understudied geographical regions are several "link areas" that historically served as conduits for linguistic and cultural influences—for example, Maharashtra, Karnataka, and Andhra—in which Indo-Aryan Sanskritic civilization interacted with Dravidian and tribal cultures. Research on these regions depends, of course, on the availability of instruction in relevant languages and is hampered at present by poor employment prospects for scholars specializing in nonmainstream traditions. Yet the multilingual culture of medieval South Asia—in which local vernaculars, as yet little affected by a spirit of regional linguistic nationalism, were molded by saint-poets anxious to place their message before a wide audience—can never be fully appreciated until some of the peripheral and link areas receive more sustained attention. In this context, it is also worth noting the continuing absence of major studies that critically examine the nature and extent of Hindu/Muslim interaction during the medieval period.

Even within the traditions that have been relatively well studied, there is need for more sophisticated analysis of the masterpieces of bhakti literature. A few signal studies (e.g., Bryant, Cutler, Ramanujan) have applied some of the insights of contemporary criticism to demonstrate convincingly that, for example, the apparent "spontaneity" and "emotion" of some of the best devotional poetry conceals the craft of self-conscious artists operating within a highly intertextual world of discourse. Significantly, these studies seem to have produced, along with critical insights, some of the most elegant and readable translations. Yet they remain notable exceptions to a scholarly agenda that still largely emphasizes historical and theological cataloging. And despite a few exceptions (e.g., Clooney, Narayanan, Timm), the study of indigenous commentarial traditions and the often highly sophisticated theories of literature and aesthetics that underlie them likewise remains in its relative infancy.

A corollary to the notion of saint-poets as unselfconscious ecstatics has been the implicit judgment, referred to earlier, that the incorporation of their songs into sectarian liturgy, ritual, and metaphysics represents a corruption of their authors' vision, and a topic less worthy of researchers' attention. Again, a few recent studies (e.g., Davis, Haberman, Prentiss) have challenged this attitude by focusing on the enactment of bhakti through formalized techniques that nevertheless function in the context of emotional worship. Similarly, Peterson and Narayanan remind us that, in the case of the Tamil saint-poets, ritual worship in temples is alluded to in the earliest texts and often appears to have provided inspiration for poets' songs.

Another neglected field, linked to the sectarian expression of bhakti, is hagiography. Several recent studies (e.g., Peterson, Hardy) have pointed out that knowledge of the legendary biography of a singer is often essential for the devotional audience to understand the meaning of a singer's song, and that the persuasive power of vernacular texts depends largely on concepts of exemplary personal witness and authority. The personalized nature of this literature warrants further investigation, yet some of the major works relevant to such research remain either untranslated (e.g., the Hindi *Bhaktamāla* and most of the hagiographies of the early Tamil saints) or little studied (e.g., the Marathi hagiographies of Mahīpati).

Ideally, the study of hagiography should be one aspect of a wider project in social and cultural history. Although scholars have long abandoned the cliché that bhakti is an "egalitarian" phenomenon, the diverse sociocultural ramifications of medieval devotional traditions and their interaction with mundane networks of power and hegemony still remain inadequately explored, and this is only partly due to scarcity of documentation. It is also true that historians of religion, despite the label, have sometimes shown surprisingly little interest in history. In contemporary South Asia, conflicting interpretations of the past championed by religiopolitical groups have become a source of increasingly violent conflict, and it is imperative that scholars seek a fuller understanding of the religious history of the premodern period.

This assumes, of course, that students of culture continue to care about such issues. At present, an often-invoked but vaguely defined notion of cultural "globalization" coupled with an assault on "area studies" (associated with old-school orientalist prejudices and a dull emphasis on texts) by some social scientists and advocates of "cultural studies," seems to have led to declining interest in the study of texts, and indeed of non-Western languages, and to a preoccupation with contemporary and often obscure theory—a kind of neo-Brahmanical world of mind-numbing pedantry that, paradoxically, presents itself as politically committed scholarship. Certainly there are works among those cited here that err on the side of a too-close focus on individual textual "trees" without any vision of a broader forest—the encompassing cultural context within which texts live and are interpreted. Yet I have found the scholarly output of the past three decades to be, on the whole, more balanced and contextualized, aware of cultural issues and debates that bracket texts and ritual practices and also increasingly sensitive to the ideological baggage of the scholar's own academic lineage. The best scholarship always appears to be rooted in a thorough training in regional languages and extensive immersion in their cultural milieu: a time-consuming, commitment-demanding training that few graduate programs at present seem to encourage.

Finally, I must sound a warning concerning the preservation of manuscripts as a resource for future scholarship. Few South Asian archives have adequate facilities or equipment for historical preservation; many lack the means, or perhaps even the inclination, to make their holdings widely accessible to scholars. Despite the pioneering labors of a few researchers (e.g., Callewaert) and the potential of computer technology to facilitate manuscript research, few major bhakti works are available in truly critical editions, and in general the potential for such research may be reckoned to grow less with each succeeding monsoon. Yet scholars need not consider themselves altogether helpless in this matter; during the 1970s, a group of Indian, British, and American scholars collaborated to establish the Vrindavan Research Institute for the preservation of the manuscript heritage of the Braj region; with support from several foundations and governments, they succeeded in establishing a modern preservation facility and archive that now houses some twenty-five thousand manuscripts. A comparable facility is badly needed to preserve the premodern literature of eastern Hindi, currently contained in such anachronistic archives as the library of the Nagari Pracarini Sabha in Banaras and, worse yet, in the private treasuries of sectarian temples, where unique manuscripts may serve as objects of veneration even while they turn to dust.

The bureacratic, financial, and cultural obstacles to establishing facilities such as the one in Vrindavan are daunting, but even where such new institutions are impossible, scholars should use what influence they have to encourage local librarians and collectors to do a more effective job of preserving the manuscript heritage. The importance of this effort grows even as standardized printed and recorded texts continue to proliferate and the number of traditional scholars and performers conversant with variant textual traditions declines. Working to prevent the disappearance of a vital component of India's cultural heritage must assume priority status for concerned scholars.

Notes

1. Eleanor Zelliot, "The Medieval Bhakti Movement in History," in Bardwell L. Smith, ed., *Hinduism: New Essays in the History of Religions* (Leiden: E. J. Brill, 1976), 143–68.

2. The manner in which internal debates in British and European intellectual circles over the nature and validity of religion influenced early scholars of Hinduism is explored in Krishna Sharma's *Bhakti and the Bhakti Movement* (New Delhi: Munshiram Manoharlal, 1987), which is further discussed toward the end of this chapter.

3. 1:48 in the version that appears as a preface to *Śrimad Bhāgavata Mahāpurāṇa*, trans. C. L. Goswami and M. A. Sastri, in 2 vols. (Gorakhpur, U.P.: Gītā Press, 1971), 6; the *Bhāgavata māhātmya* is commonly included in the *Padma* and *Skanda* purāṇas. A critical analysis of this passage that questions its historical validity appears in Sharma, *Bhakti and the Bhakti Movement*, 296–314. Sharma's argument is further extended by Prentiss in *The Embodiment of Bhakti*, 31–36.

4. I am grateful to Frederick Smith for assistance in compiling this section.

5. I am grateful to Tony K. Stewart for assistance in locating works relevant to the study of Oriya and Bengali Vaiṣṇava traditions.

NINE Modern Hinduism

ROBERT D. BAIRD

An understanding of modern Hinduism has been greatly enhanced in recent years through the work of a number of disciplines such as anthropology, sociology, political science, history, and the history of religions. No longer can religion be understood apart from its cultural context. This means that religion must be understood in the context of the social, political, legal, and historical setting in which it occurs. To understand religion (and that includes modern Hinduism) at this point in scholarly activity means to understand more than religion.

Such an understanding is also much more complex than our earlier understandings made possible. In the light of anthropological and sociological studies, facile statements about Hindu essence can no longer be made. If it is anything, Hinduism is more than a philosophical essence that is empirically unverifiable except in the religious thought of a reformer. Hinduism is also what simple householders do, which often stands in some discontinuity from philosophical essences. Readers who limit their reading to one discipline in the study of modern Hinduism are bound to receive a truncated view of Hinduism—or that to which the term is often taken to refer. It is my intention, then, to take into account a wide range of disciplines, remembering that the focus of our account is religion.

The organization of such a critical bibliography is to a large extent arbitrary. While the books and essays under consideration fit under the categories I will use, they often fit with equal comfort under other categories. Does one deal with pilgrimage in Rajasthan under regional studies or pilgrimage? When a book includes a discussion of, say, ritual, temples, and festivals, under which of the three does one deal with it? Given the nature of modern scholarly studies, this is an insoluble problem. So, knowing that there must be numerous alternative organizational schemes, in this chapter I attempt to organize modern scholarship. With a few notable exceptions, I limit this account to works that have been published since 1965.

Some works, while not claiming to be exhaustive, do attempt to cover more than one would expect from a monograph. Frequently they seek to cover a broad range of topics, thinkers, or movements. Philip H. Ashby's *Modern Trends in Hinduism* is a series of lectures given in 1968–69 under the auspices of the Committee on the History of Religions of the American Council of Learned Societies.[1] This 134-page book offers several useful studies, which are based on three underlying principles: that Hinduism does not borrow from the outside in order to displace its essence; that the standards to which modern Hinduism appeals are central to its own traditions; and that Hinduism is consciously aware of the present situation in which it lives. Ashby proposes that Hinduism has an essence and that it is continually regrouping around that essence. The change that characterizes its present existence will also be part of its future. Particularly useful are the chapters on the values of contemporary Hindu youth, the esoteric religion of Radha Soami Satsang, the Hindu religion and politics. *Religious Ferment in Modern India*, by Hal W. French and Arvind Sharma, provides an introduction to nineteenth- and twentieth-century Indian religion focusing on religion's interaction with political realities.[2] While it concentrates on "Hindu" developments, it also touches on Muslim and Buddhist developments as well. "Modern" in the title is taken to mean the period from 1800–1947.

Rakhal Chandra Nath's *The New Hindu Movement, 1886–1911* is an attempt to relate the history of ideas that are foundational for "the New Hindu Movement," a designation that Nath prefers to "the Hindu Revival," which suggests to him the undoing of the good things achieved by nineteenth-century reform movements such as the Brahmo Samaj.[3] The broader movement is characterized by rationalism, personal illumination through religion, and bringing a vision of Indian civilization into the present and future. Centering on Bengal, this study includes a discussion of

Ramakrishna and Vivekananda, ending with 1911, the year of the annulment of the partition of Bengal. That date also marked the end of a phase of political agitation in Bengal that drew its inspiration from religious ferment. Of particular interest to Nath are the ideological roots of nationalism. V. S. Naravane's *Modern Indian Thought* is organized with chapters on specific thinkers, rather than thematically.[4] Dealing with Rammohun Roy, Ramakrishna, Vivekananda, Tagore, Gandhi, and Aurobindo, along with Coomaraswamy and Iqbal, it is quite useful as an introduction to the thought of these important modern religious thinkers. Donald H. Bishop's *Thinkers of the Indian Renaissance* covers much the same ground.[5]

For years, the standard survey of modern Indian religion was Farquhar's *Modern Religious Movements in India* (1914), but Farquhar's study, while substantial, was written from a missionary perspective that is not part of the present academic method. Since the 1980s we have had the 500-page *Religion in Modern India*, edited by the author of this chapter.[6] Using historical method, *Religion in Modern India* is a collaborative effort to survey the field, with thirteen substantial chapters on modern religious movements and ten on modern religious thinkers. Another book with the same title, *Religion in Modern India*, edited by Giri Raj Gupta, offers a more sociological approach.[7] Its sixteen essays deal with such themes as popular Hinduism, mother goddess cults, and religious insulation and adaptation.

Milton Singer's collection of essays *When a Great Tradition Modernizes* is broader than the study of religion but includes a number of previously published articles that neither the anthropologist nor the historian of religions can afford to ignore.[8] Among them are "Text and Context in the Study of Contemporary Hinduism"; "Search for a Great Tradition in Cultural Performances"; "The Social Organization of Sanskritic Hinduism in Madras City"; "Urbanization and Cultural Change: *Bhakti* in the City"; and "The Radha-Krishna Bhajanas of Madras City."

Reference works that include material on the modern period should also be mentioned. The thirteen-volume *Encyclopedia of Religion* (Mircea Eliade, editor-in-chief) contains articles on most of the themes discussed in this chapter; the major articles include a brief bibliography.[9] *Hindu World*, by Benjamin Walker, is a two-volume encyclopedia of terms and movements that will be useful for understanding both the modern period and the ancient and classical periods.[10] Bibliographies of value are Maureen Patterson's extensive *South Asia Civilization* (800 pages), which includes material on modern India,[11] and Barron Holland's *Popular Hinduism and Hindu Mythology: An Annotated Bibliography*.[12] Holland's volume covers material published up to 1978 and deals with periods other than the modern. Its references include attention to sects, deities, ritual, festivals and pilgrimage, religious centers, dance and drama, and doctrine.

Hinduism and Social Change

While surveying a broad area, some books relate modern Hinduism to social reform and social change or place movements within a social context. Charles H. Heimsath's *Indian Nationalism and Hindu Social Reform* deals with social reform in the nineteenth century.[13] On the role of religion in social protest and reform, see the collection of essays edited by S. C. Malik, *Indian Movements*.[14] The volume includes "Bhakti Movement in South India," by M. G. S. Narayanan and Veluthat Kesavan; "The Virasiva Movement," by Arun P. Bali; "Saint-Poets of Maharashtra: Their Role in Social Transformation," by G. B. Sardar; "Arya Samaj Movement," by Pushpa Suri; and "Dissent and Protest in Modern Hindi Literature," by Narendra Mohan. *Social and Religious Reform Movements in the Nineteenth and Twentieth Centuries*, edited by S. P. Sen, director of the Institute of Historical Studies, is a collection of thirty-three essays that survey twenty states and union territories in a regional manner.[15] This volume is particularly useful by reason of its broad coverage. Movements are dealt with here that are not often met elsewhere.

Mark Juergensmeyer's *Religion as Social Vision* is based on the principle that the untouchables have long struggled against social oppressions that have been embodied in the creation of new religious movements.[16] Juergensmeyer concentrates on one such movement, the Ad Dharm. Kenneth W. Jones's *Socio-Religious Reform Movements in British India* is the third volume of the projected thirty-one-volume *New Cambridge History of India*.[17] The movements Jones chooses are "socio" in the sense that they attempt to reorder behavior, custom, and authority; they are "religious" in that they seek to legitimate an ideology through appeal to specific forms of authority such as scripture or a new religious leader's message; they are "movements" in the sense that they are an aggregate of individuals, sometimes loosely organized, united by the message of a charismatic leader or an ideology derived from that message. This careful work combines an extensive array of historical sources with a conceptual framework for explaining socioreligious movements.

Paul G. Hiebert's "India: The Politicization of a Sacred Society," in Carlo Caldarola, ed., *Religion and Societies: Asia and the Middle East*, is a survey of modern changes of a social and political nature. Relevant contributions to other volumes include J. T. F. Jordens, "Hindu Religious and Social Reform in British India"; Miriam Sharma and Jagdish P. Sharma, "Hinduism, Sarvodaya, and Social Change"; and Agehananda Bharati, "Hinduism and Modernization."[18]

V. Sudarsen et al's *Religion and Society in South Asia* contains essays by distinguished anthropologists in a Festscrift to N. Subha Reddy.[19] Bardwell L. Smith's *Religion and Social Conflict in South Asia*, while extending its attention to Buddhism, includes useful essays dealing with the Hindu tradition, among them his own "Religion, Social Conflict, and the Problem of Identity in South Asia: An Interpretive Introduction." Other essays in the volume include "The Izhavas of Kerala and their Historic Struggle for Acceptance in Hindu Society," by Cyriac K. Pullapilly, and my "Religion and the Secular: Categories for Religious Conflict and Religious Change in Independent India."[20] Addressing itself to both religious and social change in relationship to bhakti movements is Jayant Lele, ed., *Tradition and Modernity in Bhakti Movements*, a collection of essays on continuity and change in bhakti movements.[21]

Regional Studies

Important work is being done in regional studies. The regions receiving the most attention are Maharashtra, Bengal, and South India. Among the important works on Hinduism in Maharashtra is *The Experience of Hinduism*, edited by Eleanor Zelliot and Maxine Berntsen.[22] With twenty-one individual essays, this volume seeks to communicate what it means in human terms to be a Hindu in Maharashtra today. Included are some essays of a first-person account, others analyzing religious institutions, and several analyzing attacks on caste. The book was published as a tribute to Irawati Karve, and her firsthand account of a pilgrimage is included along with other pilgrimage accounts. The volume has a useful bibliography. Another collection of essays is Milton Israel and N. K. Wagle, eds., *Religion and Society in Maharashtra*.[23] Gunther-Deitz Sontheimer's *Pastoral Deities in Western India* (translated by Anne Feldhaus) is a study of deities in

Maharashtra and Karnataka, based on oral "texts" collected during fieldwork. The texts are placed in their social, cultural, and ecological contexts; see also Anne Feldhaus, *The Deeds of God in Ṛddhipūr*.[24]

Lawrence Allan Babb's *The Divine Hierarchy* is an anthropological analysis of the pantheon of deities, their puja, and the rites and rituals associated with the popular Hinduism of Raipur and the Chhattisgarh region of Madya Pradesh. Babb's *Redemptive Encounters* is a study of three urban movements—the Radhasoami movement, the Brahma Kumaris, and Sathya Sai Baba—based on research done in the Delhi–New Delhi area.[25] R. M Sarkar's *Regional Cults and Rural Tradition* is a study of village deities and village cults in Bengal in terms of social anthropology. Lina Fruzzetti's *The Gift of a Virgin* also gives attention to ritual and the place of women. P. K. Maity's *Human Fertility Cults and Rituals in Bengal*, a study of folk religion, is an attempt to trace the history of human fertility cults and rituals in Bengal historically and in the present; see also June McDaniel, *The Madness of the Saints: Ecstatic Religion in Bengal*.[26] For another dimension of Hindu religious change in the British period, see David Kopf's *British Orientalism and the Bengal Renaissance*.[27]

Moving from Bengal, south to Orissa, Anncharlott Eschmann et al's *The Cult of Jagannath and the Regional Tradition of Orissa* contains a rich array of essays dealing with historical and contemporary themes relating to this important tradition. Nancy Gardner Cassels, *Religion and Pilgrim Tax under the Company Raj* is a study of the relationship between the East India Company and the temple of Lord Jagannath; one might also look at Prabhat Mukherjee, *History of the Jagannath Temple in the 19th Century*.[28]

A number of volumes have grown out of the "Conference on Religion in South Asia" (CRSA). Two CRSA workshops produced *Gods of Flesh, Gods of Stone: The Embodiment of Divinity in India*, edited by Joanne Punzo Wagnorne and Norman Cutler with the collaboration of Vasudha Narayanan. Among the essays are "Creation of the Sacred Image: Apotheosis and Destruction in Hinduism," by James J. Preston; "On This Day in My Humble Way: Aspects of Puja," by Paul B. Courtwright; "Arcavatara: On Earth as He Is in Heaven," by Vasudha Narayanan; "The Devotee and the Deity: Living a Personalistic Theology," by William H. Deadwyler III; "Possession and Pottery: Serving the Divine in a South Indian Community," by Stephen Inglis; "God's Forceful Call: Possession as a Divine Strategy," by Manuel Moreno; "Founders, Swamis, and Devotees: Becoming Divine in

North Karnataka," by Lise F. Vail; and "The Holy Man as the Abode of God in the Swaminarayan Religion," by Raymond B. Williams.[29] Also emerging from CRSA (1984) was Alf Hiltebeitel, ed., *Criminal Gods and Demon Devotees*, a collection of fifteen essays on popular Hinduism.[30]

K. Ishwaran's *Religion and Society among the Lingayats of South India* is a sociological study interpreting the Lingayats as a populist religion, utilizing but not completely adopting either the Great or the Little Traditions; Ishwaran treats ethics, religion and social structure, and modernization. Fred W. Clothey, "The Yāga: A Fire Ritual," and Charles A. Ryerson's "Contemporary Śaivism and Tamil Identity" are to be found in *Experiencing Siva*, edited by Fred W. Clothey and J. Bruce Long; Holly Baker Reynolds, "The Changing Nature of a Tamil Vow: The Challenge of Trans-Sectarian Bhakti in Contemporary South India," is in Bardwell L. Smith's *Religious Movements and Social Identity*.[31]

Fred W. Clothey, *The Many Faces of Murukan* is a study of the textual tradition relating to Murukan as well as the contemporary cults surrounding this deity in Tamil Nadu.[32] *Krishna: Myths, Rites, and Attitudes*, edited by Milton Singer, is a collection of essays, the majority of which deal with the premodern periods, but three of the essays fall within the modern period and are well worth reading: Singer's "The Rādhā-Krishna Bhajanas of Madras City"; T. K. Venkateswaran's "Rādhā-krishna Bhajanas of South India: A Phenomenological, Theological, and Philosophical Study"; and McKim Marriot's "The Feast of Love."[33] Genevieve Lemercinier's *Religion and Ideology in Kerala* also deals with southern India. For a more extensive survey of work on religion in South India done since 1970, see Fred W. Clothey's "On the Study of Religion in South India."[34]

Hindu Temples

A growing number of studies have been made of Hindu temples from the perspectives of anthropology and art history. Other studies have concentrated on rituals or the relationship between temples and state regulation. Franklin A. Presler's important *Religion under Bureaucracy* is an analysis of the relations of the state, religion, and politics in Tamil Nadu.[35] It goes beyond this, however, in showing how social and economic factors are also involved. In a preface summary, Presler writes:

> The government's official policies toward religion provides a fruitful context from which to view, for example, the relation of political parties

> to sources of patronage and conflict, the effect of centralized "rational" administration on local practice and privilege, the consequences of bureaucratization for democratic politics, and the legacy of traditional theories of legitimacy in the "secular" state.

This book is a must for both political scientists and historians of religions.

Another work is anthropologist Arjun Appadurai's *Worship and Conflict under Colonial Rule*. Of somewhat shorter scope but no less significant is James J. Preston's *Cult of the Goddess*, an anthropological study that places a Devi temple in Cuttack City, Orissa, in a social, economic, and ritual context so that the reader gains insight into understanding how the goddess "assists newly urbanized people as they adjust to new conditions imposed by city life." Preston's article "Two Urbanizing Orissan Temples," written with James Freeman, is also important, and note should also be made of Nirmal K. Bhose's "Organization of Services in the Temple of Lingaraj Bhubaneswar."[36]

An important study of the Minaksi temple in Madurai is Carol Appadurai Breckenridge's unpublished dissertation "The Sri Ninaksi Sundaresvara Temple." William P. Harman's *The Sacred Marriage of a Hindu Goddess* is a careful study of relevant texts that provide the historical background for the marriage of the goddess Minaksi to Siva. Also included is description and analysis of the annual marriage festival as performed in Madurai and a determination of how this enactment touches the lives of participants. C. J. Fuller's *Servants of the Goddess* is an anthropological analysis of the Minaksi temple in Madurai. Although it concentrates on the role of the priests and their views of themselves, it also deals with temple reform and the relationship of the government to the temple. Also by C. J. Fuller are his article "The Divine Couple's Relationship in a South Indian Temple" and "The Attempted Reform of South Indian Temple Hinduism," in *Religious Organization and Religious Experience*, ed. J. Davis. Equally important is an article by André Beteille, "Social Organization of Temples in a Tanjore Village."[37]

Ritual, Festival, and Pilgrimage

The themes of ritual, festival, and pilgrimage have considerable overlap: ritual, which can take place in the home or temple, may be part of a festival; rituals, festivals, and even temples can become part of a pilgrimage. Addressing itself to ritual and festival is Fred W. Clothey's collection of essays *Rhythm and Intent: Ritual Studies from South India.*[38] Placing his particular attention to the south Indian Muruka cult in the context of ritual studies, Clothey addresses such themes as ritual space, ritual time, as well as specific festivals and rituals (a chapter addressing the "festival experience" which makes it clear that pilgrimage can also be part of festival). *Rites and Beliefs in Modern India,* edited by Gabriella Eichinger Ferro-Luzzi, comes out of the "Tenth European Conference on South Asian Studies," held in Venice in 1988. It includes such essays as "Ethnic Contrasts and Parallels in the Post-partum Period: Some Evidence from Bijnor, North India," by Patricia Jeffery, Roger Jeffery and Andrew Lyon; "Death and Defilement: Divergent Accounts of Untouchability in Gujarat," by Shalini Randeria; and "Modern Devadasis: Devotees of Goddess Yellamma in Karnataka," by Jackie Assayag. See also Stuart H. Blackburn's article "Death and Deification."[39]

Festivals have generated considerable attention on the part of anthropologists, geographers, and historians of religions. *Religious Festivals in South India and Sri Lanka,* edited by Guy R. Welbon and Glenn E. Yocum, contains a number of important essays: "The Hindu Festival Calendar," by Karen L. Merrey; "The Cycle of Festivals at Pārthasārathī Temple," James L. Martin; "The Caala's Song," by Guy R. Welbon; "Two Citrā Festivals in Madurai," by D. Dennis Hudson; "Mahāśivarātri: The Śaiva Festival of Repentance," by J. Bruce Long; "The Festival Interlude: Some Anthropological Observations," by Suzanne Hanchett; "The End Is the Beginning: The Festival Chain in Andhra Pradesh," by Jane M. Christian; and "Kaḷam Euttu: Art and Ritual in Kerala," by Clifford R. Jones.[40] A more extended study is Penelope Logan's thesis "Domestic Worship and the Festival Cycle in the South Indian City of Madurai." Suzanne Hanchett's *Coloured Rice* is a social anthropological study of a number of family festivals in two South Indian villages: the festivals are placed in a cultural and ritual setting; attention is given to the place of women in the kinship system in general and at festivals in particular. It is a rewarding study. Note also Akos Ostor, *The Play of the Gods.*[41] Articles on festivals include Paul Younger's "A Temple Festival of Māriyamma" and "Ten Days of Wandering and Romance with Lord Rankanatan," and John M. Stanley, "Special Time, Special Power: The Fluidity of Power in a Popular Hindu Festival."[42] Two chapters on festivals appear in Bardwell L. Smith, ed., *Religious*

Movements and Social Identity: Jayashree B. Gokhale's "Religion and National Awakening: The Ganapati Festival in Bombay Presidency, 1890–1920," and William C. McCormack's "Meaning System in Two Lingayat Festivals."[43]

For a broad view of pilgrimage sites, a good place to start is Surinder Mohan Bhardwaj, *Pilgrimage: A Study in Cultural Geography*, a study with an introductory survey of the literature and an appended bibliography. Among studies of specific sacred centers, of the first order is Diana Eck's *Banaras: City of Light*, which combines the study of numerous Sanskrit texts with fieldwork that provides a contemporary understanding of the city itself. The present understanding includes the city's geography, its temples, seasons of pilgrimage, and its Brahmins—the living keepers of its tradition. This book is a significant scholarly achievement; moreover, its map and carefully chosen illustrations bring Banaras to life. Other book-length studies of sacred towns are Makhan Jha, *The Sacred Complex in Janakpur*, and Rajendra Jindel, *Culture of a Sacred Town: A Sociological Study of Nathdwara*. L. P. Vidyarthi, *The Sacred Complex in Hindu Gaya* deals with such issues as sacred geography, performances, fairs and festivals, specialists, and pilgrimage. The same author's *The Sacred Complex of Kashi* deals with most of the same themes for Kashi.[44] A number of journal articles also address pilgrimage sites. Among them are Diana L. Eck, "India's Tīrthas: 'Crossing' in Sacred Geography"; Fred Clothey, "Pilgrimage Centers in Tamil Cultus of Muruka"; and James Freeman, "Religious Change in a Hindu Pilgrimage Center."[45]

On pilgrimage itself, an early study is G. A. Deleury, *The Cult of Vithoba*. More recent is *Palkhi: An Indian Pilgrimage*, a translation by Philip C. Engblom of D. B. Mokashi's day-by-day account of his experience on the Warkari pilgrimage in Maharashtra. This volume—like Zelliot and Berntsen's *The Experience of Hinduism*, mentioned above—vividly portrays the human dimension of religious practice. E. Alan Morinis's *Pilgrimage in the Hindu Tradition* explores individual behavior and experience in a microsociological study of three Bengali pilgrimages, while Ann Gold's *Fruitful Journeys: The Ways of Rajasthani Pilgrims* concentrates more on the range of motivations of the pilgrims than the pilgrimage site as such. Makhan Jha, ed., *Dimensions of Pilgrimage* contains thirteen essays on Hindu pilgrimage based on the transactions of a "World Symposium for Pilgrimage."[46] Shorter works addressing pilgrimage include Mira Reym Binford,

"Mixing the Color of Ram and Ranuja: A Folk Pilgrimage to the Grave of a Rajput Hero-saint," and Agehananda Bharati, "Pilgrimage in the Indian Tradition."[47]

John Stratton Hawley's *At Play with Krishna* provides not only an account of pilgrimage to Brindavan but also four dramas, with helpful introductions. This performance theme is continued in two recent publications: Richard Armando Frasca's *The Theater of the Mahabharata* shows how theater can transform the text into sacred time and space, thereby renewing those who sponsor and/or view such performance; and Philip A. Lutgendorf, *The Life of a Text*, captures in detail the performance techniques and the impact of the epic upon largely illiterate audiences. Lutgendorf's study contains a wealth of ethnographic detail. Finally, John D. Smith's *The Epic of Pabuji: A Study* is the study of the text of an oral epic and its performance in contemporary Rajasthan. This is part of a cult of a medieval hero who has attained the status of a Hindu god.[48]

The Feminine in Hinduism

Although there is a growing number of books on Indian women, many of them only slightly touch on religion or Hinduism explicitly. *Images of the Feminine*, by Katherine K. Young and Arvind Sharma, includes some titles useful for the study of Hinduism and women, but the number of books on women has exploded since the publication of that bibliography in 1974.[49]

A number of interesting papers are contained in *The Powers of Tamil Women*, edited by Susan S. Wadley, among them "On the Meaning of Sakti to Women," by Margaret Egnor; "The Auspicious Married Woman," by Holly Baker Reynolds; "Marriage in Tamil Culture: The Problem of Conflicting 'Models,'" by Sheryl B. Daniel; and Wadley's "The Paradoxical Powers of Tamil Women." Another article is Kim Knott's "Men and Women, or Devotees? Krishna Consciousness and the Role of Women"; and also helpful are two articles by Katherine K. Young, "From Hindu Stridharma to Universal Feminism: A Study of the Women in the Nehru Family," and "Hinduism," in *Women in World Religions*, edited by Arvind Sharma, which touches on the modern period.[50] Other important essays include David Kinsley, "Devotion as an Alternative to Marriage"; Bina Gupta, "Women's Rites and Religious Consciousness"; and Kathryn Young and Lily Miller, "Sacred Biography and the Restructuring of Society: A Study of Anandmai Ma, Lady-Saint of Modern Hinduism"; Rita M. Gross,

"Hindu Female Deities as a Resource for the Contemporary Rediscovery of the Goddess"; Kenneth W. Jones, "Socio-Religious Movements and Changing Gender Relationship among Hindus of British India"; Doranne Jacobsen, "The Women of Northand Central India"; and Susan S. Wadley, "Women and the Hindu Tradition." Also note Wadley's "Hindu Women's Family and Household Rites in a North Indian Village" and Charles S. J. White's "Mother Guru: Jnanananda of Madras."[51]

Mother Worship: Theme and Variations, edited by James J. Preston, is a crosscultural examination of the mother goddess by contemporary anthropologists. Of this book's fifteen essays, four deal with modern India: "The Goddess Kannagi: A Dominant Symbol of South Indian Tamil Society," by Jacob Pandian; "The Village Mother in Bengal," by Ralph W. Nicholas; "The Goddess Chandi as an Agent of Change," by James J. Preston; and "Pox and the Terror of Childlessness: Images and Ideas of the Smallpox Goddess in a North Indian Village," by Pauline Kolenda. G. Obeyesekere's *The Cult of the Goddess Pattini* is a detailed analysis of the goddess Pattini in terms of its textual tradition as well as its myths and rituals and its role as a mother goddess.[52]

Although abolished in 1829, the practice of suttee, or sati, continues to excite scholarly interest, perhaps as a result of a few sensational instances of it that show its remarkable persistence. The titles of the following works, one of which indicates the continuing relevance of the work of Raja Rammohun Roy in this regard, convey a fair impression of their contents: V. N. Datta, *Sati: A Historical, Social and Philosophical Inquiry into the Hindu Rite of Widow Burning*; Lata Mani, *Contentious Traditions*; Harish Chandra Upreti, *The Myth of Sati*; Santosh Singh, *A Passion for Flames*; Rajeshwari Sunder Rajan, *Real and Imagined Women*; Svapana Basu, *Sati*; Sakuntala Narasimhan, *Sati: A Study of Widow Burning in India*; Raja Rammohun Roy, *Sati: A Writeup of Raja Ram Mohun Roy about Burning of Widows Alive*; Arvind Sharma, *Sati*; and J. S. Hawley, ed., *Sati: The Blessing and the Curse*.[53]

The institution of Devadasis also continues to be a subject of analytical clarification. There is now a more nuanced understanding of their role, as indicated by the following: Jogan Shankar, *Devadasi Cult: A Sociological Analysis*; A. K. Prassad, *Devadasi System in Ancient India: A Study of Temple Dancing Girls in South India*; Saskia C. Kersenboom-Story, *Nityasumangali: Devadasi Tradition in South India*; Frederique Apffel-Margilin, *Wives of*

God-King; Leslie C. Orr, *Donors, Devotees and Daughters of God: Temple Women in Medieval Tamilnadu*.[54]

Religious Movements

David Kopf, *The Brahmo Samaj and the Shaping of the Modern Indian Mind* is the basic volume for understanding the Brahmo Samaj and its influence. On the connections with U.S. and English Unitarianism, see Spencer Lavan, *Unitarians and India: A Study of Encounter and Response* and Lavan's chapter on "The Brahmo Samaj" in *Religion in Modern India* (Baird).[55]

For the history of the Arya Samaj in the Punjab, Kenneth W. Jones's work is basic. His *Arya Dharma: Hindu Consciousness in Nineteenth Century Punjab* is a study not only of regional culture but also of a search for identity and the growth of Hindu consciousness. This is a good example of solid and insightful historical method. See also Jones's chapter "The Arya Samaj in British India" in *Religion in Modern India* (Baird) and his article "Social Change and Religious Movements in Nineteenth Century Punjab," in Rao's *Social Movement in India*. Further bibliographic references can be found in Jones's "Sources for Arya Samaj History," in W. Eric Gustafson and Kenneth W. Jones, *Sources of Punjab History*.[56]

Recent scholarly studies on the Ramakrishna movement are few. Carl Olson's *The Mysterious Play of Kali* provides some new insight into the phenomenon of Ramakrishna; Harold W. French's *The Swan's Wide Waters* traces the Ramakrishna movement in the West. Leo Schneiderman's "Ramakrishna: Personality and Social Factors in the Growth of a Religious Movement" is also useful. One might also check Claude Alan Stark's *God of All: Sri Ramakrishna's Approach to Religious Pluralism*.[57]

A fine historical treatment of the development of Vivekananda's religious thought can be found in George M. Williams's *The Quest for Meaning of Svāmī Vivekānanda*; also consult V. K. Aroa, *The Social and Political Philosophy of Swami Vivekenanda* and Binoy K. Roy, *Socio-political Views of Vivekananda*. Agehananda Bharati's "The Hindu Renaissance and its Apologetic Patterns," while broader in its subject matter than just Vivekananda, is a perceptive analysis of the apologetic dimension of Hindu-renaissance thinkers, including Vivekananda. There are also chapters in most of the edited books on modern Indian religion on Ramakrishna and on Vivekananda, such as Walter G. Neeval Jr., "The Transformation of Sri Ramakrishna," and Cyrus R. Pangborn, "The Ramakrishna Math and

Mission." Also, from a sympathetic viewpoint, see Christopher Isherwood's *Ramakrishna and His Disciples*. George Williams's two chapters in my *Religion in Modern India* are careful studies: "Svami Vivekananda: Archetypal Hero or Doubting Saint?" and "The Ramakrishna Movement: A Study in Religious Change."[58]

On the Radhasoami movement, see Mark Juergensmeyer, "The Radhasoami Revival of the Saint Tradition," in Karine Schomer and W. H. McLoed, *The Saint Tradition of India*, and Agam Prasad Mathur, *The Radhasoami Faith*.[59]

Raymond B. Williams, *The New Face of Hinduism: The Swaminarayan Religion* is a historical study of a movement that began in Gujarat but spread abroad through emigrants. It deals with the doctrine of the Swaminarayan sect along with its ritual and practices. With its useful glossary and bibliography, this is the place to start in the study of this movement. Also important is Arvind Sharma's "Relevance of Swaminarayanan and Contemporary Indian Thought."[60]

The scholarly treatment of the Theosophical Society is Bruce F. Campbell's *Ancient Wisdom Revived: A History of the Theosophical Movement*. Catherine Lowman Wessinger's *Annie Besant and Progressive Messianism, 1847–1933* analyses the thought of a subsequent leader of the society from the standpoint of messianism.[61] One may also refer to a growing number of books that offer a psychoanalytical perspective of some leading figures of modern Hinduism—especially Ramakrishna—that go beyond the kind of analysis carried out by Erikson on Gandhi. To this controversial genre belong Jeffrey J. Kripal, *Kālī's Child* and Narasingh Prosad Sil, *Rāmakṛṣṇa Paramahamsa*. Also see June McDaniel, *The Madness of Saints: Ecstatic Religion in Bengal*.[62] A recent work on the universal dimension of modern Hindu thought is Arvind Sharma, *The Concept of Universal Religion in Modern Hindu Thought*.[63]

Religious Thinkers

For the thought of Rammohun Roy, see James N. Pankratz, "The Religious Thought of Rammohun Roy"; also, by the same author, a chapter in *Religion in Modern India* (Baird), "Rammohun Roy." Two books on Roy are V. C. Joshi, ed., *Rammohun Roy and the Process of Modernization in India*, and Ajit Kumar Ray, *The Religious Ideas of Rammohun Roy*. Meredith

Borthwick's *Keshub Chandra Sen* is a careful scholarly analysis of the work of one of Roy's charismatic successors.[64]

The definitive work on Dayananda Sarasvati is J. T. F. Jordens, *Dayānanda Sarasvatī.* Jordens deals with the thought of Dayananda in its historical development, thereby giving an account of changes in his thought. He also seeks to place this history of ideas in a context of social history. Jordens uses sources that had been previously ignored or unavailable, such as the first edition of *Satyarth Prakash,* which is seen as differing from later editions in significant ways. One might also look at K. S. Arya and P. D. Shastri, *Swami Dayananda Sarasvati: A Study of His Life and Work* for an account by authors associated with the Arya Samaj. Jordens's *Swāmī Shraddhānanda: His Life and Causes* continues his study of Arya Samaj leadership into the twentieth century. Dhanpati Pandey, *The Arya Samaj and Indian Nationalism,* P. A. Parpullil, *Swami Dayananda Saraswati's Understanding and Assessment of Christianity,* and Arvind Sharma's essay "Svami Dayananda Sarasvati" deal with specific dimensions of Dayananda's thought and activity.[65]

Aurobindo Ghose was one of the most systematic thinkers of the so-called Hindu renaissance. His complete works were published in thirty volumes as *Sri Aurobindo Birth Centenary Library.* Secondary works are equally voluminous. Although specifically a study of Aurobindo's ethics, Robert N. Minor's *Sri Aurobindo* is a good historical introduction to Aurobindo's thought. Arguing against the view that Aurobindo used religion for political goals is David L. Johnson's *The Religious Roots of Indian Nationalism.* Also addressing the political dimension of Aurobindo's thought is June O'Connor, *The Quest for Political and Spiritual Liberation.* For a discussion of Aurobindo's evolutionary theory, see Rama Shanker Srivastava, *Sri Aurobindo and the Theories of Evolution.* Dealing with another facet of Aurobindo's thought is Kees W. Bolle's *The Persistence of Religion.* Other worthwhile introductions are Beatrice Bruteau, *Worthy Is the World,* Robert A. McDermott, ed., *Six Pillars,* K. R. Srinivasa Iyengar, *Aurobindo,* and R. R. Diwakar, *Mahayogi Sri Aurobindo.*[66]

The June 1972 issue of *International Philosophical Quarterly* was devoted to the thought of Aurobindo. It included essays such as "Sri Aurobindo: An Integrated Theory of Individual and Historical Transformation," by Robert A. McDermott; "The Supermind in Aurobindo's Philosophy," by Haridas Chaudhuri; "Sri Aurobindo and Teilhard De Chardin on the

Problem of Action," by Beatrice Bruteau; "Sri Aurobindo's Conception of the Nature and Meaning of History," by Grace E. Cairns; "Types of Society: The Social Thought of Sri Aurobindo," by John M. Koller; "Sri Aurobindo as the Fulfillment of Hinduism," by Jehangir N. Chubb; "The Yoga of Knowledge in the Gītā According to Sri Aurobindo," by David White; and "Life as a Battlefield: A Gītā Symbol as Interpreted by Sri Aurobindo," by Duncan Bazemore.

A bibliographic guide listing publications on Aurobindo to 1971 is H. K. Kaul, *Sri Aurobindo: A Descriptive Bibliography*. In addition to the special issue of *International Philosophical Quarterly*, among the numerous articles on Aurobindo of particular note are Robert A. McDermott's "The Experiential Basis of Sri Aurobindo's Integral Yoga," Robert N. Minor's "Sri Aurobindo's Integral View of Other Religions," Eliot Deutsch's "Sri Aurobindo's Interpretation of Spiritual Experience," and Haridas Chaudhuri's "The Philosophy and Yoga of Sri Aurobindo."[67]

As with Aurobindo, the literature on the thought of S. Radhakrishnan is voluminous. A good place to begin is Robert N. Minor's religio-historical analysis *Radhakrishnan: A Religious Biography*, which packs a great deal into a 181-page book.[68] It carefully analyzes the thought and development of Radhakrishnan to determine what if any changes took place throughout his life. There is also a useful bibliography of books, articles, and unpublished Ph.D. dissertations, as well as a chronological bibliography of Radhakrishnan's publications. This book provides an entrance to all the relevant primary and secondary material on Radhakrishnan. Schilpp's Library of Living Philosophers volume on Radhakrishnan, with twenty-three substantial essays and Radhakrishnan's "Fragments of a Confession," remains an important resource in spite of its date (1952). More recent books on a variety of themes relating to Radhakrishnan are Donald A. Braue, *Maya in Radhakrishnan's Thought*; Ishwar C. Harris, *Radhakrishnan*; Alysius Michael, *Radhakrishnan on Hindu Moral Life and Action*; Thomas Paul Urumpackal, *Organized Religion According to Dr. S. Radhakrishnan*; and John G. Arupura, *Radhakrishnan and Integral Experience*.[69]

Robert N. Minor, whose Radhakrishnan biography was named above, has also published four chapters or articles on Radhakrishnan.[70] Other articles of note are Austin B. Creel, "The Concept of Revelation in Sarvepalli Radhakrishnan and H. Richard Neibuhr"; Robert A. McDermott, "Radhakrishnan's Contribution to Comparative Philosophy"; Klaus

Klostermaier, "Some Aspects of the Social Philosophy of Sarvepalli Radhakrishnan"; Quinter M. Lyon, "Mystical Realism in the Thought of Sarvepalli Radhakrishnan"; and Ram Pratap Singh, "Radhakrishnan's Substantial Reconstruction of the Vedanta of Sankara."[71]

On the thought of Rabindranath Tagore, see A. K. Srivastava, *God and Its Relation with the Finite Self in Tagore's Philosophy*; William Cenkner, *The Hindu Personality in Education*; Bhupendra Nath, *Rabindranath Tagore*; Benoy Gopal Ray, *The Philosophy of Rabindranath Tagore*; and Mary M. Lego, ed., *Imperfect Encounter*.[72]

There always seems to be a market for one more book on M. K. Gandhi. Among recent ones are A. L. Basham's *The Father of the Nation*; William Borman, *Gandhi and Nonviolence*; Bal Ram Nanda, *Gandhi and His Critics*; Rhagavan N. Iyer, *The Moral and Political Thought of Mahatma Gandhi*; Margaret Chatterjee, *Gandhi's Religious Thought*; Joan V. Bondurant, *Conquest of Violence*; Judith Brown, *Gandhi and Civil Disobedience*; D. M. Datta, *The Philosophy of Mahatma Gandhi*; K. L. Seshagiri, *Gandhi and Comparative Religion*; and Glyn Richards, *The Philosophy of Gandhi*. Those who find psychohistory a useful method may consult Erik H. Erikson's *Gandhi's Truth: On the Origins of Militant Nonviolence*.[73] For a less well-known thinker of the Hindu renaissance, see Ninian Smart's *Prophet of a New Hindu Age: The Life and Times of Acharya Pranavananda*.[74]

Gurus, Saints, and Ascetics

A well-written book on monasticism with which one might begin is *Hindu Monastic Life*, by David M. Miller and Dorothy C. Wertz. This volume's objective as stated in the preface is "to provide for the undergraduate teacher and student a thorough description of the practice of Hindu monasticism in a medium-sized pilgrimage center as it existed in 1964." It also seeks to determine what changes were taking place in monastic life at Bhubaneswar as the result of the influence of "Westernization." The authors propose that the changes that could be determined were the result of internal shifts and reorganizations so that the traditional forms continue to exist alongside modern institutions; also see Miller's article, "The Guru as a Centre of Sacredness." Daniel Gold's *The Lord as Guru* is an analysis of a tradition that at times exalts the guru as the embodiment of God. It deals with lineage, the bonds felt between gurus and disciples, and the place of the holy man among the Radhasoamis. Also important is Gold's

Comprehending the Guru. For an introductory survey of a number of popular modern gurus, one might turn to Vishal Mangalwadi, *The World of Gurus*.[75]

Richard Gurghart and Audrey Cantlie's *Indian Religion* contains several important anthropological studies, including "The Aghori Ascetics of Benares," by Jonathan P. Parry; "The Indian Renouncer: Structure and Transformation in a Lingayat Community," by N. J. Bradford; "Initiation and Consecration: Priestly Rituals in a South Indian Temple," by C. J. Fuller; and "Vaisnava Reform Sects in Assam," by Audrey Cantlie. Also see Burghart's article "Wandering Ascetics of the Rāmānandī Sect." One might also consult B. D. Tripathi, *Sadhus of India;* Philip Singer, *Sadhus and Charisma;* and Surajit Sinha and Baidyanath Saraswati, *Ascetics of Kashi: An Anthropological Exploration*.[76]

Two important articles by Charles S. J. White on contemporary saints are "Sai Baba Movement: Approaches to the Study of Indian Saints" and "Swāmī Muktānanda and the Enlightenment through Śakti Pāt." There is also Charlotte Vaudeville, "Paṇḍharpūr: The City of Saints."[77]

Hinduism in Diaspora

In addition to J. P. Rao Rayapati, *Early American Interest in Vedanta,* which shows that interest in Hinduism in the West preceded the present century, there is a growing body of literature on emigrant Hindus. A suggestive bibliography is attached to Steven Vertovec's "Hinduism in Diaspora: The Transformation of Tradition in Trinidad," in *Hinduism Reconsidered* (see the section "Hinduism Reconsidered" below).[78] Richard Burghart, ed., *Hinduism in Great Britain* includes eleven essays on various facets of Hinduism in Great Britain and concludes with a useful bibliography with more than six hundred entries. Two useful unpublished Ph.D. dissertations are Richard Forbes, *Arya Samaj in Trinidad*, and Kim Knott, *Hinduism in Leeds*.[79]

A number of articles assist in understanding the range of Hindu expansion outside India: Marjorie Wood, "Hinduism in Vancouver"; Jim Wilson, "Text and Context in Fijian Hinduism: Uses of Religion," and, by the same author, "Text and Context in Fijian Hinduism: Religion as a Framework for Life"; K. Hazeersingh, "The Religion and Culture of Indian Immigrants in Mauritius"; Chandra Jayawardena's study of Hinduism in British Guiana, "Religious Belief and Social Change"; and Mark Juergensmeyer's "Radhasoami as a Trans-national Movement."[80]

Two important studies of specific communities are Raymond B. Williams's *Religions of Immigrants from India and Pakistan* and John Fenton's *Transplanting Religious Traditions: Asian Indians in America.*[81] The former is a study of immigrant groups and of American adaptations of Indian religions. It contains a major chapter on the Swaminarayan movement in the United States. Fenton's book is a study of Asian Indians in Atlanta, Georgia, and is based on a questionnaire, participant observation, and in-depth interviews. Neither volume is limited to Hinduism.

On the Krishna Consciousness movement in the United States and its present status, Larry Shinn has provided a up-to-date account based on interviews and observations at a number of important centers. His *The Dark Lord* includes a useful bibliography. Also treating this movement are Francine Jeanne Daner, *The American Children of Krishna;* E. Burke Rochford, *Hare Krishnas in America;* and my "ISKCON and the Struggle for Legitimation." Three others of my essays seek to understand specific doctrines in the thought of the founder of the movement, Swami Bhaktivedanta: "Swami Bhaktivedanta and the Bhagavadgita 'As it Is,'" "Swami Bhaktivedanta: Karma, Rebirth, and the Personal God," and "The Response of Swami Bhaktivedanta." Still important, though now dated, is J. Stillison Judah, *Hare Krishna and the Counterculture.*[82]

Indispensable for those seeking to keep abreast of news of the Hindu community around the world and particularly in North America is the bimonthly periodical *Hinduism Today*.

Thematic Volumes

Several important thematic volumes on modern Indian religion have been the result of conferences. Ronald W. Neufeldt, ed., *Karma and Rebirth: Post-Classical Developments*, collects papers on contemporary philosophical treatments (Austin B. Creel), Aurobindo (Robert N. Minor), Vivekananda (George M. Williams), the contemporary guru (David Miller), North Indian Vaisnavas (Klaus K. Klostermaier), the Theosophical movement (Neufeldt), Swami Bhaktivedanta (Robert D. Baird), and Rajneesh (Robert E. Gussner).[83] Another volume on karma, *Karma: An Anthropological Inquiry*, is a collection of anthropological essays on South and Southeast Asia edited by Charles F. Keyes and E. Valentine Daniel, which grew out of a workshop sponsored by the Joint Committee on South Asia of the American Council of Learned Societies and the Social Science Research

Council.[84] Among the essays on South Asia are "The Tool Box Approach of the Tamil to the Issues of Moral Responsibility and Human Destiny," by Sheryl B. Daniel; "Fate, Karma, and Cursing in a Local Epic Milieu," by Brenda E. F. Beck; "Karma Divined in a Ritual Capsule," by E. Valentine Daniel; "Karma and Other Explanation Traditions in a South Indian Village," by Paul G. Hiebert; "Vrats: Transformers of Destiny," by Susan S. Wadley; and "Destiny and Responsibility: Karma in Popular Hinduism," by Lawrence A. Babb.

Robert N. Minor's *Modern Interpreters of Bhavavad Gītā* is less an attempt at understanding the *Bhagavadgita* than an analysis of its use by modern religious thinkers and reformers.[85] It includes papers on such modern Indian interpreters of the Gītā as Gandhi (by J. T. F. Jordens), Vinoba Bhave (Boyd H. Wilson), Vivekananda (Harold W. French), Radhakrishnan (Robert N. Minor), Sivananda (David Miller), Swami Bhaktivedanta (Robert D. Baird), Tilak (Robert W. Stevenson), and the Theosophical Society (Ronald W. Neufeldt).

Religion and Legitimation of Power in South Asia, edited by Bardwell L. Smith, includes essays outside of Hinduism and outside of the modern period.[86] Among the relevant essays focusing on modern Hinduism are "Theogony and Power in South Asia: Some Clues from the Aiyappan Cult," by Fred W. Clothey; "Modernization and Religious Legitimation in India: 1835–1885," by Gerald James Larson; "Rajaji, the Brahmin—a Style of Power," by Joanne Punzo Waghorne; my "Religion and the Legitimation of Nehru's Concept of the Secular State," and "The Legitimation of Religious Policy in Tamil Nadu: A Study of the 1970 *Archaka* Legislation," by Franklin A. Presler.

Religion, Law, and the State

Several books are essential for understanding the topics of religion, law, and the state in independent India. Although outdated (1963), Donald Eugene Smith's *India As a Secular State* still contains a wealth of information on the issue of the secular state and its implications for religious liberty, state control and reform, and the relations between religion, politics, and law. *Secularism: Its Implications for Law and Life in India*, edited by G. S. Sharma, contains a series of important essays by Indian judges and law faculty. A good summary of constitutional provisions for freedom of religion and the Supreme Court's handling of the issue is V. M. Bachal,

Freedom of Religion and the Indian Judiciary. See also Trevor O. Ling, *Religious Change and the Secular State* and Chandra Y. Mudaliar, *The Secular State and Religious Institutions in India: A Study of the Administration of Hindu Public Religious Trusts in Madras*.[87]

One of the most knowledgeable interpreters of Hindu law is the British scholar J. D. M. Derrett. *Religious Law and the State in India* is a collection of his essays on religion and law: relating to modern Hinduism are "The British as Patrons of the Sastra"; "The Administration of Hindu Law by the British"; "The Codification of Hindu Law"; "Religion and Modern Indian Law"; and "Religious Endowments, Public and Private." His analysis of the "Hindu Code Bills" is in *The Death of a Marriage Law*. Derrett's earlier work, *Hindu Law Past and Present*, is an account of the controversy that preceded the enactment of that code.[88] A number of shorter works are also worth examining, among them G. D. Sontheimer, "Religious Endowments in India," John H. Mansfield, *Comparative Constitutional Law*, Derrett's "The Reform of Hindu Religious Endowments," and S. S. Rama Rao Pappu, "Hinduism, Secularism, and the Secular State."[89]

A number of essays by the author of this chapter have been brought together in *Essays in the History of Religions*.[90] Among them are "'Secular State' and the Indian Constitution"; "Uniform Civil Code and the Secularization of Law"; "Religion and the Legitimation of Nehru's Concept of the Secular State"; "Cow Slaughter and the 'New Great Tradition'"; and "Mr. Justice Gajendragadkar and the Religion of the Indian Secular State." Secularism is a contested subject in India these days. For an excellent survey of the debate, see Rajeev Bhargava's *Secularism and Its Critics*. Also useful for insight into the political dimensions are Ainslie T. Embree, "Religion, Nationalism and Conflict," and Kenneth W. Jones, "Political Hinduism."[91] A number of important essays are to be found in *Religion and Law in Independent India*, edited by the present author. Robert N. Minor's *The Religious, the Spiritual, and the Secular* is a study of the religious and legal dimensions of the development of Auroville.[92]

Hinduism and Other Traditions

Hinduism has encountered a variety of religious traditions throughout its long history. In the modern period, the chief points of contact have been with Christianity and Islam, although its relation with the Sikhs, a tradition that initially sought to overcome the conflict between Hindus and

Muslims cannot be overlooked. *Modern Indian Responses to Religious Pluralism*, edited by Harold G. Coward, deals with the ways the nineteenth- and twentieth-century Indian religious thinkers and movements handled other religions. Included are essays on Gandhi (by J. T. F. Jordens), the Brahmo Samaj (James N. Pankratz), the Arya Samaj (Harold G. Coward), the Ramakrishna Mission (Ronald W. Neufeldt), Aurobindo and the Mother (Robert N. Minor), Swami Bhaktivedanta (Robert D. Baird), modern Vaisnavism (Klaus K. Klostermaier), Saiva Siddhanta (K. Sivaraman), and philosophical responses (J. G. Arapura). Also edited by Coward is *Hindu-Christian Dialogue*, which contains a variety of essays on the interaction of Hindus and Christians, among them "The Response of the Hindu Renaissance to Christianity," by Ronald W. Neufeldt; "Trialogue: The Context of Hindu-Christian Dialogue in Kerala," by Ronald E. Miller; "Gandhi and the Christians," by John C. B. Webster; "Hindu-Christian Dialogue in Europe," by Eric J. Sharpe; "Current Hindu-Christian Dialogue in India," by Richard W. Taylor; and my "Hindu-Christian Dialogue and the Academic Study of Religion."[93]

Important for the relationship of Hindus and Muslims in British India is G. R. Thursby, *Hindu-Muslim Relations in British India*. Another work that addresses both Hindu/Muslim conflict as well as Hindu/Sikh conflict is Asghar Ali Engineer, *Communalism and Communal Violence in India*. James Warner Björknam, ed., *Fundamentalism, Revivalists, and Violence in South Asia* is based on a workshop held at the University of Wisconsin that addressed the increasingly violent role of religion in India. Included are "The Dark Side of Force: Notes on Religion and Politics" (James Warner Björkman); "Fundamentalism and Revivalism in South Asia" (Robert Eric Frykenberg); and "The Political Uses of Religious Identity in South Asia" (Surjit Mansingh). S. K. Ghosh, *Communal Riots in India* seeks to analyze the causes and dimensions of communal violence and includes a number of case studies. Walter K. Andersen and Shridhar D. Damle, *The Brotherhood in Saffron* is a study of the formation and development of the Rashtriya Swayamasevak Sangh in the light of Hindu-Muslim relations. For an analysis of the issue by a liberal Muslim, see Asghar Engineer, *Communalism and Communal Violence in India*.[94] Other books that shed light on recent developments are Richard Fox Young, *Resistant Hinduism*, Raul R. Brass, *Language, Religion, and Politics in North India*, and Asghar Ali Engineer, ed., *Communal Riots in Post-Independence India*.[95]

During 1990, one of the most emotional issues was the conflict over the Babri Masjid mosque and the argument by Hindu fundamentalists that the mosque stands over the birthplace of Ram. Their argument is that the mosque should be torn down and the temple that stood there before Muslims destroyed it should be rebuilt. For a discussion of the issue, see Koenraad Elst, *Ramjanmabhoomi vs. Babri Masjid* and Asghar Ali Engineer, ed. *Babri-Masjid Ramjanmabhoomi Controversy*.[96]

Hinduism Reconsidered

A recently published and important collection of essays is *Hinduism Reconsidered*, edited by Gunther D. Sontheimer and Harmann Kulke. Although not all of the essays that appear in this volume deal with modern Hinduism, a good number of them do. Among other issues with which they deal is the idea of Hinduism—that is, the concept and the term *Hinduism* itself. The category had been questioned by Wilfred Cantwell Smith in *The Meaning and End of Religion* (1963) and by myself in *Category Formation and the History of Religions* (1971).[97] Scholars have been somewhat uncomfortable with the category since then, but they have continued to use it under the rationale that there is no adequate substitute. It is interesting, therefore, to see the issue raised from a different quarter, in *Hinduism Reconsidered*, in 1989. Some of the essays in this important book are "Reconsidering Hinduism: What I Might Have Said (in part) If . . ." (David Shulman); "Hinduism: On the Proper Use of a Deceptive Term" (Heinrich von Stietencron); "The Emergence of Modern 'Hinduism' as a Concept and as an Institution: A Reappraisal with Special Reference to South India (Robert E. Frykenburg); "Hinduism and National Liberation Movement in India" (Horst Krüger); "Multiple Approaches to a Living Hindu Myth: The Lord of Govardhan Hill" (Charlotte Vaudeville); "Bhakti and Monasticism" (Monika Thiel-Horstmann); "Staying on the Goddess's Eyelid: Devotion and Reversal of Values in Hindu Bengal" (Serge Bouez); and "Hinduism in Diaspora: The Transformation of Tradition in Trinidad" (Steven Vertovec). These papers and others were part of a panel by the same title as the present book, organized for the Eleventh European Conference of Modern South Asian Studies in 1986.

Hindu Nationalism

The rise of Hindu nationalism in post-Independence India is now beginning to attract scholarly attention. For its place in the broader context of the rise of religious fundamentalism the world over, one may turn to the five-volume study on the general theme of fundamentalism, beginning with *Fundamentalisms Observed*, edited by Martin Marty and R. S. Appleby.[98]

The seminal work in the context of the ideology of Hindu nationalism itself, known as Hindutva, is V. D. Savarkar, *Hindutva: Who Is a Hindu?* This book introduced the word *Hindutva* into the politics of India when first published in 1923. Two other prominent ideologues of the movement are "guru" M. S. Golwalker (d. 1973) and Balraj Madhok. Golwalker's concept of Hindutva is outlined in *We, or, Our Nationhood Defined* and *Bunch of Thoughts*.[99] Madhok, in addition to being an ideologue, has also been a political activist, as is apparent from the titles of his works (e.g., *A Story of Bungling in Kashmir* and *Murder of Democracy*).[100]

Good critical studies of the Hindu nationalist movement are now available. For a good account of the RSS, see W. K. Anderson and S. D. Damle, *The Brotherhood of Saffron*. For an account of the Jan Sangh, see Bruce Graham, *Hindu Nationalism and Indian Politics*. For a comprehensive look at the Hindu nationalist movement as a whole, a useful book is Christopher Jeffrelot, *The Hindu Nationalist Movement in India*. Thomas Blom Hansen's *The Saffron Wave: Democracy and Hindu Nationalism in Modern India* brings the account right up to the end of the twentieth century. Another excellent study is by Eva Hellman, *Political Hinduism: the Challenge of the Viśva Hindū Pariṣad*.[101] For a work highly critical of the movement, see Achin Vanaik, *The Furies of Indian Communalism*.[102]

Retrospect and Prospect

Several observations grow out of the above survey of literature on modern Hinduism. The first was mentioned at the beginning of this chapter: that the study of modern Hinduism has been approached by a variety of disciplines. While this does not mean that scholars should cease to operate within the disciplines in which they have been trained, it surely suggests that they ought not to limit their reading when they seek to develop a more comprehensive understanding of modern Indian religions—in this case, Hinduism.

A second observation is that in many recently published works, the distinction between classical, medieval, and modern is virtually erased. Some studies fit exclusively in the modern period, but other studies combine the analysis of classical texts with their contemporary use; that is, they attend to both text and context. Several recent works deal with the performance or enactment of *Rāmāyaṇa* or even oral "texts." Hence, they are partly ancient or classical and partly modern or even contemporary. Works of this nature should be encouraged.

A third observation is that there is, by reason of the strong influence of anthropology and field methods, a growing attention to ritual, festivals, pilgrimage, ascetics, and monastic life. This has enriched not only our overall knowledge of modern Hinduism but has also added a dimension to the history of religions. To the extent that historians of religions do fieldwork, however, it is imperative that they receive adequate preparatory training before going into the field.

What might be considered the more fruitful areas for research in the immediate future? One must be cautious in suggesting that any area has been exhausted. There is always room for a new, insightful analysis of an already covered area. Yet it would seem that the "Hindu renaissance" and its dominant thinkers such as Rammohun Roy, Dayananda, Vivekananda, Radhakrishnan, Aurobindo, Gandhi, and others have been worked very hard. If new works in this area do appear, they must be thoroughly based not only on a mastery of primary sources but also on secondary works, so that we are not submitted to a rehash of what is already known. If there is more to do with that period, it might be with themes, rather than thinkers. There have been conferences and books on karma and rebirth, responses to religious pluralism, religion and legitimation, and treatments of the *Bhagavadgita*, to mention a few. There is certainly room for the analysis of other themes as well.

We need anthropologists and historians of religions with competence in regional languages to research oral traditions, gurus, ascetics, monastic organizations, festivals, and pilgrimages. This suggests that the growing attention to what people feel and do should be continued. And, in the process, attention to the thought systems that sometimes propel such action ought not to be ignored. Some may hold that this is merely ideology to sustain vested interests, but a case can also be made for an analysis of thought as a basis for action.

Considerably more could be done in the area of ethics. A number of recent works have sought to determine Hindu responses to contemporary ethical and medical issues. We would profit from a discussion of the religious thought that forms the basis for ethics, the content of ethics, and how classical forms are remaining constant or changing as Hindus seek to respond to contemporary ethical issues.

Finally, while we have given some attention to the methods that we use for the study of modern Hinduism, and the logic of those methods, a great deal more needs to be done in this regard. Not only should methodological discussions become a natural part of our empirical studies, but there is room for studies that address themselves to methodological issues as such.

The survey of this chapter would seem to suggest that the study of modern religious thought and activity in India has a good foundation. We are neither moving in the wrong direction nor have we arrived at our destination.

Notes

1. Philip H. Ashby, *Modern Trends in Hinduism* (New York: Columbia University Press, 1974).

2. Hal W. French and Arvind Sharma, *Religious Ferment in Modern India* (New York: St. Martin's, 1981).

3. Rakhal Chandra Nath, *The New Hindu Movement, 1886–1911* (Columbia, Mo.: South Asian Books, 1982).

4. V. S. Naravane, *Modern Indian Thought* (Bombay: Asia Publishing House, 1964).

5. Donald H. Bishop, ed., *Thinkers of the Indian Renaissance* (New Delhi: Wiley Eastern, 1982).

6. Robert D. Baird, ed., *Religion in Modern India* (Columbia, Mo.: South Asia Publications, 1981; 4th. rev. ed., Delhi: Manohar, 2001).

7. Giri Raj Gupta, ed., *Religion in Modern India* (Delhi: Vikas Publishing House, 1983).

8. Milton Singer, *When a Great Tradition Modernizes: An Anthropological Approach to Indian Civilization* (London: Pall Mall Press, 1972).

9. *The Encyclopedia of Religion*, 13 vols. (New York: Macmillan, 1987).

10. Benjamin Walker, *Hindu World*, 2 vols. (London: George Allen & Unwin, 1968).

11. Maureen Patterson, comp., *South Asia Civilization: A Bibliographic Synthesis* (Chicago: University of Chicago Press, 1981).

12. Barron Holland, comp., *Popular Hinduism and Hindu Mythology: An Annotated Bibliography* (Westport, Conn.: Greenwood, 1979).

13. Charles H. Heimsath, *Indian Nationalism and Hindu Social Reform* (Princeton: Princeton University Press, 1964).

14. S. C. Malik, ed., *Indian Movements: Some Aspects of Dissent, Protest, and Reform* (Simla: Indian Institute of Advanced Study, 1978).

15. S. P. Sen, ed., *Social and Religious Reform Movements in the Nineteenth and Twentieth Centuries* (Calcutta: Institute of Historical Studies, 1979).

16. Mark Juergensmeyer, *Religion as Social Vision: The Movement against Untouchability in Twentieth Century Punjab* (Berkeley and Los Angeles: University of California Press, 1982).

17. Kenneth W. Jones, *Socio-Religious Reform Movements in British India*, vol. 3 *The New Cambridge History of India* (Cambridge University Press, 1989).

18. Paul G. Hiebert, "India: The Politicization of a Sacred Society," in *Religion and Societies: Asia and the Middle East*, ed., Carlo Caldarola (Berlin: Mouton, 1982); J. T. F. Jordens, "Hindu Religious and Social Reform in British India," in *A Cultural History of India*, ed. A. L. Basham (Oxford: Clarendon, 1975); Miriam Sharma and Jagdish P. Sharma, "Hinduism, Sarvodaya, and Social Change," in *Religion and Political Modernization*, ed. Donald Eugene Smith (New Haven: Yale University Press, 1974); and Agehananda Bharati, "Hinduism and Modernization," in *Religion and Change in Contemporary Asia*, ed. R. Spencer (Minneapolis: University of Minnesota Press, 1971).

19. V. Sudarsen et al, eds., *Religion and Society in South Asia* (Delhi: B. R. Publishing, 1987).

20. Bardwell L. Smith, *Religion and Social Conflict in South Asia* (Leiden: E. J. Brill, 1976).

21. Jayant Lele, ed., *Tradition and Modernity in Bhakti Movements* (Leiden: E. J. Brill, 1981).

22. Eleanor Zelliot and Maxine Berntsen, eds., *The Experience of Hinduism: Essays on Religion in Maharashtra* (Albany: State University of New York Press, 1988).

23. Milton Israel and N. K. Wagle, eds., *Religion and Society in Maharashtra* (Toronto: University of Toronto–Centre for South Asian Studies, 1987).

24. Gunther-Deitz Sontheimer, *Pastoral Deities in Western India*, trans. Anne Feldhaus (New York and Oxford: Oxford University Press, 1989); Anne Feldhaus, *The Deeds of God in Ṛddhipūr* (Oxford: Oxford University Press, 1984).

25. Lawrence Allan Babb, *The Divine Hierarchy: Popular Hinduism in Central India* (New York: Columbia University Press, 1975); idem, *Redemptive Encounters: Three Modern Styles in the Hindu Tradition* (Berkeley: University of California, 1986).

26. R. M Sarkar, *Regional Cults and Rural Traditions: An Interacting Pattern of*

Divinity and Humanity in Rural Bengal (New Delhi: Inter-India, 1986); Lina Fruzzetti, *The Gift of a Virgin: Women, Marriage, and Ritual in a Bengali Village* (New Brunswick, N.J.: Rutgers University Press, 1982); P. K. Maity, *Human Fertility Cults and Rituals in Bengal* (New Delhi: Abhiav, 1989); June McDaniel, *The Madness of the Saints: Ecstatic Religion in Bengal* (Chicago: University of Chicago Press, 1989).

27. David Kopf, *British Orientalism and the Bengal Renaissance* (Berkeley: University of California Press, 1969).

28. Anncharlott Eschmann et al., eds., *The Cult of Jagannath and the Regional Tradition of Orissa* (Delhi: Manohar, 1978); Nancy Gardner Cassels, *Religion and Pilgrim Tax under the Company Raj* (Delhi: Manohar, 1988); Prabhat Mukherjee, *History of the Jagannath Temple in the 19th Century* (Calcutta: Firma KLM, 1977).

29. Joanne Punzo Waghorne and Norman Cutler, eds., with collaboration of Vasudha Narayanan, *Gods of Flesh, Gods of Stone: The Embodiment of Divinity in India* (Chambersburg, Pa.: Anima, 1985).

30. Alf Hiltebeitel, ed., *Criminal Gods and Demon Devotees: Essays on the Guardians of Popular Hinduism* (Albany: State University of New York Press, 1989).

31. K. Ishwaran, *Religion and Society among the Lingayats of South India* (New Delhi: Vikas, 1983); Fred W. Clothey, "The Yāga: A Fire Ritual in South India," in *Experiencing Śiva: Encounters with a Hindu Deity*, ed. Fred W. Clothey and J. Bruce Long (Delhi: Manohar, 1983); and, ibid., Charles A. Ryerson, "Contemporary Śaivism and Tamil Identity: An Interpretation of Kuakkuṭi Aṭikaḷār"; Holly Baker Reynolds, "The Changing Nature of a Tamil Vow: The Challenge of Trans-Sectarian Bhakti in Contemporary South India," in *Religious Movements and Social Identity*, ed. Bardwell L. Smith (New Delhi: Chanakya, 1990).

32. Fred W. Clothey, *The Many Faces of Murukan: The History and Meaning of a South Indian God* (The Hague: Mouton, 1978).

33. Milton Singer, ed., *Krishna: Myths, Rites, and Attitudes* (Honolulu: East-West Center Press, 1966).

34. Genevieve Lemercinier, *Religion and Ideology in Kerala*, trans. Yolanda Rendel (Louvain-la-Neuve: Université Catholique de Louvain, 1983); Fred W. Clothey, "On the Study of Religion in South India: An Assessment," in *Studies of South India: An Anthology of Recent Research and Scholarship*, ed. Robert E. Frykenberg and Pauline Kolenda (New Delhi: American Institute of Indian Studies, 1985).

35. Franklin A. Presler, *Religion under Bureaucracy: Policy and Administration for Hindu Temples in South India* (Cambridge: Cambridge University Press, 1987).

36. Arjun Appadurai, *Worship and Conflict under Colonial Rule: A South Indian*

Case (Cambridge: Cambridge University Press, 1981); James J. Preston, *Cult of the Goddess: Social and Religious Change in a Hindu Temple* (Prospect Heights, Ill.: Waveland, 1980); for the quote, see the preface; James J. Preston and James Freeman, "Two Urbanizing Orissan Temples," in *Transformation of a Sacred City: Bhubaneshwar, India,* ed. Susan Seymour (Boulder: Westview, 1980); Nirmal K. Bhose, "Organization of Services in the Temple of Lingaraj Bhubaneswar," in *Culture and Society in India,* ed. Nirmal K. Bhose (Calcutta: Asia Publishing House, 1967).

37. Carol Appadurai Breckenridge, "The Sri Minaksi Sundaresvara Temple: Worship and Endowments in South India, 1833–1925," unpublished Ph.D. diss., University of Wisconsin, 1976; William P. Harman, *The Sacred Marriage of a Hindu Goddess* (Bloomington and Indianapolis: Indiana University Press, 1989); C. J. Fuller, *Servants of the Goddess: The Priests of a South Indian Temple* (Cambridge: Cambridge University Press, 1984); C. J. Fuller, "The Divine Couple's Relationship in a South Indian Temple: Minaksi and Sundaresvara at Madurai," *History of Religions* 19 (1980):321–48; C. J. Fuller, "The Attempted Reform of South Indian Temple Hinduism," in J. Davis, ed., *Religious Organization and Religious Experience* (London: Academic, 1982); André Beteille, "Social Organization of Temples in a Tanjore Village," *History of Religions* 5 (1965):74–92.

38. Fred W. Clothey, *Rhythm and Intent: Ritual Studies from South India* (Madras: Blackie, 1983).

39. Gabriella Eichinger Ferro-Luzzi, ed., *Rites and Beliefs in Modern India* (Delhi: Manohar, 1990); Stuart H. Blackburn, "Death and Deification: Folk Cults in Hinduism," *History of Religions* 24 (1985):255–74.

40. Guy R. Welbon and Glenn E. Yocum, eds., *Religious Festivals in South India and Sri Lanka* (Delhi: Manohar, 1982).

41. Penelope Logan, *Domestic Worship and the Festival Cycle in the South Indian City of Madurai* Ph.D. thesis, University of Manchester, 1980; Suzanne Hanchett, *Coloured Rice: Symbolic Structure in Hindu Family Festivals* (Delhi: Hindustan, 1988); Akos Ostor, *The Play of the Gods: Locality, Ideology, Structure, and Time in the Festivals of a Bengali Town* (Chicago: University of Chicago Press, 1980).

42. Paul Younger, "A Temple Festival of Māriyamman," *Journal of the American Academy of Religion* 18 (1980):493–517; idem, "Ten Days of Wandering and Romance with Lord Raṇkanatan: The Pankuni Festival in Srirankam Temple, South India," *Modern Asian Studies* 16 (1982):623–56; John M. Stanley, "Special Time, Special Power: The Fluidity of Power in a Popular Hindu Festival," *Journal of Asian Studies* 37 (1977):27–43.

43. Bardwell L. Smith, ed., *Religious Movements and Social Identity,* vol. 4 of

Boeings and Bullock Carts: Essays in Honor of K. Ishwaran (Delhi: Chanakya, 1990).

44. Surinder Mohan Bhardwaj, *Pilgrimage: A Study in Cultural Geography* (Berkeley: University of California Press, 1973); Diana Eck, *Banaras: City of Light* (Princeton: Princeton University Press, 1982); Makhan Jha, *The Sacred Complex in Janakpur* (Allahabad: United, 1971); Rajendra Jindel, *Culture of a Sacred Town: A Sociological Study of Nathdwara* (Bombay: Popular Prakashan, 1976); L. P. Vidyarthi, *The Sacred Complex in Hindu Gaya* (New York: Asia Publishing House, 1961); idem, *The Sacred Complex of Kashi: A Microcosm of Indian Civilization* (New Delhi: Concept, 1979).

45. Diana L. Eck, "India's Tīrthas: 'Crossing' in Sacred Geography," *History of Religions* 20 (1981):323–44; Fred Clothey, "Pilgrimage Centers in Tamil Cultus of Murukan," *Journal of the American Academy of Religion* 40 (1972):72–95; James Freeman, "Religious Change in a Hindu Pilgrimage Center," *Review of Religious Research* 16 (1975):124–33.

46. G. A. Deleury, *The Cult of Vithoba* (Poona: Deccan College Postgraduate and Research Institute, 1960); D. B. Mokashi More, *Palkhi: An Indian Pilgrimage*, trans. Philip C. Engblom (Albany: State University of New York Press, 1987); E. Alan Morinis, *Pilgrimage in the Hindu Tradition: A Case Study of West Bengal* (Delhi: Oxford University Press, 1984); Ann Gold, *Fruitful Journeys: The Ways of Rajasthani Pilgrims* (Berkeley and Los Angeles: University of California Press, 1988); Makhan Jha, ed., *Dimensions of Pilgrimage: An Anthropological Appraisal* (New Delhi: Inter-India, 1985).

47. Mira Reym Binford, "Mixing the Color of Ram and Ranuja: A Folk Pilgrimage to the Grave of a Rajput Hero-saint," in *Hinduism: New Essays in the History of Religions*, ed. Bardwell L. Smith (Leiden: E. J. Brill, 1976); Agehananda Bharati, "Pilgrimage in the Indian Tradition," *History of Religions* 3 (1963): 135–67.

48. John Stratton Hawley, *At Play with Krishna: Pilgrimage Dramas from Brindavan* (Princeton: Princeton University Press, 1981); Richard Armando Frasca, *The Theater of the Mahabharata: Terukkuttu Performances in South India* (Honolulu: University of Hawaii Press, 1990); Philip A. Lutgendorf, *The Life of a Text: Performing the Rāmcaritmānas of Tulsīdās* (Berkeley: University of California Press, 1991); John D. Smith, *The Epic of Pābūjī: A Study, Transcription, and Translation* (Cambridge: Cambridge University Press, 1991).

49. Katherine K. Young and Arvind Sharma, *Images of the Feminine: A Bibliography of Women in India* (Chico, Calif.: New Horizons, 1974).

50. Susan S. Wadley, ed., *The Powers of Tamil Women* (Syracuse: Maxwell School of Citizenship and Public Affairs, Syracuse University, 1980); Kim Knott,

"Men and Women, or Devotees? Krishna Consciousness and the Role of Women," in *Women in the World Religions Past and Present*, ed. Ursula King (New York: Paragon House, 1987); Katherine K. Young, "From Hindu Stridharma to Universal Feminism: A Study of the Women in the Nehru Family," in *Traditions in Contact and Change: Selected Proceeding of the XIV Congress of the International Association for the History of Religions*, ed. Peter Slater and Donald Wiebe (Toronto: Sir Wilfrid Laurier Press, 1983); idem, "Hinduism," in *Women in World Religions*, ed. Arvind Sharma (Albany: State University of New York Press, 1987).

51. David Kinsley, "Devotion as an Alternative to Marriage in the Lives of Some Hindu Women Devotees," in Jayant Lele, ed., *Tradition and Modernity in Bhakti Movements* (Leiden: E. J. Brill, 1981); Bina Gupta, "Women's Rites and Religious Consciousness: India—Ancient and Modern," in *Indian Civilization in Its Local, Regional, and National Aspects*, ed. Dhirendra K. Vajpeyi, vol. 2 of *Boeings and Bullock-Carts: Essays in Honour of K. Ishwaran* (Delhi: Chanakya, 1990); ibid., Kathryn Young and Lily Miller, "Sacred Biography and the Restructuring of Society: A Study of Anandmai Ma, Lady-Saint of Modern Hinduism"; Rita M. Gross, "Hindu Female Deities as a Resource for the Contemporary Rediscovery of the Goddess," *Journal of the American Academy of Religion* 46 (1978): 269–91; Kenneth W. Jones, "Socio-Religious Movements and Changing Gender Relationship among Hindus of British India," in *Fundamentalism, Revivalists, and Violence in South Asia*, ed. James Warner Bjorkman (Delhi: Manohar, 1988); Doranne Jacobsen, "The Women of North and Central India: Goddesses and Wives," in *Women in India: Two Perspectives* (Delhi: Manohar, 1986); ibid, Susan S. Wadley, "Women and the Hindu Tradition"; idem, "Hindu Women's Family and Household Rites in a North Indian Village," in *Unspoken Worlds: Women's Religious Lives in Non-western Cultures*, ed. Nancy Auer Falk and Rita M. Gross (San Francisco: Harper & Row, 1980); ibid., Charles S. J. White, "Mother Guru: Jnanananda of Madras, India."

52. James J. Preston, ed., *Mother Worship: Theme and Variations* (Chapel Hill: University of North Carolina Press, 1982); G. Obeyesekere, *The Cult of the Goddess Pattini* (Berkeley: University of California Press, 1983).

53. V. N. Datta, *Sati: A Historical, Social, and Philosophical Inquiry into the Hindu Rite of Widow Burning* (Delhi: Manohar, 1990); Lata Mani, *Contentious Traditions: The Debate of Sati in Colonial India* (Berkeley: University of California Press, 1998); Harish Chandra Upreti, *The Myth of Sati: Some Dimensions of Widow Burning* (Bombay: Himalaya Publishing House, 1991); Santosh Singh, *A Passion for Flames* (Jaipur: Rissa, 1989); Rajeshwari Sunder Rajan, *Real and Imagined Women: Gender, Culture, and Postcolonialism* (London and New York:

Routledge, 1993); Svapana Basu, *Sati* (Kalakata: Pustake Bipani, 1982); V. N. Datta, *A Historical, Social, and Philosophical Inquiry into the Hindu Rite of Widow Burning* (Riverdale, Md. and London: Sangam, 1988); Sakuntala Narasimhan, *Sati: A Study of Widow Burning in India* (New Delhi and New York: Viking, 1990); Raja Rammohun Roy, *Sati: A Writeup of Raja Ram Mohun Roy about Burning of Widows Alive* (Delhi: B. R. Publishing, 1989); Arvind Sharma, *Sati: Historical and Philosophical Essays* (Delhi: Motilal Banarsidass, 1988); J. S. Hawley, ed., *Sati: The Blessing and the Curse: The Burning of Wives in India* (New York: Oxford University Press, 1994).

54. Jogan Shankar, *Devadasi Cult: A Sociological Analysis* (New Delhi: Ashish Publishing House, 1990); A. K. Prassad, *Devadasi System in Ancient India: A Study of Temple Dancing Girls in South India* (Delhi: H. K. Publishers, 1990); Saskia C. Kersenboom-Story, *Nityasumangali: Devadasi Tradition in South India* (Delhi: Motilal Banarsidass, 1987); Frederique Apffel-Margilin, *Wives of God-King: The Rituals of the Devadasis of Puri* (Delhi and New York: Oxford University Press, 1985); Leslie C. Orr, *Donors, Devotees, and Daughters of God: Temple Women in Medieval Tamilnadu* (New York and Oxford: Oxford University Press, 2000).

55. David Kopf, *The Brahmo Samaj and the Shaping of the Modern Indian Mind* (Princeton: Princeton University Press, 1979); Spencer Lavan, *Unitarians and India: A Study of Encounter and Response* (Boston: Beacon, 1977); idem, "The Brahmo Samaj," in *Religion in Modern India* (Baird).

56. Kenneth W. Jones, *Arya Dharma: Hindu Consciousness in Nineteenth Century Punjab* (Berkeley and Los Angeles: University of California Press, 1976); idem, "The Arya Samaj in British India," in *Religion in Modern India* (Baird); idem, "Social Change and Religious Movements in Nineteenth Century Punjab," in *Social Movement in India*, ed. M. S. A. Rao (Delhi: Manohar, 1979); idem, "Sources for Arya Samaj History," in W. Eric Gustafson and Kenneth W. Jones, eds., *Sources of Punjab History* (Delhi: Manohar, 1975).

57. Carl Olson, *The Mysterious Play of Kali: An Interpretive Study of Ramakrishna* (Atlanta: Scholars Press, 1990); Harold W. French, *The Swan's Wide Waters* (Port Washington, N.Y.: Kennikat, 1974); Leo Schneiderman, "Ramakrishna: Personality and Social Factors in the Growth of a Religious Movement," *Journal for the Scientific Study of Religion* (spring 1969); Claude Alan Stark, *God of All: Sri Ramakrishna's Approach to Religious Pluralism* (Cape Cod, Mass.: Stark, 1974).

58. George M. Williams, *The Quest for Meaning of Svāmī Vivekānanda* (Chico, Calif.: New Horizons, 1974); V. K. Arora, *The Social and Political Philosophy of Swami Vivekenanda* (Calcutta: Punthi Pustak, 1968); Binoy K. Roy, *Socio-political*

Views of Vivekananda (New Delhi: People's Publishing House, 1970); Agehananda Bharati, "The Hindu Renaissance and Its Apologetic Patterns," *Journal of Asian Studies* 29, no. 2 (1970):267–88; Walter G. Neeval Jr., "The Transformation of Sri Ramakrishna," in *Hinduism: New Essays in the History of Religions*, ed. Bardwell L. Smith (Leiden: E. J. Brill, 1976); ibid., Cyrus R. Pangborn, "The Ramakrishna Math and Mission: A Case Study of a Revitalization Movement"; Christopher Isherwood, *Ramakrishna and His Disciples* (Calcutta: Advaita Ashrama, 1965); George Williams, "Svami Vivekananda: Archetypal Hero or Doubting Saint?" in *Religion in Modern India* (Baird); ibid., "The Ramakrishna Movement: A Study in Religious Change."

59. Mark Juergensmeyer, "The Radhasoami Revival of the Saint Tradition," in Karine Schomer and W. H. McLoed, eds., *The Saint Tradition of India* (Berkeley: Berkeley Religious Studies Series, 1981); Agam Prasad Mathur, *The Radhasoami Faith: A Historical Study* (Delhi: Vikas Publishing House, 1974).

60. Raymond B. Williams, *The New Face of Hinduism: The Swaminarayan Religion* (Cambridge: Cambridge University Press, 1984); Arvind Sharma, "Relevance of Swaminarayanan and Contemporary Indian Thought," in *New Dimensions in Vedanta Philosophy* (Ahmedabad: Akshar Purushottam Santha, 1981).

61. Bruce F. Campbell, *Ancient Wisdom Revived: A History of the Theosophical Movement* (Berkeley: University of California Press, 1980); Catherine Lowman Wessinger, *Annie Besant and Progressive Messianism, 1847–1933* (Lewiston/ Queenston: Mellen, 1988).

62. Jeffrey J. Kripal, *Kālī's Child: The Mystical and the Erotic in the Life and Teachings of Ramakrishna* (Chicago and London: University of Chicago Press, 1995); Narasingh Prosad Sil, *Rāmakṛṣṇa Paramahamsa: A Psychological Profile* (Leiden: E. J. Brill, 1991); June McDaniel, *The Madness of Saints: Ecstatic Religion in Bengal* (Chicago: University of Chicago Press, 1989).

63. Arvind Sharma, *The Concept of Universal Religion in Modern Hindu Thought* (New York: St. Martin's; London: Macmillan, 1998).

64. James N. Pankratz, "The Religious Thought of Rammohun Roy," Ph.D. diss., McMaster University, 1975; idem, "Rammohun Roy," in *Religion in Modern India* (Baird); V. C. Joshi, ed., *Rammohun Roy and the Process of Modernization in India* (New Delhi: Vikas Publishing House, 1975); Ajit Kumar Ray, *The Religious Ideas of Rammohun Roy* (New Delhi: Kanak, 1976); Meredith Borthwick, *Keshub Chandra Sen: A Search for Cultural Synthesis* (Calcutta: Minerva, 1977).

65. J. T. F. Jordens, *Dayānanda Sarasvatī: His Life and Ideas* (Delhi: Oxford University Press, 1978); K. S. Arya and P. D. Shastri, *Swami Dayananda Sarasvati: A Study of His Life and Work* (Delhi: Manohar, 1987); J. T. F. Jordens, *Swāmī Shraddhānanda: His Life and Causes* (Delhi: Oxford University Press, 1981);

Dhanpati Pandey, *The Arya Samaj and Indian Nationalism* (New Delhi, 1972); and P. A. Parapullil, *Swami Dayananda Saraswati's Understanding and Assessment of Christianity* (Rome: Pontifical Gregorian University, 1970); Arvind Sharma, "Svami Dayananda Sarasvati," in *Religion in Modern India* (Baird).

66. Aurobidon Ghose, *Sri Aurobindo Birth Centenary Library*, 30 vols. (Pondicherry: Sri Aurobindo Ashram Trust, 1971); Robert N. Minor, *Sri Aurobindo: The Perfect and the Good* (Calcutta: Minerva, 1978); David L. Johnson, *The Religious Roots of Indian Nationalism: Aurobindo's Early Political Thought* (Calcutta: Firma K. L. Mukhopadhyay, 1974); June O'Connor, *The Quest for Political and Spiritual Liberation: A Study in the Thought of Sri Aurobindo Ghose* (Rutherford, N.J.: Fairleigh Dickinson University Press, 1977); Rama Shanker Srivastava, *Sri Aurobindo and the Theories of Evolution* (Varanasi: Chowkhamba Sanskrit Series, 1968); Kees W. Bolle, *The Persistence of Religion: An Essay on Tantrism and Sri Aurobindo's Philosophy* (Leiden: E. J. Brill, 1965); Beatrice Bruteau, *Worthy Is the World: The Hindu Philosophy of Sri Aurobindo* (Rutherford: Fairleigh Dickinson University Press, 1971); Robert A. McDermott, ed., *Six Pillars: Introductions to the Major Works of Sri Aurobindo* (Chambersburg, Pa.: Wilson Books, 1974); K. R. Srinivasa Iyengar, *Aurobindo: A Biography and History*, 3rd ed. (Pondicherry: Sri Aurobindo Ashram Trust, 1972); R. R. Diwakar, *Mahayogi Sri Aurobindo: Life, Discipline, and Teachings of Sri Aurobindo* (Bombay: Bharatiya Vidya Bhavan, 1972).

67. H. K. Kaul, *Sri Aurobindo: A Descriptive Bibliography* (Delhi: Munshiram Manoharlal, 1972); Robert A. McDermott, "The Experiential Basis of Sri Aurobindo's Integral Yoga," *Philosophy East and West* 22 (1972): 15–32; Robert N. Minor, "Sri Aurobindo's Integral View of Other Religions," *Religious Studies* 15 (1979): 367–79; Eliot Deutsch, "Sri Aurobindo's Interpretation of Spiritual Experience: A Critique," *International Philosophical Quarterly* 5 (1964); Haridas Chaudhuri, "The Philosophy and Yoga of Sri Aurobindo," *Philosophy East and West* 26 (1972):5–14.

68. Robert N. Minor, *Radhakrishnan: A Religious Biography* (Albany: State University of New York Press, 1987).

69. Paul Arthur Schilpp, ed., *The Philosophy of Sarvepalli Radhakrishan*, Library of Living Philosophers (New York: Tudor, 1952); Donald A. Braue, *Maya in Radhakrishnan's Thought: Six Meanings other than Illusion* (Columbia, Mo.: South Asian Books, 1985); Ishwar C. Harris, *Radhakrishnan: The Profile of a Universalist* (Columbia, Mo.: South Asian Books, 1982); Alysius Michael, *Radhakrishnan on Hindu Moral Life and Action* (Delhi: Concept, 1979); Thomas Paul Urumpackal, *Organized Religion according to Dr. S. Radhakrishnan* (Rome: University Gregoriana Editrice, 1972); John G. Arupura, *Radhakrishnan and Integral Experience: The*

Philosophy and World Vision of Radhakrishnan (New York: Asia Publishing House, 1966).

70. Robert N. Minor, "The *Bhagavadgita* in Radhakrishnan's Apologetics," in *Modern Interpreters of the Bhagavadgita*, ed. Robert N. Minor (Albany: State University of New York Press, 1986); idem, "In Defense of Karma and Rebirth: Evolutionary Karma," in *Karma and Rebirth: Post-Classical Developments*, ed. Ronald W. Neufeldt (State University of New York Press, 1986); idem, "Sarvepalli Radhakrishna on the Nature of 'Hindu' Tolerance," *Journal of the American Academy of Religion* 50 (1982); idem, "Sarvepalli Radhakrishnan and 'Hinduism' Defined and Defended," in *Religion and Modern India* (Baird).

71. Austin B. Creel, "The Concept of Revelation in Sarvepalli Radhakrishnan and H. Richard Neibuhr," *Journal of Dharma* 3 (1978); Robert A. McDermott, "Radhakrishnan's Contribution to Comparative Philosophy," *International Philosophical Quarterly* 10 (1970); Klaus Klostermaier, "Some Aspects of the Social Philosophy of Sarvepalli Radhakrishnan," *Religion and Society* 14 (1967); Quinter M. Lyon, "Mystical Realism in the Thought of Sarvepalli Radhakrishnan," *Philosophy East and West* 16 (1966); Ram Pratap Singh, "Radhakrishnan's Substantial Reconstruction of the Vedānta of Śaṅkara," *Philosophy East and West* 16 (1966).

72. A. K. Srivastava, *God and Its Relation with the Finite Self in Tagore's Philosophy* (Delhi: Oriental, 1976); William Cenkner, *The Hindu Personality in Education: Tagore, Gandhi, and Aurobindo* (Columbia, Mo.: South Asia Books, 1976); Bhupendra Nath, *Rabindranath Tagore: His Mystico-religious Philosophy* (New Delhi: Crown, 1985); Benoy Gopal Ray, *The Philosophy of Rabindranath Tagore* (Calcutta: Progressive, 1970); and Mary M. Lego, ed., *Imperfect Encounter* (Cambridge: Harvard University Press, 1972).

73. A. L. Basham, *The Father of the Nation: Life and Message of Mahatma Gandhi* (New Delhi: Ashish Publishing House, 1988); William Borman, *Gandhi and Nonviolence* (Albany: State University of New York Press, 1986); Bal Ram Nanda, *Gandhi and His Critics* (Oxford: Oxford University Press, 1985); Raghavan N. Iyer, *The Moral and Political Thought of Mahatma Gandhi* (Oxford: Oxford University Press, 1973); Margaret Chatterjee, *Gandhi's Religious Thought* (London: Macmillan, 1983); Joan V. Bondurant, *Conquest of Violence: The Gandhian Philosophy of Conflict* (Berkeley: University of California Press, 1965); Judith Brown, *Gandhi and Civil Disobedience* (Cambridge: Cambridge University Press, 1977); D. M. Datta, *The Philosophy of Mahatma Gandhi* (Madison: University of Wisconsin Press, 1961); K. L. Seshagiri, *Gandhi and Comparative Religion* (Delhi: Motilal Banarsidass, 1978); and Glyn Richards, *The Philosophy of Gandhi: A*

Study of His Basic Ideas (London: Curzon, 1982); Erik H. Erikson *Gandhi's Truth: On the Origins of Militant Nonviolence* (New York: Norton, 1969).

74. Ninian Smart, *Prophet of a New Hindu Age: The Life and Times of Acharya Pranavananda* (London: Allen & Unwin, 1985).

75. David M. Miller and Dorothy C. Wertz, *Hindu Monastic Life: The Monks and Monasteries of Bhubaneswar* (Montreal and London: McGill-Queen's University Press, 1976); David M. Miller, "The Guru as a Centre of Sacredness," *Studies in Religion* 6 (1976–77): 527–33; Daniel Gold, *The Lord as Guru: Hindi Saints in Northern Indian Tradition* (Oxford: Oxford University Press, 1987); idem, *Comprehending the Guru: Toward a Grammar of Religious Perception* (Atlanta: Scholars Press, 1988); Vishal Mangalwadi, *The World of Gurus* (New Delhi: Vikas Publishing House, 1977).

76. Richard Gurghart and Audrey Cantlie, eds., *Indian Religion* (London: Curzon Press, 1985); R. Burghart, "Wandering Ascetics of the Rāmānandī Sect," *History of Religions* 22 (1983):361–80; B. D. Tripathi, *Sadhus of India: The Sociological View* (Bombay: Popular Prakashan, 1978); Philip Singer, *Sadhus and Charisma* (Bombay: Asia Publishing House, 1970); Surajit Sinha and Baidyanath Saraswati, *Ascetics of Kashi: An Anthropological Exploration* (Varanasi: Bhargava Bhushan, 1979).

77. Charles S. J. White, "Sai Baba Movement: Approaches to the Study of Indian Saints," *Journal of Aisan Studies* 31 (1972):863–78; idem, "Swāmī Muktānanda and the Enlightenment through Śakti Pāt," *History of Religions* 13 (1974): 306–22; Charlotte Vaudeville, "Paṇḍharpūr: The City of Saints," in *Structural Approaches to South Indian Studies*, ed. Harry M. Buck and Glenn E. Yocum (Chambersburg, Pa.: Wilson Books, 1974).

78. J. P. Rao Rayapati, *Early American Interest in Vedanta* (New York: Asia Publishing House, 1973); Steven Vertovec, "Hinduism in Diaspora: The Transformation of Tradition in Trinidad," in *Hinduism Reconsidered*, ed. Gunther D. Sontheimer and Harmann Kulke (Delhi: Manohar, 1989).

79. Richard Burghart, ed., *Hinduism in Great Britain: The Perpetuation of Religion in an Alien Cultural Milieu* (London: Tavistock, 1987); Richard Forbes, "Arya Samaj in Trinidad: An Historical Study of Hindu Organizational Process in Acculturation Conditions" (Ph.D. diss., University of Miami); Kim Knott, "Hinduism in Leeds: A Study of Religious Practice in the Indian Community and in Hindu-related Groups" (Ph.D. diss., University of Leeds, 1977).

80. Marjorie Wood, "Hinduism in Vancouver: Adjustments in the Home, the Temple, and the Community," in *Visible Minorities and Multiculturalism*, ed. J. V. Ujimoto and G. Hirabayashi (Toronto: Butterworth, 1980); Jim Wilson, "Text

and Context in Fijian Hinduism: Uses of Religion," *Religion* 5 (1975):53–68; idem, "Text and Context in Fijian Hinduism: Religion as a Framework for Life," *Religion*, 5: 101–16; K. Hazeersingh, "The Religion and Culture of Indian Immigrants in Mauritius and the Effect of Social Change," *Comparative Studies in Society and History* 8 (1966):211–40; Chandra Jayawardena, "Religious Belief and Social Change: Aspects of the Development of Hinduism in British Guiana," *Comparative Studies in Society and History* 8 (1966); and Mark Juergensmeyer, "Radhasoami as a Trans-national Movement," *Understanding the New Religions*, ed. Jacob Needleman and George Baker (New York: Seabury, 1978).

81. Raymond B. Williams, *Religions of Immigrants from India and Pakistan* (Cambridge: Cambridge University Press, 1988); John Fenton, *Transplanting Religious Traditions: Asian Indians in America* (New York: Praeger, 1988).

82. Larry Shinn, *The Dark Lord: Cult Images and the Hare Krishnas in America* (Philadelphia: Westminster, 1987); Francine Jeanne Daner, *The American Children of Krishna: A Study of the Hare Krishna Movement* (New York: Holt, Rinehart & Winston, 1976); E. Burke Rochford, *Hare Krishnas in America* (New Brunswick, N.J.: Rutgers University Press, 1965); Robert D. Baird, "ISKCON and the Struggle for Legitimation," *Bulletin of the John Rylands University Library of Manchester* 70 (1988):157–69; idem, "Swami Bhaktivedanta and the Bhagavadgita 'As it Is,'" in Minor, ed., *Modern Interpreters of the Bhagavadgita*; idem, "Swami Bhaktivedanta: Karma, Rebirth, and the Personal God," in Neufeldt, *Karma and Rebirth*; idem, "The Response of Swami Bhaktivedanta," in Harold G. Coward, ed., *Modern Indian Responses to Religious Pluralism* (Albany: State University of New York Press, 1987); J. Stillison Judah, *Hare Krishna and the Counterculture* (New York: Wiley, 1974).

83. For Neufeldt, *Karma and Rebirth*, see n. 70.

84. Charles F. Keyes and E. Valentine Daniel, eds., *Karma: An Anthropological Inquiry* (Berkeley and Los Angeles: University of California Press, 1983).

85. For Minor, *Modern Interpreters of Bhagavadgita*, see n. 70.

86. Bardwell L. Smith, ed., *Religion and Legitimation of Power in South Asia* (Leiden: E. J. Brill, 1978).

87. Donald Eugene Smith, *India As a Secular State* (Princeton: Princeton University Press, 1963); G. S. Sharma, ed., *Secularism: Its Implications for Law and Life in India* (Bombay: N. M. Tipathi, 1966); V. M. Bachal, *Freedom of Religion and the Indian Judiciary* (Poona: Shubhada Saraswat, 1975); Trevor O. Ling, *Religious Change and the Secular State* (Calcutta: K. P. Bagchi, 1978); Chandra Y. Mudaliar, *The Secular State and Religious Institutions in India: A Study of the Administration of Hindu Public Religious Trusts in Madras* (Wiesbaden: Steiner, 1974).

88. J. D. M. Derrett, *Religious Law and the State in India* (London: Faber &

Faber, 1968); idem, *The Death of a Marriage Law* (Durham, N.C.: Carolina Academic Press, 1978); idem, *Hindu Law Past and Present* (Calcutta: Mukherjee, 1957).

89. G. D. Sontheimer, "Religious Endowments in India: The Juristic Personality of Hindu Deities," *Zeitschirft fur Vergleichende Rechtswissenschaft* 67:45–100; John H. Mansfield, *Comparative Constitutional Law*, ed. Mahendra P. Singh (Lucknow: Eastern Book, n.d.); J. D. M. Derrett, "The Reform of Hindu Religious Endowments," in *South Asian Politics and Religion*, ed. Donald E. Smith (Princeton: Princeton University Press, 1966); S. S. Rama Rao Pappu, "Hinduism, Secularism, and the Secular State," in *Indian Civilization in Its Local, Regional, and National Aspects*, vol. 2 of *Boeings and Bullock Carts: Essays in Honour of K. Ishwaran* (Delhi: Chanakya, 1990).

90. Robert D. Baird, *Essays in the History of Religions*, Toronto Studies in Religion Series (New York: Lang, 1991).

91. Rajeev Bhargava, *Secularism and Its Critics* (New Delhi: Oxford University Press, 1989); Ainslie T. Embree, "Religion, Nationalism, and Conflict" in J. S. Bains and R. B. Jain, eds., *Contemporary Political Theory* (New Delhi: Radiant, 1980); Kenneth W. Jones, "Political Hinduism: The Ideology and Program of the Hindu Mahasabha," in *Religion in Modern India* (Baird).

92. Robert D. Baird, ed., *Religion and Law in Independent India* (New Delhi: Manohar, 1993); Robert N. Minor, *The Religious, the Secular, and the Spiritual: Auroville and Secular India* (Albany: State University of New York Press, 1999).

93. Harold G. Coward, ed., *Modern Indian Responses to Religious Pluralism* (Albany: State University of New York Press, 1987); idem, *Hindu-Christian Dialogue: Perspectives and Encounters* (Maryknol, N.Y.: Orbis, 1989).

94. G. R. Thursby, *Hindu-Muslim Relations in British India: A Study of Controversy, Conflict, and Communal Movements in Northern India* (Leiden: Brill, 1975); James Warner Björknam, ed., *Fundamentalism, Revivalists, and Violence in South Asia* (Delhi: Manohar, 1988); S. K. Ghosh, *Communal Riots in India* (New Delhi: Ashish, 1987); Walter K. Andersen and Shridhar D. Damle, *The Brotherhood in Saffron: The Rashtriya Swayamsevak Sangh and Hindu Revivalism* (New Delhi: Vistar, 1987); Asghar Ali Engineer, *Communalism and Communal Violence in India: An Analytic Approach to Hindu-Muslim Conflict* (Delhi: Ajanta, 1989).

95. Richard Fox Young, *Resistant Hinduism: Sanskrit Sources on Anti-Christian Apologetics in Early Nineteenth Century India* (Vienna: Gerold, 1981); Paul R. Brass, *Language, Religion, and Politics in North India* (London: Cambridge University Press, 1974); Asghar Ali Engineer, ed., *Communal Riots in Post-Independence India* (Hyderabad: Sangham, 1984).

96. Koenraad Elst, *Ramjanmabhoomi vs. Babri Masjid: A Case Study in Hindu-*

Muslim Conflict (New Delhi: Voice of India, 1990); Asghar Ali Engineer, ed., *Babri-Masjid Ramjanmabhoomi Controversy* (Delhi: Ajanta, 1990).

97. Gunther D. Sontheimer and Harmann Kulke, eds., *Hinduism Reconsidered* (Delhi: Manohar, 1989); Wilfred Cantwell Smith in *The Meaning and End of Religion* (New York: Macmillan, 1963); Robert D. Baird, *Category Formation and the History of Religions* (The Hague: Mouton & Co., 1971).

98. Martin Marty and R. S. Appleby, eds., *Fundamentalisms Observed* (Chicago: University of Chicago Press, 1991).

99. V. D. Savarkar, *Hindutva: Who Is a Hindu?* (Bombay: Savarkar Sadan, 1969); M. S. Golwalker, *We; or, Our Nationhood Defined* (Nagpur: Bharat Prakashan, 1947); idem, *Bunch of Thoughts* (Bangalore: Jagarana Prakashana, 1966).

100. Balraj Madhok, *Hindu Rastra* [in Hindi] (New Delhi: Bharati Sahitya Sadan 1958); idem, *Indianization? What, Why, and How* (New Delhi: Bharati Sahitya Sadan, 1969; Delhi: Chand, 1970); idem, *Balraj Madhok on India's Foreign Policy* (New Delhi: Bharati Sahitya Sadan, 1969); idem, *Portrait of a Martyr: Biography of Dr. Shyama Prasad Mookherji* (Bombay: Jaico Publishing House, 1969); idem, *A Story of Bungling in Kashmir* (New Delhi: Young Asia, 1972); idem, *Murder of Democracy* (New Delhi: Chand, 1973); idem, *Reflections of a Detenu* (New Delhi: Newman Group, 1978); idem, *Stormy Decade: Indian Politics 1970–1980* (Delhi: India Book Gallery, 1980); idem, *Punjab Problem: The Muslim Connection* (New Delhi: Hindu World, 1985); idem, *R.S.S. and Politics* (New Delhi: Hindu World, 1986); idem, *Jammu, Kashmir, and Ladakh: Problem and Solution* (New Delhi: Reliance Publishing House, 1987).

101. For Anderson and Damle, *Brotherhood of Saffron*, see n. 93; Bruce Graham, *Hindu Nationalism and Indian Politics: The Origins and Development of the Bharatiya Jana Sangh* (Cambridge: Cambridge University Press, 1990); Christopher Jeffrelot, *The Hindu Nationalist Movement in India* (New York: Columbia University Press, 1993); Thomas Blom Hansen, *The Saffron Wave: Democracy and Hindu Nationalism in Modern India* (Princeton: Princeton University Press, 1999); Eva Hellman, *Political Hinduism: The Challenge of the Viśva Hindū Pariṣad* (Uppsala: Department of History of Religions, Uppsala University, 1993).

102. Achin Vanaik, *The Furies of Indian Communalism: Religion, Modernity, and Secularization* (London: Verso, 1997).

ABOUT THE CONTRIBUTORS

GREGORY BAILEY obtained a B.Ec. from Monash University in Australia, an M.A. in religious studies from Lancaster University, England, and a Ph.D. in Indian studies from the University of Melbourne, Australia. He is currently reader in Sanskrit in the Department of Asian Studies at La Trobe University. His publications include *The Mythology of Brahmā* (1983); *Materials for the Study of Ancient Indian Ideologies: Pravṛtti and Nivṛtti* (1985); *Bhartṛhari's Critique of Culture* (1995); *The Gaṇeśapurāṇa*, vol. 1: *Upāsanākhaṇḍa* (1995); and *Mythologies of Change and Certainty in Late Twentieth Century Australia* (2000). He is coeditor with Mary Brockington of *Epic Threads: John Brockington on the Sanskrit Epics* (2000). He is at present completing the second volume of his translation of the *Gaṇeśapurāṇa* and working on a major textual study of the Sanskrit words *pravṛtti* and *nivṛtti* and associated ideologies.

ROBERT D. BAIRD obtained a B.A. from Houghton College, a B.D. from Fuller Theological Seminary, an S.T.M. from Southern Methodist University, and a Ph.D. from the University of Iowa. He was professor of the history of religions and former director of the School of Religion (1995–2000) at the University of Iowa. In January 2000 he became professor emeritus at the University of Iowa and the Goodwin-Philpot Eminent Chair in Religion at Auburn University. He has published numerous articles and books in the areas of methodology and the history of religions, Indian religions, religion in modern India, and religion and law in India. He is the author of two books—*Category Formation and the History of Religions* (1971) and *Essays in the History of Religions* (1991)—and editor of and contributor to four others: *Religions in Modern India*

(1981, 1985, 1989), *Religion and Law in Independent India* (1992), *Methodological Issues in Religious Studies* (1975), and *Indian and Far Eastern Religious Traditions* (1972). He has also published more than twenty-nine scholarly articles.

MILTON "MICKEY" EDER received his Ph.D. from the Committee on History of Culture at the University of Chicago. He is currently the Academic Director of General Education at the Illinois Institute of Art–Chicago. He most recently published "The Autobiographer in Mohandas Karamchand Gandhi's *The Story of My Experiments with Truth*," in *Cultural Visions: Essays in the History of Culture* (2000). His current research is in semiotics and developing a better understanding of the concepts of globalization and international business. A book tentatively titled *Civilizational Dialogues: Translating the Bhagavadgītā as a Comparative Cultural Project* is a work in progress.

ALF HILTEBEITEL received his Ph.D. in history of religions from the University of Chicago. Columbian Professor of Religion and Human Sciences at George Washington University, he is the author of *The Ritual of Battle: Krishna in the Mahābhārata* (1976, 1990); two volumes on *The Cult of Draupadī* (1988–1991); *Rethinking India's Oral and Classical Epics: Draupadī among Rajputs, Muslims, and Dalits* (1999); and *Rethinking the Mahābhārata: A Reader's Guide to the Education of the Dharma King* (2001). He is also editor of *Criminal Gods and Demon Devotees: Essays on the Guardians of Popular Hinduism* (1989) and coeditor, with Barbara D. Miller, of *Hair: Its Power and Meaning in Asian Cultures* (1998). He is coeditor, with Kathleen M. Erndl, of *Is the Goddess a Feminist? The Politics of South Asian Goddesses* (2000) and continues to work on South Indian folk religion and the Sanskrit epics.

STEPHANIE W. JAMISON received her Ph.D in linguistics from Yale University. She has taught Sanskrit and linguistics at a variety of universities and is currently Professor at the Department of East Asian Languages and Cultures, UCLA. She is the author of *The Ravenous Hyenas and the Wounded Sun: Myth and Ritual in Ancient India* (1991) and *Sacrificed Wife/Sacrificer's Wife: Women, Ritual, and Hospitality in Ancient India* (1996). She has published numerous articles on Indo-Iranian linguistics and Vedic and classical Sanskrit literature and religion.

PHILIP LUTGENDORF has a Ph.D. in South Asian languages and civilizations from the University of Chicago and since 1985 has taught Hindi and modern Indian studies in the University of Iowa's Department of Asian Languages and Literature. His *The Life of Text: Performing the Rāmcaritmānas of*

Tulsīdās (1991) won the A. K. Coomaraswamy Prize of the Association for Asian Studies. He is also the author of several recent articles on the worship of Hanuman. His research interests include epic performance traditions, folklore, and mass media.

ARVIND SHARMA was in the Indian Administrative Service before he embarked on an academic career. He obtained a master's in economics at Syracuse University, a master's in theological studies at Harvard Divinity School, and a Ph.D. in Sanskrit and Indian studies at Harvard University. He has taught religious studies in Australia and the United States and is currently the Birks Professor of Comparative Religion in the Faculty of Religious Studies at McGill University. He has published in the areas of comparative religion and Hindu studies and is the editor of *Our Religions* (1993) and *Women in World Religions* (1987).

ERIC J. SHARPE died on October 20, 2000, while this book was being prepared. He studied at the Universities of Manchester and Uppsala. He lectured in India, Korea, Singapore, and Hong Kong and taught in the United States, Canada, Sweden, and the United Kingdom. From 1977 he was Foundation Professor of Religious Studies at the University of Sydney in Australia, retiring from that post in 1996. His major publications include *Not to Destroy but to Fulfil* (1965), *Comparative Religion: A History* (1975; 1986), *Faith Meets Faith* (1977), *Understanding Religion* (1983), *The Universal Gītā* (1985), *Nathan Söderblom and the Study of Religion* (1990), and *The Riddle of Sadhu Sundar Singh* (forthcoming). His chief research interest was the history of the East-West encounter in religion, with special regard to the influence of Eastern religious traditions on Western ways of thought, and vice versa, in the nineteenth and twentieth centuries.

MICHAEL WITZEL obtained M.A. and Ph.D. degrees from Erlangen University. He taught as assistant professor at Tübingen University, and then as associate professor (1976–79) and full professor (1980–86) at the University of Leiden in the Netherlands. He was also director of the Nepal German Manuscript Preservation Project at Kathmandu, Nepal (1972–77). He was appointed Wales Professor of Sanskrit at Harvard University in 1986. He is the author of *Das Kaṭha Āraṇyaka* (1974). *On Magical Thought in the Veda* (1979), and *Das alte Indien*. and is editor of *W. Caland, Kleine Schriften* (1989), F. B. J. Kuiper's *Selected Writings on Indian Linguistics and Philology* (1997), and *Inside the Texts, Beyond the Texts: New Approaches to the Study of the Vedas* (1997). He has published more than ninety articles and has been the editor of the Harvard Oriental Series since 1993. He is a member of the editorial board of the *Indo-Indian Journal*, *Studien zur Indologie und Iranistik*, and the *International Journal of Tantric Studies*, and also edits the *Electronic Journal of Vedic Studies*.

INDEX OF SUBJECTS

INDEX OF NAMES

INDEX OF TERMS